by the same author

A Wife for the Pretender

James Francis Edward Stuart, *de jure* James III and VIII, from a
contemporary portrait by Belle. (*National Portrait Gallery, London*)
frontispiece

JAMES

by Peggy Miller

London · George Allen & Unwin Ltd
Ruskin House   Museum Street

First published in 1971

ISBN 0 04 923056 5

Printed in Great Britain
in 11 point Plantin type
by W & J Mackay Ltd
Chatham, Kent

To my mother and father

Acknowledgement

The extracts from the Stuart Papers in the Royal Archives
at Windsor Castle are published by the gracious permission of
Her Majesty the Queen.

Contents

Illustrations

The Interrelationship of the Houses of STUAR[T] and HANOVE[R]

Marguerite de Valois = ① HENRI IV K. of France (1553–1610) ② = Marie de' Medici

LOUIS XIII K. of France (1601–1643) = Anne of Austria

Gaston Duc d'Orléans d.1660

Maria Theresa of Spain = ① LOUIS XIV K. of France (1638–1715) ② = Françoise d'Aubigné (Madame de Maintenon)

Henrietta of England ＊ = ① Philippe Duc d'Orléans (Monsieur) d.1701 ② = Eliza[beth] Charlo[tte] of the Palati[ne] ＊ ＊

Louis (Dauphin) d.1711 = Maria Anna of Bavaria

Marie Louise m. CHARLES II K. of Spain (1661–1700)

Anne Marie m. Victor Amadeus D. of Savoy

Philippe Duc d'Orléans (Regent) d.1723

Elizabeth Cha[rlotte] m. Leopold Jose[ph] D. of Lorrai[ne] d.1729

Louis Duc de Bourgogne d.1712 = Marie Adelaide of Savoy

Philippe Duc d'Anjou (PHILIP V K. of Spain) (1683–1746)

Charles Duc de Berry = Marie Louise

Louis Duc d'Orléans d.1752

FERDINAND VI K. of Spain (1713–1759)

CHARLES III K. of Spain (1716–1788)

Louis Phili[ppe] Duc d'Orléa[ns] d.1785

LOUIS XV K. of France (1710–1774) = Maria Leszczynska

OURBON, ORANGE, The PALATINATE —1542–1807

MARY Queen of Scots (1542–1587) = **Henry Stuart** Lord Darnley d. 1567

JAMES I and VI K. of England & Scotland (1566–1625) = **Anne** of Denmark

Henrietta Maria = **CHARLES I** K. of England (1600–1649)

Elizabeth = **FREDERICK V** Elector Palatine K. of Bohemia 1619 'The Winter King'

CHARLES II f England 0–1685) — **Anne** Hyde = ① **JAMES II** ② K. of England (1633–1701) = **Mary Beatrice** of Modena

Mary = **William II** P. Orange d. 1650

Henrietta m. Philippe Duc d'Orléans *

RY = **WILLIAM III** K. of England (1650–1702) nd 694)

ANNE = George Q. of of England Denmark (1665–1714)

WILLIAM III K. of England

Charles Louis Elector Palatine

Elizabeth Charlotte (m. Philippe Duc d'Orléans) **

Sophia = **Ernest** Elector of Hanover

GEORGE I K. of England (1660–1727)

GEORGE II K. of England (1683–1760)

MES **FRANCIS EDWARD** (1688–1766) = **Maria Clementina** Sobieska

Louise Marie d. 1712

arles Edward 720–1788)

Henry Cardinal York (1725–1807)

GEORGE III K. of England (1738–1820)

GEORGE IV K. of England (1762–1830)

ITALIAN STATES
1. D. of Milan
2. Republic of Genoa
3. D. of Parma
4. D. of Modena
5. D. of Tuscany

SCOTLAND

Peterhead
Perth   Aberdeen
         Dundee
   Edinburgh

NORTH

Belfast   Carlisle

SEA

IRELAND   Dublin   Preston

WALES   Derby
        ENGLAND
   Bristol   London   Amsterdam
                      The Hague   UNITED
   Plymouth   Portsmouth   NETHERLANDS   HA

English Channel   AUSTRIAN NETHERLANDS   Breda

                  Le Havre
Brest   St Germain   ROMA
   St Malo   Paris   PALATINATE   Philipps
   Versailles   NORTH   Kehl
         Fontainbleau   Bar   LORRAINE
                        le Duc   ALSACE   Sélestat

F R A N C E

SWITZ^LND

Corunna   SAVOY

         Bordeaux   PIEDMONT   1   V

Bayonne   Avignon   2   3   Parma
                                          Modena
   Burgos   Antibes   4

         Gerona   Toulon
Madrid   Barcelona   CORSICA   Civitavec
PORTUGAL   S P A I N   Ro.

                                KINGDOM
Cadiz   M E D I T E R R A   SARDINIA

★
Europe
in
1740

A F R I C A

Part One

SAINT-GERMAIN

Chapter One

For eight days the Queen of England had waited in Boulogne, but no one had come, no message had arrived. The weather remained stormy, menacing seas battered the beaches, and all the northern ports of France were closed. She tried to forget the terrors of the journey from Whitehall and to concentrate what was left of her energy into prayers for the safe deliverance of her husband so recently driven from his kingdom by his son-in-law, William of Orange, who had landed at Torbay in November 1688. After several days a rumour reached her that rebellion had spread throughout England and that James II had been taken, but still there was no confirmation. She begged those about her to let her leave the six-months-old Prince with them in safety while she returned to find the King, but they would not hear of such madness: the Duc de Lauzan had by now received orders from Versailles to deliver her and the child to Louis XIV, and nothing was going to stop him carrying them out. Taking the Prince alone did not suit his plans; he needed Queen Mary Beatrice's intercession with Louis to effect his own restoration at Versailles.

Short, prematurely wizened at fifty, by no means a figure to inspire romance, Lauzan had lived a colourful existence at the French court. Although he had been comparatively poor at the outset of his career, his Gascon wit and daring had furthered soaring ambition, and he had early attracted the notice of the King. He was known to be one of the few who were allowed to speak their minds to Louis, but eventually he had overreached himself by aspiring to marry Louis's cousin, the Grande Mademoiselle. Not only had he lost his position, but his vanity was wounded. So he left for England in an attempt to restore his financial fortune by gaming, which was as prevalent and socially acceptable at Whitehall as at any other European court. When the situation began to look really grim for the English royal family, Lauzan saw his chance of accomplishing a particularly daring 'gasconnade' and saving both them and his own destiny. If he were successful and the Stuarts grateful, surely that would go a long way towards softening Louis's obduracy towards him? He did not consider failure.

The baby Prince had been sent to Portsmouth a few weeks previously in the care of Lord and Lady Powis. King James, while Duke of York, had virtually established the Navy, and the fleet had always been loyal to him, so Portsmouth seemed a good choice. The eighteen-year-old Duke of Berwick, the King's illegitimate son, had been riding around the West Country trying to muster what army he could, so the child was received by Lord Dartmouth who was in command at Spithead. From there, James Francis Edward was supposed to go to France, and the King had commanded Dartmouth to put the Prince in the charge of Lord Dover to travel in the yacht *Mary*. Dartmouth could no longer rely upon the Navy; he knew also that if he took the responsibility of hazarding the life of the heir to the throne by sending him out of England without an order from the Privy Council, he could himself be attainted for high treason. He sent a message to the King asking him to reconsider his decision. James and Mary Beatrice were now frantic for the safety of their son. Dartmouth was told to return the Prince to London, and two new and hastily mustered Irish Catholic regiments were sent to accompany the child and ensure his safety.

Dover, whose loyalty, unlike that of Dartmouth, was never in question, feared treason, and rightly so. The usurper, William of Orange, had sent out a hundred cavalry under six officers to scour the countryside for the Prince; the plans for his despatch from Portsmouth were soon learnt, and a trap laid in the Forest of Bere. But Dover, acting upon his own intuition and initiative, sent the child back in a coach with Lord and Lady Powis and escorted by the two regiments a day earlier than had been planned. They travelled via Petersfield, and all went well until they reached Southwark, where the soldiers of the escort were recognized by the populace as Irish, and consequently 'Papists', and were forced to disband. Some stayed around the coach, others scattered looking for help and fortunately fell in with a squadron of Guards returning to Whitehall. Hell for leather, they rode back with the Guards towards Southwark and rescued the baby, conducting him safely to the palace where he was placed in the Queen's arms on Saturday, 8 December, at three o'clock in the morning.

While all this had been going on, Lauzun had arrived in Whitehall and had lost no time in convincing Mary Beatrice that it was imperative for her and the child to leave for France. King James seemed to have lost all power of making a decision; he was utterly fatigued, his speech was slurred and he was still stunned by the shock of being betrayed by his daughters, Mary and Anne. Lauzun conferred with John Caryll, the Queen's secretary, and plans were made for the escape of the Prince and his mother. At first she refused to go without the King, but he finally persuaded her that he would follow them within twenty-four hours. A few other faithful friends were admitted to the secret: Francesco Riva, the Keeper of the Queen's Wardrobe; Pellegrina Turini, her personal maid; Father Giudici, her confessor; Vittoria Davia and her brother, the Marchese di Montecucculi; Lord and

Lady Powis; and Sir William Waldegrave, the royal physician, and his wife. The Comte de Saint-Victor, Terriesi, the Venetian Ambassador, and Rizzini, the envoy of the court of Modena, were also in the secret. The Queen was disguised as an Italian laundress and, at two o'clock in the morning of Sunday, 9 December, she and her party stole out of Whitehall with the Prince bundled up like a parcel of laundry, *en route* for France.

His Most Christian Majesty of France had his own reasons besides the ties of friendship, kinship, religion and the desire to re-establish an anointed king upon a throne which had been stolen from him. While he held the Stuart royal family in his hand he held a political pawn and, at the same time, a justification in the eyes of Europe if at any time he decided to attack the Prince of Orange. William's power was growing too rapidly and too soon for Louis's peace of mind. So the unhappy Queen passed more than a week in Boulogne with nothing to do except to visit the chapel in the castle where she was lodged: she heard three masses on New Year's Eve alone.

For the rest of the time she thought about James and the happier times she had known with him in England, and devoted herself to her baby son. Although his birth on 10 June of the disappearing year, 1688, had been a sign for the Whigs to send appeals to the Prince of Orange to deliver them from the fetters of 'popery', London had, nevertheless, celebrated the birth with fireworks, while bread and wine had been distributed free to its citizens three nights running.

This had been nothing compared with the celebrations in Rome and Madrid. Cardinal Howard, son of the Earl of Arundel, had arranged three days' holiday in Rome: there were fountains flowing with wine, roasted oxen and illuminations in the streets. Wine also flowed from fountains in Madrid, and there were fireworks and banquets organized by Lord Lansdowne, the British Ambassador, as well as the Spanish court. Lansdowne was lacking in neither nerve nor wit when he presented the bill to William in the following year. All this was on account of a baby who represented to the Holy See and to the Catholic countries of Europe the possibility of the return of England to the Mother Church.

How the child survived was a miracle in itself. Mary Beatrice had had five earlier children, three girls and two boys, all of whom had died in early infancy. James Francis Edward was a normal, healthy child, but so many doctors were involved in making sure that the Prince remained in this world that all kinds of food and drink were pushed down his tiny throat. Experiments were made with various types of gruels, containing oatmeal, barley, currants and wine, as well as bread and milk. The usual course of employing a healthy wet-nurse was spurned until the Queen, made desperate by the fact that the baby seemed to be losing his fragile hold on life, and small wonder, demanded that one should be brought. Eventually a robust brick-layer's wife was found; the child responded immediately to his new diet and began to put on weight. But his general constitution had been impaired to some degree for the rest of his life and in later years he suffered from time to time with digestive troubles. In the month following his birth he was declared Prince of Wales, and in August, somewhat optimistically, Admiral of England. He was not baptized until October; this was done publicly but, lest London should show a hostile reaction, the ceremony was curtailed. It was only ten days after this, on 26 October, that William of Orange, husband of Princess Mary, sailed from Holland to usurp his father-in-law's throne.

The Queen waited, remembered and hoped. There was no improvement in the weather and now it had begun to snow hard. News seemed as difficult as ever to obtain so, urged on by Lauzun to continue the wearisome journey to Versailles, she climbed at last into one of the three ornately gilded coaches drawn by ten horses which Louis XIV had sent her for the rest of her progress. Her ladies and gentlemen followed in the other two coaches and in litters, accompanied by French pages, footmen, guards, at least one lieutenant and other officers.[1]

The snow continued to fall, and the grey fields merged with the grey horizon. The roads were in an appalling state, so detachments of soldiers were deployed along the route to clear the way for the coaches. Wherever the Queen stopped, the local dignitaries welcomed her and brought out their best for her reception. They travelled via Abbeville and Poix where a message was received from Louis offering his château at Saint-Germain-en-Laye as a home for the royal family. She stayed overnight in the bishop's palace at Beauvais and attended mass on the morning of what would have been Christmas Day in the English calendar, but was 4 January in France. As she left the cathedral, another messenger from the French king arrived with information that James had left England. This was at least something, although she still feared for his safety during a crossing in such violent weather. At Beaumont her anguish was ended when she heard that the King had landed at Ambleteuse and was safe.

The King of France was waiting for her with all his household and a hundred coaches in the snow at Châtou, a few kilometres from Saint-Germain. He descended from his carriage as the English party came into view and, when the nurse, Mrs Labardie, stepped down from the coach holding the Prince of Wales, he discarded ceremony, took the child in his arms and saluted him with a kiss. Any doubts Mary Beatrice may have had about Louis's personal welcome were completely dispelled. If the Prince of

[1] Madame de Sévigné, *Lettres*, No. 999, 27 December 1688

Wales had any thoughts at all, he was probably wondering why this huge face with its black eyes surmounted by an extraordinary amount of dark, curling hair was pressed so close to his own, blotting out the sky.

Louis made her sit at his right hand in the coach, opposite Monsieur and Madame, his brother and sister-in-law and, when they arrived, led her to the apartments which had been made ready for her down to the last expensive detail. Laid out for her was a complete and luxurious wardrobe with appropriate jewels, and a toilet set of chased silver. Always practical, Louis had also provided a golden casket filled with 6,000 golden *louis* for her own personal use. The Queen's gratitude moved her to tears.

Political considerations apart, Louis showed the very best side of his nature in his personal relations with the exiles: he spared no kindness nor expense in trying to make them feel as at home as was possible in the circumstances, and to invest them with the dignity owing to their station; every mark of protocol was scrupulously observed. James and Louis were two very different people with nothing in common but their sovereignty, but the French king had a deep affection and respect for Mary Beatrice who, for him, was an example in her beauty, dignity and goodness of all that a queen should be.

She had arrived as an unwilling bride in the English court to become the second wife of the widowed Duke of York, who was eventually to succeed his brother as King of England. Aged sixteen, her one great desire had been to become a nun and this, combined with the shock of comparison between her own strictly Catholic upbringing in Modena and the prevalent licentiousness of the court of Charles II, as well as her own inexperience, made her first years of marriage difficult. Yet it did not take her long to fall in love with her husband, and she loved him faithfully until his death. For a newly-wed young girl, she had much to accept: James had had a number of mistresses, and returned more than once to the last of them, Catherine Sedley, one of her own ladies, during the early part of his marriage and even during the first year of his accession. But the Queen, for all her obedience and love, was a high-spirited and quick-tempered young woman. In the presence of various dignitaries of the Catholic Church she made it clear to him that he either gave up Sedley or she would leave him. James knew her well enough to know that she meant exactly what she said, so he chose the wiser course.

She also had the problem of coming to terms with her two stepdaughters, both a little younger than herself, and James's two recognized but illegitimate sons by Arabella Churchill. With regard to Mary and Anne, there was really no problem at all; quite soon after her arrival they were all on the best of terms. She did not accept so unreservedly the recognition of the

25

boys, but it was not long before a mutual respect and a somewhat guarded affection sprang up between her and the elder boy, James Fitzjames. They had three qualities in common: honesty, common sense and a devotion to the King.

The Queen also possessed another enviable quality, that of being able to adapt herself to whatever circumstances in which she found herself with a grace and ease unusual in one of her background. After her arrival in France she was admired and liked by the hypercritical court of Versailles, but it never took her husband to its heart.

There was no doubt but that he was a difficult character. Never very intelligent, he was dogged and painstaking in everything he chose to do. His obstinacy, tactlessness and lack of imagination led him into situations which his 'bloody-mindedness' would not let him retrieve. He meant well but he did not have the easy personal charm of his brother. Charles attracted people to himself with the sureness of a magnet, and it may have been that James, during his formative years, had suffered by comparison with his attractive, dashing elder brother so obviously born to rule. Whatever the reason, there was a strong streak of inhibition in him which was expressed through some physical characteristics as well: although above average height, well-made and strong, with the strength that comes from sinew rather than from weight, he moved without grace and, even as a young man, showed a stiffness and constraint in his gait. There was a hesitation, not quite a stammer, in his speech. He did not stand on ceremony, although no one knew when it was necessary to observe it better than he. But there was a natural difficulty of communication between him and most of the people in his life. He also lacked Charles's gift of swift, sure and often cynical appraisal of character. James, once he had given his trust, never withdrew it, even when the loyalty was misplaced as in the case of Arabella's brother, John Churchill, and of the President of the Council, Lord Sunderland. The latter, as the Duke of Berwick was to note later, was not only responsible for many of the misunderstandings between the King and his ministers, but was also an active conniver in the Monmouth rebellion.[1]

James II was certainly a brave man, and two of the greatest of French generals, Condé and Turenne, had remarked on his valour when he had fought in Europe before the Restoration.[2] Much of his failure as a king may be attributed to the fact that the military and naval experience he gained during his youth in exile was not complemented by a political education.

He had made up his mind at last to meet the usurper, and the place he had chosen for the encounter was Westminster. But he delayed at Salisbury,

[1] Berwick, *Mémoires du Maréchal de Berwick*, Vol. I, p. 35
[2] *ibid*, Vol. 2, p. 484

and was then incapacitated by a severe nose-bleeding. When he returned to London on 29 November, having achieved nothing, it was clear that he was losing his grip on the situation; added to this, he was personally broken by the defection of his daughters.

It was the betrayals within the family which affected him most. James Fitzjames, the Duke of Berwick, was the only relative, other than the Queen, to whom he could turn, and in him he placed all his trust. His daughter Mary, the wife of the Prince of Orange, excused herself later on the grounds that she had never imagined that her father would be banished, but had supposed that there would be a regency with her husband as regent. Prince George of Denmark had already gone over to William; and his wife, Princess Anne, James's younger daughter, had fled to Nottingham in her night clothes, accompanied by Lady Berkeley, Lady Churchill and Bishop Compton of London, less through conviction of William's rights or supremacy than from an inability to face her father after her husband's desertion. The trusted and well-loved John Churchill, uncle of the Duke of Berwick, had deserted to the enemy as well as others such as the Dukes of Grafton and Ormonde and the Lords Lovelace, Colchester and Cornbury.

If he was disappointed in his daughters, he was not so in his natural son. James Fitzjames was eighteen when his half-brother, James Francis Edward Stuart, first saw the light of day. Fitzjames found that his illegitimacy had little effect on his future career: it precluded him from accession to the throne, but Berwick was enough of a natural philosopher to waste no time fretting on this score.

He had been born in France, brought to England as a small child, returned to France in 1677 for his education, and was more French than English in his upbringing. He was also bilingual. James recognized his son, as well as another younger son borne by Arabella, but it was obviously not so very convenient for both boys to be around Whitehall as a continual reminder to Mary Beatrice, then Duchess of York, of her husband's lapses. James Fitzjames returned to London for his father's coronation; he was sixteen and had decided to make his career in the army.

His father gave him permission to join the Emperor's forces in Hungary, and off went Berwick to the siege of Buda, then beleaguered by the Turks. This was his first experience of that branch of warfare and the science of tunnels, redoubts and earthworks which he was to make peculiarly his own. He returned to give an account of himself to James II later in the same year and, in token of the King's pleasure at his military progress, was created Duke of Berwick. He spent that winter in England but he responded to the call of Mars with the return of spring and rode back to 'high deeds in Hungary'. At that period war had its code of etiquette just as much as the court, and it was the practice during the winter season either to dig oneself in, call a truce, or postpone operations by heading for home. It was a practical idea: even the comparatively few good roads across Europe became quagmires and it was impossible to move supplies.

The Emperor made the young Duke a colonel and he was given command of the regiment of the Cuirassiers de Taaff. It was at this time, in the campaign of 1687, that he formed a strong and lasting friendship with the Duke of Lorraine, whose family was later to provide friends in need to the Stuarts. He shared the Duke's victory at the Battle of Mohacs and, on his return to Vienna, the Emperor proclaimed him 'Sergent Général de Bataille'.

He already possessed a regiment of infantry back in England and, when he returned there for the winter of 1687, the King gave him the governor-ship of Portsmouth and Southampton as well as a regiment of Horse Guards. So, as Montesquieu was to write many years later in an appendix to the Duke's memoirs, 'at the age of seventeen he found himself in the situation, so flattering to a man of noble mind, of seeing the road to glory stretching before him and the possibility of achieving great things'.[1]

In November the King gave him orders to reassemble the army in Portsmouth. James's ministers delayed the order on purpose until it was too late to accomplish anything. Berwick was sure of his garrison of 2,500 foot and 500 dragoons, but he was without provisions, blocked by the rebellious fleet at sea and the advance troops of William of Orange outside the town. There was nothing more to be done but, on James's orders, to surrender the town and return to the King. Disciplined, philosophic and realistic as he was, it must have been heartbreaking for an eighteen-year-old governor to be forced to surrender his own town and a key position through no fault of his own. As he dismounted wearily in the courtyard of Rochester Castle on the night of 19 December 1688, the young Duke doubtless wondered what state of affairs he was going to find within.

When he entered the King's bedchamber it was to find a man looking much older than his fifty-five years, a man weighed down by care, with a very tenuous grasp on the realities of his position. The King told his son of his plan of escape and the part he was to play in it. He also learnt of his six-months-old brother's escape with the Queen and of Lauzun's assistance in the affair.

When James had received the news of the safe departure of his family to France he had sent a deputation consisting of Sidney Godolphin, the Lord Chamberlain, the Earl of Nottingham and the Marquis of Halifax to William, who was taking his time about proceeding to London. Perhaps he

[1] Berwick, *op. cit.*, p. xix. Tr. Author

hoped that he would be saved the embarrassment of having to depose his own father-in-law by the latter's leaving the throne vacant of his own accord; in any case, his only reply was that he would talk with James when he arrived in London.

Panic hit James: he feared arrest by the Prince of Orange, and probably also thought that he would stand a better chance of recovering what he had already lost by going to France and then descending upon England with a larger and better organized army. He disguised himself in a dark wig and set out for the coast, accompanied by one of his gentlemen, Sir Edward Hales.

At Faversham in Kent he hoped to take a small boat but the weather, so often the enemy of the Stuarts, betrayed him: a gale rose and the small craft had to remain in the harbour. Stirred up by rumours of a Jesuit, possibly James's confessor, the much hated Father Petre, trying to escape, some of the local people boarded the boat, rough-handled the King in disguise and dragged him ashore. He was robbed of his money, gold watch and sword and thrown in the local gaol. The distraught Hales had made the mob uneasy by insisting that this was the King, and he was finally allowed to get a message through to the Earl of Faversham in London. Eventually Faversham arrived with some of the Royal Bodyguard and took James back to Whitehall.

The temper of the London crowd changed as suddenly as the wind veers and, on the way back to the palace, James was cheered along his route with cries of 'Long live the King!' If he had only known how to take advantage of it, then was his golden opportunity to rally his subjects and take a stand against the usurper. But James was a poor student of psychology and in any case lacked the personal persuasion necessary to carry out such an action. When William heard of this triumphal return, he demanded that James should leave London at once and, in spite of the pleas made by the faithful Earl of Balcarres and Viscount Dundee, the King complied. William then sent to Whitehall a detachment of his own Blue Guards who ordered the English guards to retire, which they did without fighting. James sailed down to Rochester on 17 December, escorted by William's guards, and sent for Berwick, then in Portsmouth.

The King's *coucher* was carried out as usual on the night Berwick arrived. Once in bed, the King dismissed the other gentlemen, requesting his son to remain. He then dressed again, and left with the Duke through a secret door from his chamber and made for the river. There he went aboard a *chaloupe* made ready for him by two sea captains, Trevannion and Macdonnel. He had only two others with him beside Berwick: Biddulph, his gentleman of the bedchamber; and his valet, Labardie, whose wife was nurse to the Prince. On Christmas Day they disembarked at Ambleteuse, and the weary, disorientated man sent his son to Versailles to ask Louis officially for asylum. Berwick noted of Louis's reception: 'I was received with every imaginable courtesy and kindness, and it was patent to see, by the way he spoke, that his heart was speaking as well as his lips.'[1]

Three days after Berwick, James himself arrived at Saint-Germain, travel-weary and defeated by the sudden onslaught of events which had taken their toll of his appearance. Gone, completely gone, was the warrior who had earned praise from Condé and Turenne as the young Duke of York; disappeared for ever was the admiral who had led the British fleet to victory against the Dutch in 1665.

Although she did not yet realize it, it was Mary Beatrice who was gradually to take over the direction of the fortunes of the small family after the first few years of exile. For that moment, at last defeated by all she had endured during the past month and unable to cope with any more emotion, she had taken to her bed, and it was the Dauphin who waited at the foot of the grand staircase to greet James with the deference due to a reigning sovereign. Together they mounted to the *Salle des Gardes*, rivalling the Banqueting Hall at Whitehall in its magnificence, where Louis himself waited in his sun-splendour. With his acute sense of tact and his natural courtesy, he raised James who, as a suppliant and in gratitude, would have gone on one knee before him, and embraced him warmly. Then he took him to the Queen's bedside, saying: 'Madam, I bring you someone whom you will be very glad to see!'[2]

In their mutual joy, and careless of the surprise of the French court, so frozen in its etiquette at the expense of its emotions, the royal couple kissed in view of all. Then the two Kings retired while the Queen dressed before joining them again in the Prince's nursery. As James embraced his little son, the King of France said: 'I have taken great care of him, you will find him in good health.'[3] It was 6 January 1689 – the Feast of the Kings.

[1] Berwick, *op. cit.*, Vol. I, p. 41
[2] Marchesa Campana de Cavelli, *Les Dernier Stuarts à Saint-Germain-en-Laye*, p. 3
[3] *ibid.*

Chapter Two

James Francis Edward's birthday fell on 20 June,[1] the same day as that of his ancestor and namesake, the Black Prince, who had been responsible in 1346 for the razing of the original château of Saint-Germain-en-Laye built two centuries before. Rebuilt to a large extent in the fourteenth century, it was completed in the sixteenth and the Château Neuf added close by. The latter gradually fell into disuse, with the exception of the two *pavillons*, in one of which, the Pavillon Henri IV, Louis XIV was born.[2]

There was something forbidding about the Château Vieux as it towered, vast in yellow brick and stone, from an eminence above the winding Seine. Visible for miles around, it was a menacing giant threatening the peacefully undulating countryside of the Île-de-France surrounding it. Whilst it looked as if it had nothing to do with spring, it was easy to see that it was an edifice to withstand any onslaught the winter might bring. Not only was it proof against the elements: it had been built as a fortress and as such had well served its purpose in the past.

This severity was lessened to a degree by the beauty of its gardens and surrounding parkland. In front of the deserted Château Neuf, soon to become the quarters of the Jacobite officers and courtiers, were hanging gardens and pleached alleys sheltering grottoes. Here were statues of classical divinities and the remains of marvellous hydraulic automatons installed in the reign of Henri II and since fallen into disrepair. There were fountains, a bowling-green and an ornamental lake; and there was Le Nôtre's beautiful terrace, finished in 1673, running arrow-straight for a mile and a half along the side of the park, overlooking the Seine. This had cost Louis 850,000 *livres*. In 1664 he planted 5,585,000 trees in the Great Park,[3] and both the park and the surrounding country provided the finest hunting-grounds that he possessed. And yet, in spite of all this natural beauty, an atmosphere of sadness and nostalgia drifted over the château – a sense of desertion, of being frozen in a moment of past time: *le son du cor au fond des bois* sounded as plaintively for the shade of the Vert-Galant as it did for the Sun King. Two Stuart queens, Mary of Scotland and Henrietta Maria, had lived in exile there before Mary Beatrice crossed the inner court on a bleak winter day in 1689.

[1] New style calendar
[2] Jacques Levron, *The Royal Châteaux of the Île-de-France*, p. 47
[3] *ibid.*

Louis XIV had never cared for Paris or its inhabitants, but he liked the Château Vieux even less. Twice, in his minority and during the troubles of the Fronde, he and his mother had been obliged to camp in the empty, ice-cold halls, without beds or furniture, for the building had been scarcely used since the death of his father. This was an unpleasant memory for the luxury-loving monarch he had later become; yet, after his marriage in 1660 until he settled himself and the seat of government at Versailles some twenty years after, he had frequented Saint-Germain more than any of his other palaces. From the terrace with its superb panorama of Paris could be seen the outline of Saint-Denis, the mausoleum of the kings of France – a constant *memento mori* to Louis of the transience of worldly power and splendour. By the time the Stuarts arrived he had already made Versailles his chief residence, and it was not altogether a sacrifice to relinquish to them the château of Saint-Germain.

The luxury and elegance of the building far exceeded that of the palace of Whitehall, and James II was given a guard of honour composed of some of the finest soldiers of Europe. After he had to some degree recovered his health, he was delighted to find that he had for his personal use a hunting establishment fit only to rival that of Louis himself. Besides an army of huntsmen and beaters there was a complete arsenal of guns and spears, as well as hundreds of tents, nets, horns, dogs for chasing deer, wolf, fox and bear, hawks for herons and falcons for wild duck at his command, while Louis's Master of the Hunt, the Duc de la Rochefoucauld, was as anxious as the King himself to satisfy James's every wish in this direction.

With a great deal of ceremonial on both sides, the English court settled in. Visits were exchanged and the all-important points of etiquette were ironed out – such as whether the Queen should salute Monsieur in French or English fashion, and whether her lady-in-waiting, Vittoria Davia, now created Countess of Almond, should take precedence over other ladies of the French court.

The château was never intended to house an entire court, yet in the beginning the small Stuart court was almost lost in it, and had to be supplemented by French courtiers. Gradually, however, when refugees from England, Scotland and Ireland poured in, not only were the French attendants no longer needed, but Louis's pension to the Stuarts began to appear dangerously small, since few of the Jacobites were able to bring any money with them and nearly all were dependent on the bounty of James. At first, the financial situation appeared to be adequate: thanks to Riva, the Keeper of the Queen's Wardrobe, Mary Beatrice had most of her personal jewels, and James had recently sent out of England gold roughly approximating to £23,000 in modern sterling. The late Duchess of Modena had left her daughter a salt rent in the Île de Ré, and Louis had made over the Château Vieux to James rent-free. In addition, he gave the exiles a monthly pension of 50,000 *livres*. As the demands on their resources became heavier and more frequent, one by one the Queen's jewels were sold, although she retained to her old age the exquisite diamond pendant ear-rings which Louis had given her on the occasion of their first meeting, during her bridal journey to England.

Strong, wise and resigned, the beautiful Queen did everything in her power to disguise her unhappiness in the face of the care and consideration which the King of France offered her. It was not only the more spectacular efforts at distraction, such as balls and *fêtes*, which touched her, but also the little things – the provision of a layette for James Francis Edward which was a replica of that of the Duc de Bourgogne, Louis's grandson, and the removal of a Le Brun tapestry representing the family of Darius at the feet of Alexander when one of the Queen's ladies tactfully hinted that she had noticed it distressed her mistress.

From the beginning the Queen was on good terms with the French King's morganatic wife, Madame de Maintenon. Each respected the other, and recognized each other's spiritual aspirations. For the greater part of the French court a perfunctory appearance at the masses for Easter and Christmas were considered sufficient, while even the Archbishop of Paris derided James for having lost his kingdom for a mass. It was a strange fact that whereas, sincere as he was, James's religious observances were treated almost with contempt, Mary Beatrice's faith was always taken seriously.

The court of Versailles had much of the quality of a diamond: it was brilliant, hard and cold. Success was its only criterion, and sympathy was rarely wasted on failures. If misfortune hit one of their number, he or she stood a much better chance of regaining their place in that tightly-knit society if they disappeared for the time being with a flourish or a witty 'curtain-line'. But James, in French eyes, was a sorry and dull failure; they would have been more forgiving if he had shown himself to possess an intellect or a social wit to recommend him, to say nothing of a sense of humour. He had none of these things, and was thought to be graceless for retaining the ancient English title of 'King of France' as well as those of the three kingdoms of Britain; while his custom of illustrating his position as 'Defender of the Faith' by standing with his sword, point uppermost, in his hands before him during the Credo, was considered to be indeed bizarre. James was tolerated by Versailles, but Mary Beatrice was loved.

Yet a life of ease did not satisfy him for long. His restoration to better health and the long days of hunting with his friend, the Dauphin, did nothing to compensate for the loss of a kingdom. The Dauphin was a large, friendly creature – ill suited to the task of eventually succeeding to his splendid father – who did not demand much in the way of intellectual brilliance from his friends: if they hunted well that was sufficient.

With time on his hands the King had an opportunity to think and plan – plans to which Louis XIV lent a sympathetic ear. James's old tenacity came to the fore again. For some time he had been receiving optimistic reports from Richard Talbot, Duke of Tyrconnel, as to the present state of disaffection in Ireland, and Viscount Dundee's Highlanders were a constant thorn in the flesh to William of Orange in Scotland. Furthermore, John Churchill, created Earl of Marlborough on William and Mary's accession, wrote to James in terms of remorse for his past betrayal and, begging forgiveness from their exiled Majesties, obtained it.

How far this was his true reason for attempting to re-establish friendly relations is open to question. Ambition had always been Marlborough's overriding passion, a passion shared by his beloved and loving wife Sarah, who completely dominated the Princess Anne. He was not achieving enough under William, and possibly he thought that if he became responsible for the re-establishment of James II, then there would be a reasonable chance, with an ageing King, of making himself virtually master of the country later on.

An impoverished scion of a West Country family, John Churchill had come a long way since he had arrived at the court of Charles II. His looks and grace soon ingratiated him with Charles's mistress, the Duchess of Cleveland, while his sister was the mistress of the Duke of York. He accompanied James when he was sent by the King to Scotland, and continued to be a favourite with him when he ascended the throne. He was a member of the Privy Council and a Major-General of the army, but began to detach himself from the King when his liberal attitude towards the Catholics and other dissenters became too suddenly apparent.

He did more than anyone to persuade the officers of the army to adopt the cause of William and Mary, and thereby to remove any effective resistance from the time of William's landing in Torbay. The army had complete confidence in him, and for the first few years he enjoyed the royal favour. Suddenly a difference seemed to arise between William and himself and he was deprived of his offices about the court; yet, despite the displeasure of her sister and brother-in-law, Princess Anne would not abandon the Marlboroughs.

When Marlborough's offer of assistance came to Saint-Germain, James received it with more caution than he would have done in earlier times; he had at last begun to learn the lesson of misplaced trust. Still, Marlborough offered to raise the army for James and to bring Anne back to a sense of her filial duty. He had already won over the Catholic Earl of Shrewsbury and, apparently, was successfully intriguing with the Marquis of Caermarthen.[1] Provided that he accepted with caution Marlborough's offer of becoming his *chargé d'affaires* in England, James had little to lose in listening to his counsel.

He preferred however to base his invasion attempt upon Ireland. He gratefully accepted the French offer of money, ships and officers and left Saint-Germain for Ireland in February 1689. With him Louis sent the Comte d'Avaux as ambassador to the court of France and also General von Rosen, later replaced by de Lauzun, as military adviser. Berwick also went with his father. The King of France came to Saint-Germain to give James a diamond-hilted sword as a parting gift. Years later, in his *Ebauche d'Eloge Historique du Maréchal Berwick*, Montesquieu was to describe the Irish campaign as 'an unfortunate war where valour was never lacking, but discipline always'.[2]

On arrival in Ireland it soon became obvious that Tyrconnel had been oversanguine about success: the Irish troops were untrained and lacking in experience; there was dissension among their leaders and confusion was paramount. The French troops, reasonably enough, had no particular desire to fight on foreign soil for a cause which was not their own. All they wanted to do, according to Montesquieu, was 'to arrive, fight and go home',[3] and who could blame them?

Berwick distinguished himself and, at the age of nineteen, was made Lieutenant-General, replacing Tyrconnel who left for France. William himself was in the field and, after the Battle of the Boyne on 1 July 1690 had finished all James's hopes, he raised the siege of Limerick, which had been invested by the French, and returned to England. He sent out Marlborough as his replacement with 8,000 men who were harried by Berwick who was doing his utmost to re-establish the Irish army, break up the existing factions and generally restore morale. When Tyrconnel went back to Ireland in 1691, Berwick returned once more to France.

Viscount Dundee had meanwhile done all in his power to raise Scotland for James, and the Highlanders, who would follow wherever Bonny Dundee chose to lead them, came flocking to his banner. The Queen in Saint-Germain pawned more of her jewels to send him £2,000 for supplies. He had far greater success than James had experienced in Ireland but, sixteen days after the Battle of the Boyne, Dundee was killed at Killiekrankie, at the very moment when the tide seemed to be turning in the Stuarts' favour.

[1] Berwick, *op. cit.*, Vol. 2, p. 474 and note 3 to p. 157
[2] *ibid.*, p. xx
[3] *ibid.*

With their leader gone, the Highlanders lost heart and returned to their homes in the north.

During the absence of her husband, Mary Beatrice found the routine ceremonial of court life too much for her and retired with the four-year-old Prince to a convent at Poissy. Seeking an even greater seclusion, she moved again after a little while to the Convent of the Visitation at Chaillot on an eminence overlooking the Seine just outside Paris. This convent had been favoured by the King's mother, Henrietta Maria, during her exile and had been presented with her heart after her death. Mary Beatrice rented a suite of rooms from the nuns, and it was to be her frequent and favourite retreat at intervals during the rest of her life. The nuns, civilized and learned women for the most part, belonged to the order founded by St Francis de Sales which she had longed to enter as a young girl, and the Superior, Mother Angélique Priolo, became her personal friend.

She returned to Saint-Germain just before James's return from Ireland, sharing her time between looking after her little boy and a continually growing correspondence with supporters of the Stuarts in Europe, her brother, who was the Duke of Modena, and, at longer intervals, with Sidney Godolphin, Lord Treasurer in England. He had been Chamberlain during their reign and still loved and respected his former Queen. From him she was able to obtain some news of conditions across the Channel.

On 21 April 1692 James set off on another expedition, backed by French troops, money and ships. This time he had the humiliating experience of seeing his fleet, under Admiral Tourville, soundly defeated off Cape La Hogue. He returned only a few days before the birth of his daughter, Louise Marie, on 28 June 1692. Louis XIV was godfather to the baby and Madame, his sister-in-law, was godmother. James said that she was his 'consolatrice' for all his trials, and soon was to find in her the loving daughter that neither Mary nor Anne had become.

After another abortive attempt in 1696 which ended off the coast at Calais, Louis seemed to lose all interest in contributing materially to an invasion on James's behalf. It was evident that William was consolidating his position in England and that he had the money and support of the Whigs behind him. Apart from the extremist group of Jacobites, there was no real strength and certainly now no leader for royalist support among the Tories. Someone far more invigorating than James could ever be was needed to lead a rebellion guaranteed to succeed.

By this time Louise Marie was four, and she was to confide later to the nuns of Chaillot that when she saw her father returning to the château in a blue cloak instead of a victorious scarlet one, she knew that her England was destined to be there, at Saint-Germain.[1] Louis in no way lessened his care and friendship for the Stuarts, but they were now only useful to him as a tool for harrying the House of Orange although he still did not recognize William as rightful king of England.

At last James seemed to accept the fact that nothing short of a miracle would put the crown of England on his head again. What hopes there were lay in the person of his son, James Francis Edward, and he was determined that the future James III of England and VIII of Scotland should become a good Catholic and a good king – in that order.

The Marchioness, later Duchess, of Powis was the Prince of Wales's first governess. The latter was a natural appointment, considering that she and her husband had been responsible for saving the Prince's life in the first instance. Small as he then was, the Prince had his own suite: after the death of the Duchess of Powis his governess was the Countess of Errol, assisted by Lady Strickland. They looked after him until he was seven and then he passed into the hands of governors. His first was Lord, later the Duke of Perth, assisted by Mr Edmund Perkins until his death in 1697, and then Colonel Dominic Sheldon of whom Saint-Simon wrote: 'One of the rarest, finest and most cultured minds in all England – brave, pious, wise, learned, an excellent officer and of unswerving loyalty.'[2] He also had his own groom of the bedchamber and his personal valets.

William Fuller, who was for some time page to the Queen before he returned to England to reveal what he knew about the exiled court and a lot more besides which he had invented about the circumstances of the Prince's birth, described the infant James in 1696 as

. . . very Brisk and Airy, no ways deformed in his Limbs, but a Ruddy Complexion, fair Hair, and Dark coloured brisk Eyes. He, when but Two Years Old, was a great Lover of Musick, and could distinguish several particular Tunes when Played; he is a notable Fighter; and does not only beat his young Play-fellows on the least Distaste; but the Dauphin of France, going one Day to Kiss his Highness, and his Welch or Irish Blood being up, he gave the Dauphin a Blow on the Face with all his Might. None dare cross him, for he is so Refractory, that upon the least Occasion he will hold his Breath to that degree, that the Queen and all about him have thought him really Dead.[3]

It was a strange life for a child, full of contrasts and overcharged with ceremonial. Born late into one of the greatest dynasties of the Western

[1] Campana de Cavelli, *op. cit.*, p. 247
[2] Saint-Simon, *Mémoires*, V, Ch. 22, pp. 417–18
[3] William Fuller, *A Brief Discovery*, pp. 18–19

world, his inheritance was a title without a crown, a court without a kingdom, an allegiance without a country. Living in the shadow of the splendour of Versailles, he had gradually to learn how to maintain the outward show of royal dignity on the slenderest of material resources. When the only hope for the restoration lay in the unity of its supporters, he was to witness from his earliest years petty bickerings and jealous intrigues among those who served him. But he was sustained as his father, uncle and grandfather before him by the absolute conviction of his Divine Right to rule: even if his father had been deposed, he was still the monarch by virtue of the right passed down the royal line in legitimate succession and confirmed by the sacrament of the coronation.

Chapter Three

In 1697, when young James was nine, the eight years' war between France and the Grand Alliance composed of England, the Holy Roman Empire, Spain and Holland came to a grinding halt in the Peace of Ryswick. It had put an end to the struggle which had been consuming the vital energies of France and Holland, and, simultaneously, an end to any remaining hope that James II may have entertained regarding a restoration with French help.

The basis of the peace was that all territorial acquisitions made since the Treaty of Nijmegen in 1679 should be restored. Louis had to give up Breisach, Freiburg and Philippsburg, but kept Strasbourg and regained Pondicherry and Nova Scotia. Spain recovered Catalonia and the fortress towns of Courtrai, Luxembourg and Mons. The duchy of Lorraine was taken from France and given back to a son of the duke Charles V: Holland was to garrison strategic points, such as Namur and Ypres, in the Netherlands.

But far more important to the future of the Prince of Wales was the clause by which William of Orange was to be recognized as King of England, Scotland and Ireland. By signing the treaty, France had necessarily to subscribe to this clause as well, but Louis XIV did his best to settle his private conscience by recognizing William only *de facto* and not *de jure*. He may also have had some private understanding with William regarding the English succession. There was no doubt but that William's health was failing; he was a widower now, and without children. Although relations between himself and his sister-in-law, Anne, were maintained for the sake of appearances, it was clear that he did not welcome her as his successor.

Berwick throws some light on this possible attempt at agreement between Louis and William in his memoirs:

A little while after the Peace of Ryswick, His Most Christian Majesty had proposed to the King of England that, if he would allow the Prince of Orange to enjoy the Realm peacefully, he would ensure its passing to the Prince of Wales after his [William's] death. The Queen, who was present at the conversation, did not give the King, her husband, time to reply, and said that she would rather see her son dead than 'possess the Crown to the prejudice of his father; thereupon His Most Christian

Majesty changed the subject. It appears that what he had said had been concerted with the Prince of Orange; and it was, if I may say so, a great imprudence to refuse such an offer.[1]

Although he was writing with hindsight, it was probably about the time of this conversation that Berwick, who was now twenty-seven and a good judge of character, was beginning to realize that when the Queen's heart spoke before her head, as it often did, the results were not always what could have been wished in terms of diplomacy. But, knowing her views on the subject of the Divine Right, Louis could hardly have expected a different reaction.

A secret and verbal clause of the treaty – the repayment of Mary Beatrice's dowry of £50,000 – was soon to be refuted by William on the grounds that the money was only to be paid if and when Louis XIV ordered James, his family and his supporters out of the French dominions. But Louis was adamant that they should remain at Saint-Germain. If the Prince happened to be playing with his sister on the roof-terrace of the château, he might still see the bulky iron cart, surrounded by musketeers and outriders trundling along the road from Versailles, bearing their monthly stipend from the coffers of France. At times, preoccupied with more important things, the Treasury forgot, and nearly everyone at the château, with the exception of his parents, tried to borrow from somebody else, or took to poaching in the surrounding woods to provide the next few meals until the money should arrive.

He was being brought up to understand that there could never be enough money for his father to be able to maintain his supporters in the everyday necessities of life, while the luxury to which some of them had been accustomed was out of the question. He had first become aware of how meagre a prince's resources could be when he had met a group of Scots who had been officers under Dundee, at the entrance to the château. Two years before, after the Highlanders had returned to their hills, these gentlemen had finally found their way to Saint-Germain. When they realized that they could only be an extra financial burden on James, they asked his permission to join the French Army as privates. They came to bid him farewell and passed before him in review as he wished them God-speed. At his request, they had returned to see him again, and this was their first sight of the Prince of Wales already known to many 'over the water' as 'the bonny Blackbird' owing to his long, black Modenese eyes, and curling hair which had darkened since William Fuller had last seen him.[2] Without prompting,

[1] Berwick, *op. cit.*, Vol. I, p. 172
[2] See above, p. 37

the child gave them his hands to kiss, then welcomed and thanked them for all they had done for his family. Then he took his purse which contained 12 pistoles and gave it to them. Twelve pistoles among so many hungry men – but they cheered him as if the gift had been twelve thousand.[1]

Both he and his sister were beautiful children and their portraits by Rigaud and Larguillère were not mere flattery. Apart from his mother's colouring, James Francis Edward had also inherited her slender grace: his height, long oval-shaped face and indefinable air of distinction tinged with mystery and melancholy were purely Stuart. So were his hands – the long-fingered, fine-boned Stuart hands so similar to those of Berwick.[2]

At first, the ladies of Versailles had been shocked to see that from a very early age the Prince and his sister were dressed like little men and women; but they came to accept the fashion as more and more children arrived from the other side of the Channel, and gradually a generation was born that had never seen any of the three kingdoms. In any case, it was a practical fashion since little girls' dresses and their brothers' breeches could be cut down from their parents' clothes when every penny counted.

As the hundreds of exiles poured in from England, Scotland and Ireland, a shadow court was formed at Saint-Germain. Lord Melfort was the first Secretary of State, at first assisted and then replaced by Lord Middleton. Neither was acceptable to all the Protestants and Catholics of all three nationalities. Both were civilized and learned men of old families: Melfort had money of his own in France and possessed a house in Paris in the rue des Petits Augustins where he kept his collection of paintings by Rembrandt, Van Dyck and other masters, as well as drawings by Michelangelo.

Of Melfort, the Earl of Ailesbury wrote in his memoirs:

He was a pretty plausible gentleman and had flights of fancy, adorned a court well enough, but in Cabinet he was not true steel, which proceeded only from not being endowed with a consummate head for politics. His style was easy but too notional. In a word he did one great state action, and it was just that he should have the glory of it, and if he did no other that came up to that, perhaps it never lay in his power. That action was his treaty with the French Ministers, in so secret and efficacious a manner, that the French fleet in 1692 was ready to sail, wind had permitted, before the Court in London had due notice.[3]

Middleton, a Protestant with a Catholic wife, was the more likeable and sociable of the two, with a sharp wit and easy sophistication. All the royal

[1] A. Shield and A. Lang, *The King over the Water*, Ch. 4, p. 39
[2] Berwick, *op. cit.*, p. xxiv
[3] Ailesbury, *Memoirs*, p. 322

family liked and esteemed him, and the young Prince learned much from him about the outside world.

But it was not the personal qualities of Melfort and Middleton which caused trouble. The former was an intransigent Catholic who demanded an absolute, or 'non-compounding' restoration to the throne, whereas Middleton was prepared to settle for a restoration with a general amnesty and religious toleration for all. This 'compounding' attitude was adopted by many of the Catholics surrounding the King, including Berwick, as well as by Protestants, as being the only reasonable hope for success. The feud between Melfort and Middleton was to provide the basis for most of the unfortunate friction in Jacobite circles.

After his return from Ireland the King had found that, mostly through the Queen's organization, the court was complete. The Lord Chamberlain was the Marquis, later Duke, of Powis. Lord Dunbarton was Lord of the Bedchamber; the Vice-Chamberlains were Colonel Porter and Robert Strickland whose brother Roger was also one of the King's gentlemen. Another was Sir Edward Hales, created Lord Tenterden, who had been with James since his escape from England. The Lord Chancellor was Sir Edward Herbert, later Lord Portland; Lord Waldegrave was ambassador to the Court of France and Cardinal Gualterio was appointed by the Holy See to watch over Stuart affairs at Saint-Germain and to further the restoration by all possible means. This last appointment was not entirely acceptable to all points of Jacobite view, particularly in England: domination by Rome was an ever-present fear in the minds of most Protestants supporting the Stuart cause.

Mary Beatrice, as faithful as her husband to those who had sacrificed so much for them, kept Pellegrina Turini, Francesco Riva, the Countess of Almond and Lady Waldegrave within the intimate circle of her attendants. John, later Lord, Caryll was to serve her loyally for many years as her Secretary of State.

The face of Saint-Germain was altered now: where it had once been a quiet village deserted by its previous royal occupants, it now possessed an aura of royalty, albeit an impoverished one, and its streets echoed to the sound of French spoken with exotic accents, while uniforms of every rank and in varying stages of preservation and deterioration coloured them. Although the court was maintained in dignity at the Château Vieux, the delapidated Château Neuf had been handed over to the ex-army officers and men, and it was not long before a gay, ramshackle barracks atmosphere made itself felt. In 1693 the French Ministry of Works complained because the moat was allowed to be filled with rubbish by the English. Even in the orchard of the Château Vieux etiquette was relaxed enough to allow the

Queen's ladies to dry their linen in the sun while the children of Lords Melfort, Middleton and Marischal played with the junior Skeltons, O'Briens Plowdens and Dillons, as well as the three little Oglethorpe girls whose Jacobite parents were somehow managing to escape notice among the mercantile worthies of the City of London.

Most of the exiles at this time were brave, gay and ebullient in their adversity; they had a common hope and, to a large extent, a common faith; they were insulated by their isolation against the fears which a realistic appraisal of the way things were going over the water might have aroused. And if the King withdrew from them more and more in favour of the monastic seclusion of the abbey of La Trappe, seeking a fulfilment in things spiritual which he could no longer find in things temporal, they had to admit that he was ageing now – but they could see the 'White Rose' of their hopes in the shape of the young Prince.

He was growing and learning fast how to become a king. It was difficult because he had to be two people at the same time: a normal boy, quick, alive and eager, and the Prince of Wales, self-controlled, aware of his responsibilities and his status owing to God. He loved his parents, not only dutifully, but from the heart; their circumstances had made them a closely-knit family. Mary Beatrice's exile may have taken away from her the rights and duties of a reigning queen, yet it yielded her one great blessing in that she was able to spend so much time with her children.

Louise Marie was perhaps nearest of all to the Prince, despite the gap of four years between them. Not that the difference in their age was so noticeable. The Queen had always treated her little daughter with the respect owing to an adult and never condescended to her: Louise Marie was what, at a later point in time, would have been described as 'old for her age'. She was very intelligent, lively and with keen powers of observation; she could be serious at one moment and gay as a bird the next. If James Francis Edward was the 'White Rose' of the Jacobites, she was the Red.

The years 1698 and 1699 were eventful for the Prince from the social point of view. In the May following the Peace of Ryswick, William of Orange sent his personal friend Bentinck, Lord Portland, to Paris as his ambassador. One of the chief objectives of the visit was to protest formally to Louis XIV against the protection which he was giving to the Stuarts. Even Versailles was impressed by the magnificence of the state he kept, the carriages he maintained and the clothes he wore. This was how William had planned it should be. He was determined to let Louis see that money and power were not lacking in England and that fashionable taste was not the prerogative of Versailles.

The French King entertained the ambassador courteously and regally:

if the English display impressed him, he did not seem to show it, and he certainly did nothing about removing the Stuarts. One of the set-pieces of the entertainment was a royal review of the troops at Grésilles, near Poissy. Whether Louis's exquisite manners got the upper hand of his sense of diplomacy, or whether he wished to make Bentinck realize that no one dictated the terms of his own personal conduct to him, the fact remains that he invited King James and young James to the review as honoured guests.

On that bright, cold January morning the sun shone, the trumpets blared and the cannons pounded. It was an occasion to make the heart sing for the glory of France and to lift an eleven-year-old boy to the threshold of paradise. When Bentinck's party arrived the Prince was delighted to see that the ambassador's son, Lord Woodstock, a boy of about his own age, was also of the company. He was always avid for news of England, and now there appeared to be a first-hand source of information within reach, but it was soon clear that Bentinck was not going to allow even an interchange of the merest civilities. The young lord was recalled smartly to his father's side, and James followed his own father obediently to the little eminence from where Louis XIV was to review his army.

The three mounted men and the two boys, accompanied by the Dauphin, took their positions on either side of the Sun King. Behind them, in a crescent, were nearly a hundred carriages containing the ladies of Versailles. Already an excellent rider, young James, wearing the dark-blue ribbon of the Garter, sat his horse erect. In front of them marched and countermarched the infantry in their coloured coats – black for the German contingent, red for the Swiss and blue for the Italians. Then, wheeling and orbiting in formation, came the light grey cavalry with their red facings, followed by the gold-laced blue of the *élite*: the *Maison du Roi*, composed of the *Garde du Corps* and the *Mousquetaires*. This was the company in which every strong, brave and right-thinking young aristocrat longed to serve, but rigorous was the selection of applicants and demanding the discipline, for these were the men who surrounded the King and his family in battle, fighting under the white standard powdered with the gold *fleurs-de-lis*.

The deportment of the Prince of Wales on that day was such as to gladden the hearts and hopes of those near to him, and none could surely have been prouder of him than his personal groom, Charles Booth, who watched and fussed over him in the same way that a hen might have fostered a fledgling peacock. He came from Herefordshire, of a yeoman background, and was fearless in speaking his mind to the young Prince. His devotion to his young and royal master was often tried but it never faltered. He was always within call of the Prince and frequently in situations where he, personally, would far rather not have been, such as the boar-hunt at Poissy in the November of 1699.

There was a convent there, separated by a large wood from the château and its abbess, Madame de Chaulnes, was a friend of the King and Queen of England. The Prince often visited her, and she had given him permission to hunt in her park and woods for hares and rabbits. The woods were normally quiet and secret, the silence broken only by a convent bell or the harsh cries of rooks. On this particular afternoon, the grey monochrome of the trees and the Seine was torn by sudden flashes of blue, silver and scarlet, while the air began to fill with hunting-calls, the voices of men and the whinnying of horses.

Across the river, from the King's glassed-in balcony high in the château, a watcher could have seen two groups of men, each forming and re-forming around two boys, Prince James and Charles, Duc de Berry, grandson of Louis. All were carrying guns. In spite of their accoutrements, any approach or retreat by one of the dozen or so men to either of the children was accompanied by a reverence and a balletic flourish of the hat.

In appearance the boys showed a strong contrast: Berry was small and fair, with quick, almost feminine gestures; he chattered incessantly. James, although two years younger, was much taller than he, slender and graceful in his movements and less volatile in action and in speech. There was also a strong contrast in the clothes they wore: Berry's velvet suit far outshone James's serviceable one which showed long usage.

Their sport had been poor, and a light drizzle was setting in again, making the château even more forbidding in the failing light. Berry called his men around him and prepared to mount for home. James, followed by Booth, wandered away from the main party back towards the wood in a last hopeful quest for quarry.

On the edge of the clearing he saw a boar track. He could not pretend that it was a fortuitous find since a lay-brother at the convent had told him that there was a boar in the wood. He followed the tracks further into the trees, with Booth protesting respectfully behind him. His other attendants caught up with them and they too begged him to proceed no further. Nothing they said made any impression on the boy who moved so lightly and with such determination through the trees.

He ran on further, leaving the others behind, seemingly propelled partly by fear which must be conquered, and partly by daring. Near enough to hear the snorts and grunts of the animal ahead, he steadied himself to take aim. A crashing of undergrowth, and he was confronted by a solid brown mass of energy mounted on four stubby legs, its evil little eyes glinting behind the vicious yellow-white tusks.

Boy and beast regarded each other. Fractionally, James was the quicker, and he had already taken aim as the boar rushed at him, tusks lowered. The bullet travelled along the top of its spine and lodged in the lower part of its back. Squealing and grunting in pain and anger, the boar, luckily for James, turned a complete circle and began to run through the wood towards the convent. He followed it, and after him, thrashing through the trees, came Booth who had only arrived in time to see the bullet find its destination.

James kept up the pursuit until he reached the moat which he knew was too deep for him to ford. He could not swim and take aim at the same time, so he waited for the others to catch up with him. Then he made the unfortunate Booth wade into the icy water, carrying him on his shoulders. The boar was swimming frantically. The other men had reached the moat and two of them jumped in the water. By splashing and yelling at the frightened animal, they managed to exhaust it and drive it back into the small canal which led into the river. Once there, too tired to attempt to swim, it floated on the current almost into the side of a small fishing-boat.

The fisherman had been watching the activity on the bank and was poised ready for the moment when the prize should come his way. There was a flash of a knife, a final desperate shriek and the river around the boat ran red. The man leaned over the side, tied a rope around the boar and pulled it behind him until it reached the bank. Once there, he beached the boat and then fell on his knees before the Prince who was now well known by sight to most of the country people of the neighbourhood.

Freed from his usual shyness by the excitement of the hunt, James thanked the man with warmth and Dominic Sheldon gave the fisherman a piece of silver he could ill spare but appearances, as the sub-governor well knew, had to be maintained.

They were going to be late: two hours could hardly be called 'an hour or somewhat more' stipulated in the 'Rules for the Education of the Prince of Wales' drawn up by the King himself. Rule Twenty-four decreed:

> After dinner there must be allowed an hour or somewhat more for play, and about two hours more in the afternoon must be allotted for his studies, either before he goes abroad or afterwards, or part before and part after, according as it should be found convenient considering the season of the year.[1]

The whole of the Prince's life was governed by the Rules. James II was doing his best to ensure that the omissions and errors of his own education during his childhood exile were not repeated in that of his son. Fear of outside corruptive influences dominated the list of instructions from

[1] HMC Stuart Papers, Vol. I, pp. 114–17

beginning to end, and this meant that the Prince had few close friends among the Jacobite children.

No children were allowed to visit the Prince in his apartments with the intention of playing with him unless they were summoned by his governor, the Duke of Perth or, in his absence, by Sheldon. And then not more than two or three at one time were permitted into the royal presence: 'The proper and usual time for such children will be after dinner and supper, and at such other times when the Prince is allowed to recreat, and when the Governor, or in his absence, the Under-governor in waiting thinks fit to send for them.'[1]

No one was permitted to whisper or to run into corners with the Prince if Perth or Sheldon were unable to hear or see what they were doing, and the two men received direct orders from the King as to which children were suitable to play with James or to travel in his coach. This curb on the quick and easy friendships of childhood isolated the boy to a certain extent, and emphasized his innate reserve. He did not give himself readily: he did not have the easiness of manner and confiding charm of Louise Marie, and he was aware of it. Both lessons and personal relationships seemed to come easily to her, whereas James had to work steadily at both, but he was possessed of an extraordinary determination and would not rest until he had achieved what he had set out to do – there was in him more than a streak of his father's stubbornness. Even at eleven years old, he had a great dignity, and he was self-contained to an unusual degree. But his temper flared up and then disappeared as suddenly as it had arisen: this was part of his Italian inheritance.

From the time of the arrival of the Stuarts in France there had been plenty of spies for the English government around Saint-Germain, and always present in the minds of the King and Queen was the fear that he might be kidnapped or, at the very least, carried off by overenthusiastic Jacobites from Scotland who were impatient for the arrival of the King or the Prince of Wales on their shores. So he was hardly ever alone, except in his half of the confessional box. When he rose at half past seven, he was dressed by the groom of his bedchamber, either Nevill, Bellasis or young Strickland, as he had been undressed the night before. The groom slept in his room, waited on him with two waiters at table, and otherwise attended him.

Before his breakfast at nine o'clock he said his prayers and waited upon his parents. This audience frequently took place in Mary Beatrice's room which had belonged to the late Queen of France. The light and airy chamber with its white and gold decoration, mirrors, porcelain and chandeliers was

[1] HMC Stuart Papers, Vol. I, pp. 114–17

so unlike the rest of the château's stately and gloomy rooms that it made a good and pleasant beginning to the day. At nine precisely, the boy went, attended by his suite, to the children's chapel to hear mass in the company of the other Catholic children of the court,

> . . . which done, his studies may begin, and be continued so long as his Preceptor shall judge proper for his improvement. When his book is done, there will be time between that and dinner, which will be about twelve and a half, for his dancing, writing or any other exercise that costs but half an hour.[1]

He was a very good dancer; in fact anything which required physical exercise gave him pleasure: in addition to being an exceptionally accomplished horseman, he excelled many older than himself in fencing and shooting. From his uncle Charles he had inherited a love of walking at such a pace that his companions were hard pressed to keep up with him; this was a habit which was to last well into his old age.

As for his studies, he acquitted himself well, although he, even then, would have considered excessive his father's assessment of him as a 'genius capable of arriving at the highest accomplishment'.[2] He had grown from a baby with the French language ever in his ears; from the age of seven he began to study it seriously, although he was not able to speak it freely for a few years to come. In his teens he was highly proficient in both French and Italian. Mathematics were taught him by Father Michael Constable who also gave him his religious instruction. Other subjects were divided between his tutor, Doctor Betham, his sub-tutor, Doctor Ingleton and later, Mr Francis Plowden. Keeping an eye on all this and responsible for his general deportment and behaviour were Lord Perth and Dominic Sheldon. Both were good men and loved James with a warmth of feeling which was perhaps even greater than his father allowed himself to give to the boy.

James II was sixty-six now – old enough to have been his son's grandfather – and he had never been a lovable man or one easy to approach. Remorse for the dissipations of his earlier life had crowded in upon him, and he spent more and more time in Normandy at the Cistercian abbey of La Trappe until it seemed that he had come to accept, if not welcome the loss of his kingdom as a just price to pay for his future salvation. When the King went to La Trappe the Queen very often visited the nuns at Chaillot, so the two children, although well cared for and guarded, had frequent periods when they were the first lady and gentleman at Saint-Germain. Not that Middleton allowed anything to get out of hand: the lessons of the

---

[1] HMC Stuart Papers, Vol. I, pp. 114–17
[2] A. Shield and A. Lang, *op. cit.*, Ch. 4, p. 43

Prince and the Princess were carried on as if their parents had been present.

In spite of his age and his personal limitations, the King loved his son with a deep affection and for that reason had laid down the Rules which left nothing to chance. In its earlier days the court contained some of the liveliest minds in the three kingdoms, so there was little fear that the Prince would lack general instruction. As well as connoisseurs such as Melfort, there were always painters visiting the court, among them Rigaud, Laguillère and Gobert, while Perth, Middleton and John Caryll, besides being cultured men, were also writers of no mean ability.

His studies were balanced by a thorough programme of physical exercise. If the King had given up ideas for his own restoration, he was determined that when, and there was little of 'if' about it, his son should inherit the crown, he should be a complete being, mentally and physically.

> The proper time of his receiving company will be at his *levé*, and at his dinner, and in the evening after his studys are done, and at supper. But orders must be given not to let in all sorts of people without distinction and care must be taken that those who are admitted may not talk with the Prince too familiarly without observing that distance which ought to be kept.[1]

With his friends measured out to him and, even then, held at a distance, he must have been a lonely child, whether he realized or not the full extent of that loneliness. The visits exchanged with the young French princes were nearly always on a formal footing, heavily charged with the top-heavy etiquette of Versailles.

The lives of princes are usually artificial to a certain degree, but that of young James was more artificial than most. If he had been in his rightful place in London, even if he had not been allowed more friends or to mix freely in company of his own choosing, at least he would have seen the people and the vitality of the capital as he passed from Whitehall to St James's, Richmond Park or Greenwich. He would not have lived within a closed cultural society, but would have been subjected to the ebb and flow of the largest cosmopolitan city in the world. As it was, he passed in procession from Saint-Germain to Versailles, to Marly or Fontainebleau, all of them beautiful but artificial towns in miniature. There was very little contact with the common people when Louis, with the horrors of the Fronde still vivid in his memory, fell upon the simple expedient of removing the seat of government from Paris to Versailles. Paris was left to the people, but it was a capital without a crown, a body without a head. This did not mean that James grew up without an idea of the struggles of the poor: he

[1] HMC, Vol. I, pp. 114–17

saw poverty all around him among his supporters and he was comparatively poor himself, but it was a poverty which had been for the most part deliberately chosen, a poverty which would be alleviated if and when the King came into his own again.

With his studies, recreations and friends all carefully considered, weighed and planned, and his 'Holy Days' filled with the reading of good books, Catechism and Christian doctrine, it is to be marvelled at that he was not an impossible, model child, but the essential boy survived. The strong characteristics of simplicity and common sense belonging to Mary Beatrice had been born into both of her children. And James was a lively child in spite of all the loving attention to his upbringing which might have had a dampening effect on a less resilient boy, and the sound of children's laughter floated unabashed through the long corridors of the château. The Queen had a very strong influence over her son, albeit a good one but, with an ageing penitent for a father who was more given over to the spiritual kingdom than an earthly one, James could easily have lacked a masculine stiffening in his development. He needed someone close to him, nearer to his own age, but not too young, someone to be a hero for him: he needed Berwick.

Chapter Four

While the infant legs of James, the Prince of Wales were carrying him in a staggering course around the formal *parterres* and lawns of Saint-Germain, James Fitzjames the warrior was away fighting for the French against the Dutch, English and Bavarians. On the few occasions when the Duke of Berwick was not campaigning he spent most of his time at his father's court. Then there were three Jameses under the château roof: the King, the young Prince and his half-brother. The latter was eighteen years older than the Prince; yet they had one thing in common – both had spent most of their lives in Europe.

Berwick was tall, as were most of the Stuarts, and very handsome. He had the long, oval face, the sculptured hands and the good figure which belonged to his line. He had the same dignity, but not the aura of mystery which seemed to float around the boy James. Where the Prince was pale and dark-haired with black eyes, Berwick was lighter in colouring, with large blue-grey eyes and light-brown hair inherited as much from the Churchills as from his father.

He was a much more intelligent man than his father: direct, uncomplicated and methodical. He was a leader of men and a pragmatist. The flair for organization which he possessed was inherited from both sides of the family: James II had proved this side of his character when he had established the Navy, while strategy in military affairs was the undoubted gift of his uncle Marlborough. There was a warmth in this man which made the rank and file follow him with the same faith his intimates had in him: from his earliest years as a commander he had inspired a great devotion in his men and their confidence in him was never misplaced. Not only did Berwick look strong, he *was* strong and born to command, and in this quality of leadership he most resembled Marlborough.

There were other resemblances too: both possessed a remarkable flair for assessing people and situations quickly and accurately and for making vital decisions in the minimum time. Neither used the spoken or written word unnecessarily; both had a telling terseness of phrase. But James Fitzjames differed from John Churchill in that he was completely devoid of material interests. Money was of no great interest to him and was useful only in so far as it served his vital needs and those of his family.

Marlborough was probably no more and no less religious than any other man of his time and situation who conformed to the Established Church. Berwick was religious and a Catholic, but his was a tolerant Catholicism, and he realized very early in exile that if the King were ever to regain the crown he would only do so by tolerating other creeds. Jesuits were never allowed to interfere in Berwick's affairs, public or private: this may have been owing to the disastrous influence exercised upon his father by the Jesuit Father Petre before the Rebellion, and also to the King's ever-increasing withdrawal from the material world just when his physical presence and leadership were so needed at Saint-Germain.

When he returned to France after the failure of the Irish campaign in 1691, he asked for the King's permission to join Louis's army as a volunteer for the campaign then under way in Flanders. Permission obtained, he set off for the siege of Mons, and continued to fight under the Maréchal de Luxembourg at the Battle of Steenkerk. In 1693 he was made *Lieutenant-Général* in France and rendered distinguished service at the Battle of Neerwinden where he was taken prisoner by English and Bavarian troops. He had attempted to make his escape by taking the distinctive white cockade off his hat and pretending to be an English officer. As he was bilingual this ruse might have succeeded, but he was recognized by his other uncle, Brigadier Churchill, and taken to William of Orange who was commanding in person.

It must have been a strange meeting: the older man no doubt curious to see this brilliant young general of twenty-three who, in terms of personal capability, provided the strongest threat to his peaceful tenure of the throne of England. As for Berwick, looking at the man who had usurped his father's kingdom: 'The Prince made me a very polite compliment, to which I responded only by a low bow: after looking at me for a moment, he put on his hat again, and I did the same; then he gave an order that I should be taken to Leuwe.'[1]

Once there, the tide of battle turned again, and negotiations were put in hand in the usual way for the exchange of Berwick against some important English prisoners of war. Apparent in this account of the meeting is the Duke's immense pride. Not a word did he utter in response to what he admits to have been a polite approach on William's part, and the covering of his head in William's presence emphasized that he did not recognize any superior in the Prince of Orange. William was sensitive and vindictive about such things; Berwick's attitude would have been neither forgotten nor forgiven.

He continued to fight in Flanders under Luxembourg and later under Villeroy. In 1695 he made a love-match with Honora Bourke, the daughter

---

[1] Berwick, *op. cit.*, Vol. I, p. 224

of the Earl of Clanricarde, and it must have been a wrench to leave his young wife the next year, when their son was born, and travel to England on a secret mission for which he did not greatly care.

The King asked him to go to England to find out the real state of affairs there and to see how much support he could count upon from the English nobility. Berwick did not think much of the idea: 'a rather bad affair, of persuading the lords to act against their good sense. It did not succeed.'[1] Whether the King was privy to any definite plot is a matter for conjecture, but it appears to have been a surprise for Berwick. When he realized that his presence in London was also being used as an inspiration for a group of Jacobite hotheads who were planning to execute William, he hastened his return. Not before time, since his 'cover' was wearing thin, and he was recognized by at least one Englishman who, fortunately, was a Jacobite, by his height, his strong family resemblance and the length of his fingers. The man murmured 'May God bless you in all your enterprises!'[2] and passed by.

Honora, his Duchess, was well liked and formed a welcome addition to the inner circle of Mary Beatrice's ladies. But the winter air of Saint-Germain was often raw and unkind, and Honora was not the only one affected by it. The harsh winds sweeping across the plain from Paris, the draughty corridors of the château and the frequently ill-balanced diet enforced by necessity did not combine to make the royal refuge the healthiest of places. The young Duchess never fully recovered from the birth of her child, and gradually fell a victim to tuberculosis. Distracted, Berwick removed her to the milder air of Languedoc, but all to no use. She died in June 1698. There is no mention in any record of any other woman in Berwick's life before his marriage, and certainly no scandal was ever attached to this man in a period when scandal was commonplace. He was to marry again: he had to do so, since he now had an infant son in need of a mother, and one son in those days was but a poor insurance against the disappearance of a family name.

He came back to Saint-Germain for a few months after the death of his wife, and it was probably about this time that James Francis Edward and he became really aware of each other. The Prince was eleven years old and was reaching an impressionable age. What he unconsciously looked for and could not find in his father he found in his half-brother: he was the right age for a hero – not too young at twenty-nine and not too old; he looked and behaved well; he was obviously not self-seeking; and above all, his fearlessness, his air of command and his military prowess combined to make him a boy's ideal. And for all his straightforward, no-nonsense approach

[1] Berwick, *op. cit.*, p. iii
[2] *ibid.*, p. xxiv

to life in general, Berwick was also the fortunate possessor of that personal charm which, like a streak of sunshine on a grey day, had occasionally flickered in the character of his grandfather, Charles I, was so patently missing in his father, but had blazed to its fullest extent in his uncle Charles II and his aunt Henrietta. Most people who had dealings with him, unless they had reason to fear him, liked Berwick. And his dry and succinct conversation, so very much to the point, was of the kind to recommend itself to a child who demands logic above all things. He had no illusions about himself and gave himself no airs. Being a Stuart, he subscribed to the theory of the Divine Right of Kings and, for him, James II was his only monarch and young James was the heir.

It must have been with a special mixture of pride, affection, obedience, even amusement – for Berwick had a sense of humour – that this tall soldier looked down upon the dark and slender boy to whom he gave his allegiance. Because he had few opportunities of spending much time with boys of his own age, James, like his sister, was older than his years in many ways, with a lively curiosity, and Berwick was not likely to have been bored in his company. They shared a number of interests: the Prince learned much about campaigning from his brother, and they both delighted in riding and fencing.

They did not see much of each other during the year 1699, since Berwick, partly to distract himself from recent unhappy things and partly to obtain an idea of the kind of support the Jacobites might expect made a long journey in Italy. He returned to marry Miss Bulkeley, a daughter of one of the Queen's ladies. She too was liked by the Queen and the court, and was to make Berwick a good wife.

Saint-Germain had no longer settled down after Berwick's wedding than it was thrown into a second flurry of excitement by the imminent début of the Prince of Wales at the French court. The early summer of 1700 saw the end of the real childhood of James Francis Edward: at twelve he was henceforth to live in the limelight directed upon kings and the sons of kings. His father was spending more and more time in his Trappist retreat and, although he relinquished nothing of his royal state, he may have thought that it would be useful to have young James as an understudy for some of the more time-consuming social rituals of Versailles.

So the enormous coach which, with its horses, was the only personal belonging the rancorous Prince of Orange had allowed to be sent from England for the use of Mary Beatrice, lumbered out of the courtyard of the château one morning early in May carrying the royal family on a journey of approximately forty miles to Fontainebleau. Louis did not often stay there, most of his time being divided between Versailles and Marly, and the château was now largely given over to the entertainment of foreign princes who were visiting France.

After the bone-shaking coach journey, neither the old man nor the boy could have felt much inclined for the social ordeal awaiting them, and the Prince would have been no more than a normal child if he had not felt some flutterings of nervousness as he mounted the marble stairs with their wrought-iron balustrades twisting and twining into the royal and inter-laced 'L's and the lilies of France. Down the unfamiliar galleries they went, watched by silent, marble groups of godlike men, tall, slender, high-breasted women, smiling angels and cherubic babies, linked to one another by garlands of fruit and flowers. James II presented his son to Louis in the ballroom, over twenty great chandeliers making the boy's only remarkable jewel, the insignia of the Garter, flash and dance as they approached His Most Christian Majesty. The Prince performed all the niceties of royal etiquette to perfection, and delighted the ladies of the court. Louis in him-self was formidable but, surrounded by what must have seemed to a child of a small-sized family to have been cohorts of relatives, the effect was overwhelming. But Louis could be kind to young people, especially if they pleased him by their looks, deportment and conversation, and he felt a warm regard for the handsome, sloe-eyed child on whose slender shoulders the burden of kingship would probably be resting before long. They had seen each other on many occasions before, but then James Francis Edward had had to keep a respectful distance and he had remained almost ignored by his elders in company, since the Queen's sensible upbringing of her two children precluded any hint of precociousness of display.

Although he would not come of age until he became eighteen, the boy was now accepted as a responsible being in his own right: in theory, at any rate, he was almost the equal of the King of France. In practice, of course, no man set himself up to be the equal of the Sun King – no man, that is, who wished to retain Louis's approval. In so far as James II was concerned, in spite of his failures, it probably never occurred to him to consider himself as less than the King of France: they both shared the Divine Right of Kings and therefore were equal in the sight of God. Louis recognized this too, up to a point. He was more realistic than the English King, and could see that the Stuarts' chances of regaining the throne were slight. But in themselves at this time they were invaluable to him as pawns on his chess-board, and his chessboard was Europe.

If the Duke of Berwick had had any qualms about his young half-brother's capabilities to deal with such brilliant social gatherings, or if he had had any fears for the Prince being able to keep his social success in perspective, they must have dissolved as snowflakes in the morning sun when he watched his assured but modest demeanour at his reception by the Archbishop of Paris on the parvis of Notre Dame on 22 May. The great bells clanged, and the people of Paris turned out to welcome him, for this was a civic acknowledgement as much as a religious one. Not only the Parisians were there in force, but practically every English visitor taking advantage of the unusual peace to visit Paris rushed to look at the boy about whom they had heard so much but had had no chance of seeing until then. Close by, eight-year-old Louise Marie was delighting in the affection of the French crowd which welcomed her brother so warmly.

This should have been the boy's summer. Louis had organized a great hunt to take place in the forest of Compiègne in August, in his honour. Nothing would have given him greater pleasure, but it was to be one of his earliest grand disappointments. The sickly, hydrocephalic Duke of Gloucester, the sole surviving child of his half-sister, the Princess Anne, died suddenly. James, of course, had never seen this 'half-nephew' who was a little junior to himself, but Louis put Versailles into mourning – as much a sign of expediency as regret, for it cost him nothing to be polite to William, whose heir the boy had been. Some of the Jacobites and French courtiers had had the bad taste to demonstrate publicly their feelings of joy at the disappearance of the heir to the English crown, although this was frowned upon by both the kings in France. But nothing could destroy the hopes of the more superficially thinking Jacobites that, when the now invalid and failing William died, the English government and people would have a reversion of feeling and recall the Stuarts from their exile. Anne was considered to have neither the strength of character nor body to present a serious challenge and, in any case, certain informed circles reported that she was inclined to think favourably of her young half-brother, so there was a possibility that, even if she did not hand the throne over to him, she might consider him as her successor now that her son was dead. But Anne was more resilient than anyone guessed.

There were those, too, at Saint-Germain who felt that whereas the old King did not stand a chance of being reinstated by the subjects who had so blithely got rid of him, an attractive young prince was a much more pleasing prospect than the elderly Sophia, Electress of Hanover, the next in Protestant succession. The next in legitimate succession (after Louise Marie) was Anne Marie of Savoy, a Roman Catholic. She was a daughter of Henriette d'Orléans, James's aunt, but she was not interested in pursuing the claim. Sophia was a daughter of Elizabeth, the sister of Charles I of England, who had married the Elector Palatine, the 'Winter King' of Bohemia.

The Jacobites who followed this line of thought felt that if young James were to adhere to the Non-Compounding policy and promise toleration for all denominations in England his task would be a relatively simple one. What they did not realize, with the Channel between them, and their consequent necessity to rely upon hearsay, was that neither the Whigs nor the Tories would welcome a king who would rule without prejudice for any one party or religion. After William's firm line of government the party leaders were hungering for scope to exercise their personal power under a weaker monarch as they hoped Anne would be: each side wished to gain her for their own.

Perhaps no one at Saint-Germain realized this better than Berwick. His earlier education and experience in Europe had made him less insular in opinions than many of the other Jacobites, and he was able to weigh facts impartially and realistically. His *sortie* into England and his later journey to Italy gave him the opportunity of hearing and seeing things denied to the Stuarts and their adherents cooped up in Saint-Germain. But, at this time, there were other things on his mind as well as the question of the English succession.

On 9 November 1700, just as Louis was preparing to go hunting in the Forest of Fontainebleau, news was brought to him of the death of the childless Charles II of Spain. In his will Charles had named Louis's grandson, the Duc d'Anjou, second son of the Dauphin, as his successor. Both the French monarch and the Emperor had the nearest claims to the Habsburg throne of Spain which they had previously renounced. Yet the hopes still lingered that if they personally could not add all the Spanish territories (comprising the Catholic Netherlands, part of Italy, most of South America, Mexico, the Balearics and the Antilles) to their own, then at least one of their descendants would do so. It was not feasible that the rest of Europe would sit by and acquiesce in either the Dauphin or the Emperor's heir taking over this immense source of wealth and power without a struggle. Both Louis and Leopold knew this, so the French candidate was Louis's second grandson, and the Emperor put forward his second son, the Archduke Charles. On the whole, Spanish opinion seemed to favour the Austrian claimant; they had shared an Emperor with Austria before, and it was a case of 'the devil you know' being preferable to any representative of their old enemy across the Pyrenees. And meanwhile the rest of Europe waited, biding its time to unite in a common onslaught against France in a final effort to break her supremacy.

King James was now living in a world of his own, remote from reality. In the preceding five years he had been to La Trappe ten times for sojourns of four days and was, in fact, learning how to die. Soon he was thanking God for having taken away his three kingdoms so that he might become a better man. While the question of the Spanish Succession was in the air a new pope, Clement XI, was elected and the old King sent his elder son to congratulate him. So far was James out of touch with reality that he instructed the Duke of Berwick to inform the Pope that if France levied an army including Irish troops from Saint-Germain he, James II, would lead it in person. This would maintain the state of neutrality in Italy were it to be threatened by the events in Spain. But the Pope 'thought the task rather too great for him, and the Duke of Berwick returned'.[1]

Whilst the Duke had been away, in the February of 1701, Melfort had written to the Duke of Perth a letter concerning the considerable number of Jacobites to be reckoned upon in Scotland. Why he chose to write to someone so close to himself and the King and on so confidential a matter was a mystery. Even more mystifying was the fact that this letter was sent, allegedly by accident, with some mail destined for England, where it fell into the hands of the Government, and they immediately took alarmist measures against suspected Jacobites. There were many at Saint-Germain and in England who thought that Melfort had betrayed the cause; the King himself could not be sure. This extra worry did nothing to improve his rapidly deteriorating state of health, and he was taken ill in the chapel while the choir was chanting the last chapter of Lamentations: 'Our inheritance is turned to strangers, our houses to aliens',[2] and fell down unconscious. After a few hours he became better but suffered a slight stroke a week later while he was dressing. He lost the use of his right hand and at first had difficulty in walking, although this did improve to a certain extent after a few days. But Mary Beatrice and the children were concerned for him; so was Louis who sent him his own doctor, Maître Fagon. Fagon suggested that the waters of Bourbon might be beneficial, so Louis advised King James to spend some time there during April, gave him money to defray the cost and sent the Marquis d'Urfé to accompany him and the Queen. He seemed to have improved a little when he returned to the château, but in August he began to spit blood. For some time past he had been praying daily that God would remove him from this world of troubles, in spite of Mary Beatrice's protestations. He appeared to have made his peace with God and to be actively welcoming the approach of death. To his wife he said that 'God Almighty would take care of her and her children, and that his life gave him no capacity of doing anything for them'.[3]

On 2 September he fainted again in chapel; two days later there was another seizure and this time Fagon had to open his mouth forcibly and the blood flowed. When he was fully conscious again, he asked for his

[1] Berwick, *op. cit.*, p. xxv

[2] de Bosq de Beaumont, *La Cour des Stuarts à Saint-Germain-en-Laye*, p. 218

[3] Rankine, *Memoirs of Chevalier de St George*, p. 24

confession to be heard by the Jesuit Father Sanders and for communion. By this time Berwick had been sent for and, so far as young James was concerned it was not before time, because he was now going through the first major emotional upheaval of his life.

One of the first things to strike Berwick on his return was the public manifestation of the act of the demise of the crown: the King, his father, lay with the doors to his bedchamber unguarded and open to every passer-by. The curtains round his bed were left open so that his long, emaciated outlines could easily be seen from the corridor as he lay there with his eyes closed and the unaccustomed beard, which had grown so quickly during this illness, flowing on to his breast. The courtiers of Versailles who had used him with disdain during his lifetime, now began to treat him as a saint as he stood on the threshold of death. They crowded into his room with the sorrowing Jacobites to witness the passing of a man who had resigned three kingdoms to God. The Prince de Conti told Berwick that he wished to remain there all the time, so deeply was he moved by the manner of the King's dying.[1]

He received daily communion and on Tuesday, 6 September, made a general confession and forgave all his enemies, including the Prince of Orange, and his daughter, Princess Anne. Never once did he mention England. Then he called for his son. James Francis Edward was waiting in an antechamber with the Queen, surrounded by a group of weeping men and women, for this was a period when men were not ashamed to weep publicly as well as copiously.

As the boy crossed the threshold of his father's room he was greeted by a cloud of incense which served the double purpose of religious observance and of dispelling the odours of a sickroom. The priests and doctors around the bed stood aside to allow the Prince to approach. As he did so, the King, who had once again been vomiting blood, sat up in bed with an almost superhuman effort and held out his arms to his son. This was a scene which the boy was hardly likely to forget for the rest of his life; the old man with the long beard whom he scarcely recognized straining towards him, his face covered with blood, looking already like some ghastly apparition from the grave. Yet he did not hesitate nor let any feelings of repugnance or horror which he might have felt convey themselves to the King. He ran straight to him and was embraced in the long thin arms and held to the bloodstained nightshirt.

His father blessed him, and made the sign of the cross upon him. Then he recommended him above all things to adhere to his religion and the service of God, and 'to have always for the Queen all the respect and sub-

[1] Berwick, *op. cit.*, Vol. I, p. 169

59

mission due to the best of Mothers'.[1] Given over to a flood of tears, she was half lying on the floor on the other side of the bed, her head resting upon the coverlet. The King turned his head towards her, and gently told her to refrain from weeping with the words: 'Think, Madam, I am going to be happy for ever!'[2] He had already severed all his earthly ties, but she was still involved with her love for this strange, brave, obstinate, charmless man who was dying with so much more grandeur than which he had lived.

Returning his mind to the boy beside him, he motioned to him to give him a manuscript lying on a nearby table, and this he passed to the Prince with instructions to read often after his death. Then he charged him never to forget the debt which he owned to the King of France, and embraced him again. Fearing lest he should become over excited, the doctors tried to remove the boy, but he held on to him, crying out: 'Do not take my son from me until I have given him my last benediction!' He advised him then again, never to separate himself from the Catholic Church. At last he let him go, and the Prince made his way back to his own apartments. As the crowd parted before him at the doors, he saw Louise Marie, small and, even if she did not show it, probably very frightened, approaching with her ladies down the corridor towards her father's room. There was nothing he could do for her: she, too, would have to undergo the same emotional torment as he had done.

Once in his own apartments, James Francis Edward opened the manu-script which was to be the blueprint for his life from that day forward. It took him a very long time to read it all and some of it he could not entirely understand. It began clearly enough:

> Kings not being responsible for their actions, but to God only, they ought to behave themselves in everything with more circumspection than those that are of an inferior condition; and if subjects owe a faith-ful obedience to their King and his laws, the King is likewise obliged to take a great care of 'em, and to love them like a father. Then as you hold the first rank among 'em, and that you must be one day their King your-self, I believe it to be my duty, as your King, and your father, to give you the following advice: and I find myself yet more obliged to it, when I reflect on your age, my own, and the present state of my affairs.

This document accounted for many of the hours in which the King had remained with his study door closed against all comers, writing late into the night. There were eleven articles and in all of them the Prince could hear the voice of his father speaking to him. Although James Francis Edward did

[1] Rankine, *op. cit.*, p. 23
[2] Berwick, *op. cit.*, Vol. I, p. 169

not realize it then, this instruction was the result of experience dearly bought, and it could have formed the basis of the wisest reign of any English king. He read on, from the beginning to the end:

Article One – Serve God as a perfect Christian, and like a worthy child of the Roman Church, let no humane [*sic*] consideration of what ever nature so ever, be ever capable to draw you from it. Remember always that Kings and Princes, and the Great Ones of the Earth, shall give an account of their conduct before the dreadful Tribunal of God, where every one shall be judged according to his works. Consider that you are come into the world to glorify God, and not to seek your Pleasure. . . .

The third paragraph enjoined him to govern mercifully: 'A king cannot be happy if his subjects be not at ease, and the subjects also cannot securely enjoy what belongs to them if their King be not at his ease, and in a capacity to protect and defend them.' He was advised to live at peace abroad, and

. . . to endeavour to establish by a law the liberty of conscience; and whatever may be represented to you about it, never leave that design until you have compass'd it. It is a grace and particular favour that God does them, whom He enlightens with His Knowledge in calling them to the true religion; and it is by mildness, instructions, and a good example, that they are won, much more than by fear or violence.

Was this the king who had incurred such venom in England for his religious policies? Was this the leader in exile who had inclined towards the Non-Compounders more than a little? His hours of solitary contemplation and his conversations with the Trappist Abbot, Le Rancé, seemed to have done much to bring him to a more liberal frame of mind. This was to prove to be probably the most important advice which James II left to his son; it was to figure again and again in the declarations which James Francis Edward was later to send across the Channel.

There followed three counsels of a more personal nature which, to a boy of thirteen, in his circumstances, could only have been of an academic interest: nevertheless, he noted and digested them well. Paragraph 5 read:

If you begin early to live well, it will be much easier to you to preserve your innocence than to recover it after you shall have lost it. Forget not the good instructions that have been given you, to shun idleness, and bad company. Idleness will expose you to all sorts of temptations, and bad company will be a poison to you of which you will hardly escape the influences. Suffer no persons to come near you that talk obscenely or impiously, and by their railleries endeavour to destroy Christianity itself, and turn into ridicule the most Holy and religious practices.

His father then declared:

> Nothing is more fatal to man, and to the greatest men (I speak with a deep-bought experience) than to be given over to the unlawful love of woman, which of all vices is the most seducing, and the most difficult to be conquer'd, if not stifl'd in its birth. It is a vice that is but too universal and too common in young people. . . .

The awful example of King David who progressed from lust to adultery to murder was held up as a warning. How much of his father's past affairs was known to the Prince at this age remains a mystery. Certainly the Queen would have done everything in her power to protect him from anything which she might have thought would have detracted from his respect for his father, but when time hangs heavy on the hands, as it did for so many unemployed Jacobites, there is always room for gossip and reminiscence. On the other hand, the boy was cut off from contact with anyone whose presence was not sanctioned by his preceptors, so it was quite conceivable that he was still innocent of most of his father's past.

Next came warnings against anger – 'that passion offends God and is grating to Man' – and excessive indulgence in feasting and drinking. Then the King returned to things of a political nature: he warned the Prince against being drawn into offensive wars which were not just, and against exceeding his revenue. He must also dismiss ministers who abused their powers, and he had to take great care in knowing the British Constitution: 'Further, be instructed concerning the trade of the Nation, make it flourish by all lawful means. It is that which enriched the Kingdom, and which will make you considerable abroad.' And then, last of all, came the plea which had always been so near to the heart of James II: 'But, above all, endeavour to be and to remain superior at sea, without which England cannot be secure.'[1]

The Duke of Perth, James Francis Edward's governor, tried to keep the royal household running along accustomed lines, but he could do little to prevent the atmosphere of growing tension and sad excitement which began to swirl around the person of the young Prince who, perhaps, was more unconscious of it than anyone else. He was involved in the death of his father, but the bystanders were already recognizing in him the future King of England. Still King James floated between life and death; at times he was half unconscious, half asleep, at others he was alert enough to attempt to convert some of his Protestant courtiers. He told Lord Charles Murray to reflect upon his present state: 'It is not natural courage nor my own strength which sustains me in such misfortune and such sufferings; only

[1] Rankine, *op. cit.*, pp. 39–41

the true faith can effect a thing so much out of proportion to my own resources . . .', so Perth later reported one of the King's exhortations to the abbot of La Trappe.[1] He also expressed a wish to be interred as a private gentleman in the parish church of Saint-Germain-en-Laye, but when the King of France visited him he reasoned against this, saying that it would suit neither the King of England nor himself.

Louis had already visited his cousin, leaving his carriage outside the château, lest the noise of its wheels and the hoofs of the horses on the flag-stones of the inner courtyard should disturb him. James's imminent death brought its own problems for Louis too, beside that of his natural and sincere sorrow. For months past Mary Beatrice had been exerting all her efforts to obtain the good offices of her friend, Madame de Maintenon, seeking to influence Louis to recognize James Francis Edward as the future monarch. Apart from anything Louis might have felt personally, such a course would have violated the Treaty of Ryswick which acknowledged William of Orange as King of England, and it required an extremely courageous man, if not a foolhardy one to do so. Louis XIV was courageous, he was also a devout believer in the Divine Right of Kings and a loyal friend. For him, however, this issue was not only a personal and a religious one, but a constitutional one. Both he and his grandson, the Duc de Bourgogne, fought their Chancellor, Torcy, and the rest of the Privy Council long and hard over the fact that, whereas William could be, and was recognized *de facto*, only James Francis Edward could be recognized as the *de jure* king. Nothing in the Treaty of Ryswick had referred to the removal of the title of 'king' from James II, and Louis had only undertaken not to harass William in the possession of the kingdom. He ignored all the wise advice his ministers sought to give him, and rode out from Marly to Saint-Germain to inform Mary Beatrice of his decision.

Taking care not to enter the Queen's chamber by way of the King's, Louis went along the balcony to find her distraught with grief at the coming separation from the husband she had loved so much and in such adversity. When he told her of his decision, gratitude and relief transformed her countenance as she thanked him and asked him to let her husband know his decision from his own lips. Louis called the Duke of Perth from where he had been standing discreetly by the french windows leading on to the balcony and asked him to send first for the Prince of Wales. When the Prince arrived he said gently to him: 'Monsieur, you are going to lose the King your father, but you shall always find another in me, and I shall look upon you as my own child.'[2] He continued: 'I am come to tell you that I

[1] Archives Nationales, Paris, K.1717, No. 26
[2] Rankine, *op. cit.*, p. 26

shall recognize you as King of England when it shall please God to take your father.'[1] Upon this, the Prince, by now completely unable to cope with the weight of emotion forced upon him, threw himself at Louis's feet and wept his thanks. Louis raised the boy and then, leading him apart from Perth and the sobbing Queen, spoke with him in a serious and intense fashion: no one was a witness to this conversation. As soon as Louis had passed on into the King's chamber, James Francis Edward seated himself at the Queen's writing table and began to write, oblivious of those around him. Perth approached the table and asked him what he was writing. 'I am writing down', he said, 'everything that the King of France said to me, so that I may read it every day and never forget it so long as I live.'[2]

When Louis XIV entered the King's room everyone there stood back as he came near to the bed. He said to James: 'Monsieur, I am come to see how your Majesty fares today.' The King appeared to be almost asleep, so one of his gentlemen stepped forward and, leaning over him, told him that the King of France was there. James raised himself in the bed, asked where Louis was because he could not see him. Then his sight cleared, and he thanked his cousin for coming. Louis replied: 'I have done little; what I am going to tell you now is of greater consequence.' The courtiers began to go to the door in order to leave the two kings in privacy, but Louis said to them all in a loud voice: 'Let no one leave! I am come, Monsieur, to tell you that, when it shall please God to take you from this world, I shall take your family under my protection, and shall treat your son, the Prince of Wales, in the same manner as I have treated you, and recognize him as King of England, as he surely will be.'[3] He added that in the young Prince he perceived 'those early appearances of vertue and honor that could not but strengthen His Majesty in his affection to him, besides the obligations of conscience and affinity which he had always indispensably thought himself under'.[4]

Then pandemonium broke out: notwithstanding the dying man in the bed who was striving to make himself heard by the French king, the British and French alike burst into tears of gratitude, loud sighs of admiration and even applause. The Jacobites threw themselves at His Most Christian Majesty's feet, and the wave of emotion was so great that even Louis scarcely refrained from tears. Finally, he caught the words which James was trying to convey to him: 'May God render to you a hundredfold, in this world and the next, everything which you have done for me; only He

1 de Bosq de Beaumont, *op. cit.*, p. 226
2 *ibid.*
3 Berwick, *op. cit.*, Vol. 2, p. 473, note 4
4 Rankine, *op. cit.*, p. 26

1. Eighteenth-century view of the château of Saint-Germain-en-Laye. (*Radio Times Hulton Picture Library*)

2. James Fitzjames, 1st Duke of Berwick, in his early twenties, engraved from a portrait by Genaro. (*Radio Times Hulton Picture Library*)

is capable of recompensing you!'[1] Then everybody cried 'Vive le Roi!' Dominating his emotion as best he could, Louis then took his final leave of his royal cousin with the words: 'Adieu, mon frère, le meilleur, le plus outragé des hommes!'[2]

He left the chamber and descended the great staircase, crossed the inner courtyard attended by all his suite, and then proceeded to the outer one, on the confines of which his coach awaited him. At the main gates he stopped. Calling for the officer of the guard, he instructed him that when the King should die he should render immediately the same service and honours to the Prince of Wales as he had done previously to the King. Which done, he climbed into his carriage and returned to Marly, an old man who had been looking on death.

The visits of the Queen and the Prince of Wales had been kept to a minimum for fear of overexciting the King; on Wednesday, 14 September, however, the Queen insisted on seeing him, knowing that it could very well be her last opportunity for doing so. She agreed not to upset him by weeping and sat by his bedside, wiping his face and eyes with a sponge. He asked her how she was, and she replied that she wanted to stay with him night and day; then she asked what she could do for him. 'Anything that is the best for your health,' he replied. 'Am I in your way?' she asked. 'Not at all Madam, providing that all is well with you'[3] – he knew how much she was suffering through him.

As he seemed a little better, he was allowed to see young James again. As soon as the boy appeared on the threshold, the King held out his arms to him and said as he ran towards the bed: 'I have not seen you since His Most Christian Majesty has been here and promised to recognize you after my death. I have sent Lord Middleton to Marly to thank him.'[4] Then, after a little while, his strength began to diminish and he began slowly to sink: as his brother had done, James took a long while to die.

While the young Prince waited near the chamber doors that long Friday morning, he could hear the litanies being intoned and the singing of the penitential psalms. During the early part of the morning the King, surprisingly, had taken some sustenance, but in a little while he was shaken by spasms and a general trembling of the body. At three o'clock he lost consciousness, and about twenty minutes past three he smiled and died.

By the end the Queen was resigned to the will of God, but she was devastated by her loss: for days she had hardly eaten until she had reached

[1] de Bosq de Beaumont, *op. cit.*, p. 227
[2] *ibid*. Tr. 'Adieu, my brother, the best, the most wronged of men!'
[3] *ibid*.
[4] Berwick, *op. cit.*, Vol. 2, p. 473, note 4

such a degree of thinness that her ladies began to fear for her life. Immediately after the death, the representatives of the Pope, the King of Spain and her brother, the Duke of Modena, kissed the Prince's hands and recognized him as king. Then she, with Berwick at the head of a group of English lords, had an audience of him and saluted him as their king. It must have been a poignant moment for her as she made her reverence to him and said: 'Sir, I acknowledge you as my King, but do not forget that you are my son.'[1] Her influence was to remain with him as long as she lived.

Berwick, with the help of Middleton, took charge of the arrangements and the Queen retired to the convent at Chaillot for the time being. On the evening of the King's death, towards six o'clock, the body was exposed to public view in the death chamber. In the light of the tall candles the French princes and princesses slowly swept past in a silken line, scattering drops of holy water upon the dead man as they murmured prayers for the repose of his soul. Everybody at the court of Saint-Germain did the same, and they were followed by the inhabitants of the town. All night psalms were sung and, on the following morning, two altars were set up in the room and masses were said for the peaceful passage of the late King's soul. At four o'clock the body was opened and embalmed, whereupon some of the royal bodyguard took off their cravats and others took their handkerchiefs and dipped them in their late master's blood. In accordance with the macabre ritual of the time, the heart and entrails were placed in separate urns. Part of the latter were left in the parish church of Saint-Germain-en-Laye, part at the English College of Saint-Omer and the brain was left to the Scots College in Paris. The remains were placed in a coffin of wood which was placed inside one of lead and then inside another of wood. The whole was draped in black velvet. A plaque was placed on the bier: 'Ici est le corps du très-haut, très-puissant et très-excellent prince Jacques II, par la grâce de Dieu Roy de la Grande-Bretagne, né le 24 octobre 1633, décédé en France au château de Saint Germain en Laye le 16 septembre 1701.'[2] Then the coffin was lifted on to a black-draped carriage, drawn by sable horses with high, black plumes and taken to Paris that night, followed by two other coaches carrying Berwick, Middleton and other courtiers, the almoners, the prior and the curé of Saint-Germain. The bodyguard escorting them carried great candles of white wax, and they moved at a slow and dignified pace, surrounded by crowds of mourning French people as they progressed to the chapel of the English Benedictines in the Faubourg

---

[1] de Bosq de Beaumont, *op. cit.*, p. 230
[2] Tr. 'Here lies the body of the most high, most powerful and most excellent prince James II, by the grace of God King of Great Britain, born 24 October 1633 died in France at the château of Saint-Germain-en-Laye on 16 September 1701.'

Saint Jacques. On the way they stopped at the Convent of the Visitation at Chaillot and presented the heart of the King to the community who did their best, but in vain, to prevent the Queen hearing the arrival of the mourning cavalcade. On presenting the body to the Benedictines, a discourse was pronounced in Latin and the prior of the Benedictines replied in the same language; then it was laid to rest under a dais in the chapel.

The King had died on the Friday and the Queen remained at Chaillot all the weekend, neither eating, nor seeing anyone, completely stunned by her grief. Young James, meanwhile, was left to deal with his own emotions as best he might in the château which had probably never seemed more forbidding than it did at this time, with autumnal leaves falling to the long, sad terrace and the scent of death still within doors. On the same day as his father died he was proclaimed in front of the gates of the château by James Tyrry, the Athlone King of Arms, in English, French and Latin as James III of England and VIII of Scotland. The townspeople and courtiers gathered there cheered him as the last trumpet-note faded, and all the exiles acclaimed their new sovereign. He was thirteen years old.

Chapter Five

The sound of James Tyrry's trumpet outside the gates of Saint-Germain did much to disturb William III in Whitehall. He already had matters of considerable weight upon his mind: following the taking over by France of the Spanish forts in the Netherlands in March 1701, England and France were virtually at war, although it was not until the following year that it was made official. In June 1701 the English Parliament had approved the Act of Settlement which provided, in default of issue to William or to Anne, for the crown to be passed to 'the most excellent princess, Sophia, electress and duchess dowager of Hanover', the granddaughter of James I, and to 'the heirs of her body, being Protestant'. But the political climate in London in 1701 was equivocable in the extreme. The London Tories, who included a number of Jacobites, were in power, with the Queen Regent's admirer, Sidney Godolphin, as Lord Treasurer, and Robert Harley as the Speaker. In addition, a party of Scottish lords, led by the Duke of Hamilton, showed their enthusiasm for the Stuart cause by sending their representative, Lord Belhaven, to Saint-Germain where he stayed for several weeks. He dealt, however, only with the Queen Regent who did not entirely trust him, and with reason since he had been pro-William in 1688. Once she had firmly scotched the idea of her son's turning Protestant – in which event, said Belhaven, there would have been no difficulty about his succession at all – it was proposed that, if he undertook to leave the established religion unchanged, he would stand a good chance of regaining the throne, providing he crossed the Channel at once for Scotland. Mary Beatrice, although agreeing to the proviso, refused to let the King go to Scotland because he was too young. This was not only a mother's fear for her child venturing into the unknown but a total lack of confidence in the venture.

The 'non-juring' element in the Church of England, that is that section of the clergy which refused to take the oath of fealty to the *de facto* monarch, sent their representative, Doctor Charles Leslie to Saint-Germain. He was intelligent and efficient and the young King liked him. He too asked for a guarantee that the Established Church would be left undisturbed in the event of his succession and, in addition, that the King would leave the preliminary selection of candidates for higher holy office to the archbishops and bishops, only confirming their choice and making the final selection. They also wanted him to promise that he would allow Parliament to regulate

68

the laws prevailing against Catholics and that he would guarantee liberty of conscience. To all of this James, through his mother, agreed. Much of what had been demanded was in line with his late father's final advice anyway.

If Louis had been able to spare more time and thought for the young King's political situation, he might have been able to organize and make something viable of the various strains of enthusiasm for the Stuart cause but, like William, he had the question of the Spanish Succession on his mind. If he had been able at that time to sift these possibilities at their true value and to back an invasion attempt with money and men, it might well have succeeded.

Immediately after the French recognition and making matters much worse in William's eyes, the representatives of Spain, Modena and the Papacy pledged their support to the Stuart succession and, just as swiftly, James was proclaimed King of England by all the French ambassadors to the courts of Europe. When Mary Beatrice, approved by the Privy Council and by Louis XIV as Queen Regent, and assisted by Berwick at the head of the Council, published and sent to England a manifesto declaring James Francis Edward king, William became even more disturbed and recalled his ambassador, Lord Manchester, refusing to allow him even to make his formal *adieux* at Versailles. In retaliation, Louis withdrew his representative, Monsieur Poussin, from London.

The manifesto, dated 3 March 1702,[1] from Saint-Germain, declared that King James III would protect 'all his own subjects of the Church of England as it is established by law' in their legal rights and privileges, and in possession of their churches, schools and universities. He would also select with care worthy men of the Anglican religion for all posts in the Church. If the churchmen helped to return the country to obedience to him, he would waive his right of selecting the dignitaries of the Anglican Church which he would hand over to a council of bishops led by the archbishop of Canterbury. He promised also to forgo his title to the 'first fruits' and tenths paid to him by the clergy. It was understood that he would not persecute Catholics or other dissenters and the question of toleration of worship would be given to Parliament to settle.[2]

The manifesto was countersigned by Lord Middleton, and it was one of those instances of pure bad luck which seemed to dog the Stuarts that it was about this time that he made it known that he had been converted to the Catholic religion, apparently persuaded thereto by the shade of his late master, James II. This, naturally enough, did not help James's cause with his Church of England supporters.

[1] New style calendar in France, i.e. 21 February old style in England
[2] HMC Vol. IV, pp. 3–4

With James's proclamation the Tories fell from power and the Whigs returned, but Godolphin was reinstated as Lord Treasurer. The Whigs were eager for war with France and Spain, whereas the Tories who were pro-Jacobite were loath to fight the defender of their rightful king. Louis's championship of his young *protégé*, of whom he seemed genuinely fond, was undoubtedly the match to the fuel William had been preparing for the largest conflagration which Europe had yet to experience. No single member of the Grand Alliance was enthusiastic, brave or strong enough to attack the all-powerful France on its own but, together under the leadership, of England, most of the German states as well as Austria and Holland felt safe enough to do so. William's entire military career had been moving towards this moment, and he had had little trouble in persuading the States General in Holland to attempt to seize the Spanish Netherlands from Louis's grandson, the King of Spain, or in persuading the Holy Roman Emperor to try for the former Spanish territories in Italy. Much as he wanted to give all the attention he could to James, Louis soon found that he had enough on his hands where his own affairs were concerned.

On 7 March 1702, William signed an Act of Attainder and Abjuration against James. On 8 March he died. His death followed swiftly upon a fall from his horse, and Saint-Germain was taken entirely unawares. Versailles seemed, for the time being, to have lost interest in the Stuart cause and Anne was proclaimed Queen of England, Scotland and Ireland without any trouble at all. Now James shared with his late uncle the debatable distinction of being an exiled monarch with the death penalty on his head in his own country. William's anger had been directed more against Louis for his recognition of James than against the boy himself.

The greater part of England had become alarmed at the thought of possible invasion, and the Whigs took full advantage of the atmosphere prevailing. War was declared on 4 May 1702, and on 2 July Marlborough sailed for Europe and the command of the allied armies. Louis put his grandson, the Duc de Bourgogne, nominally in charge of the French troops, although Maréchal de Boufflers was there to do most of the fighting.

Louis's support of the exiled English king worried many at Versailles, and they questioned the wisdom of his action. But with regard to James himself they said that

. . . they shou'd be glad of any opportunity to serve him, whose interest they cou'd never think of deserting, were not that of their own country in the scale, the inevitable commencement of a war depending from the express terms of a peace very lately concluded. And therefore if they did not think this a proper season to proclaim his title, they cou'd not but doubt that they shou'd merit his Majesty's and the P[rince]'s excuse in what they said.[1]

In this they were probably sincere, for James and Louise Marie were loved by the French to whom their youthful attractiveness and gaiety appealed. They liked the boy's social grace and accomplishments, and the Marquis de Dangeau was to describe him in his diary as 'a very pretty prince who made himself much beloved'.

Yet, beneath his lively, sophisticated exterior, behind the boy who liked to fence, hunt and dance in the company of some of the most courtly people in the world, there was a darker side, a hidden reserve, an introspection. In all his portraits there is a hint of a secret sorrow: from the very moment of his proclamation and before that, James III plucked the bitter rue of adversity. He knew that everyone who was with him was also subject to the Attainder and automatically forfeited all that they had left across the Channel as well as their titles of nobility. If they returned they were under sentence, most probably of death; anyone in the three kingdoms who held any communication with him or contributed to the furtherance of his plans in any fashion was to be penalized in the same way. From the time when he had first been able to think for himself, his parents had made him aware of the weight of the enormous debt which he owed, not only to those immediately around him in the château, but also to all the soldiers from the highest to the lowest ranks, scattered across Europe, who had offered their services to states friendly to the Stuarts in order not to be a burden on the King's privy purse. He was to live with the debt for the rest of his life, and it coloured all his future thinking.

Apart from gratitude, one of the most outstanding characteristics of James was a sensitivity which his father had so conspicuously lacked: this he had inherited from his mother along with her quick intelligence and temper. He learned to control his temper more and more as time went on, and it was necessary to do so, since there was a great deal to try his patience in the intrigues of the court surrounding him. From his father came his bravery, although he was obdurate where James II had been only obstinate; from his uncle Charles came his unbiased judgement of men and, so some degree, his clear thinking. But Charles had kept his throne through petty shifts and personal compromise, and this was something which his nephew never considered. He was prepared to allow his subjects religious toleration but, where his own religion was concerned, there could be no compromise. In addition, he had also inherited the background of the long chain of mistakes which four kings before him had made, mistakes which had

[1] Rankine, *op. cit.*, p. 41

toppled two of them from their thrones and which invested the name of Stuart with suspicion in the minds of so many Englishmen.

His first act as king was to receive all the lords, with his half-brother at their head, as they knelt before him and took the oath of fealty. Then his servants kissed his hands. He confirmed in their appointments the ministers who had served his father, as the Queen had recommended him to do, and returned the Seal to Lord Middleton who had given it back to the new king in the usual way. Middleton was head of his cabinet, and the Duke of Powis was Lord Chamberlain. The ceremonial wheel had begun to turn again.

It is fairly certain that Berwick, as leading member of the Council, was not far from the young king's side when, on 20 September, four days after the demise, Louis XIV paid a mourning visit to Saint-Germain. He was received and led to an audience chamber by James who was wearing the great violet cloak of royal mourning. James then conducted His Most Christian Majesty to his mother. Afflicted by grief as she was, she had expressed a wish for no ceremony and did not wear the violet cloak herself. Respecting her wishes, all the members of the French royal family were also dressed informally, although in mourning. Louis let them return home to Versailles before him, but he stayed until the last and talked for a long time with the Queen and James, remaining standing the while. The next morning James returned his visit as etiquette demanded, and set off in his long cloak in the enormous and cumbersome coach which was now beginning to look old-fashioned beside the later, lighter models then in vogue at Versailles. But there was no question of changing it, even now that he was king, because the money for such an unnecessary expense did not exist. Louis met him at the top of the main staircase and took him to a room where, as an ultimate mark of respect and rank, he placed him in an armchair on the right of his own. They talked privately for a while until they were joined by the Duchesse de Bourgogne.

The French king took seriously his promise of looking after the young King of England and reviewed his domestic establishment at the château. This resulted in James being given a detachment of fifty French guards in addition to his twelve Yeomen of the Guard and six personal bodyguards. A staff of domestics was assigned to him at a cost of 50,000 *livres* a month, plus a personal allowance of nearly the same amount.

Touching him even more closely was Louis's own supervision of his education. Not only was instruction in the embellishments of fencing, riding, dancing and shooting intensified, but much stress was laid upon his lessons in European languages, and to these were added hours of instruction in mathematics, navigation (at which he excelled) and fortification. For all these lessons Louis XV paid. James was a good 'all-rounder', not a genius, but he was already developing those sides of his character which would make him one of the cultivated and discerning gentlemen so frequently found in the more civilized courts of eighteenth-century Europe.

At the back of his mother's mind there was always the fear that her son might be suborned by visiting Jacobites into heading off for his kingdom in a solitary attempt to win back the crown, and risking death if it failed. He was, after all, only thirteen years old and the romance and adventure of the situation in which he found himself were likely to appeal to any imaginative child. But if he was secretly approached, he resisted the temptation.

Mary Beatrice would never have been popular as Regent in England since she was a Catholic and so, in one way, Louis's preoccupation with his own affairs at this time was not inopportune as it allowed the King to come nearer to his majority. It also gave time, if used wisely, for Queen Anne to come to terms with her young half-brother whom she was reputed to consider favourably although she herself had given him the title of 'the Pretender'. Such terms could only be achieved on a private and personal basis while England and the Grand Alliance were engaged against France in what was to become the twelve-year-long War of the Spanish Succession.

Although his mother and Berwick at the head of the Council did their best to lessen the day-to-day demands upon the King's time in order to leave him as free as possible for his education and natural development, he still carried an enormous burden for a young boy. In addition to the emotional situation facing the solitary task of kingship, there was also the natural impatience of youth to be reckoned with. The sooner he came of age to engage actively in the business of regaining his own, the better James would be satisfied.

It was about this time that the young Earl of Derwentwater, also called James, came into his life. He was three years younger than his sovereign and the owner of large estates in Northumberland, the family seat being Dilston Hall at the confluence of the Devilswater and the Tyne. His mother had been a natural daughter of Charles II by the actress Mary Davies, so that he was a first cousin to James. He was a good-looking, fair-haired boy, generous, amiable and loved by all who knew him: he was the kind of friend for the King to whom no one could object. There was a different atmosphere in the château after the death of the old king; a new generation was growing up with new hopes for a young and well-favoured king, and the air of religious gloom which had previously made the court such a depressing place was rapidly being dispelled. There was every reason to be optimistic for a restoration, even if activity seemed suspended for the moment. But there was also activity of another kind: espionage was rife and there was a constant coming and going of both English and Jacobite spies at Saint-Germain. In 1696 William Fuller, on his return to England, published an account of his existence as a Jacobite spy: 'Several letters I carried to and brought from France were made up as the Mould of a Button, and so work'd over with Silk or Silver, and worn on my Cloaths: Others I brought over in the Pipes of Keys, and some writ Obscurely.'[1]

Berwick had only eight months in which to guide James in the first steps in statecraft. In May 1702 he left with the Duc de Bourgogne for active service in Flanders. It was evident that if Louis could take him away from James at such a time during the King's minority, then he must consider Berwick to be more his servant than that of James. This was the beginning of a situation disturbing in its implications.

It has to be remembered that Berwick had lived until his early manhood without a country of his own, although he acknowledged his father as his sovereign. All his childhood had been spent in France and his youth in the service of the Holy Roman Empire. Not until he returned in 1688, just before the Revolution, did he spend any considerable time in England and, all in all, that sojourn barely amounted to the space of a year.

He thought and wrote as easily in French as in English. Because his allegiance was a purely personal one to his King, and because the eighteenth century was a period when a good soldier could sell his services honourably in most of the European kingdoms, the modern conception of nationalism would probably have meant very little to someone such as Berwick. Now he may be recognized for what he was, a citizen of Europe rather than an exiled Englishman. There was probably not all that amount of surprise, at least in Versailles, when he announced his intention of taking French nationality, with James's permission, at the end of the Flanders campaign of 1703. So far as can be ascertained, there was no outward expression of resentment from Saint-Germain either. In 1704 he was naturalized as French, James having been advised by his ministers, and presumably the Queen Regent, to grant his request to become so. But in the licence which he granted to Berwick a clause was inserted stating that the Duke should always and everywhere be at James's service when he needed him. It was obvious that ambiguity could arise and eleven years later it did. But that day was still distant and in 1704, so Montesquieu reported in his *Eloge Historique* to Berwick's *Mémoires*, admittedly on information presumably received later from the Duke himself, all was achieved 'du contentement de la Cour de Saint Germain'.[2] In the same year Louis sent his new subject to Spain to assist his grandson, Philip V. His mission was to tidy up the

[1] *A Brief Discovery*, pp. 26–7
[2] 'to the satisfaction of the Court of Saint-Germain'. Berwick, *op. cit.*, p. xxv

situation of internal intrigue rife in the Spanish court which Louis, knowing that Philip was not the strongest-minded of men, had reason to fear. The Queen, who had been the Princess Marie Louise of Savoy, was inclined to rule her husband and she, in her turn, was ruled by her ex-governess, now chief adviser, the Princess Orsini, or Madame des Ursins as she was better known to the French. She had her favourites, Count Orry and the Abbé d'Estrées, who sought to influence her purely for their private gain. As for Berwick, who arrived with eighteen battalions and nineteen squadrons, 'he only regarded private interests as private interests; he considered neither Madame des Ursins, nor Orry, nor the Abbé d'Estrées; neither the wishes of the Queen nor the inclination of the King; he only considered the Monarchy'.[1] Louis had asked him to send Madame des Ursins back to France and, in spite of all her protestations, back to Versailles she went to give an account of her activities. She returned, chastened, but Berwick had other things to occupy his mind by then. With an army one-third the size of the Portuguese force, which was backed by the Alliance, he stopped their advance to Madrid and thus saved Spain and its monarchy. He returned to France in 1705, having been made Governor of Languedoc; in the same year he successfully besieged and took Nice which was the property of the Duke of Savoy, the father of the Queen of Spain and the Duchesse de Bourgogne.

While Berwick was away putting Spain in order as much for Louis as for Philip, life at Saint-Germain was proceeding in the usual way. If the King had decided to think no more about the Divine Right and his inheritance, it could have been a pleasant leisurely life for him and his mother in the château. If money were scarce among their followers they had only to shut their eyes and hearts and live upon the bounty of Louis XIV. But neither James nor Mary Beatrice were made in that mould. Always uppermost in the mind of James was the idea of his restoration as King of the Three Kingdoms, and whatever pension or monetary aid they received from Louis was shared among the needy Jacobites. The French king, knowing well the way their money tended to disappear, did not slacken his efforts to make their poverty bearable in other ways: regular deliveries of fruit and flowers were made to the château every May and September, and the two hundred pots of shrubs carefully maintained in the Orangery, while small personal gifts, such as a beautiful *prie-dieu*, were made to the Queen.[2]

In 1703 James became the centre of a small *brouhaha* affecting those closest to him. One of his tutors was Doctor Betham, accused of Jansenism and, what was worse, of infecting the King with his ideas. Jansenism

[1] Berwick, *op. cit.*, p xxvl
[2] Carola Oman, *Mary of Modena*

stemmed from the doctrines of Jansenius, a Dutch divine who advocated a return to the simple and practically Spartan principles of the early Christian Church, and had its headquarters at the convents of Port-Royal in Paris and Port-Royal-des-Champs not very far from Versailles. Louis detested any divergence from the conventions of Catholic worship and held Jansenism in particular abhorrence, but the prime instigator of the investigation into Doctor Betham's methods was Madame de Maintenon. She sought the advice of the curé of St Sulpice and of the bishop of Toul. Eventually, the matter was handed over to the urbane and learned Archbishop of Paris, Cardinal de Noailles, who cleared Betham of the charges laid against him. But, whether owing to his teaching or otherwise, James's approach to his religion was much simpler and more sincere than that of most of the French court.

The last two years before James's majority in 1706 were some of the happiest that he was to know. He had got over the initial shock of his father's death although he still mourned him and, as he inched more and more out of the chrysalis stage of child into man, he was becoming very definitely a personality in his own right. None of the Stuart kings before him had been content to remain mere royal personages, and he was no exception.

Time spent within the panelled walls of his study with its sombre dark green and gold decoration were compensated for by hours danced away at Marly and Fontainebleau. Louise Marie was growing up enough to be a companion and partner at the many social events to which the French king invited them. She had made her first communion in 1704 and her presentation to Louis XIV took place later in the year at Marly. She was good-looking, vivacious and intelligent, and her very existence must have been a blessing where Mary Beatrice was concerned since she removed any embarrassment or inhibition in the selection of a partner for the young king on social occasions. He loved her and loved to be with her. She was quick-tempered as he was, and more impatient than he. Music, entertainments and *fêtes* delighted her as well as the social pattern of the most brilliant court in the world. On the other hand, like James, she had a serious side and enjoyed staying for short periods with her mother at the Convent of the Visitation at Chaillot. This was not to be compared with the austerity of her father's sojourns at La Trappe. The nuns, with whom she became very friendly, let out quite comfortable apartments to ladies of quality, and neither they nor their tenants were exactly cut off from the outside world.

There was no doubt that the physical situation of Saint-Germain did not suit James any more than it had the first Duchess of Berwick. His chest was never strong, and the cold winds sweeping across the plain from Paris and buffeting the château walls were filled with danger for him. About this time he developed his first symptom of quartan ague which was to plague him, usually at the most inopportune moments, for the rest of his life. This malady, with its recurrent fever every four days and consequent debility and depression, was a form of malaria which responded to treatment by quinine. When the stagnant pools and moats around the château are taken into consideration, together with the lack of sewage, as it is understood today, the King's illness was not surprising. As he grew older it was notice-able that the ague attacked him whenever any major act or decision was imminent, and it is difficult not to surmise that much of James's illness sprang from nervous origins. Even today, it is apparently not unknown for a chronic malaria sufferer, when faced with a crisis, to worry himself into a malarial condition.

The Queen Regent, too, was ill now from time to time, and the doctors suspected a malignant growth in her breast. She recovered enough to go with James to Fontainebleau on a state visit lasting a fortnight, in the autumn of 1704, but did not participate much in the social activity, prefer-ring the peace and quiet of the royal chapel to the sounds of hunting-horns and violins. Hunting, in earlier days, had been the only sport for which she cared, and this against her husband's wishes. The situation was repeated with Louise Marie who also loved hunting, although James, fearful for her safety, disapproved of her following the hounds. As it was, she was thrown on one occasion and suffered a bloody nose.[1]

On this Fontainebleau visit during the last half of September 1704 the Stuarts could have hunted boar and stag every day had they had a mind to do so, and James nearly always did so. Louis delighted in organizing entertainments of every possible kind – balls, theatricals, treasure hunts with costly prizes, and other games to fill in the evenings for the young people – while Madame de Maintenon played cards with the Queen, a pastime for which the latter, unfortunately for her, never greatly cared.

Derwentwater and the three young princes, Bourgogne, Anjou and Berry were his constant companions in the daily sport, but on 30 September he was unable to hunt as he felt ill. Whether he had overtaxed his strength or damaged himself internally in some way when taking a fall from a horse, or whether it was the effect of a severe chill, the fact remained that he was not strong enough to ride. For a few days he followed the hunt in a carriage and merely watched its progress, but soon he had to stay indoors. By his departure on 6 October it was clear that his lungs were affected in some way. At home he became worse and began to spit blood. To his own sorrow and that of everyone around him, he was unable to accompany the Princess

[1] Archives Nationales, Paris, K.1302

to Marly for her *début*. At Versailles it was said that the young man could not last very long, and Louise Marie was regarded as his natural successor.

Indeed, it was the opinion of some in England that the girl might have made a better choice for restoration than her brother because, providing Parliament could have made her accept certain conditions as to the religious upbringing of any children she might have, a marriage could have been arranged with one of the eligible Protestant princes. She would have proved less of a problem than James as a possible heir to poor, childless Anne.

The snow-laden winds of January hurled themselves at the glass of James's roofed-in balcony and the gilt filigree of the railings was fringed with white as he lay in his bed coughing, spitting blood and seemingly growing taller and thinner every day. The young laughter was stilled in the château, and the King's few close companions, such as Derwentwater, knew by 20 February that he was near to death. The hushed, apprehensive atmosphere recalled the period of the old King's dying.

Then there occurred what seemed to be a miracle. He suddenly rallied and, as rapidly as he had fallen sick, so he as quickly recovered. Five days after being reported as at death's door, he was opening the ball with Louise Marie at a splendid reception at Marly.

The next twelve months or so was the halcyon period in James's life. Both he and his sister were very friendly with the Duchesse de Bourgogne, Louis's beloved granddaughter-in-law, and she was adept in arranging hunting-parties, water-picnics, masques and balls. These were days when the season seemed always to be high summer and the time, the golden afternoon. Mornings were for hunting; then, after dinner in the afternoon, parties formed of the Bourgognes, the Duc de Berry, the Stuarts, and their friends and attendants would float in gondolas on the waters of Versailles to the sound of violins. War may have been raging between Louis and the Grand Alliance at sea and on land in July 1705, but this did not deter the happy young duchess from chaperoning a party of eighteen young people and sailing down the lake at Marly to the Ménagerie where they ate, drank, danced and sang. They sailed back again in the blue twilight from their Cythère to the myriad candles of the Château de Marly.[1]

Yet James did not neglect his reading nor his regular sessions with his tutors and the Duke of Perth. He had grown much stronger since his illness but his doctors decided, after the scare about his health and as he was still growing, that he should not abstain from meat on fast-days, so he had his own separate table when he visited Louis at such times. He was simple and practical in his approach to religion, pious but not fanatical: he went to weekly confession and communion, and heard mass daily. At this time he

[1] Dangeau, *op. cit.*, Vol. 2, p. 229

was thrown much more upon his own resources than he ever had been before. The Queen did not diminish her efforts and care for him and looked after much of his correspondence still, but she was now becoming more of an invalid and, by virtue of her frequent retreats to Chaillot, less of a constant companion than she had been. He was missing Berwick too.

The Duke had spent most of 1705 reducing Nice, part of the territory of the Duke of Savoy. His more frequent presence during these two or three years would have been helpful to the Queen Regent and the General Staff, as well as personally to James. But now the Duke had to go where Louis sent him, and the French king's whole effort was directed against the Alliance; the Stuart cause had to wait.

There had been more than one sinister visitor to the château whom Berwick would have seen through far more quickly than Mary Beatrice could do. As Montesquieu wrote: 'The misfortunes of the King, his father, taught him that one exposes oneself to great error when one has too much credulity for people, even those of the most respectable character.'[1]

Few Scots would have credited that most dangerous of intriguers, Lord Lovat, with a respectable character. At first the Queen had been inclined to trust him, and none of her advisers had spoken out strongly against him. Perhaps some feared the damage his enmity might do to the cause, for Simon Fraser, who had wrongfully assumed the title of Lord Lovat, could be one of the most cunning and most vindictive men in Scotland. He could also be one of the most charming when it suited him to be so. Be that as it may, the fact remains that for a time he had the ear of the Queen and also of Lord Middleton.

The Scots wanted action, particularly the Highland clans to whom warfare was a way of life; they also wanted to see the 'bonny Blackbird', but once again the Queen resisted this demand to send her son. But she became more interested when Lovat told her that 12,000 Scots would rise if Louis would only send 5,000 men from France.

Torcy, the French Foreign Minister, naturally enough wanted to know more about such a possible commitment, so a John Murray was sent back with Lovat to see what the state of affairs really was in Scotland. This was at the turn of the year 1702–3. Saint-Germain had already sent over another Murray, James, to investigate on its behalf a few weeks previously. After Lovat and John Murray had left for Scotland, Middleton sent James Murray back to Scotland in their wake. He carried credentials and un-addressed letters to be given to such Jacobites as proved loyal, worthy and likely to be useful in raising a rebellion. Lovat obtained one of these letters, put the name of his detested enemy and brother-in-law, the Marquis of

[1] From Montesquieu's *Eloge* in Berwick, *op. cit.*, p. xli

Atholl, at the head of it, and gave it to the Duke of Queensberry who was a supporter of the British government.

Atholl, fortunately forewarned of the plot against him, was able to appeal to Queen Anne and was cleared of any complicity. Nothing deterred, Lovat also gave the names of three other Jacobites, David Lindsay, Sir John MacLean and one named Keith. All this time John Murray had innocently been acting as a 'cover' for Lovat's treacherous activities which the other Murray (James) barely escaped. The Earl Marischal, the Duke of Hamilton and the Earl of Home were also implicated, but managed to make cases for themselves. Sir John MacLean panicked and told all he knew, bringing out a number of names of probable supporters of the Jacobite cause: those of Marlborough and Godolphin included. The Whigs in the Lords wanted proceedings taken against these two peers, but they were not strong enough to combat the ministry led by the same two men.

It is hard to imagine what Lovat's aims had been, other than to revenge himself on Atholl and create as much harm as he could to all concerned. The affair itself fell to the ground, but it was the means of putting a match to the powder magazine already existing within the English Parliament, and also of bringing suspicion on any other suggestions for French aid to the Stuarts. Middleton's son, Lord Drummond, came to France in the early summer of 1704 with another and better organized project, but this was rejected by Torcy. Men came and went between Scotland, Saint-Germain and Versailles, some more serious than others but, according to Louis and Torcy, the time was not yet ripe.

James was becoming impatient, but there was nothing he could do about it, even though he was king. He had been brought to see through the unfortunate Lovat affair that his concerns in Scotland needed to be properly organized and that, loyal though some might be, others were equally treacherous. Without the aid of France it was courting disaster to set forth for Scotland.

So he bided his time, filling it in with work and play. On 3 November 1705 a great hunt was held at Marly in honour of St Hubert and attended by James and Louise Marie. She, at the age of fourteen, was entering upon a period of great beauty, and was celebrated in verse by Anthony Hamilton:

> Offrons à l'astre d'Angleterre,
> Au lieu des fleurs, ces nouveaux vers,
> Offrons les voeux de l'Univers
> Au plus digne objet de la Terre.[1]

[1] 'Let us offer to the Star of England these newly-penned lines instead of flowers: let us offer the good wishes of the World to the most worthy object on Earth.'

Shortly after the St Hubert hunt, James had another attack of the quartan ague and this left him weakened for the rest of the year. But he was more or less recovered by January 1706, the year of his majority. He desperately wanted to learn the art of war as his half-brother had done, and asked Louis for permission to join his campaign in Flanders or, failing that, to fight with the brilliant young general, Charles XII of Sweden. But Louis was not satisfied yet that his health would stand up to the rigours of a campaign, and he did not want to be held responsible for the death of his *protégé*. Also Louis had far too much on his hands in the war against the Alliance at that time to give the subject his complete attention.

In March 1706 Anne's ministers made it plain through their inter-mediaries that they would not consider peace before Louis had banished James from France and had promised to destroy the fortifications of Dun-kirk, to neither of which demands he acceded. In May the French were roundly defeated by Marlborough at Ramillies, and Louis was more than ever preoccupied with his problems.

Berwick was made a Marshal of France in 1706 and sent back to Spain to command an army against Portugal. Derwentwater had departed with James's permission on a grand tour of Europe in 1705 and, deprived of action for himself, James threw himself into the voluminous correspondence with which his mother had previously dealt. Shortly after his birthday, now known to all loyal adherents as 'White Rose Day', Middleton was able to write to Torcy on 28 June: 'Le Roy mon maître s'applique au travail presentem[en]t avec l'habileté d'un maître ouvrier.'[1] A master workman he was to be all his life: whatever he did, whether it was work or play, he threw himself into it wholeheartedly. The King might not have come into his own yet, so far as the Three Kingdoms were concerned, but he had certainly come into his own at Saint-Germain. He was now, at eighteen, indisputedly King, and a new factor was brought into play at both the English and the French courts, the personality of James the monarch.

[1] Tr. 'The King, my master, gets down to work at the present time with the ease of a master workman.' Thomas Carte papers, MS. 238, fol. 16

Part Two

IN THE FIELD

Chapter Six

Each of Marlborough's victories lessened the dissatisfaction of the English with their lot. Proportionately, their desire for a change of rulers diminished: they were more inclined to accept Anne than to run the risk of national disaster by inviting her brother, who was an unknown quantity, to take his rightful place on the throne.

In June 1706 James wrote to the Scots to say that nothing could be achieved at that moment; all they could do was to hinder by everything in their power the negotiations of the proposed Act of Union between England and Scotland and to keep themselves in readiness for a suitable occasion to rise. Meanwhile, he did not endear himself to the English Protestants by nominating Cardinal Caprara in Rome as Protector of England.

Berwick might have counselled him against this last action if he had been there, but once more he was away on Louis's business. Conditions in Spain were desperate again. Philip had raised the siege of Barcelona and had had to return to Madrid through France. Berwick persuaded the Queen of Spain to withdraw to Burgos with part of the army and the Privy Council, and her husband joined her there with the rest of their army. The Portuguese, on the side of the Alliance, rushed to Madrid, hoping to encounter them there, but they had already left. Berwick, 'leading them step by step as a shepherd leads his sheep',[1] enticed them out of Castile without giving a single battle. This was his genius – to make defensive war. He claimed that 'it took two to make a battle, and that a general should only resort to it when he could do nothing else, because the outcome was always uncertain, and that one should not risk the success of a campaign, of a war, or even less the destiny of a State when one could equally well, by good emplacements and clever manoeuvres, achieve one's object without giving battle'.[2] There was nothing of the coward in Berwick, but there was plenty of common sense.

In this campaign he took more than 10,000 prisoners. From this he went on to conquer Valencia and Aragon, to lead his men to the glorious victory of Almanza and to take Lerida by siege. In gratitude Philip made him a Grandee of the First Class and gave him the dukedoms of Liria and Xerica which he, in turn, was to give to his elder son on his marriage to Doña

[1] Montesquieu's *Eloge* in Berwick, *op. cit.*, p. xxix
[2] Berwick, *Memoires*, Vol. 2, p. 387

Catarina de Portugal, sister and heiress to the Duke of Veragua. On his return for a brief spell to France, Berwick was given the governorship of the Limousin. He was nearer to James, but still not near enough.

It was a long, dry summer in 1706 and the strain was beginning to tell on the nerves of both the courts. In Saint-Germain people seemed more edgy and quarrelsome than ever, and it needed all James's patience to iron out the petty bickerings and jealousies. It was probably with some feelings of relief that he went to Lauzun's house at Passy from whence he set out *incognito* on sightseeing trips into Paris which he as yet hardly knew. While he entertained himself thus under the guardianship of the sprightly little duke, the Queen Regent and the Princess stayed for a time at the Chaillot convent which was quite near to Passy.

As for Louis XIV, he took the hitherto unprecedented step of considering making peace with the Alliance. He consulted first with James and the Queen Regent, assuring them that

> . . . he wou'd never depart from their interest, tho' the present exigency of affairs and the pressing instances of his subjects had oblig'd him to make some overtures of peace to the enemy. They return'd his Majesty's compliment with sighs; and the (pretended) Prince himself replied, 'That not only his interest, but even his life itself was too small a consideration for his most Christian Majesty to put in composition with the good of his Kingdom.' 'I am content', says he, 'to leave my Cause to Providence, being entirely assur'd of your Majesty's sincere affection to me.'[1]

The war, however, dragged on, and in a desperate effort to make everyone forget it, Louis saw that there was a gay winter in all his palaces that year. Everyone danced, including Saint-Germain. About this time Anthony Hamilton wrote to Berwick, away at the wars:

> The King, our master, increases daily in wit and the Princess, his sister, becomes more and more charming. Heaven prevent her from being stolen from us.
>
> A painter might choose the figure of our young King for a model of the God of Love, if such a deity could dare to be represented in this saintly court of St Germain's. As for the Princess, her hair is very beautiful, and of the loveliest shade of brown; her complexion reminds us of the most brilliant yet delicate tints of the fairest spring flowers; she has her mother's eyes. She has the roundness one adores in a divinity of sixteen, with the freshness of an Aurora; and if anything more may be said, it must be said in praise of the shape and whiteness of her arms.

[1] Rankine, *op. cit.*, p. 46

Even allowing for the poetic licence of the age, an impression of two attractive young people remains.

The next year, 1707, was a little better: the Allies had been checked in Flanders, Berwick had been victorious at Almanza, and the enemy had had to retire before Toulon. Whether the King of France was feeling more sanguine than he had of late about his chances of victory, or whether he perceived an opportunity for drawing off some of the Allies' forces back to England, the fact remains that he did view more sympathetically another idea for raising Scotland. The Scots were generally irked by the Union of England and Scotland, and a party of Scottish lords had been in correspondence with Saint-Germain. Following their reports on the unrest, Louis sent a courier to Scotland to spy out the land, and ordered him 'to bring back the best intelligence possible, not only of the truth of what had been laid before him, but what force wou'd be required to put it into action, and what strength the English wou'd be able to send thither on a sudden'.[1]

The report was favourable; the affair received Louis's blessing and was sent to the Pope for his. The proposed expedition was promoted by Louis to the Pope as furthering the cause of the Catholic religion, which was not the best way of ensuring the support of the Protestant Jacobites, but so far as James himself was concerned, he wisely confined himself to sending the Scots a declaration of his intentions, dated 1 March 1707, promising to deliver them from the oppression of the past eighteen years and to maintain them and protect them in their independence. Now they were to muster and to obey the commander he would be sending them, seizing the castles and fortresses which opposed them. He also wrote to Lord Granard in Ireland along the same lines. As soon as possible he would join the Scots in person. He was eager to get on with the matter or, as Rankine put it, 'he was charmed with this new opportunity of putting himself into the world, having a secret impulse of glory that spurr'd him forwards to appear in something worthy of the character that was given him; and of putting in action those rudiments of honor which he had learned with so much pleasure'.[2]

In March 1707 an attempt was made by a party of English soldiers garrisoned at Coutrai to kidnap James while he was travelling between Paris and Versailles, but one of his staff was carried off by mistake. Both the English and the French courts were justifiably alarmed for the safety of the King and also of the Princess, and their protection was intensified. This did not seem to ruffle James in the slightest, and he stayed mostly at Saint-Germain looking after his ever-increasing correspondence and business matters both foreign and domestic. He attended to nearly everything himself. Early in his life he had learnt that although delegation had its

[1] Rankine, *op. cit.*, p. 48   [2] *ibid.*, p. 49

advantages, yet if he were to move swiftly and sure-footedly he had to keep everything under his own hand.

The plan for the invasion began to get off the ground in the autumn of 1707. Colonel Nathaniel Hooke, a Jacobite agent, had sailed in a frigate to Scotland to put the machinery of the affair in motion, but he found there less enthusiasm than the recent report had led everybody to expect. The Dukes of Atholl and Hamilton and the Earl Marischal claimed to be too ill to see Hooke, but Hamilton did make it known to him that the 5,000 men which the French proposed to put in the field would be of no use at all: at least 15,000 were necessary to ensure success. Also, they were not prepared to make a move until they showed themselves willing. So there was a checkmate. The Duchess of Gordon wrote that the Scots were weary of waiting and that something had to be done soon. Through Ogilvie, an English spy who pretended to be in the service of the King of Sweden, much of the Jacobite plan was reported to Queen Anne's government.

Still the young King had to contain his impatience and wait upon Louis's decision. There was nothing else he could do: he had no troops of his own and very little money. If he went alone to Scotland, the hastily mustered troops lacking in accoutrements, provisions and, above all, trained leaders would not withstand the opposition of the English trained forces for more than a day or so. If he were taken, he would be executed and that would be the end of the Stuart cause. So, whether he wanted to or not, he had to dance.

Whether or not to distract the thoughts of the court from the war against the Alliance which was costing so much and not doing so well, or whether it was because he wished to stave off for as long as possible the coming dark, Louis XIV seemed to wish that the young people about him should be entertained more than ever; even a young man or girl would have needed a very good stamina to withstand the marathon of late nights, dancing and hunting that was so thoughtfully provided for Versailles, Fontainebleau and Marly that year.

Generally speaking, it was innocent entertainment. Madame de Maintenon, who had brought up the young princess with such a firm hand, had lost none of her capacity for inspiring respect and obedience to her wishes, and riotous behaviour would certainly not have been to her liking. And, as he grew older, the King of France fell in more and more with the inclinations of his morganatic wife.

With mornings devoted to hunting and nights to dancing, the afternoons were for taking *promenades* such as the one on 28 September 1707 to the romantic ruins of the lonely Ermitage at Franchart which Princess Louise Marie wished to see. King Louis, the Queen Regent and the dowager

Duchesse d'Orléans were together in one coach. James, the Princess Louise Marie, Monseigneur, the Duchesse de Bourgogne, the princess and all the young people at court rode beside the coach in magnificent riding-habits with waving plumes or the white cockade of the House of Stuart in their hats.

For Twelfth Night, 1708, the famous Long Gallery at Versailles was lit by two thousand candles and the King and Princess of England danced until 4 a.m. Louise Marie was dressed in yellow velvet with her bodice and petticoat flashing with jewels, most of which were the remains of her mother's collection. In her soft brown hair she wore a diamond aigrette and other precious stones.[1] She and James opened the ball in the presence of Louis XIV, and great was the admiration accorded to the beautiful young brother and sister. When they left to return to the cold of Saint-Germain, Louis's Swiss Guard turned out to salute them as they entered their carriage in the flaring torchlights of the Cour de Marbre.

A fortnight later there was another ball at Marly to which the Princess brought Lady Betty Middleton and the daughter of the Earl of Melfort who, according to Dangeau, were 'remarkably pretty and danced well'. Both girls were close friends of the Princess and may well have received her confidences with regard to the Duc de Berry, for it was no secret to the court that she was falling in love with him. He was certainly an eligible young man, being Louis's youngest grandson and the one he seemed to prefer. He was reasonably good-looking, amiable, well-behaved, and although not religious, satisfied Madame de Maintenon's requirements in this regard more than the other grandchildren of the King. He was also a great friend of James. But Louise Marie's future was a question-mark and Berry's was not one to be gambled with. James himself was apparently not entirely heart-free either, for there is one report of his looking 'for some time with such passionate eyes' upon 'Mademoiselle de C.' 'as made it whisper'd at Court that they too apparently betrayed something more than a common respect due to so celebrated a Beauty'.[2] Who 'Mademoiselle de C.' was is open to conjecture. Among the young girls of the two courts at that time were Mademoiselle de Charolais, who was second daughter of the Duc de Bourbon; Mademoiselle de Conti, another of Louis's granddaughters; and also Mademoiselle de Clare, or 'Miss Clare', the niece of Berwick's second wife. Whoever she was, the Queen Regent saw to it that the matter was not discussed at court owing to 'perhaps the reasons of State that moved in the necessity of dissipating such a match'.[3]

Dangeau reports another ball, a masked one, at Marly which was not so exclusive and to which many people came from Paris. All were masked

[1] Dangeau, *op. cit.* (F), p. 50, note   [2] Rankine, *op. cit.*, p. 49   [3] *ibid.*

except Louis; even James, who was very plainly dressed, wore a mask and went *incognito*, accompanied by a very few members of his suite. He was hard to mistake, with his height and slenderness: Louis certainly recognized him, but pretended not to do so, in order to leave him greater liberty. Then the Queen Regent who had not attended the other balls gave a large ball at the château. This had to be given as reciprocal hospitality to Louis, and the townspeople were also invited. Needless to say that it must have cost far more than the depleted coffers of Saint-Germain could afford.

Lent put an end to all these gaieties. It began on 22 February that year. Six days later the plan for the invasion of Scotland was put into action.

Chapter Seven

If Berwick had had any say in the matter, Monsieur de Chamillart, the French Secretary of State for War, would not have been allowed anywhere near the plans for James's invasion of Scotland, nor would he have valued the capabilities, such as they were, of Monsieur de Pontchartrain, the Secretary of State for the Navy. Of the former he wrote later:

It must be admitted that he was a good man who had very good intentions: but he had so little genius that it is astonishing how the King [of France] possessing such a deep insight, could have chosen him for Minister, or at any rate, kept him so long, to the peril of all the business that daily came his way. He had a wonderful opinion of himself, and always used to say when you began to speak to him 'I know', although it might be about something quite other than what he imagined. He believed himself to be a born general and so he said once to Maréchal de Tessé that if he had been at the head of a body of five or six thousand horse, he would not have failed to have carried out some splendid manoeuvres. The first time the King met him was on the occasion of a game of billiards; he was one of the best players in the Kingdom, and as the King liked to play very much, this gave him the opportunity to come often to Court and be of the royal party. So he became charged with a post in the Department of Finance and, being in favour with Madame de Maintenon, he was made Contrôleur-Général when Monsieur de Pontchartrain became Chancellor. Shortly afterwards, on the death of Monsieur de Barbefleur, Secretary of State for War, they gave him that post as well. It is not surprising that he was not very good at it, since Messieurs Colbert and de Louvois, two of the greatest Ministers ever known in France, both found themselves with enough to do with only one of these posts. In 1708, no longer knowing what he was about, he begged the King to take Finance away from him and this was given to Monsieur Desmaretz; and finally, seeing that there was no means of leaving him in his position without risk of losing everything, the King gave him a large pension and handed over his job to Monsieur Voisin.[1]

Although this served to show that Louis too could be only human when judging his fellow men, it was to cost James dear, but he was so grateful to

[1] Berwick, *op. cit.*, Vol. 2, pp. 73–4

be setting off at all that he did not argue about his benefactor's choice of ministers. There was no one to advise him: Berwick was on operations in Spain that spring and, although the Queen Regent and Middleton were not entirely sanguine about the affair, they did nothing to prevent his going. It would have taken a very hard-hearted mother to try to deter her son, a courageous, clear-headed young man of twenty, from attempting to regain his kingdom when there was at least a possibility of success.

Whether from accident or design, Berwick was not informed of the venture until it was all over. The English government, through its spies, were much better informed than he. They knew that there was regimental movement in the Dunkirk area, that the Scots were liable to rise in great numbers, that the Duke of Atholl would probably join them, and that there was a plan to surprise Edinburgh Castle. They thought that 10,000 men were to be sent, whereas Louis had in reality promised only 6,000, and in fact only 5,100 materialized after Chamillart had begun to organize everything. He was at loggerheads with Pontchartrain, and neither the Chevalier de Fourbin, who was in charge of the operation, nor the Comte de Gacé, who was Ambassador Extraordinary to James and in charge of the troops, were whole-hearted about the venture. Possibly, they thought it an ill-planned idea, or that they had little chance of success anyway, or they mistrusted the Scots' claim that thousands would rise, or they felt that the troops and ships involved could be put to better use elsewhere, now that Louis's position was becoming more desperate. The only man who was really happy and convinced of victory was James.

On 29 February 1708 he sent an agent to Lothian and the country north of the Forth, to prepare the Jacobites for his arrival. Meanwhile the invasion fleet was being assembled: 2 men-o'-war were converted into transport carriers and these were escorted by 5 men-o'-war plus 21 privateers. Twelve thousand arms were embarked, but no saddles for the Scottish cavalry as promised.[1] It was not until this stage that the French court knew that Louis was definitely proposing to help the King of England. Not everybody was pleased with the news, especially when it was learnt that English ships were lying off Dunkirk, but their fears were to some degree allayed when these retreated to the Downs before the equinoctial gales then raging.

Before James left for Dunkirk to join his troops he drew up a Declaration to Scotland, the first which he had addressed to that country alone. In it, he repeated his father's offer of pardon of 1696 and added that he would leave the settlement of the Scottish Church to the Parliament of Scotland which he would also ask to confirm all judicial proceedings, apart from those taken against the Jacobites, since the Revolution of 1698. Ever practical, he

[1] C. H. Jones, *The Main Stream of Jacobitism*, p. 78

promised to pay the arrears of pay outstanding to officers and men who deserted from the other side to join him. And there was another important clause: 'We do hereby promise that the Vassals of such who deliberately persist in their rebellion, shall be deliver'd from all servitude they were formerly bound to, and shall have Grants of their lands to be held immediately of the Crown, provided that upon our Landing they declare for Us and come in to our Service.'[1]

Most of James's staff preceded him by about a week, making their various ways to the coast. It was noised abroad that his own few coaches were being prepared for a hunting expedition to Louis's château at Anet. On 7 March, Louis XIV came to say good-bye. Rankine describes the scene as James welcomed the elder monarch:

He received the King in the most dutiful and affectionate manner, having a great crowd of courtiers about him, and began with expressing some extraordinary sentiments of thanks for what the King had been pleas'd to do for him in this affair. The King told him very gayly, that he came not to receive his thanks for it, but to wish him good success, and likewise to furnish him with a sword, which he desired him to wear in the cause he went on, and to remember if it prov'd successful that it was a French sword. The Chevalier return'd the compliment, by assuring His Most Christian Majesty, 'That if it were his good fortune to get possession of the throne of his ancestors, he wou'd not content himself with returning him thanks by letters and ambassadors, but wou'd show him gratitude by his actions.' The King likewise ask'd if he was satisfied in the choice of officers and servants that he had made to attend him? To which the Chevalier reply'd that, as in everything else, so even in that he left it entirely at His Majesty's disposal.[2]

The sword, similar to that which Louis had given James's father before the ill-fated Irish expedition, was beautifully fashioned, with a hilt of diamonds.

After James had said good-bye to the Prince and the Princesses of the Blood, his last adieux were for his mother and sister. Shortly afterwards Louise Marie wrote to her brother: 'I am not unaware of what I owe to you as my king, yet believing myself allowed to speak to you as my brother, I feel myself obliged to say that, on this occasion, you must gather together in yourself all the virtues of our ancestors and you must conquer or die.'[3] First his mother, then his sister embraced him while weeping copiously, but

[1] HMC CSP, Vol. I, pp. 218–21
[2] Rankine, *Memoirs of Chevalier de St George*, p. 50
[3] *Journal Historique de Verdun* (1708)

it really would have been better if Louise Marie had been a hundred miles away at the time, as events were to prove.

So, on the evening of 7 March 1708, James left for the coast accompanied by the Duke of Perth and Lord Middleton, Dominic Sheldon, Lord Galmoy, Anthony Hamilton and Captain Gaydon, who later was to play such an important part in James's life. Several others had gone on before. A few miles out of Saint-Germain he dismissed his French attendants and took off his decorations so that he should not be betrayed by them.

His feelings at that moment must have been mixed: the exultation that it was all happening at last, the determination to succeed, the desire to be worthy of the trust that so many had placed in him. Doubtless the tears of the Queen were in his mind as she gave him some of her remaining jewels and 'expressed very dreadful apprehensions she conceived of his safety'. Whatever his thoughts may have been, they would have received an unsettling jolt when the carriage broke down at Amiens. Superstitious people may well have taken this as some form of omen, but James does not seem to have paid any attention to it. He spent the night at Amiens and, the nearer he drew to the coast the fiercer grew the wind because the equinoctial gales were still blowing. The next night he slept at Boulogne and on Friday, 9 March, he reached Dunkirk.

Now that the young king had departed, Louis XIV thought that the time had come to inform his representatives in Geneva, Rome and other neutral capitals:

I have long been of opinion that the assisting the King of England to possess the throne of his ancestors wou'd be for the general good of Europe; I believe that a peace would be consequence of its success; and that this Prince's subjects will esteem themselves equally happy to re-establish him in the place of his predecessors, and in being themselves deliver'd from the continual impositions, wherewith they are over-whelmed, to maintain a war altogether foreign to them.

As the Scots have got more reason than the English to be dissatisfy'd with the present government of England, it appears to be a convenient opportunity to restore that nation their lawful Sovereign, and to enable the Prince to deliver it from the oppression it has suffer'd since the Revolution, which happened under the late King of England, James II.

These are the reasons which have determined me to equip a squadron of my ships at Dunkirk, and to furnish the King of England with a considerable number of my troops to accompany him to Scotland to support those his faithful subjects who shall declare for him.

He left this place yesterday, to go to Dunkirk, in order to embark and get with all expedition to Scotland. His intention is not to enter the Kingdom by right of conquest, but to oblige them to receive him as legal possessor of it. He will behave himself in like manner with respect to all his Dominions, who shall pay the obedience they owe him, and his subjects will only be distinguish'd according to the zeal and affection they show for him, without examining what religion they profess'd in which he leaves them in their entire liberty.

I have not thoughts of enlarging my power by assisting to re-establish this Prince. 'Tis sufficient that I do an act of justice in vindicating the honour of crown'd heads, highly affronted in the person of the King his father; and my wishes will be entirely accomplished, if by God's blessing on the endeavours, the success become means of procuring a lasting peace, so necessary to all Europe.

As this Resolution of mine will soon spread itself thro' Europe, my will is that you speak of it in the manner I direct you.

Given at Versailles, this Eighth of March, 1708[1]

If Louis did not have, as he so ingenuously asserted, any thoughts of enlarging his power by assisting James, he was none the less very happy to learn that there was a panic run upon the Bank of England and that English troops were being withdrawn from Flanders to cope with a possible invasion in Scotland. The latter information, on the other hand, was not encouraging for the Jacobites. However, the Catholics among them were heartened by the news that the Pope had ordered public prayers to be said for a period of forty hours in the English, Irish and Scots churches in Rome for the success of the enterprise.

The sea had its own special malice for James: it had not welcomed him in his early infancy when he had first come to France and it did not welcome him now. The English admiral, Sir John Leake, had been on his way to support the Allied troops in Portugal when fortuitous gales blew him to Torbay. He had hardly put a foot ashore before being ordered back in his ship again to see what was going on off the French coast; so he lay off Dunkirk, effectively blockading the port. Thereupon the French soldiers were disembarked from James's ships.

This was the situation he found on his arrival at Dunkirk. He also found further tokens of Louis's consideration for him: there was finely-wrought gold and silver plate for his table, strong tents and clothes and liveries for his household and personal guard. There were standards in plenty, displaying suitable devices, such as '*Nil desperandum Christo Duce Auspice Christo*', '*Dieu et mon Droit*' and *Q'ui Venti et Mare obediunt, impera Domine et fac*

[1] Rankine, *op. cit.*, pp. 51–2

Tranquilitatem'. But when he arrived, he was scarcely in a position to appreciate all this, for he was very tired and had a mounting fever. He did not know yet that shortly after his sister had embraced and wept over him in loving farewell, she had fallen victim to the measles, and now it was his turn. It could not have been more badly timed.

With the harbour blockaded, the French admiral, Forbin, was not inclined to risk his ships, and nothing James himself or Perth or Middleton could say would move him. No one but the King of France could give orders to his fleet or his army. His decision was reinforced when another English squadron under Admiral Byng took up position off Gravelines. James argued and pleaded, but all in vain. Finally he sent a messenger back to Versailles. Forbin sent one also, stating that he might get the troopships out, but he could not be responsible for the safety of his fleet when he landed the troops, *if* he landed them. Louis told him to get on with the work.

By now it was 17 March, and James was in a high fever, suffering very much from that childish ailment which is not merely humiliating but dangerous when experienced in adult life. His doctor told him that it was impossible to proceed, but the King would not be deterred. For the first time the wind had turned in his favour; the British ships had been forced to quit their positions and were being blown towards the coast of Brittany. By now they had been at sea for some time and were carrying a weight of water in their timbers, whereas the French fleet had not only recently put to sea but was specially composed of light, fast-moving vessels, so Forbin had the advantage of speed. Willy-nilly, he re-embarked Grace's troops and James, wrapped up in blankets, was carried on board. On 18 March James wrote in French to his mother: 'At last I am on board. My body is weak but my courage is so high that it will uphold the weakness of the body. I hope that when I write to you again it will be from the palace at Edinburgh where I reckon to arrive on Saturday.'[1] With the wind in their favour, they sailed out of the Flemish Roads, but then it changed and their destiny with it. They were forced to stay in Newport Pits until 27 March when they set course for Scotland. Their delay had not passed unnoticed by the English Intelligence, and Byng was ordered to leave Gravelines and follow the French.

Great confusion reigned in Scotland, and communications between one group of Stuart adherents and another was rapidly coming to a standstill. Both the Duke of Atholl, representing the Highlands, and the Duke of Hamilton for the Lowlands, considered themselves the leader of the Scots Jacobites. It was for this reason that the Scots expressed to Colonel Hooke,

---

[1] Dangeau, *Journal de la Cour de Louis XIV*, (D), Vol. XII, p. 101

during his reconnaissance, that they wanted Berwick for their leader but, as we have seen, Louis had taken care that he should be engaged elsewhere: from Spain he had been sent to Germany to harry Prince Eugène, the brilliant military genius of the Alliance.

There was an extraordinary dichotomy in Louis's attitude over this whole affair. Much as he genuinely loved James, much as he respected the Divine Right of Kings and wanted to see the English monarchy restored, it suited his own purposes only too well if the invasion plan did not succeed, providing enough hope was left for the Jacobites to be an ever-present thorn in the flesh of the English government. With Berwick their chances of success would undoubtedly have been much higher, for the one thing which was lacking above all others was a competent leader.

Meanwhile ten battalions of English troops were rushed back from Flanders, in a war-weary condition 'We had continual Distruction in ye fore-top; ye Pox above board; ye Plague between Decks; Hell in ye fore-castle, and ye Devil att ye Helm':[1] so wrote a soldier in one of the battalions sent immediately to Scotland. They were soon joined by a squadron of horse grenadiers, two regiments of dragoons, two troops of guards of the Duke of Northumberland's Regiment of Horse and several regiments of foot.

The French transports were carrying ten battalions and their supplies, plus an extra four hundred non-commissioned officers for the troops they expected to find in Scotland. James was on board the *Mars* with Maréchal de Gacé, the Duke of Perth, Lord Middleton, Lord Galmoy and other officers and gentlemen. In spite of his illness, in spite of Forbin's obstinacy and all the delays, he still believed fervently in what he had set out to accomplish and his hopes were sanguine enough, as his note to his mother showed.

On the *Salisbury* were the two sons of Lord Middleton, the Marquis de Lévy, Colonel Francis Wauchope and the elderly Lord Griffin among others, and the ship's company of nearly 300 men and officers. Griffin was a devoted follower of James – a bluff, courageous old gentleman, not very intelligent according to the Earl of Ailesbury, 'he understood dogs and horses, and that well; and being refused the place of Secretary of State there (and if he could write his name that was all) he stuck to the Count of Toulouse, a natural son of Louis the fourteenth, a passionate lover of hunting, and he kept a good table, which this lord delighted in'.[2] He was hurt to the quick when he learned that he had been kept out of the invasion plan because of his age, and remonstrated bitterly to the Queen. He did not

[1] J. M. Deane, *A Journal of the Campaign in Flanders*, p. 6
[2] Ailesbury, *Memoirs*, p. 605

stop at words, however, but leapt on his horse and galloped off in the wake of the younger men, towards the coast.

Owing to the delay, when the French fleet did reach the mouth of the Forth on the early morning of 23 March, having first overshot the Firth of Forth, there was no one to welcome them and, what was worse, no pilots to guide them in. The Scots had given them up. The Comte de Gacé described the situation in a letter to Monsieur Chamillart:

> . . . with a strong gale we made the Frith [*sic*] of Edinburgh the 23rd in the morning, and in the evening cast anchor at the mouth of it. The 24th in the morning as we made ready to enter the Frith, we discover'd a great number of ships which we soon found to be the enemies' squadron to the number of twenty eight sail, who we judg'd to be the same that appear'd off Dunkirk, whereupon Monsieur de Fourbin resolv'd to bear off by the favour of a land breeze, which very luckily carried us from the enemy; the latter pursuing us very close all that day [24th] and four of their best sailors being come up with our sternmost ships, the enemy's foremost ship attack'd at four in the afternoon, the *August* with whom she exchang'd some shot, for some time after the English bore down upon the *Salisbury*, which was more a stern, and endeavoured to put her between herself and another English ship that was coming up to her.[1]

The *Salisbury* put up a great fire with her small arms, and the fight between her and the English ship lasted until nightfall. But by that time, all the French ships were scattered, and Admiral de Forbin's ship which was carrying the King found itself surrounded on all sides. The darkness proved to be their friend because the *Mars* was able to take evasive action and, on the morning of the 25th, it picked up with twenty of their own ships at a considerable distance from the enemy. After consultation with both Gacé and James, Forbin decided to set off for Inverness, but they had no pilots with them who knew how to put in to that port. Finally, the admiral sent off a frigate to fetch pilots from the nearest point which was the Cape of Buccaness. The wind favoured them on a fairly straightforward course to the north of Scotland during the day, but towards midnight a gale arose and continued with such violence during the next day that the Frenchmen were obliged to tell the King of England that if they continued on that course they would inevitably be scattered again with the possibility of either falling into the enemy's hands or being driven on to the rocks. Even if they managed to land successfully, their provisions had almost run out.

In vain did James plead and argue; in vain did he ask to be put ashore with one or two of his gentlemen in a small boat, so that he could make for

[1] Rankine, *op. cit.*, p. 61

Wemyss Castle and chance fortune alone. Forbin took no notice and continued to act in what he considered to be the best interests of France. If he saved the ships, they could sail again – and this time along the Flemish coast where they were badly needed. So they turned back for France.

An 'officer of distinction' (anonymous), actually Lieutenant de Rambure who was in charge of a frigate, wrote from Dunkirk on 12 April 1708 to a friend in Paris, giving an account of the expedition. His was one of seven privateers which, as they could not be prepared in time to go with the King, followed him four days later, intending to catch him up in the Leith Roads. They were surprised to find no French ships there, and so they flew Dutch colours and went in close to Leith to discover what had happened. Two pilots came out in a boat and told them that the French had never put in there, but that the English ships, which took them to be Dutch East India-men, were lying off the Firth of Forth. They kept the pilots on board and got out of the Firth as quickly as they could, keeping to the south, to avoid the English. They caught up with the main body of the French fleet two days later,

... all scatter'd and revolving homeward. I went on board the *Mars* where I was told the Prince and Privy Council were, to receive further orders, and give an account of my expedition, and there heard of their narrow escape by the luckiest accident in the world. They had got into the Firth on Friday night, having heard nothing of the English fleet, and anchor'd off Pittenweem and Creil, with design to land near Leith in the morning, when in the night, they heard the English fleet give the signal for their ships to come to an anchor. Monsieur Fourbin, knowing the meaning of it, immediately sent a boat on board of every ship in his squadron, ordering them to put out their lights, and to sail one by one out of the Firth, and steer a north-east course till they shou'd come off the town of St Andrews, which accordingly they did, but the wind and tide being against them, the English made them in the morning and pursued them. In the pursuit, which lasted three days, they lost the *Salisbury*, the *Blackwall*, founder'd since at sea, the *Deal, Castle, Sun,* and *Squirrel* we are afraid are lost on the coast of Holland, and the *Triumph*, which we thought also lost is got in, but much shatter'd. On Thursday, out just off of Zealand, our small squadron fell in with four English third rates which frighten'd us out of our wits, for we were in so dismal a condition that we could not make any defence, and we must have surrender'd; but they knowing nothing of our circumstances, bore away from us and we got that afternoon into Dunkirk Road, and next day our Prince arriv'd with the rest in so miserable a condition as all of us, that the soldiers when they crept on shoar [*sic*] look'd more like rats than men.[1]

The objective of the whole expedition had been Edinburgh. The anonymous officer told his friend that

. . . the plan of the castle was laid before a Council of General Officers at Versailles, and it was unanimously concluded that with the troops, mortars and bombs, which we carry'd, it cou'd not hold above 3 days. We design'd to have made a false attack at the postern gate, while 3 battalions shou'd enter the outworks that front the City, and lodge under their half-moon, which wou'd oblige them the next day to surrender. By the taking of the Castle we shou'd have had the Regalia; and I am told, two Protestant Archbishops wou'd have crowned the Prince in the High Church. The equivalent from England being also in this Castle, wou'd have been a great supply to us for raising of men. We have 400 officers with us for that purpose, all pretty fellows, that have serv'd in the wars of Italy and Spain, and above 100 chests of money. Some were for landing in Murray Firth, if it had been only to refresh our troops, but you know how nicely the French King's orders are to be obey'd, and how little power he gives of his troops to any ally, but always secret ones to his own generals. We Scots and Irish might have landed but the French were restrained to Musselburgh and Leith, or nowhere.[2]

If Forbin had agreed to James's plea to be put ashore, this impetuous action might well have succeeded, and all Scotland might have rallied to the young man who was willing to risk his life for his cause. Unfortunately, Jacobite history is full of such 'ifs' which could have turned the course of history. But Forbin was adamant. His orders were not to risk the life of the King, so he was going back to Dunkirk. With a battered squadron which had been two weeks in high seas, with the wind and the admiral contrary to him, there was nothing James could do.

He returned to Saint-Omer, where he stayed a little while with some English gentlemen there: 'who in the welcome they gave him, cou'd not but mix with sad and dejected looks, some sighs and affectionate expressions of sorrow, for the unfortunate disappointment he had met with: but he had learned so much of the hero, as to show a perfect unconcernedness at what they said, and with a becoming serenity, very rare in one so young, turn'd the discourse to other things'.[3] He was not yet twenty, but already he was developing a self-control and a philosophic turn of mind well beyond his

[1] Rankine, *op. cit.*, p. 67   [2] *ibid.*   [3] *ibid.*

years. Some who did not know him well enough were liable to interpret this attitude as lethargy, but if James were anything at all, he was realistic, and this was an achievement in that court which was built so much on hope and wishful thinking. If, on the return to Dunkirk, he had shown bad temper or wept tears of bitter regret, how would it have benefited his royal position? If he had lost control, how could he expect it in those around him? He had come a long way from the small boy who had held his breath until bursting point in an Italianate tantrum.

The Duke of Berwick placed the blame squarely where it belonged:

This affair had been very badly organized on France's part, owing to the stupidity and jealousy of Messieurs de Chamillart and de Pontchartrain, the former, Minister of War and the latter, Minister of Marine. They also say that if the Chevalier de Fourbin, who commanded the squadron, had agreed to run the risk of losing his ships, the young King would have been able to put a foot on shore, because it only depended on his entering the river of Edinburgh and beaching there, upon which the troops would have disembarked. Admittedly, the English would prob- ably have been able to burn the ships before all the supplies and ammuni- tion on them could have been got off. But this consideration should not have been an obstacle, because the essential thing was that the body of the troops and the young King were disembarked. All Scotland awaited him with impatience, ready to take up arms in his favour, moreover, England was then entirely denuded of troops, so that he could have marched without hindrance on the North, where a number of worthy persons had promised to join him. It also seemed that even his half- sister, Queen Anne, fearing a civil war, might be seeking to reconcile herself with him, so that he would have been sure of being re-established on the throne of his ancestors. Consternation was so great in London that the royal bank almost crashed with everybody running to withdraw their money, but the news of the unsuccessful outcome of the enterprise soon re-established the government's credit. Only the Comte de Gacé was made happy by that expedition. Monsieur de Chamillart, his close friend, had him nominated General of the French Army, and he received on board the brevet of Marshal of France. The Scots had asked for me with insistence; but the King [Louis XIV] did not want this, saying that he needed me elsewhere; this was the result of an intrigue by de Chamil- lart on behalf of the Comte de Gacé.[1]

Both James and Berwick realized that they might never have another such opportunity as this one; writing with hindsight, Berwick knew that

[1] Berwick, *op. cit.*, Vol. 2, p. 58

time had proved them right. The Scots were still smarting from resentment at the Act of Union of the year before, Anne was more or less willing to swallow her pride in any attempt to avoid civil war and ready to accept her half-brother as her heir, and James was a handsome young king fit to fire the imagination of the Scots and backed by the resources of France. In so far as England was concerned, however, they were likely to resent any monarch imposed upon them by the French, for this was how they interpreted James's position. This was his dilemma: he could not do anything without the aid of France.

It was probably not all Machiavellism on Louis's part; much of the failure of the expedition was the result of internal politics waged by petty men in ministerial positions which were too much for them, as Berwick realized. Probably Louis had not intended to go as far as he had: caring for James as he did, he would not have risked his person. He had most likely meant to use the threat of the invasion as a means of drawing the English forces out of Europe to defend their own country, but his bluff was called by the cautious Scots who refused to move an inch towards causing the commotion he needed until he had sent James to Scotland, backed by French money and men.

When it put in to Dunkirk, the remainder of the fleet was in a very poor condition: the gales and tempests had taken their toll, not only of the ships but of the men in them as well. The King's father had been a sailor, but the Queen had always detested the sea; James himself seemed to steer a middle course, but on this occasion, as with most of the gentlemen accompanying him, he had been very sea-sick indeed and, what with the after-effects of measles, exposure to the elements, frustration and fatigue, he looked thin and tired when he came ashore. The occasion and James are described by the 'officer of distinction':

> The Prince suffer'd much in his health, and what with fatigues and chagrin look'd very thin, but to put a good face on the matter, dress'd himself in an embroider'd suit, and a blue feather in his hat; when he went ashoar, where he was receiv'd by an abundance of ladies in the coaches with looks that put me in mind of an English funeral. When he went off, the noise was all over, 'Long live the King!'; but at our return shrugging of shoulders and shaking of heads gave a different welcome.[1]

On the journey home from Saint-Omer to Saint-Germain how could he have helped but compare the high hopes with which he had set out with the utter failure he would now have to present not only to his family and the court of Saint-Germain, but also to his royal substitute-father and patron?

[1] Rankine, *op. cit.*, p. 66

He was young to have to adjust to a failure of such magnitude which was not of his own making.

On Friday, 20 April, he reached Saint-Germain and, on the following Sunday, he paid a formal visit, accompanied by Mary Beatrice and the Princess, to the Sun King whose radiance was by now a little diminished. Saint-Simon described the meeting thus:

> It was a beautiful day; the King, followed by everybody, went out to meet him. As he was about to descend the steps of the terrace we saw the Court of Saint-Germain at the end of the Allée of the Perspective, approaching slowly. Middleton alone approached the King in a most unusual way, and embraced his knees. The King received him graciously, spoke two or three sentences to him, looking at him fixedly during each, in a way that would have embarrassed anyone else,[1] and then went on into the Allée.
>
> The two kings greeted each other as they drew near, then at the same time, each detaching himself from his Court, they walked side by side as equals, and with the same equality embraced each other warmly several times. Distress was painted on the faces of all these unfortunate people. . . . Afterwards they returned in the direction of the Château with a few indifferent words which died upon the lips. The Queen, with the two kings, entered Madame de Maintenon's apartment, the Princess remaining in the salon with Madame la Duchesse de Bourgogne and all the Court. Monsieur le Prince de Conti, seized with a natural curiosity, took Middleton aside; the Duke of Perth did the same with the Duc de Beauvilliers and Torcy. The few remaining English, welcomed more warmly than usual in order to make them talk, dispersed themselves among the courtiers who got nothing from their reserve other than a pretended ignorance which said much, and general complaints about fortune and set-backs. The two kings were *tête-à-tête* a long time, in which time Madame de Maintenon entertained the Queen. They left at the end of an hour: a brief and sad promenade followed which terminated the visit.[2]

Either during this visit or shortly afterwards, James asked and obtained permission from Louis to join the campaign in Flanders.

Queen Anne had been more lenient than could have been expected with regard to the Scots who had been waiting for their king to arrive. The English intelligence had done its work as thoroughly as usual, and most of

[1] Saint-Simon seemed to think that Louis thought Middleton had betrayed the expedition, as did many others
[2] Saint-Simon, *Mémoires*, V, 22, pp. 417–18

the Jacobite leaders were apprehended and imprisoned in Edinburgh Castle, among them the Duke of Gordon and the Lords Seaforth, Errol, Murray, Marischal and Traquair. The Duke of Hamilton was imprisoned for a short time, but released when he gave an apparently satisfactory account of his movements. The Duke of Atholl was summoned but did not choose to answer to the summons. Most of the leaders were released after varying periods of time. Of those taken on the *Salisbury*, Lord Middleton's two sons were not imprisoned but kept on parole in England until 1713. This detention was pleasant enough as they were accepted everywhere socially. Poor old Lord Griffin was sent to the Tower, but was let out daily on parole, so that it became a kind of hotel for him. But he was never to see his beloved King nor the Comte de Toulouse again, for he died there two years later. The general leniency was partly owing to Anne's feeling towards James, partly to the fact that some of those arrested had friends among the landowning Whigs, and partly because an election was approaching. At that moment the Whigs were in the ascendancy, although the leaders of the government, Godolphin and Marlborough, were of Tory inclination. Quite a number of the French prisoners were allowed to return to France on a parole which was to last until the death of Queen Anne.

As usual in such cases, it was the Scots crofters who were to feel the strictures most, and they were severly chastised in ways which exceeded the measure of their transgression since, after all, in most cases they had answered a summons from the chief of their clan which they were in duty and honour bound to answer.

This aspect of the defeat affected James deeply. He asked the goodwill of Spain in financial help to the Scottish Catholics who had suffered for their religion, and sent Charles Farquharson secretly to Scotland with a commission written in his own hand:

You are to assure them of the concern and trouble we are in . . . that this last enterprise has failed. . . . You are to assure them that, far from being discouraged with what has happened, we are resolved to move heaven and earth and to leave no stone unturned to free ourselves and them: and, to that end, we propose to come ourselves into the Highlands, with money and arms and ammunition, and to put ourselves at the head of our good subjects, if they are in arms for us.[1]

He had not relinquished the dream.

[1] Carte CLXXX, 198, pp. 281–2. Dated 25 April 1708

Chapter Eight

Action had now become a necessity for James and to return to the old life at Saint-Germain after this first attempt, abortive as it had been, was wellnigh impossible for him. By the time he returned the two courts were buzzing with the news that Louis had decided to send his dark, melancholy and religiously inclined grandson, the Duc de Bourgogne, to command his army in Flanders.

It was no secret that Louis was dissatisfied with the way in which his general, the Duc de Vendôme, was conducting the Flanders campaign which was now going badly for the French, and the arrival of a young unseasoned prince as the Duke's commander was guaranteed not only to insult him, but also to spur him to greater efforts. The Duc de Berry wanted to accompany his brother, and what Berry wanted he usually got. So, when James did return, the first news of importance to him personally was that his two companions were off to the wars. He pleaded with Louis to allow him to go with them and, probably not unaware of the young man's state of mind, the French king gave permission for him to join the campaign as a volunteer.

Accompanied by faithful Charles Booth and a few gentlemen, he set out for Flanders *incognito*, determined to fight as a private gentlemen: it was now that he used, perhaps for the first time, the title of 'Chevalier de St George'. There was much to occupy his mind as he rode through the spring of the Île-de-France until he came to Chantilly where he took his main meal of the day. Afterwards, he walked for a long while in the woods, deep in thought, and then spent a considerable time in conversation with his mother's cousin, the Prince de Conti, who, out of favour with Louis, had retired to his estate there. James showed an independence here which could not have met with approval by the French court, but it was characteristic of him that if he liked a person as he did Conti, no one else could have altered his opinion.

He travelled on to Senlis and Péronne, and thence to Valenciennes where he joined his two cousins and Vendôme. Once there, it was soon made apparent, and very clearly so, that his presence was not welcome to either Bourgogne or Berry. Perhaps his recent meeting with Conti had nettled them; perhaps Berry, who by now knew only too well the depth of Princess Louise Marie's feelings for him, felt ill at ease since he realized that, whatever they might feel for each other, nothing could come of it while the Sun King had other plans for him. Or it may have been that the Princes considered that too much money had been wasted on James's invasion – money which could have been used to far greater effect on the campaign in which they were presently engaged. Neither of them had their grandfather's generosity of spirit or of purse and, so far as they were concerned, charity began at home.

So James was received with little courtesy, treated strictly as the private gentleman he gave himself out to be, kept waiting when he desired to see either of his 'friends', and was obviously barely tolerated at the Princes' table which he was obliged to use until his own equipment arrived. When it did, he was able to set up a table for sixteen persons daily, but took pleasure in dining out with his fellow officers of the Scottish regiment he commanded. This regiment had been his own choice when he arrived in camp on the first day to find that no particular duties had been assigned to him.

Although he mixed and talked easily with his officers, he could never surrender himself entirely in friendship: there was always a reserve, an aura of kingship of which he himself was probably unaware. But, for the very first time, he was living a life which he enjoyed: he was active among men, and wanted to get as near to the scene of action as he could, which was very unsettling for poor Booth.

It was not a happy campaign: Bourgogne and the old libertine Vendôme were continually at loggerheads. Both the Princes and James were unaccustomed to the attendant horrors of war: it was one thing listening to returning captains singing the glories of 'arms and the man' when surrounded by the luxury of Anet or Marly, but quite another to watch Vendôme's men pillaging the countryside before battle had even commenced. Because Bourgogne had never been interested in military glory he was sickened by it, and disgusted with Vendôme who thought that the young prince was a coward and took no notice of anything he said. This, naturally enough, made for division in the army, half of which was obeying the orders of the Duke, the other half, those of the Prince. There was no such split in the Allied camp under Marlborough, where men of several nationalities fought as one.

On 8 July 1708, Vendôme took Ghent, and they entered the town in state. At night they celebrated the victory with a great feast and, on the following day besieged the small town of Oudenarde. There their luck broke, and it was really their own fault. Instead of engaging with the Allies at once, Vendôme and Bourgogne indulged in another of their arguments and in the meantime Marlborough was able to cross the Scheldt and draw up his men in battle order. This the French should never have allowed to happen; now they had lost their advantage.

A French officer, writing the day after the battle, described it thus:

> The French foot charged the Enemy 5 or 6 times but was unable to be supported by the Cavalry who were hampered because the Ground was so full of 'Inclosures'. We Dragoons were oblig'd to endure the continual Fire of the Enemy's Foot and Cannon, without daring to stir, because we were on the Right of the King's Household, who suffer'd as much as we. Towards the Evening we were fallen on by a great number of the Enemy's horse, to hinder us from reassuring the rest, who were put to the Rout; and of Seven Regiments of Dragoons we lost above half. . . The Dukes of Burgundy, Berry and the Chevalier de St George staid at the Head of the Household during the whole Action, and retreated with them to Ghent, where we are just now told they are arrive'd.[1]

James was certainly receiving his baptism of fire as he charged time and again with the *Maison du Roi*. Thanks to his plain dress, he was unrecognized by the British who would have been only too eager to take such a prize had his identity been known to them.

Gradually the night began to close in, and the white coats of the tired French became more conspicuous with every flash of surrounding mortar fire. Confusion was increased by refugee Huguenot officers, fighting with the Allies, calling out their regimental battle-cries so that French infantrymen fought or stumbled towards those whom they thought to be their standard-bearers, only to find themselves prisoners in the Allied hands. Darkness was complete when the rain began to fall – a steady downpour which added to the misery of those who were trying to escape and helped to muffle the cries of the wounded and the dying. Finally, even the *Maison du Roi* was forced to retreat, and the Princes and James turned their horses in the direction of Bruges and the comparative safety of its canal-line.

Marlborough exaggerated when he described the numbers of the enemy dead, wounded, captured and deserted as 20,000, but the French had certainly suffered enormous losses at Oudenarde. What was even more devastating, their morale was shattered as well: the greatest power in Europe was overthrown. James was also to see the more sordid side of war when the recriminations began. Bourgogne had never envisaged making war in the enclosed space of Oudenarde and the surrounding villages and, because it was almost a matter of principle for him to gainsay Vendôme, had opposed the idea. Vendôme had gone ahead, and this crashing defeat was the result. He got the remainder of his men safely back behind the

[1] Rankine, *op. cit.*, pp. 73-4

Bruges Canal, it was true, but that was a small compensation for his enormous losses. Putting his faith in the doctrine of attack being the best line of defence, he sent a most unfair report of the battle to Louis XIV, placing the blame for the disaster on Bourgogne. He was generous, however, in his praise of James's conduct in battle and he was not the only person who noted the brave bearing of the Chevalier de St George. Berwick had every cause to be proud of him.

The French marched on to the relief of Lille which was being held at great cost by General Boufflers against the Allied troops. James advanced with them. He was feeling fit and, as always when active, in a contented state of mind. On more than one occasion he was asked to move out of harm's way. Once, when reconnoitring near Marlborough's camp with Vendôme and Bourgogne, they were fired upon and Vendôme insisted that James had been recognized by the English. He begged him to retire but he, with a polite stubbornness, refused. Bourgogne, for once, was of Vendôme's opinion and rode out of danger. As he did so, his equerry was killed at his side. Upon this, the entire party retired, but still James was the last to go.

It seemed that he had a need to prove himself to himself as well as to others. Also he knew for a certainty that, if he had been recognized, the fact that he had retreated before danger would have been used as very bad publicity against him in England and Scotland. All the same, for whatever reason he acted thus, it was clear that he had thrown to the four winds every vestige of the caution which had been instilled into him by his careful education. For once in his life he was really enjoying himself in the company of brave men, and poor faithful Booth had as much trouble in restraining him from throwing himself into the cannon's mouth as he had had in keeping him from impaling himself upon the boar's tusks a decade before.

The siege of Lille proved very difficult, and Louis did not sweeten Vendôme's temper by recalling Berwick from the Rhine and sending him to assist him. This was the first time that James had met his half-brother since before the attempted Scottish invasion and at least some of the brief time they spent together must have been devoted to the discussion of what went wrong and why. Later, in his memoirs, the Duke was to write of James's behaviour at Oudenarde:

'. . . he showed much bravery and *sang-froid*, and gained the friendship of everyone by his affability.'[1]

Domestic matters were a worry to James at this time; foremost of these was the problem of economy. Campaigns were costly items for princes; not only did their clothes, accoutrements and horses have to be the best which money could buy, but they were expected to provide for their suite and to

[1] Berwick, *op. cit.*, Vol. 2, p. 58

entertain in a manner befitting royalty. When the royalty belonged to Versailles, the standards were necessarily higher. At Saint-Germain the cost of keeping the Jacobite court and refugees was far outstripping the personal means of the Queen and James. Their pensions from Louis were often months behind in payment, and the Queen had still not received the repayment of her dowry from the British government. This was always the pot of gold at the end of the rainbow where the Stuarts were concerned, and it was a dream which was never to materialize. James did everything he could to cut his personal expenses at the front and at home to a minimum which was no small achievement for so young a king. An idea of the court economy may be obtained from the following letter written by Mary Beatrice to Mr Dicconson, the comptroller of her household, on 1 November, All Saints' Day, 1709 from the convent at Chaillot:

I send you a thousand thanks for letting me see plainly the sad account of our poor affaires as to money, and your thoughts upon them, which tho' good, I cannot make my own to the King, having already approved his not sending away his equipage upon a notion he has, which I think is well grounded, that his doing so, befor the Princes do it, would look as if he were weary to stay there, and impatient to com back, which I think would be a great prejudice to him, if it were so thought. This I have writt to him two days ago, and I realy think it was reasonable he should make no step homewards, till the Princes do. Therefore I shall not mention what you say, but I will send him tomorrow the account of the money you have sent me, and press him to save all he can tho' I must own I don't see how anything can be saved without he lessens his equipage, so that I believe I shall be forced to sell the rest of the jewel, but I will not tell him so.[1]

Poor Queen, for ever concerned with keeping up appearances for the sake of her dearly loved son! In his absence she kept the machinery of the court running as smoothly as it was possible to do on so small an income and, although it was contrary to her inclination to pursue a social life, she was the necessary link between James and the French court when he was away. Some thought that she controlled him too much, but without her at this time of his campaigning, his position would have been much undermined left to some of the intriguers at Saint-Germain. He relied a great deal on the good sense of his mother, but never to the point of being entirely dependent upon her: he was too much of a Stuart to delegate his authority so easily.

It was apparent to everyone on the spot, and most of all to Berwick, that

[1] WSP 2. 50

the siege of Lille would be a hopeless task. He was not very pleased at being recalled from his own campaign on the Rhine to help Vendôme who was not even a prince of the blood. Illegitimate though Berwick was, he was universally acknowledged as the son of James II and, although in so many matters he was the most modest of men, in matters of precedence he was meticulous. In this he was a child of his time: not only was he a brilliant soldier, he was also an accomplished courtier and forms of protocol were the corner-stones of Versailles. So he would not be seen to serve *under* Vendôme, and announced that he had brought his troops along to assist him and that was all; he took no command. When he realized that nothing could be done to retrieve the situation in Lille, he returned to the Rhine, seeing no sense in wasting more men and energy on an operation which was already doomed.

Both he and James had a strong streak of common sense and realistic appraisal which Charles II had also possessed, but which their father had so conspicuously lacked. Either, given the opportunity of an untroubled succession to the crown of England, might have ruled with more feeling and good sense than many kings who were yet to be born.

When Berwick rode back to the Rhine, James remained behind to sit out the fruitless siege which, nevertheless, he regarded with interest, since it was his first experience in that military art. In the intervals of occasional activity he dealt with letters and accounts from home: on 9 December, Lille fell and two days later he was lying in the quarters to which the French had retreated behind Mons, alternately shivering with cold and burning with fever. In the periods between the bouts of ague, he would eat almost to excess (to the despair of Booth) as if to make up for the starvation of the previous four days. But however much he ate, nothing made any difference to the lean and lithe elegance of his figure.

While he had been ill, Bourgogne and Berry had returned to Versailles, since winter was approaching and the time for making war was over for that year. Berry sent his horses back for James; this may have been a gesture of atonement for his earlier incivility, or an expression of his more customary good nature but, whatever spirit prompted the action, it was gratefully accepted by James to whom transport was always an economic question.

During the next few months the ague returned again and again, leaving him weak and depressed. He lay in his bed in the sombre heavily-gilded room at the top of the château while the worst winter France had known for centuries crept in from the western seaboard. While his head and limbs were seared by the fever, everything in the outside world had been forced to a standstill by the incredible cold. No one had ever known anything like it: the Seine was frozen over as well as the sea along the Atlantic coast; children froze to death in their wretched village beds and cattle became blocks of ice as they died standing in their byres. Soldiers returning in rags and tatters from the front had nothing to protect them against the severity of this most cruel of winters. A thaw came with the early spring and then the cold returned as bad as before but with worse results, for the growing crops were destroyed and now starvation stared France in the face. Everywhere people demanded the end of the war, although the Sun King still maintained his personal popularity, despite an attempted march of the women of Paris on Versailles. They were turned back by a military detachment at Sèvres without harm to anyone involved. The crowd cried out for bread and Louis melted down his plate, but it did not suffice. Only the end of hostilities could provide the necessary money to feed the hungry nation.

Both sides put out feelers regarding peace negotiations, but the price Louis would have had to have paid was too great for him; a declaration of war against his grandson, Philip of Spain. So there was nothing to do but to continue the war as soon as the season permitted. In the meantime James slowly began to regain his strength, although he was having to take quinine five times a day.

His half-sister Anne, though only in middle age, was a chronic invalid by this time and it was obvious that she would not rule for many years more. Her husband, George of Denmark, had recently died and she was reputedly still looking across the Channel towards James to take up the succession where their father had left it. She hated the idea of the Elector of Hanover succeeding her. In spite of the past, the ties of blood were strong and these were reinforced with the cement of remorse. However, after the failure of the peace feelers, she seemed to waver in her inclination towards James, and when Lord Townshend went to the Hague to meet the French Foreign Minister, Torcy, in another attempt to end the war, one of the most stringent conditions was that James would have to leave France and Louis's protection. Now he was referred to as the 'Pretender' to the throne in all English official documents.

James had no wish to become a reason for the prolongation of the war, so he expressed his willingness to go anywhere except to the Swiss cantons or to the Papal States. Either would have been fatal to him or his cause: he was physically threatened by mountains and, as a Catholic, would have felt ill at ease in the Calvinist cantons. On the other hand, once his cause was identified with Rome he knew that he would never gain the great majority of the English people to his side. He offered to go to the Low Countries, or elsewhere, provided he could be free to come and go as he pleased, without passports. He reverted to the old question of the Queen's dowry, but when

Torcy passed on this request, Townshend said that it would not be possible, but that James would be granted a pension by Anne on his departure from France. Even someone less sensitive than James would have found this proposal humiliating: he rejected it.

The year 1709 was becoming an increasingly lonely one for James. For some time past, various of the Saint-Germain refugees either sought or were offered a pardon if they returned to England and gave up the Jacobite cause. There were different reasons for their so doing, both good and bad. For those who returned for perfectly valid reasons it was natural and courteous to obtain a licence from the King to do so, and one of the licences he gave was to his boyhood friend and companion, James Derwentwater who had never seriously harmed the administration in England or Scotland, and now had vast estates to manage in Northumberland with many tenants dependent upon him. He had grown into a much-liked, amiable young man whose good looks formed a strong contrast with those of the King: he was of middle height, with fair hair and grey eyes. Always a pleasant and useful person to have around at the Court's informal social occasions, he had a charming baritone and accompanied himself on the guitar. So it was with some regret that James gave Lord Derwentwater his licence to return to Northumberland.

If some returned to England, there were still others who came to the château from other parts of Europe when they discovered that they could not earn enough to make ends meet, and it was becoming more and more necessary for James and the Queen to limit their alms. It was about this time that Mary Beatrice and her son had their first difference of opinion; it was not clear to others what it was about, but it was apparent that she was not well. She was feeling the strain of the illness which was eventually to kill her. Whether she herself suspected its malignancy is open to conjecture; if she did, she does not appear to have passed on her fears to her son.

On 22 April, Berwick left to command on the Piedmontese frontier with eighty-four battalions of foot and thirty squadrons of cavalry, and a hard time he had of it: there was no money for the campaign and he sent courier after courier back to Versailles pointing out their perilous position with hardly any provisions while the enemy had made great preparations for the campaign. If they did not send him immediate assistance, said Berwick, he would have to put only the number of troops proportionate to the amount of provisions in each outpost and send the rest of the men back to France. The sole response that this brought from the Ministry of War was that they would speak to the suppliers and do their best to satisfy him. So he acted on his own initiative and wrote to all the Intendants of the surrounding departments asking for supplies of wheat and grain, which he received. Lack of money was even greater than lack of provisions, and there was absolutely nothing to be hoped for in this direction from the court. So he took command personally of every *sou* that he could lay his hands on, either in the military coffers or that he could raise from the Intendants. Monsieur Desmaretz, the Comptroller-General of Finance, wrote to him

> . . . pointing out that this was against all kinds of rules, but I replied it was still more so to let an army perish while it was barring the way to France's enemies and he said no more. I also stopped a wagon containing a hundred thousand *écus* which was going from Marseilles to Paris: M. de Trudaine, Intendant of Lyons also found a way of making another hundred thousand *écus*, and in this fashion I began to feel a little less worried.[1]

Finally he cut off the Duke of Savoy, who was at that time on the side of the Alliance, with only a small army and was able to send twenty battalions home to Louis – 'which was a great gift at that time'.[2]

On every front the French army was without money and without provisions; the soldiers were starving and their clothes were in rags; moreover their morale was beginning to show signs of wear and tear. All this James could see as he set off for Flanders on 17 June 1709 for his second campaign. For economic reasons he had a much smaller staff than on the previous occasion: with him were his well-loved Dominic Sheldon, Lord Middleton and two or three others.

He was attached to the intrepid Duc de Villars this time. The latter was a typical, large Gascon whose extrovert character and daring address made many more conventional courtiers consider him mad. He must have been greatly in contrast with the Versailles that James knew, and probably all the more appreciated by him for that. In any case, James seems hardly to have left his side from 27 July, when Tournai fell to Marlborough and Eugène while the French were at Lens. Villars did all he could to relieve the citadel which resisted for another week, but in vain. When the Allies moved on to invest Mons, it was apparent to Louis that something would have to be done to help Villars and he gratefully accepted the offer of old General Boufflers to serve under the Duke.

While Villars and Boufflers were relieving Mons, James was forced to remain at Cambrai suffering from another of his malarial bouts. Ill as he was, this enforced stay of three weeks or so in the luxury of the archbishop's palace at Cambrai brought its own compensations for it was there that James met Fénélon, the Archbishop of Cambrai, who was to confirm him in the philosophy of life which he was devising for himself.

[1] Berwick, *op. cit.*, Vol. 2, p. 65
[2] Montesquieu's *Eloge* in Berwick, *op. cit.*, p. xxxvii

In 1697 Fénélon had published his *Explication des Maxims des Saints*. One of its tenets was that Christ was regarded by a true saint not as his personal Saviour, but as the Saviour of all men. This wax attacked by his former teacher, Bossuet, Bishop of Meaux, and Fénélon appealed to Rome. The Pope, Innocent XII, decided against the book and consequently Fénélon was exiled to his archbishopric of Cambrai because Louis sided with Bossuet.

The Archbishop's inspiration was the doctrine of Quietism which was, roughly speaking, based on the theory that all good deeds proceeded from a passive state of soul open to the reception of direct inspiration by God; any good deed consciously thought out could only therefore derive from the working of the sinful mind. Rome frowned upon the doctrine, sensing in it – and justifiably – a danger to its own bureaucratism. This doctrine formed the basis of Fénélon's *Maxims*. James seems to have imbibed much of the Quietist doctrine, evolving it in his own case to a form of Christian stoicism which accounted for much of his calm acceptance of the blows of Fate, an attitude which was sometimes mistakenly interpreted as apathy.

Tolerance was one of Fénélon's greatest qualities and it was the cornerstone of James's proposed restoration. Fénélon believed also that kings existed for the sake of their subjects and not subjects for the sake of kings. This chimed exactly with the advice given by James's father in his testament:

> A king cannot be happy if his Subjects be not at ease, and the Subjects also cannot securely enjoy what belongs to them if their King be not at his ease, and in a capacity to protect and defend them. Therefore preserve your Prerogatives, but disquiet not your Subjects, either in their Estates or their Religion. Remember the great Precept, Do not to others what you would not have done to yourself.

A bond of sympathy was immediately established between the two men, and in November 1709 Fénélon was to write to the Duc de Bourgogne.

> I have seen the King of England many times and freely, and I must tell you, Monseigneur, the high opinion I have formed of him. He appears thoroughly sensible, equable and gentle, loving virtue and religious principles, by which he wishes to rule his conduct. He keeps his head and acts quietly without temper, without caprice or variableness, without fancifulness. He is always anxious for and amenable to reason; eager to do his duty by all men and full of consideration for all. He shows no weariness of submitting himself nor impatience of restraint that he may be alone and independent; nor is he absent and self-occupied in society. He is thorough in whatever he does. He is dignified, without hauteur.

He pays due attention to rank and merit. His gaiety if the gentle and moderate mirth of a mature man. He seems to enter into amusements only out of duty; for necessary relaxation, or to give pleasure to the people about him. He is easy of access to every one, without betraying himself to any; yet there is no suspicion of weakness or levity in this complaisance for he is firm, decided, exact. He takes his share in brave actions regardless of cost to himself. I saw him leave Cambray, still greatly reduced by his recent fever, to return to the army upon a vague rumour of a coming battle. None of those who were about him would have dared to propose that he should delay his departure until more certain news arrived. If he had shown the least sign of irresolution, they would have insisted upon his waiting one day longer, and he would have lost the chance of a battle where he displayed great courage and won high reputation even in England. In one word, the King of England is generous and unselfish, unvaryingly reasonable and virtuous. His firmness, his equability, his self-possession and tact, his sweet and gentle seriousness, his gaiety devoid of boisterousness, must win him the favour of all the world.[1]

The battle which James was hastening to join despite the protests of Charles Booth and of his equerry, the Chevalier Michael Ramsay, was to take place on 11 September 1709 at Malplaquet, roughly ten miles south of Mons. Saint-Simon described James as having arrived in haste 'with the remnants of a fever, showing no concern for his health'.[2]

This was to be Marlborough's last great victory for the Allies, and the French defended their position, mainly centred around the wood of Sars, with 80,000 men. Against them, Marlborough threw 100,000 Allied troops. At seven o'clock in the morning the attack began in a dense white mist which gradually rolled away towards the wood, revealing at first, to the waiting French, wave upon wave of coloured silk as the standards of all the Allies were borne aloft. From the English side their troops seemed to disappear into the mist overhanging the wood, but the sounds of the cannon and the cavalry charging through the trees and crashing through the undergrowth betrayed the intensity of the action. Ten of the enemy's forty cannon were trained at close quarters upon the French cavalry with devastating effect; Villars received a crippling wound in the knee, and then the French left wing was defeated, 'in spite of the endeavours and the example of King James of England', according to Saint-Simon. He also described him as living very wisely, but very much in the world, seeking to

[1] Fénelon, *Lettres*, ed. McEwen, pp. 163–4
[2] Norton, *Historical Memoirs of the Duc de Saint-Simon*, Vol. I, p. 480

please and succeeding. He gained even the respect and the affection of both troops and generals by his application and his determination.[1]

The *coup de grâce* was administered by General Withers coming up with fresh troops from Tournai; eighteen infantry battalions and six squadrons of horse then fell upon the French from behind Sars and sealed their fate. Between three and four in the afternoon, Boufflers took over the command, and at four o'clock the *chamade* was sounded and the French withdrew. This time there had been no division in their command and they respected their leaders; their morale was still high. Comparatively speaking, the French losses were low, as they left behind few prisoners, with the exception of about fifteen hundred wounded whom they were unable to save in time. Dominic Sheldon was one of the officers taken prisoner and, when interviewed by Marlborough, was told by the latter how much he had admired the courage of James during the battle. General Villars was also very impressed with his conduct and took him under his wing as he trundled around on his stretcher-carriage, or *'guinguette'*, with his wounded leg stretched out stiffly before him. The French were now entrenched behind the River Ronelle, between Valenciennes and Le Quesnoy, and James accompanied Villars on every round of duty that he could, riding by his side when he visited the lines or reconnoitred the enemy, and there must have been something about him which appealed to such brave, experienced and forthright men such as Villars and Boufflers.

In spite of all this physical activity, he still found time to write home and as usual his thoughts were forcibly channelled along economic lines. On 11 October 1709 he wrote to Dicconson from the camp at Ruesne:

Although I reckon soon to be with you, yet I cannot differ till then telling you how sensible I am of all the pains you take for the Queen's and my service, and particularly for the help and care you are to her amidst all the misery of St Germains, which amongst all the obligations I have to you for so many years past I shall not look upon as the least. I find you are in no hopes of any money at all, but our army beginning to be paid more regularly, the rest will, I hope, come in time. If as, I believe, I return this month, I shall not want more than the 4,000 *livres* for October, and upon the whole, I think my expence [*sic*] this campagne has not been extravagant for me. Before I went none of you thought I could make it without retrenching or selling, but, thank God, we have rubbed it out without either, by the Queen's help and your care, for which, tho' I can only thank you by words I hope the time will come in which I may do it by effects.[2]

[1] Norton, *op. cit.*, Vol. VI, ch. 2, p. 29   [2] WSP, 2. 54

Mons fell, despite Villars's efforts, and now the autumn was with them, bringing mist and rains: the time for campaigns was over for that year. Even James was not sorry to return: he had been ill again and, although recovered, he was tired, and the gloomy château would, for once, provide a welcome change from the long hours in the saddle churning through the Flanders mud, lashed by wind and rain.

He was also anxious to return for another more positive reason. It seemed that Louis XIV was once more inclined to look favourably upon the idea of a further invasion attempt. Some of the prisoners taken on the *Salisbury*, captured in the 1708 attempt, had been returned, and brought with them stories of dissension in England. The Government was at sixes and sevens; Anne's relations with her former friend, Sarah, Duchess of Marlborough, were becoming more and more strained and consequently Marlborough himself was out of favour. There would obviously have to be a change of ministry and, if Anne continued to be antagonistic to the Hanoverians, it might be one favourable to James.

From talks with Torcy, James learned that perhaps Louis would provide three regiments of cavalry, eight battalions of foot and two of dragoons and a good supply of weapons. But nothing came of it: the New Year festivities at Versailles were relatively subdued, and Louis gave no New Year presents that January. Instead he turned over 40,000 pistoles to the needs of his men in Flanders. In view of the economic state in which France found itself, it was obviously not practical to risk any loss which would always be inherent in a plan to invade Britain. Dejected and depressed, James had to make do with the knowledge that he had the moral support of the kings of France and Spain but nothing else for the time being.

On 5 November 1709, the anniversary of the Gunpowder Plot as well as the landing of William of Orange at Torbay, Dr Henry Sacheverell preached a sermon in St Paul's based on the doctrine of passive obedience and non-resistence involving the non-toleration of dissent. Because he referred in this sermon to 'wily Volpones' which the congregation rightly or wrongly inferred to include Godolphin, the Chancellor, he was impeached by a nervous ministry and brought to trial in February 1710. Their nervousness lay mainly in the implication that Sacheverell's doctrine of non-resistance meant the 'Glorious Revolution' of 1688 should never have taken place and everything which had happened since was illegal; this included the Act of Settlement which involved the Hanoverian dynasty.

The Whig impeachment of the doctor had the effect of uniting the Tories throughout the country and Anne herself showed that her sympathies lay with Sacheverell. Even if many of the Tories were not inclined to restore the Stuarts, they were, in any case, banded together against the

Hanoverians. Thirteen bishops sat in judgement on Sacheverell and the case obtained the utmost publicity. Six of the bishops voted him innocent, seven guilty. His sentence was mild: he was to refrain from entering the pulpit for three years, and his sermon, which had been widely circulated already, was to be burned by the public hangman. Such a light sentence was interpreted as a defeat for the Whigs. Sacheverell was hailed as the moral victor and cheered all the way to his new living in Shropshire.

The news of dissension in England was sweet music to the ears of the two courts in France: it served to encourage James and to keep Louis's interest in the Stuart cause lively. So long as France held the Stuarts, she held a threat to England's peace.

In March 1710 peace negotiations were reopened at Gertruydenberg, and one of the main objectives of the Allies was the removal of James from France. James asked the French Foreign Minister to make certain representations on his behalf and sent his own man to the peace conference. He wanted to know why, if he had to go, he could not go to a place of his own choosing, what his subsistence would be, how it would be paid, whether he could travel freely with passports and whether his correspondence would be free or regulated. But the conference broke down and the war was resumed.

Nothing short of an invasion of Britain could keep James now from joining his old friend, Villars, at the front, so he left the château in May 1710 on his third campaign. Middleton did not join him this time, but remained behind at the château, no doubt relieved in one way that James was going away for a time, as a letter written by him on 1 May showed: 'We have heard with indignation of the advances that some women have made to Mr Snow. We wonder at their imprudence and hope that everybody will be on their guard against such temptations.'[1] 'Mr Snow' was one of the ciphers used for the King. Considering James's looks and bearing and given his romantic situation, it would not have been surprising if some of the ladies of Saint-Germain had not attempted to throw themselves at his head. As for the ladies of Versailles, they probably had a very shrewd idea of James's prospects and would not have been so hasty as to risk their reputations in the eyes of Madame de Maintenon, and consequently in the eyes of Louis, and to invoke their wrath. In these matters, had James been in need of outside protection, there were Lord Middleton and the Queen Mother at Saint-Germain and Madame de Maintenon at Versailles ready to repel unwelcome approaches, but he was fully capable of dealing with them himself.

He had, it was true, the blood of Charles II and James I in his veins and

[1] Carte CCXII, 12, p. 89

118

the virility of his years, but the words of his father's testament were burned deep in his mind and Berwick, his hero, had always been an example of the virtue of moderation. The latter had loved his first wife dearly, and had a great affection for his second wife and his sons. He was a model of the domestic virtues and there is no reason to think that James would not have hoped to emulate him in this fashion as in others.

Over the past two years, as James had advanced more into manhood, Berwick had become his chief adviser and closest friend; he seems to have been the only person, with the exception of his sister (who naturally understood little of military matters), to whom he could talk with complete trust. Unfortunately, as we have seen, Berwick was forced to be absent from France for long periods of time; but he was to be present on this third campaign.

For Charles Booth, who was accompanying his master as usual, it was going to be the most trying campaign of all. Early in the morning of the 16th they swung into their saddles and pointed their horses' heads in the direction of Paris. There James dined with Archbishop de Noailles, and Booth's worries began at once because the King ate too much. But after dinner they all took horse again for Péronne and in a little while the King discovered that a hard gallop did wonders for the digestion. On his arrival in the camp at Péronne he found Villars sick and in bed, 'but his heart and hand as ready to destroy the foe as ever',[1] as Booth wrote to Middleton in one of his frequent reports. He wrote about the state of his master's health and the state of the war; sometimes he acted as James's amanuensis, and he was always very deeply involved in his confidential affairs. He was one of the few outside the family who were very close to the King's heart. The dictum that no man is a hero to his valet did not apply where they were concerned: to James, the King, Booth gave an unswerving devotion – to the young man who was his master he also gave a deep affection mixed with a fussy attention to detail which, in another age, another environment, another sex would have made out of the steadfast Hereford yeoman an admirable nanny.

Three days later the army reached Cambrai and James stayed again with Archbishop Fénélon. He held a *levée* in the Archbishop's palace to which a great crowd of sightseers flocked. Some English people, curious to see him, managed to get themselves employed as waiters at the reception.

On 27 May, James was up on his horse at four in the morning with Arras as his destination. The enemy had been battering briskly at Douai, and it was evident that their next objective would be Arras: they were superior in number to the French by about 30,000 men. He rode more asleep than

[1] Carte CCX, 58, pp. 112–13

awake at first, but this did not bother either him or his horse. Berwick was beside him and they were in the saddle for eleven hours. Booth was not overworried by this because he had discovered that a long day on horseback had a very good effect on his master: the strenuous exercise made him sweat and gradually dissipated any recurring attacks of fever.

They rode close to the enemy's lines for most of the time and reached Arras in the late afternoon, whereupon the indefatigable Berwick set about looking for fording-places in the river. They made this inspection on foot, and then snatched a brief two hours' rest, wrapped in their cloaks and lying by their tethered horses. Then Villars came along in his little cart and, after they had crossed the river again near Arras, going back towards Douai from the other side, he was nearly captured in an English ambush from which he was saved by James and Berwick arriving with a company of dragoons they had found encamped nearby. Shortly afterwards a party of French dragoons took a larger number of English hussars. This kind of guerrilla warfare upset Booth considerably.

But he was not the only one in the camp to be worried. It was very obvious that the administration at Versailles had neither the faintest idea of the condition of the army nor of the difficulties presented to them by the terrain on which the next battle would be fought. James wrote that 'the repeated and positive orders sent from Court to our Marshals make them all at their wits end. They expect, by the next courier, orders to take the Moon with their teeth.'[1]

They reached Arlieu on 1 June and James lodged in the town, so high up in an old house that the gentleman of the bedchamber, who had a lyrical turn of mind at times, was able to write home that 'the tiles do not hinder us from seeing the stars'.[2] The King was tired on arrival because the weather was very warm and fighting clothes were not light wear for June. He looked well but was stooping a little owing to tiredness. Booth's main worry was that the King would not consult his doctor because, as he said, apart from tiredness he was feeling fitter than he had ever done before. He was also enjoying himself. He wrote to Middleton, who was at Saint-Germain while the Queen was at Chaillot:

I find 'tis enough to be out of St Germain's to have one's health for I don't ever remember to have had it better than 'tis now. The queen finds it so too, and I hope you do the same in your hermitage. Our general has a guingette in which he goes everywhere, he manages himself but not enough. If Coridon [Berwick] were left alone he would do

[1] Carte CCX, 69–79, pp. 126–36
[2] *ibid.*

much better: he has no equipage and so is forced to spung upon us by turns.[1]

Berwick's 'spunging' does not seem to have worried him overmuch. They were constantly together and, although the Duke kept a brotherly eye on his King, he did not interfere with his riding around with Villars and himself. On one occasion they were watching an enemy detachment for about thirty minutes and no one paid any attention to the gentleman of the bedchamber's appeals for the King to be taken to a place of safety. 'Had Sheldon been here,' wrote Booth, 'he would have taken our Master's horse by the bridle',[2] and so he would have done himself, he added, but for the presence of his superiors in rank about the King. But Hamilton was not his superior, and Booth considered that he had failed in his duties when he did not prevent James from accompanying some of the other gentlemen 'in their follies' on one occasion. It was all the more galling then when, on this occasion, Hamilton laughed at him. Then the enemy suddenly saw the watchers and rode straight at them. They wheeled and turned, riding back like the wind, with their cloaks streaming after them, chased by the bullets of the enemy.

This was the end where Booth was concerned, and he determined to take a firm line with the Duke of Berwick, but, 'I spoke to the Duke to order us to stop the King, should he come into like circumstances. He looked blanke, shook his head and said nothing. . . .'[3] Nevertheless, it did seem to have had some effect on the taciturn Berwick, because he did thereafter decree that the King should not take part in foraging forays, but he realized at the same time that James was making up for all the days in which he had longed for action. While they were encamped at Télu he told James that he could ride up and down the lines to see the charges, if he liked, but his life was too precious for him to be allowed to charge with the French; he did, however, give him a position to take up in the event of action.

If James was impatient at being kept out of the main action, Berwick was even more restless with the whole campaign. He could see that nothing could be done for Douai: there was a drought and food and water were in short supply. The English were firmly dug in and were in much better shape than the French. Much was waiting to be done in the province of Dauphiné which, very much against his will, he had left to come to Flanders. James remarked that his brother was 'becoming as weary of this country as Mme Byerley was of her Convent and like her would do anything to be out

[1] Carte CCX, 69–79, pp.126–36.
[2] Carte CCX, 74 and 78, pp. 132–5
[3] *ibid.*

of it'.[1] We learn no more of Mme Byerley, but we do know that Berwick got his way. There was apprehension in the camp at his imminent departure but he, like James, was wearied of the irresolution of the French generals 'always disputing and never resolving: just as at Mons'.[2] The Duke had always pursued a clean-cut line of action and any other approach was impossible for him. Villars found it hard to understand that he should want to leave and took it as a personal affront when it was made clear on 14 June that the Duke was soon to depart.

By now Marlborough was clearly indicating that he would be interested in promoting James's designs if the latter would do equally well by him. Returning prisoners exchanged against English captives bore messages of goodwill from Marlborough to the King. Although Marlborough was still in command of the Allied armies in Europe at this time, his position at home was becoming more and more precarious, and this makes more understandable his attempt to gain a stake in the possible restoration of the Stuarts.

The English Secretary of State, Henry St John, also began to sound out Saint-Germain, but tentatively, and at the Channel's distance. He communicated with Torcy through the relatively insignificant Abbé Gaultier who had once been attached to the parish church at Saint-Germain and had been religious adviser to the wife of St John's colleague, Lord Jersey.

Berwick was a great deal involved in all these matters and was consulted on most of them by Torcy. Therefore it was of the utmost importance that he should have the opportunity of giving James the benefit of his experience before he left him for an unknown period of time.

Meanwhile Middleton, who was still looking after affairs at Saint-Germain and answering to the Queen, was somewhat put out by a letter which had reached him from England. He mentioned this in a letter to his correspondent in Rotterdam,[3] knowing that anything written in clear to the Low Countries would pass through the hands of at least one English spy. The English writer had complained that the King's continued presence on the battlefield was prejudicial to the consideration of claims which might be advanced for him during the peace negotiations. Middleton defended the King, explaining that he made his campaign for self-discipline, to make himself a reputation by winning honour in the field and to increase his knowledge of man. He would have joined any army to gain this experience, but the French was the only one open to him.

On 20 June, his birthday, both armies were encamped on either side of

---

[1] Carte CCX, 87, p. 146
[2] Carte CCX, 79, p. 136
[3] Carte CCX, 100, pp. 100-1

the River Canihe, the French being based on Haucourt. It was a memorable day for the King. On each of the last two days he had ridden out, accompanied by Captain Murray and his two gentlemen of the bedchamber, and had sat motionless on his horse for a long time, looking across at the banners blowing on the other side of the river.

A little further down the bank on their side, a group of French soldiers were resting and cleaning their accoutrements, unaware of the exalted personages behind them. They were interested in the goings and comings of the English soldiers on the opposite bank who were equally casually employed during the respite from battle. Their voices carried across the water from one camp to the other and, before long, both sides were exchanging greetings and pleasantries in a confusion of language common to soldiers the world over. James was amused by this, and when a small party of officers appeared on the English side, he sent Booth to see if there were any English or Scots among them. Obediently, Booth rode along the bank and called across to the other group. He found that there were some Scottish gentlemen there and that he knew some of their relations who were fighting with the French. They exchanged messages for friends on both sides, and the officers then asked after James. Booth pointed him out as he sat on his horse apart, and one of the officers bowed very low towards the solitary horseman. Hamilton joined Booth and, as usual, according to the latter, went too far by sending 'his service to the Duke of Marlborough'.[1]

The English encampment intrigued James very much: it represented all that he had never known, the country he had scarcely seen, over which in his Divine Right he was born to rule. Small wonder then, that he took every opportunity, and they were very rare, to look at these men who were his subjects and to listen to their colloquial speech which was not entirely the English as spoken at Saint-Germain. He rode along the bank again, and then, accompanied by Hamilton, approached the enemy's entrenchments at a bend in the river which brought the two banks very close together. Although the entrenchments were manned, there was no fire, and James rode on undisturbed. Booth scolded him when he returned, and he agreed with this chastisement, asking, with a smile, why he was not deterred from being so foolish, which probably maddened Booth all the more.

But James was not being foolhardy, nor was he indulging in exhibitionism. Describing the incident in a letter home he wrote that they were preparing to do the same thing again, 'not to seek glory but conversation; for we hope to get more by talking with the English than by fighting with them'.[2]

[1] Carte CCX, 98, p. 162
[2] Carte CCX, 105, p. 172

When Roger Strickland, one of his gentlemen, and Booth rode along the bank on another occasion, no shots were fired although there was only about twelve yards of water between them. English officers came up to meet them and they asked the English for news of Douai, but there was none, and so they discussed the weather. Then James rode up and addressed a few words in English to the men. Booth declared that everybody showed as much civility 'as a new married lady's wont to do'.[1] Two days later James came back again with Villars and again, Booth and Hamilton were with him. Booth pointed to the King and the English and Scots on the opposite banks took off their hats and bowed very low. One of the officers on the English bank who said his name was Montgomery, called out that he had seen Lord Middleton's sons two weeks before and they were both well.[2] Then the question of peace was raised and a Major Hamilton on the English side said that it was not a subject to be mentioned in front of Prince Eugène but 'when with the Duke [of Marlborough] they talked of nothing else'.[3]

About this time Booth was also able to encourage his master with news of support from his local home front in Hereford whence his two sisters wrote that a Jacobite correspondent of the Duke of Beaufort had said in course of conversation about the 'Exiles' that 'we are working for them'.[4]

But on 26 June Douai sounded the *chamade* and capitulated, and the French subsided once more into gloom. This was relieved for James when General Lumley sent across a trumpeter from the Allied side with friendly messages for the King, asking him to endeavour to be on the bank of the Canihe at four o'clock in the afternoon. Within a few hours of getting this message, as if a malignant force were playing against him, James felt the first shivers of the quartan ague and four o'clock found him in his bed in a high fever. That this should happen when the feeling for James, always present in certain sections of the English army, was at its zenith was a major disaster, and typical of the fortunes of the Stuarts.

Through his febrile rantings he reiterated again and again that he did not want to miss any part of the next operation, although it was Booth's own determination that he should. Everybody was of the opinion that it would be better all round if he were moved to Arras where he could be lodged in a house and receive proper medical attention. But Arras was likely to be besieged, thought Booth, and then where would they be? Villars and the others did their best to dispel these fears, and James was

[1] Carte CCX, 105, p. 172
[2] They were taken prisoner on board the *Salisbury*, 1708
[3] Carte CCX, 108, pp. 177–8
[4] Carte CCX, 101, pp. 164–5

moved into the house of Maréchal Montesqieu at Arras. Just before
setting out he made Booth write home that he was convinced that if but a
score of shots were fired 'we lose three Kingdoms if we have not our share'.[1]
To this Booth added that he had been bold enough to tell the King that, for
his part, he was of another mind; presence in a general action was, indeed,
more essential than life, but small matters might be allowed to pass quietly.

For ten days James lay in bed, high with fever and sweating profusely
the whole time. When the fever had subsided a little, Booth was able to
massage him according to the doctor's instructions. The patient liked his
doctor and had confidence in him. On the whole, he was a good patient,
principally because he realized that the sooner he obeyed instructions and
recovered, the sooner he would be back in the field.

Peace talks began again between the generals on the campaign. According to James's dictation, Villars hoped that Prince Eugène would be there,
but James was sceptical: 'It seems that his head is not so light as ours,' he
wrote.[2] If Eugène was not present, the Duke of Argyll was, and Villars
sent Colonel Nugent to him with his compliments and the enquiry, 'Do
you not regard the French as fools for so continually gazing at you all?'
To this the Duke answered, 'You do us much honour; and we doubt not
your Generals will presently make both armies better acquainted with each
other and so content all curiosity.'[3]

Colonel Nugent told James all this as they sat with Lord Talbot playing
ombre. He was feeling so much better that he was getting bored with
playing cards and following the doctor's orders as well as heeding Booth.
He laid a bet of one hundred to twenty with Nugent that there would be no
battle that year and he wrote that 'either general would have paid the money
to be sure of it'.[4] On 4 July he ended his letter to the Queen via Middleton
by declaring that it was a fine evening and he was going to take a walk in a
prettier place, I believe, than you have in your palace at Chaillot, though I
hear it is very magnificent.'[5]

The Queen was not well at all, although she continued her stewardship
for James. It was a grey summer for the Princess and herself because of the
bethrothal of the gay little Duc de Berry to Mademoiselle de Chartres,
Louis's great-niece, on 5 July. They were married the next day. There was
no doubt but that Louise Marie was in love with Berry and he with her, but
love counted for nothing in Louis's dynastic schemes. However, realizing
something of what the Princess must be feeling, he excused her and her
mother from attending the wedding ceremony, and made sure that, when

[1] Carte CCX, 111, p. 185
[2] Carte CCX, 112, pp. 191–4
[3] *ibid.*   [4] *ibid.*   [5] Carte CCX, 123, p. 344

they came on their formal visit of congratulations the day after the wedding, they were received with the state due to them on such an occasion.

While James was away, the Queen and Middleton were also busy considering his marital future. The sisters as well as the daughter of the Emperor Joseph were viewed as possible brides. Since the daughter, Maria Josepha, was only eleven years old, she was out of the question so far as James himself was concerned; of the two sisters one was eight years older than he, and the other a year younger. But while the war was still progressing and general affairs in Europe were so unstable, it seemed dangerous to become wholly committed to the Stuarts. Anyway, the plans fell through – which was a pity so far as Booth was concerned, because he wrote to Middleton that the King had recovered so well and was now so handsome that, in Herefordshire phrase and custom, the Emperor's ladies 'would throw dirt through a ladder for him' in their eager rivalry if they were only to see him.[1] He also had a tart word for Louis XIV regarding Berry's marriage, which Middleton most probably did not relate any further: 'If the King of France knew the state of his army and that of the enemy's, it would, perhaps, abate the great joy he is in that one of his grandchildren has married another of them. . . .'[2]

There was no doubt but that the French army was in a terrible condition: lack of supplies and provisions was causing daily desertion. The conditions which Berwick had found in Dauphiné were typical of the whole theatre of operations, but other commanders were not so daring and did not turn to such desperate remedies as hi-jacking a wagon-load of money. Looking at the ordinary soldier, James found his heart touched with pity: 'Such creatures, I thank God, I never saw before, looking like devils, having beards indeed, but no flesh.'[3] This he wrote from Arras on 27 July, and he continued with a description of the preparations made for a sortie from the garrison of Béthune as a desperate endeavour to prevent the taking of it. To such straits had the once invincible army of France fallen while a handful of men sat in wilful ignorance of the situation, miles away in Versailles.

During his convalescence, James had not been entirely idle, and he had ordered a number of medals to be struck and sent to him from Saint-Germain. These showed his likeness on one side with '*Cujus est*' and, on the obverse, '*Reddite*'.[4] Ostensibly they were struck for those who were serving close to him in this campaign yet, when Marlborough's trumpeter visited the French camp on one of the many comings and goings over peace

[1] Carte CCX, 124, p. 211
[2] Carte CCX, 131, p. 223
[3] Carte CCX, 155, pp. 255–6
[4] 'Restore to whom it belongs'

negotiations, it was natural that he should take several back with him for some of the officers well disposed to the Stuarts. The trumpeter himself was unaware of what he was carrying but, when he returned to his camp he was shown the medal. Shortly afterwards he came to the French camp again with a request for thirty more medals for English officers serving with the Allies.

The Queen Regent viewed Marlborough's attempts at a *rapprochement* with a certain favour mixed with reservations. Whether they could rely on a man who had shown himself to be a first-class opportunist was a risk which they might have to take, but there was no doubt but that if they could secure his adherence against future promises on their side his greatest value would be his influence over the English army.

If the war was going badly for the French in Flanders, rumour had it that things were much better in Languedoc, and there was also news that Berwick might be returning any moment to the north. Villars had almost been captured in a wood where two hundred of the enemy's hussars were posted, but managed to escape with a mere dozen men. At the beginning of August they all moved to Berlé, and James told Middleton, writing of Villars, 'Our general seems to be in his senses at present,'[1] but Villars's recall appeared to be imminent.

For the time being there was nothing to do in Berlé but to play cards and hope for an engagement. The King was badly lodged now, and Booth was worried in case he should fall ill there. If the army had to march in a hurry he would be unable to keep up with them if he were once more smitten with the ague. He had already shown a few symptoms already, and now other people were beginning to be anxious as well as Booth.

The King wrote some verses 'the merit of which the writer professes to be no judge' and sent them home to his sister.[2] This may have occasioned the extraordinary outburst 'to all Christian people' 'of Charles Booth, formerly of Brampton in the county of Hereford of his entire abhorrence and detestation of all poetry and of all poets and scribes whatsoever'.[3] Clearly, the campaign was getting on Booth's nerves; all he wanted to do was to get his royal master home in one piece and in good health. He made little attempt to disguise his dissatisfaction with the world in general: when the Intendant of Picardy, on a visit to the King, attempted to describe the English Constitution; he declared in his letter to Middleton of 25 August that the attempt was 'as like what it is as an oyster is like an apple'.[4]

[1] Carte CCX, 163, p. 276
[2] Carte CCX, 181, p. 315
[3] Carte CCX, 164, p. 272
[4] Carte CCX, 181, p. 315

On 27 August 1710 the camp moved to Arras once more. James was not in the best of health and, on arrival, caught cold. While he lay ill he was busy planning in his head another invasion. This time he thought that he could manage without French troops and rely solely on the Irish regiments in the service of France. He also hoped that eventually the Church party in England 'now so much in earnest will end by bringing home the King',[1] as Monk had done in the case of his uncle. In Versailles, Torcy was receiving reports from Middleton of the readiness of the Irish for another effort on behalf of the Stuarts, and was seriously considering whether another invasion attempt might be worth while.

But in so far as the present campaign was concerned, there seemed to be little point in James remaining there while there was no action. There was great sickness and mortality in the camp, Berwick had still not arrived, and the King spent most of his time listening to Villars's stories. The French generals wanted to keep James at the front if possible, because his return would have been a too overt admission of the prevalent inactivity. But Arras itself was stricken by fever which had been brought to it by the soldiers. James was lodged over the gatehouse and looked down from his windows on carts carrying coffins as they passed out of the town on their way to the cemetery. Booth and his doctor watched him like hawks, and he was not allowed to go beyond the garden of the gatehouse. Somehow he managed to keep clear of the fever, but it seemed to be only a matter of time before his recently weakened constitution yielded again. And even he was not entirely sorry, as the first leaves of autumn floated down over the doomed town, to be leaving Arras. On 14 September 1710 he returned to the Queen and Louise Marie, who were then at Chaillot.

[1] Carte CCX, 194, p. 335

3. James II from a contemporary portrait by Kneller. (*National Portrait Gallery, London*)

4. Mary Beatrice of Modena, consort of James II from a contemporary
    portrait by Wissing. (*National Portrait Gallery, London*)

Chapter Nine

From Flanders James went straight to the Convent of the Visitation at Chaillot where he knew that he would find his mother and sister. They spent a great deal of time at the convent now, particularly the Queen who, as her health deteriorated, found the social demands of the French court more and more exhausting. Added to which, they did not have anywhere near enough money to dress or ride in the fashions held to be indispensable by Versailles.

Louise Marie was acutely aware of this, as was only natural in a beautiful and intelligent girl of eighteen who, despite her sojourns with the nuns, was devoted to music, dancing hunting and all the other social pleasures which Louis XIV knew so well how to provide for his court. Perhaps the diversion she valued most was hunting, although she knew that James did not approve. She was a brave and fearless rider and had taken at least one serious fall. Had suitable mounts been available there might have been some contention in the Stuart family but, as the Queen, who had herself been a daring rider to hounds, pointed out: 'Your necessity settles that, since you haven't a horse fit to ride.' 'We lead such a needy life,' the Princess said to her mother, 'that if we were in happier circumstances we would not know how to live a princely one!' The Sisters of the Visitation, who faithfully recorded the sayings and doings of the two royal ladies,[1] praised her attitude to adversity: one one occasion she remarked: 'It seems to me that those who are born into misfortune as I am are less to be pitied than the others: they have never tasted good fortune: they fear bad the less, they always have hope.' But she could not restrain herself from adding: 'All the same, it is a very sad fate to spend the best of one's youth in such a difficult situation.'

As James did, she loved her mother with a great devotion and, if she were apart from her for only a day, would write to her such a letter as the one to Chaillot dated 10 September 1710 which ended: 'I see that I have gone on too long, but you must forgive me because once I begin to write to Your Majesty it is only with a great deal of effort that I can stop.'[2] As their circumstances tightened, so the love of each of the three for the others became more intense. It was fortunate that James had gone campaigning when he did, otherwise he might have been smothered under a weight of

[1] Archives Nationales, Paris, K.1302
[2] *ibid.*

motherly and sisterly love; for this reason alone, his relationship with Berwick was of the utmost importance.

On the day after his arrival at Chaillot he took them both to the Benedictine Church in Paris for a requiem mass in commemoration of his father, and the next day he and Louise Marie went back to Saint-Germain, leaving the Queen in her apartments in the convent because she did not feel very well. The following day, 17 September, her daughter wrote:

> We arrived here on the stroke of nine. The King, thank God, is very little tired and has had a good supper. Please be good enough to excuse my scribble, but as I have only just arrived, my inkstand is in a very bad state. I hope that this will find Your Majesty much better than when we left you and that you have had a restful night. I am, with more respect than ever, the very humble and very obedient daughter and servant of Your Majesty,
>
> *Louise Marie.*[1]

The day after, James had to visit Louis at Versailles and this was the first of several visits within the next few weeks, during which time the Princess was left alone for the better part of the day. On one such occasion, deprived of an outing to Récollets since the King could not accompany her, and bored with walking up and down the roof-terrace, she summoned a number of young people in the château, sent for a violin-player and they danced counter-dances until the King arrived in time for supper.

But James himself did not feel very much like dancing at this time – there was so much at stake. The English Parliament had been dissolved on 21 September and there was a new Tory ministry headed by Harley as Chancellor of the Exchequer and Henry St John as Secretary of State. The Duke of Ormonde was Lord Lieutenant. Over half of this parliament supported the established Church of England. This did not mean that religious feeling necessarily ran very deep at that time, but it did signify that they were decidedly against the Lutheran Church and consequently against the House of Hanover. The Tories, amongst whom were a number of Jacobite sympathizers, wanted a cessation of the war with France, but the Whigs pressed to continue it. Now that the Tories were in the ascendancy, there was a renewal of effort to come to terms with France. Louis badly wanted peace: the coffers of France were exhausted, but he was equally determined to keep his grandson on the Spanish throne. Part of the prize he would have to pay for this would be the expulsion of James from France. The King of France was now on the horns of a dilemma: he had given his word to James and his father that he would support the Stuarts; on the

[1] Archives Nationales, Paris, K.1302

other hand the ties of Bourbon blood between France and Spain made them a formidable unit in Europe.

The Duc de Lauzun was sent by Louis first of all to Saint-Germain to warn the Queen Regent that, in order to set the wheels of peace-making in motion, her son would have to leave France. It was ironic that Lauzan who had been instrumental in bringing the infant James to France in the first place should be the first person to present the request for the King's departure from it. James had been half expecting this for some time, but did not resist the proposal as violently as he might otherwise have done, had Berwick and he not felt that some amelioration of his position might ultimately come out of it. For it was still rumoured, and with some cause, that the disposition of Queen Anne and her ministry towards James was such that it might be reasonably expected that the latter was more likely to succeed to the English throne than the newcomer from Hanover. The Abbé Gaultier was used as the intermediary between the Court of St James's and Versailles.

At the beginning of 1711 Gaultier was sent back to France by his patron, Lord Jersey, by Harley and the Duke of Shrewsbury with a message to Torcy suggesting that peace negotiations should be opened. At the same time, he sought out Berwick secretly and began discussions with regard to James's restoration. In January 1711, Marlborough had been dismissed as Supreme Commander and replaced by the Duke of Ormonde and, as the French and English drew closer together, so the rest of the Alliance gradually retreated from the latter. Eventually it became clear that England would be the prime mover in the peace negotiations.

Berwick advised James that his best course would be to accept Anne's position as Queen of England for the rest of her reign which, after all, could not last for very long, in return for her assurance and that of her ministry that the crown should be his when she should die. This the King did and at the same time added his own promise that religious and civil freedom would be preserved. He was deeply sincere about this, but it was always the stumbling-block in all relations he was to have with England's representatives. On 2 May 1711 he wrote to Middleton: 'They must not take it ill if I use the same liberty I allow to others, and adhere to the religion which I in my conscience think best.'[1]

Gaultier advised Berwick that it would be better if he returned to his command in Dauphiné as if nothing had happened and that the conclusions reached by St John and Harley should be sent to him there.

Berwick and James agreed that it would be a good idea to be together when these papers should arrive, and therefore it would seem most natural

[1] Carte CCX, 202, p. 409

that the King should use the pretext of making a tour of France to call upon Berwick in Dauphiné.

Marlborough, in spite of repeated assurances of his attachment to the Stuarts, was becoming less and less a figure to be reckoned with. Middleton was not entirely convinced that either St John or Harley, made Earl of Oxford and Mortimer in May 1711, could be completely trusted. Certainly nothing much seemed to be coming out of the peace talks in Holland which would prosper the King's interest. This fact made James draw up a manifesto asserting his royal right and assuring his subjects of his religious tolerance and his agreement to Anne's continuing as sovereign with the reversion of the crown to himself after her death. He also reserved the right to be called King and made it a condition that both their names should appear on all official documents.

He followed this on 2 May with a letter to his half-sister, written in a characteristically beautiful English:

Madam
The violence and ambition of the enemies of our family and of the monarchy have too long kept at distance those who, by all the obligations of nature and duty, ought to be more firmly united, and have hindered us from the proper means and endeavours of a better understanding between us, which could not fail to produce the most unhappy effects to ourselves, to our family, and to our bleeding country. . . . The natural affection I bear you and the King our father had for you till his last breath; the consideration of our mutual interest, honour and safety, and the duty I owe to God and my country, are the true motives that persuade me to write to you and to do all that is possible for me to come to a perfect union with you.

And you may be assured, Madam, that though I can never abandon, but with my life, my own just right, which you know is unalterably settled by the most fundamental laws of the land, yet I am most desirous rather to owe to you than to any living, the recovery of it. The voice of God and nature calls you to it; the promises you made to the King our father enjoin it; the preservation of our family, the preventing of unnatural wars require it; and the public good and the welfare of our country recommend it to you, to rescue it from present and future evils; which must to the latest posterity involve the nation in blood and confusion, till the succession be again settled in the right line.

. . . In the meantime, I assure you, Madam, and am ready to give all the security that can be desired, that it is my unalterable resolution to make the law of the land the rule of my government, to preserve every man's right, liberty and property equally with the rights of the crown: and to secure and maintain those of the Church of England, in all their just rights and privileges as by law established; and to grant such a toleration to dissenters as the Parliament shall think fit.

. . . Your own good nature, Madam, and your natural affection for a brother from whom you have never received any injury, cannot but incline your heart to do him justice; and, as it is in your power, I cannot doubt of your good inclinations. And I do here assure you that, in that case, no reasonable terms of accommodation which you can desire for yourself shall be refused by me. But as affairs of the moment be so well transacted by letters, I must conjure you to send one over to me, fully instructed and empowered by you, or to give security for such a one from me; for by that way only things can be adjusted to our mutual satisfaction, which shall be managed on our side with the utmost secrecy.

I have made this first step towards our mutual happiness with a true brotherly affection, with the plainness and sincerity that becomes both our rank and relation, and in the most prudent manner I could at present contrive, and will be directed by you in the presentation of it, relying entirely on your knowledge and experience as to the means and instruments.

And now, Madam, as you tender your own honour and happiness, the preservation and re-establishment of our ancient royal family, the safety and welfare of a brave people . . . who have no reason to complain of us and whom I must still and do still love as my own, I conjure you to meet me in the friendly way of composing our difference, by which only we can hope for the good effects which will make us both happy; yourself more glorious than all the other parts of your life, and your memory dear to all posterity.[1]

Anne did not answer this – why is not clear. Merely from courtesy she could hardly have done less but, although James may have hoped for a reply before he set out on his tour of France, none came. On Sunday, 14 June he went with his mother and sister to make his formal good-byes to Louis at Marly. The Dauphin had died on 14 April and the court was still in mourning. Both James and Louise Marie had been attached to the fat, kindly, well-intentioned Dauphin who was not cast in the heroic mould and never seemed to match up to his father's idea of what a successor to the throne of France should be.

There seemed to be no real reason for this jaunt, so far as the French court was concerned, and they were puzzled by it. How much Louis

[1] Carte CXX, 180, pp. 303-4

guessed is open to conjecture, but he in no way tried to restrain James. Once more, hope burned brightly for the King as he rode out of the court-yard of Saint-Germain on Tuesday, 16 June, leaving behind a worried Queen Regent and a disconsolate Louise Marie who would miss him not only for his own sake, but also as her partner on social occasions. His suite was small, both on account of economy and for the sake of security. The Earl of Middleton accompanied him as far as Strasbourg which they reached after staying with the Intendant of Burgundy at Dijon. From Strasbourg he travelled through the Franche Comté as far as Lyons where he ordered a riding-skirt of the finest silk brocade for Louise Marie, in spite of the fact that he did not approve of her going hunting. But the skirt was never to be worn.

Berwick, meanwhile, was waiting down in Provence:

> . . . We agreed that King James, under the pretext of making the tour of France, should, at the beginning of August, be in Dauphiné where I was commanding the army and stay there as long as possible with me. In fact, the King came; but I did not receive the papers in question, and I heard no more of them until the winter; Gaultier just wrote to me to say that he would soon be arriving with satisfactory instructions.[1]

James arrived in Berwick's camp at Barraux on 23 July and about that time the English poet and diplomatist, Matthew Prior, was sent by the Earl of Oxford and St John to speed the peace negotiations in Paris, unknown to the two men in Dauphiné. This was the beginning of the double game which St John was to play with James.

As one condition of the peace, the English insisted on the return of Dunkirk. Against this, France was to get the return of Lille and Tournai. England was to get certain fishing rights with the award of Newfoundland and to retain Gibralter and Port Mahon; she was also to win the slave trade from France.

> When Gaultier returned to France [wrote Berwick] I thought that he would be more explicit with me, but he only said that one must still be patient until the peace was finally concluded; that the slightest hint of the good intentions of Queen Anne towards her brother would furnish the Whigs with material for complaint against the Court, and might not only destroy the work necessary for peace but also cause a possible upheaval within the Ministry and in the country; that, moreover, they must be assured of the army, which could only occur when, the peace once signed, they could proceed with the reforms, and that then he

[1] Berwick, *op. cit.*, Vol. 2, p. 196

[Oxford] would be careful to keep only those officers of whom he was sure.[1]

And still the two brothers waited in Dauphiné. That summer the weather was bad, but, in spite of this and of his disappointment with Oxford, James enjoyed being in camp with his brother again. They were joined by Berwick's fifteen-year-old son, Lord Tynmouth, who followed James everywhere, evincing for him the kind of admiration James had shown for his own father at the same age. The King found further disappointment in the fact that there was no military action around him, but he managed to pass the time pleasantly enough, dining with the officers and riding out with young Tynmouth. Then rumours began to fly around the camp that arms were being landed in Scotland and that the Earl of Mar would swear allegiance to King James.

But Berwick had had no official confirmation:

The Jacobites and other well-inclined people were continually pressing Oxford to take advantage of the favourable moment; they pointed out to him that there had never been a House of Commons more favourably disposed, and thus that he had only to propose to them to revoke the acts in favour of Hanover and without doubt they would pass it. His reply was that they had to go more gently about it, that he was working seriously on the matter and that they should not be troubled about it.[2]

[1] Berwick, *op. cit.*, Vol. 2, pp. 196–208
[2] *ibid.*

Chapter Ten

If James had been inclined to forget that Berwick belonged to a country other than his own, he must have been forcibly reminded of it when he saw the Duke's tall figure striding about the camp at Barraux in the long mantle of royal mourning. It was typical of Louis's strange protectiveness towards the Stuarts that he wanted to spare them any unnecessary reminders of sadness, and so he decreed that they should not wear mourning for the Dauphin as he was not a ruling monarch. Berwick, of course, he regarded as a Frenchman.

Both brothers were impatient now for any word from England, but the older man came to realize more and more that they would indeed be fortunate if any practical good came from that quarter:

> In this fashion Oxford played with us, and it was difficult to do anything about it; because to break with him would have meant destroying everything, seeing that he held the power, and completely managed Queen Anne. So we had to pretend to trust him, but we did not cease to work under cover with the Duke of Ormonde and many others, in order to conclude this affair by their means if Oxford failed us.[1]

Seeing that there was nothing to be hoped for at that particular moment, James left Berwick before the camp at Barraux was struck in October. In any case, the army was liable to be recalled at any moment as the peace negotiations progressed. The damp seemed to have eaten into his very bones, and he was not feeling at all well, so for once he listened to his doctor and went to Grenoble to take the waters for a month. He returned to the Île de France by Languedoc and Guienne and was sumptuously entertained at Montpellier by the Duc de Roquelaure, governor of Guienne, for three days. Thence to Toulouse, and then down the Garonne in a beautifully decorated barge to Bordeaux. On this part of the trip he was joined by Lord Tynmouth and, as he neared home, his spirits began to rise again, although it was certain that Saint-Germain would not maintain them at a very high level for long.

He arrived at Chaillot in the early morning of 4 November, and his mother and sister came from their beds to greet him, exclaiming how well he looked. He rested for a while and then rose and greeted the community

[1] Berwick, *op. cit.*, Vol. 2, pp. 196–208

who gathered around him to listen to the account of his travels: he was undoubtedly the hero of the convent, who had taken the royal family to their heart. In the early afternoon, after dinner, he took his womenfolk back to the château.

The winter passed comparatively cheerfully. Louise Marie was so happy to have James back that nothing could dim her gaiety; together they were an equally matched pair: young, handsome, full of hope for a golden future. Their court that winter was probably the gayest since the Stuarts had arrived at Saint-Germain, and one of the causes of its increased optimism was the fact that Queen Anne seemed more likely than ever to declare James her successor, since the Electoral Prince of Hanover and the Whigs had openly joined forces and Anne still loathed the Whigs.

On 29 January 1712 the peace conference opened at Utrecht, and on 12 February the young Dauphine died, followed by the new Dauphin on the 18th and their elder child, aged five, on 9 March. This left the younger child, not yet two, as heir to the Sun King and the throne of France.

These events virtually marked the end of that great spirit which was synonymous with the court of Versailles: from then onwards Louis himself seemed to lose heart and to age rapidly. All happiness fled, and this atmosphere was naturally conveyed to Saint-Germain. From a practical point of view, it was disquieting. Louis was an old man with a baby as his heir; if, as seemed likely, the Duc d'Orléans was to become Regent, the personally well-disposed intentions of the French King could very well be lacking in his nephew. Anxiety slowly mounted during the month of March but was dispelled when there was talk of the possibility of Louise Marie marrying the warrior Charles XII of Sweden; if this came to pass, James's chances of a restoration would be considerably strengthened with the army of Sweden at his back.

On Maundy Thursday, 31 March, James went hunting in the Bois de Boulogne and, on the way home to Saint-Germain, called for the Queen and the Princess who were staying at Chaillot. He had had a satisfactory hunt but had not felt too well after it. Fearing another attack of the ague which he knew so well, he took to his bed. On Easter Saturday it was confirmed that he had smallpox. Anxiety seized the court, although everything that was possible to be done was being done. He was given Extreme Unction but, strangely enough, refused to confess to the Jesuit, Father Eyre. This may have been because James's Jansenism was still a large part of his spiritual life, and the Jesuits were at the other end of the scale from the Jansenists. The parish priest of Saint-Germain was sent for and James confessed to him.

It is conceivable that, while so much was being done for the King, not so

137

much attention was being paid to the Princess; on 10 May she discovered signs of the illness while at her toilet. The Queen, who had had the disease, was closeted with her son, since James was still in a critical state, but realizing the next day that something was indeed wrong with her daughter, she came to her. The Princess had been bled in the foot which had only made her uncomfortable and given her a bad night. She was then given opiates which robbed her of any will to resist. She made a general confession to Father Gaillard, and then said to the Queen: 'You see, Madam, the happiest person in the world; I have just made my general confession; I think that I have done it as well as is possible for me, and if I was told that I would die in a little while, I could not do otherwise than I have done. I have placed myself in the hands of God. I do not ask Him for life, but that His Will may be accomplished in me.'[1] On the night of 17 April, which was a Sunday, she had another bad night and was bled again. Her fever mounted and her respiration was difficult. About 5 a.m. she told the Queen that she was dying.

A distraught Berwick waited at Saint-Germain for news of his half-sister, and on the Monday morning he was allowed by the doctors to tell James that she was in great danger. News of her illness had been kept from him so far, in view of his own grave state. Having comforted him as best he could, Berwick then had to leave him to ride to Versailles to inform Louis. When he returned to the château about midday, he met a messenger riding through the main gate who told him that the Princess had died between ten and eleven.

At a time when James was still very seriously ill she was buried quietly in the chapel of the English Benedictines at Paris, by the side of her father. No public funeral oration was possible because of the delicate atmosphere engendered by the peace negotiations: no one wished to offend the English. This was a cause of sadness to the Queen. No visits of condolence could be paid by the French court, either, because of possible infection.

A French nobleman wrote to a friend at Utrecht:

My Lord, I send you by these the sad and deplorable news of the much lamented death of the Princess Royal of England who died of the small-pox the 18th of this month at St Germains who as she was one of the greatest ornaments of that afflicted court, so she was the admiration of all Europe; never Princess was so universally regretted. Her death has filled all France with sighs, groans and tears. She was a Princess of a majestical mien and port; every motion spoke grandeur, every action was easy and without any affectation or meanness, and proclaim'd her

[1] Archives Nationales, Paris, K.1302

a heroine descended from the long race of so many paternal and maternal heroes; majesty sat enthron'd on her forehead; and her curious large black eyes struck all that had the honour to approach her with aw [*sic*] and reverence; but all her external glories, though the greatest of her sex, were nothing to her internal, and she seems to have establish'd the opinion of Plato who asserts that the soul frames its own habitation, and that beautiful souls make to themselves beautiful bodies. She had a great deal of pleasant wit, joined with an equal solidity of judgment; she was devout, without the defects that young aspirers to piety are sometimes incident to; and though she comply'd with the diversions of the court, her greatest pleasure was in pious retirement. She was very affable, and of a sweet, mild temper, full of pity and compassion, which is the distinguishing character of the royal family of the Stuarts. To sum up all in a few words, she was a dutiful and obedient daughter, an affectionate sister, tenderly loving and belov'd by the hero, her brother. On both their countenances were divinely mingled the noble features and lineaments of the Stuarts and the D'Estes and beauty triumphed over both, with only this difference, that in him it was more strong and masculine as becoming in his sex, in her more soft and tender as more suiting with hers, in both excellent and alike.[1]

When James rose from his bed of sickness, all that was most sweet and colourful in his life had disappeared. He was twenty-three, but it seemed as if his youth had vanished with Louise Marie. On 14 May 1712 he wrote in Latin to Pope Clement XI from Saint-Germain: 'Among the many misfortunes which, in almost all our past life, we have endured, with the help of God, nothing has touched us with more grief than that Her Royal Highness Princess Louise Marie has been taken from us in this way by sad fate . . . amidst the many troubles of fortune she was our special ornament and joy.'[2]

[1] Rankine, *op. cit.*, p. 78
[2] HMC, Vol. I, p. 244 (Book I, p. 97)

Chapter Eleven

The year 1712 was a decisive one for the King: not only had he lost the one person of his own age whom he loved above all others but now it was rapidly becoming apparent that the time for the Jacobites to strike was imminent. Queen Anne was failing at a comparatively early age and was still repulsing every suggestion of a meeting between herself and the Electoral Prince of Hanover.

Marlborough's star was waning swiftly, both with Anne and, on the other side of the Channel, with Saint-Germain. Middleton had written to a correspondent in the previous year: 'He had it in his power to have been good and great and now can only pretend to the humble merit of a postboy, who brings good news to which he has not contributed.'[1] Yet if Marlborough counted for little now, and if Oxford's procrastinations maddened both Berwick and James, new hope seemed to be embodied in the person of St John, now Viscount Bolingbroke. During the peace negotiations he visited Paris and was a guest of Torcy. He made a courtesy call on Louis XIV at Fontainebleau and, according to Dangeau, happened to find himself in a box at the Opéra near to that of James, although there is no indication that they met.[2] But he did meet Berwick and, from this time onwards, maintained correspondence with him.

James had every reason to feel fairly optimistic with regard to his chances of restoration. There were now a fair proportion of Jacobites within the Government; the West Country and a great part of Scotland were reputed to be disposed favourably towards him, and if Marlborough's pathetic assurances that he would be ready to come to James if the charges raised against him since his fall from Anne's grace were dropped by the Tories did not amount to much, one of the most popular peers in England, the Duke of Ormonde, declared his interest to Berwick. The Earl of Mar also made approaches to James and Berwick during the spring of 1712. On James's twenty-fourth birthday, 10 June (Old Style Calendar), White Rose Day, bonfires were lit in Edinburgh, toasts were drunk to James VIII of Scotland, ships at Leith were dressed over-all and crowds surged up to Holyrood singing 'The King shall enjoy his own again'. And there was an increasing atmosphere of excitement in London and the south generally as the spirit of Jacobitism began to show itself abroad.

[1] HMC, Vol. I, p. 226   [2] Dangeau, *op. cit.*, XLV, pp. 205–15

Berwick was certain that the only sure way for his brother to succeed Anne would be for him to go secretly and alone to London and be presented by the Queen of England to Parliament as her heir in his incontestable right, both divine and human. At the same time she would assure Parliament that no harm was intended to the established religion. Telling Gaultier how much he regretted the slowness, irresolution and coldness of Oxford, the Duke charged him with this new message and patiently awaited the Treasurer's answer. But answer came there none. Oxford was becoming too submerged in his personal battle with St John and too confused by drink to take a resolute stand upon anything.

Bolingbroke, on the other hand, was capable of very cool and calculating thought. Avid for power, he did not care whether he achieved it through James or through Hanover. He had to get rid of Oxford and then, he reasoned, the reins of government would be in his hands. Anne was tired and very ill and the overt quarrels between these two ministers both dismayed and exhausted her.

It may be as well to summarize briefly the subdivisions of the two parties as Bolingbroke was to do a little later, on 27 February and 2 March 1714, in two conversations with Torcy's representative, d'Iberville. The Tories were divided into four main sections. First were the Jacobites and a few Quakers and Non-Jurors who wanted James to succeed Anne even if he did not change his religion. The 'Hanoverian' Tories were zealous for the English Church and wished for a limited monarchy. They would not have accepted James even if he had changed his religion because they maintained that he would not be able to forget the maxims of despotic government and of the Catholic Church in which he had been brought up. Then there were the Tories who were anti-Hanoverian, either from fear that under the Electoral Prince, so soon to become Elector, they would have no share in government, or from a dislike of his person or of Germans in general, or from a fear of civil war. They wanted James, but wanted him as a Protestant – some from religious zeal, some from the age-old fear of the Papacy and some from fear of losing Church lands which they possessed. Lastly, there were the Tories with merely self-interested motives, and it is difficult not to imagine that this was the group to which Bolingbroke himself belonged.

The Whigs fell into two categories. There were those who preferred a republican form of government or a monarchy in which the king would be a puppet figure; these were often Presbyterians, French refugees and Nonconformists in general. The other Whigs did not desire republicanism because they feared that they would lose their rank if they were of the nobility or otherwise socially distinguished. It was the Whigs' boast that they had the fullest purses, best swords, best heads and the fairest women.

If Bolingbroke were acting in self-interest, no less could be claimed for Oxford. His plan was to gather as much Jacobite support as he could to the Tory party by empty promises to James and his followers, thereby ensuring his own continuance in office.

If the Tories remained in power, then the chances of the peace negotiations bearing fruit were more likely than if they had been in the hands of the Whigs who sought the furtherance of the war. These negotiations dragged on for over a year, and for James himself they contained a major set-back. The English became more and more insistent that the Stuart exile should remove himself from the court of France, if not from France itself. The young king was not surprised by this, but saddened. On the other hand it seemed to come as a tremendous shock to the Queen, but the hands of Louis XIV were tied, and this time he was powerless to help his friends if he wanted peace.

On 6 September 1712, James said good-bye to the Queen Regent, who was at Chaillot, and set out on the first stage of his exile. He passed the winter at Châlons-sur-Marne, mostly in the bishop's palace, scarcely noticing the dreary provincialism of the surrounding town, so preoccupied was he with his correspondence with the Queen, Middleton and Berwick. At last the papers for which he had been waiting arrived: it was impossible for him to travel without some kind of safe-conduct and he had applied to the Emperor for a passport which came in the middle of February. At the same time Queen Anne sent a personal guarantee of safe-conduct and, armed with all these documents, he left for Bar in Lorraine, which was the nearest neighbour to France and ruled by Berwick's old friend, the Duke of Lorraine. Just before leaving for Bar he wrote in terms of the warmest gratitude to Louis XIV, who had been his adviser and the nearest he had known to a father for the past eleven years.

Châlons, 19 February 1713

With what words can I express to Your Majesty my gratitude before leaving the refuge which your paternal care has afforded me almost since my entry into this world and which you allow me to leave only in order that I may find another more suitable for the present situation of your affairs and mine? If words fail me, my heart is filled with the memory of your benefits and past kindness to which the care which you take of me and all that concerns me is the culmination, and reassures me in the sad situation in which I find myself by the confidence I have in a generosity unequalled in its duration, in a wisdom accustomed to accomplishing the widest designs and in a kindness never weary of extending its benefits to me and my family. It is my most earnest entreaty that it should continue towards myself and the Queen, the only one remaining to me of those who were most dear and who, deserving everything of me as the best of mothers, yields nothing to me in the feelings of gratitude which I have for Your Majesty which she has instilled into me from my most tender years.

It only remains for me to assure Your Majesty of my warmest and most sincere wishes for your happiness and prosperity, and to beg you to believe that you will always find in me the respect, the attachment and, if I may dare to say so, the tenderness of a son: a will always prepared not only to follow but also to anticipate your own in all things during the terms of my exile, and if ever I find myself restored to my kingdom, a faithful ally who will make it his glory and his happiness to concur in the great and just designs of a king who does so much honour to loyalty.

James R.

He sent this to Berwick[1] for him to hand personally to Louis as a mark of deepest respect and, at the same time, he addressed a letter to Madame de Maintenon:

Little content, Madame, with the letter which I have written to the King in which I have only feebly expressed the feelings which I have for him, where better may I address myself, Madame, than to you to beg to add thereto for me all that is missing? I dare to ask this of your kind heart and of the friendship which you have always had for the Queen and for me, while requesting its continuation for both of us. Allow me to assure you here of mine, useless though it may be to you, as well of the high esteem and deep gratitude that I have for you, Madame, to whom, after the King, I believe myself to owe everything.

Touched and charmed by the sincerity and the good manners of the young man, for he was under no real obligation to write thus to the French king's morganatic wife, Madame de Maintenon wrote to his mother, complimenting her on her son: 'The king, your son, Madame, has combined in his letter to the King, the politeness of an academician, the tenderness of a son and the dignity of a king.'

The Queen was James's greatest personal care: they were desperately short of money at Saint-Germain and she was reduced to making economies even in small items of dress, such as using old ribbons in her shoes. She was frequently ill, and Berwick kept an eye on her state of health, reporting to James. He was convinced that she would do better at Saint-Germain than in the icy cloisters of Chaillot and urged James to request her to return

[1] HMC, Vol. I, p. 256

to the château[1] – both for her own sake and because her influence would go some way towards restraining the petty intrigues and quarrels which thrived in the atmosphere of boredom prevalent there. With both James and the Queen gone, the Jacobites of Saint-Germain began to lose confidence and, with time hanging heavily on their hands, some of them resorted to the comfort to be found in a bottle and this, in turn, frequently ended in senseless duels.

Middleton no longer had control over the various factors in the château. While James had been at Châlons, Oxford in his dealings with Berwick had hinted that the Earl's removal might be a good thing. No one had served James and the Queen more faithfully than Middleton: he was wise and perspicacious as well, but his situation was such that he could please no one. The Scottish Jacobites thought that he had approved the union of the two kingdoms in 1707; the Irish disliked him because he was a Scot and therefore, through his influence on the court, might gain advantages for Scotland. This applied to the English as well, and the Protestants disapproved of his conversion to Catholicism. It was comparatively easy for James to remove his well-loved counsellor by calling him to his side, and Middleton travelled to Bar with him. The King had a small suite with him which was composed, for the greater part, of Protestants. As soon as he was settled in Lorraine he provided a Protestant chapel for those of his adherents who were of that persuasion, and sent for Doctor Charles Leslie who had impressed him on his visit to Saint-Germain a few years previously. The doctor arrived in August 1713 and, after a warm reception by the King, began his duties as Protestant chaplain. This had been an idea close to James' heart for some time, but while he was in France such a move had been impossible.

The Duke of Shrewsbury had come from London in place of the Duke of Hamilton as ambassador to the French court. Hamilton had been killed in a duel engineered, so it was said, because it was known that he was friendly disposed towards the Jacobites. Shrewsbury, for all that he was a son-in-law of the Earl of Middleton, was not. But when Villars, who still retained the most cordial memories of James from their campaigns together, met him at the French court, he did not hesitate to tell the ambassador what a good opinion he had of the young King. He told this to James in a letter wishing him God-speed, and received the following reply, dated 28 March 1713:

You cannot but realize that I received your letter of the 22nd of this month with much satisfaction since the thought of my General always

[1] HMC, Vol. I, p. 249

ames Francis Edward, Prince of Wales, and his sister, Louise Marie, in
695, from a contemporary portrait by Larguillière. (*National Portrait
Gallery, London*)

6. James III and VIII, from a contemporary portrait by Mengs. (*National Portrait Gallery, London*)

pleases me, and I put much value on such an amiable friendship. What you have said of me in the company which you entertained to dinner was most civil on your part, and I beg you to believe that I appreciate keenly all these marks of your zeal and of your affection, and that I reciprocate with a great esteem on my side. If you cross the Rhine on this campaign I hope that it will be to carry there the confirmation of the peace, and that you make the last campaign in Flanders.[1]

While he was at Châlons, practically destitute, James had an unexpected stroke of luck: the Queen had had two bills paid, amounting to a total of 32,000 francs and she was, at long last, able to send the King money. So he was able to make his way to the court of Lorraine at Lunéville, *en route* for Bar, with a little more affluence than he had imagined would have been possible.

The Duchess of Lorraine was the sister of the Duchesse d'Orléans and therefore not entirely unknown to James. Her husband, Leopold, was a ruler of the kind most likely to appeal to him: liberal in his opinions, he had done a great deal to further the growth of commerce in the Duchy and for the welfare of his people.

It was fortunate that the King had spent more than he could really afford on a limited but good wardrobe before leaving France, since he arrived in Lunéville just as the Lenten Carnival began. Outside the Duke's palace the lashing rain and early March cold heightened the contrast with the candlelight and warmth within and, for a brief while, a little of the old gaiety returned to him. But a scene so reminiscent of nights spent dancing with Louise Marie at Fontainebleau and Versailles could not but have brought its own moments of melancholy. His pleasant manners, affability and attractive voice brought him many admirers and he was considered a social asset to the court of Lorraine. But to Bar he had to go, and there seemed little sense in postponing the day of his arrival there and, as soon as it was polite to do, he set out with Middleton and the rest of his suite.

Most of the journey was through thickly wooded country and the Duke insisted that a body of his guards should accompany the King: outlaws and robbers lurked in the dark forests and royalty would have proved a rich prize. As they approached Bar the country became hilly and more gently wooded, and James's first view of his home-to-be was of the castle rising above the town which clung to the side of the steep valley created by the River Ornain.

The town of Bar was small, sleepy, provincial, but pleasant to look upon. The castle, which had once sheltered James's ancestress, Mary Stuart,

[1] HMC, Vol. I, p. 261

raised itself proudly above a winding conglomeration of grey stone streets. There were a number of monasteries and convents and many churches in the town, and a thick wall surrounded it, pierced by eleven gates which were locked at night to keep out brigands and any other undesirables.

Gradually James began to settle in; he could never accept his removal from France but, with the stoical resignation recognized by Fénélon which grew within him from year to year, he saw the necessity for it where Louis was concerned. In any case he was too absorbed in his plans for recovering his crown to spend much time regretting his present lot. With the arrival of spring he felt the old urge for activity which had sent him our campaigning and, when he had finished several hours of correspondence, he would gather the most limber of his court of forty or so around him and ride his horse until rider and mount were exhausted. Or, with his characteristic, swift Stuart stride, he would take long walks, often with his dog, Missy, running at his heels.

Although James had gone, Berwick did not slacken his continual drive to get some action from the English, Scots or French. Marlborough was now definitely out of the picture: a self-declared exile he was wandering uneasily in Europe while Ormonde carried on his command with Prince Eugène in Flanders. Eugène seemed determined to continue the war in Europe until the ink had dried on the last word to be written in the Peace Treaty which was taking more than a year to negotiate. Nothing definite had come from Oxford or Bolingbroke; when Torcy joined his voice to that of Berwick and demanded to know what, if anything, Oxford suggested that they should do in the apparently imminent event of Anne's death, he finally replied that when Queen Anne died, the hopes of the Jacobites and of his own party would also die. In condemning this lethargy, Berwick blamed it on neither lack of intelligence nor on lack of courage. He was convinced now that Oxford had been acting solely from self-interest. The wonder was that he never fully admitted to himself that Bolingbroke could be playing the same game. From time to time Oxford sent messages exhorting James to change his religion and thereby remove the greatest obstacle to his acceptance by the English government and people, but Versailles as well as Saint-Germain, knew that henceforth Oxford was a cipher where the restoration of the Stuarts was concerned.

Priest though he was, Gaultier had had no scruples in conveying the exhortations of both Oxford and Bolingbroke to James that he should become a Protestant. The King considered Gaultier's interference as unpardonable and complained to Cardinal Gualterio, that he was behaving in a 'terrible fashion' for he not only had advised the King to abjure the Catholic religion, but to inform the Pope that he had done this only as a matter of expediency and that his heart was still with the Catholics. Clearly, the quondam curé of Saint-Germain was beginning to exceed his original brief to act as a go-between with the English Jacobites and Versailles.

The King was incapable of that kind of strategy, and he was determined to the point of obstinacy. His father had lost a throne through devotion to his religion and it was possible that he himself might never regain it for the same reason, but nothing would make him change his mind.

On 11 April 1713 the peace was signed at Utrecht: in return for the acknowledgement of his grandson as Philip V of Spain, Louis had had to recognize the Hanoverian and Protestant succession in England. This meant the end of his declared support for the Stuarts and the continuance of James's exile. Already, in the previous November, Anne had written through her ambassador to the Duke of Lorraine complaining of his sheltering the 'Pretender'. It says much for the Duke that he took no notice of this protest and regretted that he could not do as she wished and send the King away. He had given him a promise of protection and would not abandon to his enemies a prince whose only crime was to belong to the same family as the Queen of England herself belonged.

Some of the Jacobites were sanguine about the depth of the French King's commitment to the Peace of Utrecht and thought that he would only pay lip service where his support of the English Protestant succession was concerned. But James knew better and realized that Louis was cornered: not only was it vitally important that the Franco-Spanish bloc be maintained, but Louis's strong family feeling would never allow him to abandon Philip. He loved James as a son but, in the last extreme, blood was thicker than water. So James was under no illusion as to how his chances stood.

Three things were necessary for a successful invasion of England or Scotland: the support of the whole of Scotland, his own presence, and the support of France in arms and men. Without the third, the other two could not effect very much.

He went to Lunéville to stay with the Lorraine family in May and they did their best to comfort him because they were sincerely fond of him, but depression took hold of him and, as it often turned out now, this ended in sickness a little later. Some of his court thought that the air of Bar did not agree with him but at that moment nowhere would have suited him. He went for a while to take the waters at Plombières when he was a little better, but fell ill again in September and returned to Plombières. He was tired of the bad weather prevailing that summer, and felt that if he could only get into the sun he would soon recover. Italy was suggested, but he knew that it was paramount that he should not be too far distant from France and the Channel coast, so he stayed in Bar. There was a flutter in the quiet little court when Lord Middleton's two sons returned from captivity in England in June 1713 as a result of the Peace. The intriguers at Saint-Germain had been hard at work for over the past year and in December they achieved their objective: Middleton was more or less forced to resign his seals of office to the King, who did not want to take them and was furious that such an old and trusted servant could be so ill-used. Sir Thomas Higgens was appointed in Middleton's place, and Middleton returned to the Queen's service at Saint-Germain. One of Middleton's sons, Lord Clermont, entered the King's service as a gentleman of the bedchamber.

Gradually, James was becoming convinced that if France were no longer able to support him he would have to strike alone. The Hanoverian minister in London was continually pressing the cabinet to allow the Electoral Prince of Hanover to take his place in the House of Lords with the English title of the Duke of Cambridge, but Anne was adamant that he should not step on English shores while she was alive. Nevertheless, if the Prince did manage to achieve his objective, he would be ready to take his place on the throne immediately it became vacant. Shortly afterwards he succeeded as Elector of Hanover.

With the possibility of the Hanoverian succession so likely, many more people of Jacobite inclination were leaving England and seeking 'the King over the Water', a number settling in Saint-Germain and, welcome though they certainly were, they were an additional financial burden on the King. The Queen, still carrying on the administration at the château, wrote to her secretary, Dicconson, who had gone to Bar to see the King in April: 'It is certain that I want you more than you can imagine, but I suffer it not only with patience but with pleasure, when I think that your being with the King is of so great a satisfaction to him, for there is nothing in this world I would not do (but a sin) to procure him some in the dismal circumstances he is in, since I myself cannot be so happy as to be of any to him.' Some idea of the hand-to-mouth existence in the château which, in the King's absence and with his mother so preoccupied, seemed often to result in a lowering of standards to the point of petty pilfering, can be gathered from postscript to the Queen's letter: 'Pray ask the King if it be true that he has given Daniel Mackdonal the clock that stood on the chimney in his chamber.'[1]

Berwick wrote of his final acceptance of the fact that Oxford would do nothing for them, on 27 April 1714 from Saint-Germain: 'I find M. Oleran [Oxford] is in a tottering condition, and I do believe M. Albert [Anne] will part with him ere it be long, of which I should be very glad, for that gentleman's behaviour seems not very current, however one must

[1] HMC, Vol. I, p. 316

keep fair with him to the last.'[1] He followed this letter with another, dated 4 May, telling James of the death of his young friend the Duc de Berry, the love of his dead sister: 'His death has been occasion'd by his own fault, having concealed a sprain he had a week ago a hunting that had broke a vein in his body. The King is very much touch'd at his death, but, thank God, is very well. There is no news from England . . .'[2]

Although Berwick had given up hope of obtaining help through Oxford, he was still convinced that Bolingbroke was sincere in his offers of assistance. James, however, placed no more trust at this stage in one than in the other. So he proceeded with his idea of acting on his own and wrote to the Scots in February to thank them for their loyalty. He also took, on his own account, the not entirely wise step of writing to the Vatican for financial assistance for an expedition to Scotland. It was just as well that it was not very forthcoming at the time, since the more involved he became with Rome, the less attractive he would appear in English eyes.

Just when it was becoming more essential than ever that the King should be able to obtain good advice whenever he needed it, his brother was sent to Madrid by the King of France in May. He bore the condolences of Louis to his grandson, Philip, on the death of his young wife, Marie Louise of Savoy. He was then obliged to remain with the Spanish army in Catalonia until October 1714.

Coinciding with the departure of Berwick, a sudden fever sent James back to Plombières, but he stayed no longer than 2 June when, apparently unable to remain inactive any longer, he left for Lunéville, accompanied by Lord Newcastle and, once more, by his nephew Lord Tynmouth. About this time Berwick asked to be allowed to return because he had urgent business with his son: marriage plans were in the air. This, at least, was the excuse he used to be somewhere within the reach of the King. But his request to leave Spain was granted neither by the King of Spain nor the King of France. So James was still absolutely alone as far as advisers of any worth were concerned. On 23 May the Electress Sophia died and George, her son, became the Elector and heir to the English throne. Not as popular as his mother had been at home and abroad, it was surmised by the ever-optimistic Jacobites that his chances in so far as the Queen and the British people were concerned, were much lower than those of James.

Three days after the King's birthday on 20 June, the English Parliament put a price of £5,000 on James's head. It was now clear that, in order to secure the succession, he must marry, so he again asked the Emperor for the hand of his daughter, Maria Josepha. He affirmed that, if he should regain his throne, he would renounce any claim to the Imperial throne but

[1] HMC, Vol. I, p. 318   *ibid.*, p. 320

once more the Emperor declined: the fortunes of the Stuarts had not yet shown the improvement he required. There was also talk of a union between him and Casimira Sobieska, granddaughter of the great Polish king and patriot, John Sobieski, but she was not considered suitable in the final event.

When the price had been laid upon his head, James had been staying with the Prince de Vaudémont, illegitimate son of the Duke of Lorraine, at his palace in Commercy. His father had joined him there with his duchess, and a heavy programme of army manoeuvres and less strenuous entertainments were staged for the family party and their royal friend. What with the fluidity of the political situation in England, the realization of what his outlawry really meant and the problem of making a marriage which would not only be dynastically suitable but also personally at least acceptable, distracting James must have been no easy task.

While he was in Commercy and Berwick in Spain, the English Parliament was prorogued on 9 July 1714, and Oxford and Bolingbroke had a violent quarrel in the presence of Queen Anne. It led to Oxford's resignation, if not actual dismissal and, at last, Bolingbroke was free to form his own cabinet. In this he proposed to include a number of known Jacobites, but the cabinet was still incomplete when Anne fell into her last illness. For some reason or other, Bolingbroke seemed to lose either his head or his nerve, and sought the support of the Whigs as well: a privy council was called for 30 July. To the great dismay of Bolingbroke and others present, the Dukes of Argyll and Somerset arrived and were instrumental in carrying the Whigs along with them to give support to the Duke of Shrewsbury who was known to have more regard for the Act of Settlement than for the exiled House of Stuart. Shortly afterwards Queen Anne died, and Shrewsbury was heading a cabinet largely composed of Whigs.

Berwick summarized the situation afterwards as follows:

> I was then in Catalonia, too far away to be able either to act or to give advice; and even if I had been in Paris, I should have been very embarrassed, in view of the then present state of affairs. It was in nowise our fault if we had not made any arrangements with regard to the situation which arose, and France, whatever good will she may have had, was in no way in a condition to risk a new war for upholding the interests of the young King. No measures had been taken, nor could they have been from this side of the water; it was for the well-intentioned in England to advise us what we should do, and not yet being the absolute masters, they had not had time to arrange the matter.[1]

[1] Berwick, *op. cit.*, Vol. 2, pp. 196–208

It was said that Anne had had a sealed envelope under her pillow when she died and that this had contained her will naming James as her successor. The will, if so it was, was destroyed by the Privy Council, and the Elector of Hanover was brought to England without any difficulty. James was still at Commercy when the news of Anne's death was brought to him. He left immediately, and *incognito*, for Chaillot.

Chapter Twelve

James arrived on the outskirts of Paris in the evening and went to Lauzun's little house in the woods at Chaillot which was near to the Convent of the Visitation. He had barely greeted his mother the following morning when Torcy arrived to request him, on behalf of the King of France, to return to Lorraine. His presence within the French kingdom was enough to imply the destruction of the Treaty of Utrecht, and this Louis could not afford. So little had been arranged or provided for on the other side of the Channel that even James had to admit to himself that it would have been madness to proceed further. He returned to Bar a little more coolly and pragmatically than he had set out.

From Plombières he issued a manifesto referring to himself as 'the only born Englishman now left of the royal family' and this, of course, was strictly accurate. On 26 September he sent a message to the Scots assuring them that he would come to them at the first possible opportunity, but the extreme caution and lack of concert on the part of his English adherents made it difficult for him to say positively when this would be. He begged the Scots meanwhile not to incur trouble with the Government and to try to maintain a complete agreement and intelligence between themselves, without which nothing would be of any value.

To maintain continuity of government until the Elector of Hanover should arrive to take his place on the English throne, a regency was elected of twenty-five lords, including Oxford but not Bolingbroke. It must have been about this time that the latter made up his mind to leave for France. Ormonde also began to feel disquieted. Everyone was on the alert because it was realized that if James were to make a successful landing it had to be soon. On 15 September the price on his head was raised to £100,000.

Berwick was not able to return to France until October 1714 owing to the demands upon his services in Spain. This was the first time he had not responded immediately to his brother's call, and there was time enough between August, when James first summoned Berwick, and October, when he arrived, for the King to reflect upon the depth of the implications inherent in Berwick's French naturalization. Certainly the Duke had had no intention of deserting his brother, but he may have considered himself more in the light of a War Minister than a commander taking active service abroad. He was convinced that the *coup* had to be a swift one, and was persuaded that their design could only succeed by means of a sudden revolution: 'that is to say that George must be put to flight inside three weeks or all will be finished with us, seeing that the French are unable to support us with troops and the English will have to carry it out by themselves'.[1]

If they gave George time to think, he would send for troops from Hanover and Holland, and the Stuart cause would be lost. They had to act soon and quickly, and to this end he pressed Ormonde and the rest to take action, but their only reply was that, however well they meant by James, they could do nothing until he arrived with three to four thousand men. Nothing Berwick could say would induce them to change their minds. In March 1715 Bolingbroke, learning that the House of Commons proposed to impeach himself, Oxford and Ormonde for high treason, fled to France. He conferred with Berwick in Paris, assuring him of the good disposition of their affairs in England. Even now, Berwick and James could not be absolutely certain that Bolingbroke was not playing a double game, since he saw the English ambassador, Lord Stair, in Paris before he saw the Duke. Perhaps realizing that he had indeed burnt his boats and that nothing more was to be gained from the British government, he then finally decided to declare for James. But he seemed reluctant to commit himself irrevocably and delayed going to see the King at Bar. That was probably Bolingbroke's general policy *vis-à-vis* the restoration. His was an overweening ambition, and he was determined to be the real power in England. He was prepared to help James to recover his own, but he wanted to hold the King in the palm of his hand; therefore it was politic for him to make it clear from the outset that he did not come running when summoned. He had no time for Lord Middleton nor, for that matter, for the Queen, and made no attempt to include her in the discussions which he was having with Berwick.

There was also a danger for Bolingbroke in going to Bar, for Lord Stair's espionage system was very effective, and none of his men would have had the slightest scruple in disposing of anyone who could have been of the remotest use to James. But if the Hanoverians had their network, the Stuarts possessed just as involved an organization of couriers and spies operating from all the chief cities in Europe. Messengers were continually posting to the shores of France in all weathers, there to take cockle-shell boats which would land them on the English, Scottish or Irish coasts. The Earl of Mar had been dismissed by George of Hanover, and he returned to Scotland to rally chieftains such as Lochiel, Glengarry and Clanranald. Letters and arms were transported between Saint-Germain and the

[1] Berwick, *op. cit.*, Vol. 2, p. 109

Highlands; money for the future use of the rebels was conveyed to Drummond Castle and arms were hidden near Fort William.

Things were moving in the Highlands but the situation was less happy south of the border: still the English Jacobites were not ready to rise without the assurance of French troops behind James. Rise in a body, that is, for there were sporadic small uprisings throughout the country, particularly in the west. Enthusiastic though the Highlanders were, their promises were based on wishful thinking: their cavalry were few in number, their infantry ignorant of the discipline needed in an army which was to be successful and their weapons often old and of the most primitive design.

Nevertheless they were anxious to receive their king and continued to send him messages, urging him to come. All he could do, until he knew that the time was propitious, was to counsel them to be patient and rest assured that he would come at the earliest possible moment when all was in concert. He could not control the weather and he could not order his state of health but, so far as was humanly possible, James was determined that this time nothing should go wrong, and he was prepared to wait for the right moment to set forth. In some quarters he was blamed for what was considered to be lethargy, and it was to these charges that Berwick replied in a memorandum to Bolingbroke written in July 1715 and quoted later in his *Mémoires*:[1]

> The King has no friend or ally from whom he may hope for any assistance: not because he has not taken the necessary steps to win these, but because usually Princes do not interest themselves in the causes of others, unless their own advantage is involved. For twenty-six years Europe has been engaged in a bloody and burdensome war which has exhausted its finances, ruined its commerce and even diminished its peoples, so that the whole world, being tired of war, wants only to live in peace and it is only an absolute necessity which would cause any Prince to break it. King James then may only count upon the help of his own subjects for the great task of his restoration. Let us see what he may expect of them.
>
> I shall begin with Scotland which, since the revolution, has always shown itself to be for the Royal Family, and a great number of its principal Lords have actually taken measures to rise as soon as they shall be ordered to do so. They undertake to put in the field eight thousand Highlanders and ten thousand foot from the other Provinces; but they lack arms for the latter: they also need money to pay these Troops, without which they cannot contain them: the country would be pillaged and the army itself would disappear. They can at most levy one thousand horse or Dragoons, and those of rather bad quality. They have some hope

[1] pp. 214–20

154

of being able to seize the castles of Edinburgh, Sterling and Dunbarton [*sic*]; but the success of this kind of plan is always very uncertain.

The greater part of the English Nation is so well disposed that one may say that out of six, there are five for King James. Truth to tell, this is not entirely owing to his incontestable right so much as to hate for the Hanoverian race and to prevent the total ruin of the Church and the liberties of the Kingdom, but, whatever may be their motives, it is certain that a number of Lords, Ecclesiastics and Gentlemen have given guarantees of their good intentions. Some of the most considerable, the most accredited and the best men have assembled to agree upon a means of restoring the King; but until the present they have concluded that, without the assistance of at least four thousand men, many weapons and a large sum of money, it would be foolhardy if not impossible to attempt a rising in his favour. Their reason for this is that, only being able to collect an unarmed and undisciplined people, regular troops, however small in number, would nevertheless be sufficient to dissipate them the moment that they reveal themselves. Added to which, in all England, the only arms are those held in magazines in places of which George is the master.

The Duke of Ormond, Lord Bolingbroke and many others have tried to interest the Court of France into giving the necessary help: nothing had been omitted which might persuade them, but the end has not been achieved; so that the King may at present only count upon that which he has found means of borrowing on his own credit: the whole consists of 10,000 stands of arms and one hundred thousand *écus*. I ask then if a man of sense would advise the King to venture his person as well as the lives and possessions of his friends on such slender preparations against a Prince who is in possession, who has on his side the laws of the time, however unjust, who has at present an army filled with Whigs and who, moreover, has powerful friends as his Allies, from whom he may draw as many troops as he wants, besides those which he can summon from his own State.

The King has not enough arms for Scotland and for the various places in England which demand them. He has no strongholds where his friends may assemble in safety; and even given the time to form an army, he has not the wherewithal to arm them nor to pay them.

I conclude that the King should hasard his person but not fling himself into certain ruin. Even if he had an army of Highlanders, other Scots and English people, he would have, in the end, to fight against an army of regular troops and I think that he would then run a somewhat large risk: but I do not see that he may even hope for this chance; for until now he has not any agreement on this with England, nor even any desire to act without foreign aid. Is it reasonable, therefore, in face of that, that the King should go on ? and can one describe as grandeur of soul, or as heroism a form of behaviour which can only produce an empty tumult ? The same people who now accuse him of timidity, would call him rash and ill-advised when he had failed. In a word, I have never been of the opinion that he should leave until the persons most to be considered in England shall have promised to gather at a certain time in a certain place to receive him with a number of friends; because, to believe that with the Scots alone he will succeed in his enterprise has always been regarded by me as madness.

No one could have put the King's case better than this; certainly not James himself who was beginning to feel the strain of the past year. For the first time he felt insecure in his relations with his half-brother: he had asked him, anxious to know at first hand of Berwick's dealings with Bolingbroke, to join him at Bar, but the Duke had pleaded a bad cough which prevented him from travelling. It is a mystery why Berwick should have chosen this particular moment to become diplomatically inaccessible to the King; perhaps, having taken the reins in his own hands to a certain extent, he wanted to be able to present James with a *fait accompli* or with all the facts at once, and for some he was still dependent on Bolingbroke.

Knowing Berwick as he did, James felt it would have needed more than a cough to keep him away if he had really wanted to come. From Bar in March, James made his first big mistake by creating Ormonde his Captain-General in Britain. Berwick commented flatly that he had not the necessary qualities for such an undertaking. The state which Ormonde kept, his generosity and affability made him much loved by many in England, and he was a brave man without doubt, but he was not a leader of men, not of the calibre of Marlborough or Berwick. His value to the King lay in the fact that he seemed to be the one man who could raise the West.

There was little doubt but that the West was for the legitimate King and, as Sir Charles Petrie has pointed out, 'the part of England selected for the raising of his standard, namely Bath, was in the very centre of that district which had felt most severely the weight of his father's hand only thirty years before',[1] that is, during the Monmouth Rebellion and the Bloody Assizes which followed it.

As always, Oxford was for the Stuarts: there were demonstrations there on George's birthday, 28 May, and a number of peals of bells went unrung because the churchwardens said that they had lost the ropes. On the follow-

[1] *The Jacobite Movement: The First Phase*, p. 160

ing day, Royal Oak Day was celebrated with illuminations in Oxford, and James's health was drunk on his birthday, 10 June, Old Style Calendar, and known in England as 'White Rose Day'. In May a party of people in disguise and on horseback proclaimed James at Manchester and Plymouth. James had long been convinced that the main rising would take place in England and that the Irish and Scottish ones would be subsidiary. This was the time when Ormonde should have consolidated the Jacobite strength and attempted to obtain some cohesion among them, but he chose instead to retire to his house at Richmond in July, fearing impeachment. He told James that he was prepared to raise the West at any time but, meanwhile, he stayed in the south of England without any real plan of action.

James was consumed by impatience, especially as the King of Spain had recently shown some interest in the idea of an invasion of Britain, and Spain could perhaps draw in France on their side. Negotiations had also been begun with Charles XII, the young warrior king of Sweden, who was only six years older than himself. In return for 50,000 crowns from James, Charles was to support the Jacobites in an invasion by sending troops to Newcastle; there were seven to eight thousand Swedish troops encamped near Gothenburg and the necessary transport to convey them directly to Britain. Berwick did his best to interest the French in the idea, although they were at first inclined to regard it as a chimera. Later, after Torcy had spoken with the Swedish ambassador in Paris, they approved it and gave Berwick permission to continue negotiations. But Charles, as usual, was engaged in the long protracted war against his enemies who, from one time to another, were either the Russians, the Poles or the Saxons. At the time Berwick was making his proposals he was besieged in Stralsund and communication, to say the least, was difficult. Berwick felt sure that if he could have explained, face to face with Charles, the advantages which would accrue to Sweden from a securely established House of Stuart in Britain, Swedish help would have materialized but, with Charles bottled up in Stralsund, this was impossible. The Swedes decided that, after all, they could not risk adding the name of the Elector of Hanover, alias the King of England, to their list of enemies at such a time, and Charles XII, with great regret, had to let Berwick know that he could not help.

Berwick felt that the King of Sweden had lost a great opportunity to free himself from oppression because, once James was established, he would have had money, men and ships enough to get back what Sweden had lost. At that moment the Jacobite cause would have been definitely successful, providing that some regular troops could have been added to the well-intentioned, according to the Duke.[1] George was universally disliked and

[1] Berwick, *op cit.*, Vol. 2, pp. 230–1

had only a few troops on hand in England. Later, in 1716, Charles offered to mount an invasion for James, but then events had completely changed the situation.

Berwick was being extremely active in negotiations on James's behalf but, owing to the distance between James and the Court of France, it was becoming increasingly evident to the exile in Bar that he stood in danger of becoming nothing more than a signature on documents. He had always completely trusted Berwick. Now they had been separated for a long time, and there was no one near him who had his brother's knowledge of the situation or of himself. He was worried, lonely, impatient and chafing at the restriction of the little court at Bar. He hated being inactive, and all he could do was to ride around the pretty, but not particularly inspiring countryside as an alternative to long days at his desk.

After Bolingbroke had visited the English ambassador in Paris with little effect, and had been told more or less diplomatically that he was not very welcome at Versailles, and after he had learned of the Act of Attainder issued against him in England, he decided that he had little to lose by visiting James at last. The meeting was a secret one, but if the King reproached Bolingbroke for his late appearance, it did not seem to make much difference in his attitude towards him, since he gave him the Seals of State and nominated him his minister in Paris working in close conjunction with Berwick; officially he was to be known as the Secretary of State. It was an appointment which was not approved by the Queen who had been consulted by neither her son nor Berwick on the matter.

The King's impatience to be on his way to Britain was breaking through his normal self-discipline. He wrote to Berwick on 9 July: 'Neither time nor pains must be spared that I may bee once set a flotte.'[1] He was in correspondence with the Earl of Mar who had once more assured him of the readiness of the Scots to rise and of the high state of their preparations. On receiving a message, through a Dominican, Father Callaghan, from Mar urging that he should come to Scotland at the earliest possible moment, James committed his first foolhardy political move, and one which was to influence all subsequent Stuart history. Without consulting either Berwick or Bolingbroke, and entirely on his own initiative, he sent a message back to Mar fixing the date for the rising for 10 August 1715 and promising his own presence at the earliest possible moment.

He planned to arrive in Le Havre-de-Grâce on 30 July and gave orders for a ship and escort vessel to be prepared for him. He also asked Bolingbroke to meet him there. The latter, seeing that the young King had now got the bit within his teeth, fled to tell Torcy who immediately informed

[1] HMC CSP, Vol. I, p. 374

Louis who sent for Berwick to come to Marly. Louis, considering the plan dangerous, did not want to give his consent to it until he had seen the Duke. Berwick felt certain[1] that Ormonde would have specified James's point of departure had he really sent such a message, and that the King should postpone his journey until they had made sure. Louis told Torcy and Bolingbroke to write to James along these lines. Nearly eight days later a gentleman courier arrived from Ormonde, Mar and several other Scots nobles with messages repeating what had been said so many times before, namely that without men, arms and money they did not feel confident in raising their country but, if the King positively commanded them to do so, they would do it; in any case, it could only take place towards the middle of September when Parliament would be prorogued and the members returned home. No one knew what to make of the message James himself had received but, in any case, whether Mar received the next message telling him to wait or not, he left London on 1 August (Old Style) with General George Hamilton for Scotland. It was about this time that clashes of personality began to make themselves felt.

James and Berwick were still anxious to obtain the services of Marlborough if it were at all possible, although Bolingbroke, apart from telling Berwick to do his best to secure Marlborough, did not exert himself in this direction. There was no doubt that Marlborough, Prince Eugène and Berwick were the three greatest soldiers in Europe and the idea may have been forming itself in James's mind that if Berwick were to fail him (only a few weeks before, such an idea would have been inconceivable) then Marlborough would be the man to take his place as general in command. Failing either of the two, there then remained the Duke of Ormonde and the Earl of Mar.

Berwick wrote later of Ormonde: 'To carry out such a plan, another kind of genius was needed; so great a design demands a hero and the Duke of Ormonde was not that because, although personally very brave and for some time past well-intentioned, he had very few of the qualities necessary for such an enterprise and very little knowledge of making war.'[2] After Ormonde had been accused of high treason, he retired to his splendid estate at Richmond which became a focus for Stuart supporters in England. He assured the Stuarts in France that he would remain at Richmond unless the situation became too dangerous for him whereupon he would retire to the Jacobite strongholds in Northumberland or in the West, such as Oxford or Exeter. In the latter place and in Plymouth and Bristol there were efficient espionage networks: all three places would provide good arms bases and, of

[1] Berwick, *op. cit.*, Vol. 2, pp. **220–3**
[2] *ibid.*, pp. 225–6

course, the two ports were alternative points of embarkation for the King. Even Berwick admitted that Ormonde was so popular that if he had declared openly against George of Hanover he would have received support from all quarters. But he acted disastrously and, instead of remaining at Richmond as he had said, he panicked and fled to France. He left no orders, plans or instructions behind him and, as best he could, Lord Lansdowne took in hand the half-completed arrangements and based the aborted operation on his house at Longleat. All through that autumn sympathizers with the Stuarts were taken up in the West and North, tried, condemned and sentenced to imprisonment, extradition or hanging. This effectively cancelled all hopes of obtaining help from the French, who could see no sense in assisting such an ill-organized movement apparently doomed to failure. Ormonde arrived in Paris on 7 August.

Berwick did not learn of James's correspondence with Mar until 19 June when he wrote, reasonably enough, a letter more in sorrow than in anger to his King and younger brother, and also complained of a confusion of Old and New Style dates on the King's letters. James replied with some sharpness on 23 July:

Father Calahan [*sic*] has decided all things as you will know before this comes to you, so that I have nothing to say in answer to yours of the 14th, only to explain that I meant the 10th of August new stile. Nairne had orders also to acquaint you with all particulars, and therefore in the hurry I am in I shall not repeat them here. I heartily wish your health may be soon established, and then, in acting as your heart wishes you will certainly act as I could wish, for, after all, differing your journey eight days after me, is putting yourself in great danger of never getting over at all, and your presence at first in Holland will be, if possible, of yet more consequence than in the suite. You know what you owe to me, what you owe to your own reputation and honour, what you have promised to the Scotch and to me, of what vast consequence your accompanying of me is, and at the same time none can know as well as yourself what Mr Rose's [Louis XIV] intentions are at bottom and what he thinks in his conscience and in his heart. All this being, I cannot but persuade myself that you will take on this occasion the right partie, and it would be doing you wrong to think otherwise. I shall not therefore bid you adieu for I reckon we shall soon meet, and that, after having contributed as much as you may do to my restoration, you may in a particular manner share of the advantage of it.[1]

There was no doubt but that here was the beginning of what must have

[1] HMC CSP, Vol. I, p. 376. Dated 23 July at Bar, but endorsed on copy 27 July

seemed to the Queen, and to those nearest the King at Saint-Germain and Bar, as a rupture between the two brothers who until then had been so close. Two days later Berwick replied from Marly:

Give me leave, with all respect and summission, to speak freely to your Majesty; nothing but your own honour and welfare are my motives; the affairs now on foot are of a nature that admit of no wrong stepp, which would ruin forever yourself and your friends, so that I should humbly conceive no resolution should be taken, without the advice of those whom your Majesty knows to be properst to advise: Sably [Bolingbroke] and Taler [Torcy] are certainly the fittest, the first for his knowledge of Alençon [England] as well as his credit there, the second, for his true zeal and good sense, beside that by his canal [channel] Mr Rose [Louis XIV] will be managed to advantage: whatever happens your Majesty can not be blam'd, when you act with such advice, and otherwayse reflections will be made, and even friends at Alençon discouraged; for my share, I shall not be wanting in giving my poor advice, and your Majesty may have observed that of late Sably and I had the same thoughts, though we could know nothing of one another. Sably is hearty and we are very free together.

I am for losing not a moment, but I own that I am not for making more hast than good speed: a concert must be had twixt your friends and yourself, tell them, *ce sera une charrue malle attelée*[1] [*sic*], and instead of advancing affairs it will be their destruction. I beg your Majesty's pardon for speaking so freely, but I should betray you if I said not what I thought.[2]

The seemingly immortal Louis XIV fell ill during August: he was now an old man and it was very possible that, when he died, French help for the Stuarts would die with him. Apart from his personal feelings, James also had to realize what the change in France's government might mean to him. And so he wrote to Berwick on 23 August: 'I am in great pain for Mr Rose whose state of health requires that Raucour [himself] should lose no more time. If you are at Paris you will know all I think of matters from Orbee and Sably [Ormonde and Bolingbroke] to whom I write so fully that I shall add no more here, but that I think it more than ever *now or never*.'[3]

A note of impatience which had never been there before had crept into James's correspondence with Berwick: he was beginning to chafe at what appeared to him to be a certain high-handedness on his brother's part

[1] Translated literally: 'it would be a badly harnessed carriage'
[2] HMC CSP, Vol. I, p. 377
[3] *ibid.*, p. 399

while he himself was so far away and so desperate to be involved in the action. Both of them had inherited a large share of the Stuart pride and also of their father's obduracy which could so easily turn into obstinacy. At this stage James did not yet know of Ormonde's flight and the subsequent putting down of the insurgents in the West. He was still resting securely on Father Callaghan's report and assuming that operations in Scotland were in a much higher state of preparation than they actually were, while negotiations with Sweden were still in hand. And most remarkable of all, money was beginning to come in: the King of Spain sent 428,520 French *livres*; a wealthy French banker, Antoine Crozat, gave 50,000 *écus* in return for the promise of a title when the King should come into his own again; the Duke of Lorraine gave 25,000 golden *louis*; the Pope gave the equivalent of £20,000 in the two years beginning in March 1714; and although Marlborough was chary of committing his presence he did at least contribute £2,000 to the Jacobite funds.

The death of Louis XIV on 1 September meant a great deal to James, both personally and politically. He had lost, at a critical point in his career, a loving father-figure, and it is probable that the old King of France during his lifetime had received from the young King of England more love and gratitude than he had had from any of his own descendants. And he had been a wise counsellor to James and a strong supporter when the demands and requirements of his country permitted.

Berwick had also lost a dearly loved relation, and his account of Louis's last hours throws an unusual light on the character of the latter which, in this way at least, had changed so much over the long span of the years:

Never did a man show more resolution and less fear of death; always submissive and resigned to the will of God. He gave all the orders which he thought necessary, and then awaited his last moment in tranquillity. He had been for a long time past occupied with serious thoughts; and he had said several times to the Queen of England, that he realized being old, he must soon die, and so he prepared himself every day for it, so as not to be surprised. There was quite another opinion of him current in the world, because it was believed that he would not let anyone discuss death before him. I learned, however, what I have just related from the very lips of the Queen, a most truthful Princess.

It must be admitted that never has a Prince been so little known as he. The Protestants made him pass in Europe for an inaccessible, cruel and faithless man. I have often had the honour of an audience with him and of meeting him very familiarly and I can assert that the only proud thing about him was his appearance. He was born with an air of majesty which so impressed itself upon everybody that no one could approach him without being seized with a fear and respect, but as soon as you spoke with him, his face softened, and he had the art of putting you immediately at ease with him: he was the most polite man in his kingdom; he used his own language to perfection, and in his discourse he put so many obliging things that, if he gave something, you thought that you had received double; and if he refused, you could not complain of it. In all the Monarchy, you will not find a more human king.[1]

Not only was James deeply grieved by the death of one who had been closest to him after the members of his own immediate family, but he had now to count the cost of what Louis's death would mean to him politically. The new king, Louis XV, was five years old and the Regent was the Duc d'Orléans, the late King's nephew. There was an opposition faction to Orléans led by Louis XIV's illegitimate son by Madame de Montespan, the Duc de Maine.

Berwick declared himself to be for Orléans 'by right and in the interest of the State'.[2] Orléans, on his side, was more pragmatic than even Louis XIV had been in his dealings with the Stuarts. The British government, represented by their ambassador to France, Lord Stair, paid court to the Regent, who did not, however, entirely succumb. Stair impressed upon the Regent the necessity of forbidding James to pass through France should he ever decide to strike out for the Channel coast. But the Regent had heard rumours that George did not intend to abide by the Treaty of Utrecht, so he told Stair that he would be prepared to enter into closer relations with Britain, provided that she gave assurances of being resolved to keep the last peace treaty, and that they should form a defensive alliance together with Holland. Stair replied that the best method of getting such a negotiation going would be to take measures against James: 'The Regent, seeing, by this answer that Stairs [sic] was only fencing, answered him likewise in a vague fashion and resolved, not only not to oppose the plans of King James; but to assist them as much as he could privately, without making it apparent because, knowing the bad state of the Realm, he was intent on avoiding all war.'[3] In other words, Orléans was going to play the same chess game that Louis had played.

[1] Berwick, *op. cit.*, Vol. 2, pp. 231–2
[2] *ibid.*, p. 242
[3] *ibid.*, p. 245

Chapter Thirteen

James's plan was to give Ormonde the command of the English troops, to send Berwick to command Scotland, and to keep Bolingbroke in Paris to look after the administration of the invasion. Berwick would also have been in general command of the whole operation in the field. James had tried to obtain Berwick's consent to his own part in the plan but with singularly little success, and he found the Duke's attitude increasingly difficult to understand.

There was no doubt but that Berwick was in an equivocal position: which allegiance took precedence of the other? On the one hand he had, with James's knowledge and approval, become a naturalized Frenchman and therefore his first duty would seem to be to France; on the other hand, not only was he part of the Stuart family, but he had been involved with their misfortunes since his adolescence. The King had been fourteen when he had given his consent to the Duke's naturalization and it is difficult to conjecture whether or not he had made up his own mind or whether his Privy Council had advised him to allow it. The Queen Regent may have thought that it would be useful to have a Stuart as an inmate of, and not merely a visitor to, the French court. However it was, the royal consent had been given. Another point to bear in mind is that James was twenty-seven in 1715, whereas Berwick was forty-five. By now the Duke had taken on great responsibilities: he was close to the French Regent, he had a large estate in France and both he and his elder son were grandees of Spain. He had always been able to see clearly ahead and to appraise a situation from the outset. They had been deceived before by reports of the situation in Scotland, and they might be again. Whereas the Regent and the French might have overlooked a transgression on Berwick's part if the final outcome were successful; they were not so likely to be forgiving if a distinguished French subject were discovered to be involved in an unsuccessful invasion in a country lately their enemy but with whom they were now trying to find a method of living in peace. It would have been an embarrassing situation for them, to say the least: he was proscribed in Britain and, if he had been taken, France could hardly have declared war upon England for Berwick's sake; this would have put the peace of all Europe in jeopardy once more, and how could Berwick have taken such a responsibility? In his *Eloge* to the Duke's memoirs, Montesquieu declares: 'France had now based its political system

164

on peace. What a contradiction if a Peer of the Realm, a Marshal of France, a Governor of a Province had disobeyed the law against leaving the country, that is to say had, in fact, disobeyed in order to make it appear to English eyes alone that he had not disobeyed!'[1] Certainly his attitude would seem to prove that the Duke of Berwick had little personal ambition: there could have been no greater aim than to restore the Stuarts to the British throne; he loved his family very much and he would have been happy to have had an establishment in England, even if his illegitimacy prevented himself and his heirs from sharing in the succession.

   Had James but known it, this was the watershed in his life: every decision he was making or trying to make at this time was to influence Stuart history ever afterwards. The situation in which he found himself was one of either being overwhelmed with conflicting advice or of receiving none at all. And he still had no commander-in-chief. It was apparent that, apart from expressing his good intentions towards the Stuarts, Marlborough was no longer much more than a cipher; Berwick still evaded commitment; Charles of Sweden was busy on his own affairs; and the Regent of France was getting impatient with what Berwick called '*cabales*' among the Jacobites:

. . . and to tell the truth, I think that the Regent, who was beginning to have a bad opinion of this enterprise, was not too exercised to carry out what had been hoped from him: moreover, there were *cabales* among our people which contributed not a little to ill-success. Bolingbroke was hated by the Irish who did not cease to complain about him. The Duke of Ormonde, a weak man, gave himself up to jealousies inculcated by others, as if Bolingbroke did not have enough regard for him. The Queen and those in whom she had most confidence at Saint-Germain were very dissatisfied because he [Bolingbroke] did not consult them continually and did not report regularly to them what he was doing. Some women in Paris, who wanted to be ministers and who had managed to introduce themselves into the circle of the Duc d'Orléans by underhand methods, did their utmost to denigrate Bolingbroke to that Prince. In fact, I found in several conversations with him, that he was unhappy about Bolingbroke; and the most extraordinary thing was that the only reason which he gave for this was that he used these women to pester him from morn till night. I assured him that he only did so because he did not know where to go in order to reach His Royal Highness. Upon which, he told me that he should address himself to the Maréchal d'Uxelles and nobody else; in this way he would willingly listen to him. Bolingbroke immediately broke off all contacts with these women; and they, already badly disposed

[1] Berwick, *op. cit.*, p. xlvii

towards him, and irritated by the change in his conduct, unleashed themselves against him. The Regent himself told me so and, at the same time, ordered me to assure Bolingbroke that he was pleased with him. However, nothing was done for King James by France and it all ended in hopes which were never realized.[1]

It seems unlikely that if James had known a great deal about Bolingbroke's personal character he would have finally acquiesced in Berwick's seemingly unquestioning acceptance of him. Brilliant he undoubtedly was, both as a man and a politician, but he was also recognized as a libertine. When he had attended the peace conference in Paris in 1713 one of his most frequent female companions was Claudine de Tencin, an ex-nun who was also the mistress of the Abbé Dubois, later to become a cardinal and minister under the Regent. Dubois favoured the English government and was an enemy of the Stuarts.

Madame de Tencin also captured the fickle heart of the Regent himself and, in this circumstance, she possessed a rival in Miss Olive Trant, a Jacobite adherent. The latter was a constant visitor at the house in the Bois belonging to Mademoiselle de Chausseraye, an ear neighbour of the Duc de de Lauzun, where the King had been wont to visit from time to time. The Chausseraye house seems to have been a meeting-place for ladies working for the Jacobite cause, such as Miss Trant and the three Miss Oglethorpes who had known the King at Saint-Germain when they had all been children. James certainly knew about the feminine chatter and the gossip which was dispensed through the mail carried by the couriers from one Jacobite outpost to another, but he was then inclined to discount it: he wrote to Bolingbroke on 2 August 1715 from Bar:

> Here is also a long letter to myself from Mrs Oglethorpe, the first part is very odd and I cann make no answer to it without your advice, the rest of it is most of it stuff. Mr Inese cann give you an account of that correspondence which has never signified much, and is embarassing [*sic*] enough, but in my circumstancy's wee must heare everybody, disgust none if possible, and without trusting too many, draw from all sides all the light and help wee cann gett. The Duke of Berwick and Mr Inese will tell you all they know, so that I have no more to add here but that I rely entirely on your penetration, good sense and advice, of all which I never stood in more need.[2]

Mr Inese, or Innes, was the Queen's secretary at Saint-Germain.

Some of the Jacobite ladies' gossip may have been idle, but a great deal

---

[1] Berwick, *op. cit.*, Vol. 2, pp. 262–3   [2] HMC CSP, p. 382

of it was picked up by the British government spies and, whether drunk or sober, Bolingbroke revealed much of what was discussed between Berwick, the Regent and himself to his mistress, and she, in turn, passed it on to the Abbé Dubois who forwarded it to the British ambassador, Lord Stair. In this way information about the rising in the West had reached the British in time for them to forestall it.

Apart from such leakages endangering their security, the Jacobite courts at Bar and Saint-Germain were infiltrated with British spies. Security checks were doubled and servants threatened with dire penalties if they admitted anyone into the castle at Bar without the necessary authorizations. In spite of this it became known later that a suspicious character called Colonel Douglas, professing ardent Jacobite sympathies, had managed to stay at the court for five days at the beginning of August 1715. In the correspondence forwarded from Saint-Germain to Bar during the same month was an anxious memorandum from the Queen: 'To beg of the King to take care of his person, and not so suffer any strangers to stay at Barr if they cannot give a good account of themselves.'[1]

With Ormonde in Paris when he should have been in the West of England, Bolingbroke in Paris when he would have been more useful at Saint-Germain, Marlborough somewhere in Europe but not in France or Lorraine, and Berwick nowhere near him at all, it was only reasonable that the King should look towards John Erskine, Earl of Mar, and towards Scotland. The eleventh Earl of Mar came of one of the oldest and most noble houses in Scotland, and one which had been devoted to the Stuarts. Be that as it may, he had supported the Act of Union in 1707, and later became Secretary for Scotland. It seems very likely that he had been one of the Tories favouring Queen Anne's selecting James as her heir and that he had been in some form of contact with Saint-Germain. However, on the accession of George I he offered his services to the new ruler but was snubbed by him at a levée on 2 August. Not slow to take offence, he sailed the next day on a collier from London to Fife and went thence to his extensive estates in Aberdeenshire. There he arranged a 'tynchal', or a great hunt, as a cover for the meeting of a large number of Scottish nobles and of Highland chieftains on 27 August. Present were the Earls Errol, Traquair, Marischal, Carnwath, Seaforth and Nithsdale, the Marquis of Tullibardine (eldest son of the Duke of Atholl) and the Marquis of Huntly (eldest son of the Duke of Gordon). Viscount Kenmure was also there, prepared to lead the rising in the Border country.

It was not until 6 September, nearly one month afterwards, that James learned of Mar's arrival in Scotland, and it was on 6 September (Old Style)

[1] HMC CSP, p. 409

that Mar raised James's blue and gold standard at Braemar. It was a stormy day, and many saw an ill omen when the golden ball at the top of the standard was blown down. James was proclaimed as king in Aberdeen, Brechin, Montrose, Forfar and Dundee, and soon all Scotland north of the Tay was held by the Jacobites: all that was still lacking was a leader.

Mar was by no means Berwick's idea of a leader:

Meanwhile Mar was busy forming his army and ordering everything as if he were sure that he had the necessary time to do so. If he had marched as soon as he had assembled eight or ten thousand men, he would certainly have encountered no opposition, and Argyle would have been obliged to abandon Scotland and fall back upon [the town of] Berwick. Then he could have put his army in order, called a Parliament and marched on the borders, whether to defend them against George's troops, or to march into England to join King James's friends there, assuming that they had formed party there as one had been led to suppose; but his little experience of war caused him to miss his aim, and this gave time for the troops who were marching on all sides to join the Duke of Argyle. You can have a great deal of spirit, much personal courage, be a clever Minister, and still not have the talents necessary for an enterprise of this nature. It is certain that Mar did not have them; and therefore it is not to be wondered at that he did not succeed. After having drawn the sword, he had no idea of what more was needed to press onwards and thereby lost the most favourable moment which had presented itself since the revolution of 1688.[1]

Mar had begun his campaign in friendly country, and everything was on his side. He was supported by a large number of the nobility of Scotland and by many of the landowners who, in the Highlands, were able to raise troops immediately through the chieftains of their clan. The men, wild, ragged and poorly shod, often came unwillingly to join a cause of which they understood little, but they were bound by almost feudal terms to serve their chieftains.

The English government had been concentrating on the West of England and had few forces available in the north for use in Scotland. The Duke of Argyll, with the Campbell Clan, was loyal to George who sent him straight to Stirling to await what Mar could do. Simon the self-styled Lord Lovat, the Earl of Sutherland and Forbes of Culloden were also for the Government, as were most of the Lowland landowners. Mar had about 5,000 men in the early part of September, but he lacked trained cavalry and artillery. In the beginning Argyll had only 1,500 men when he went to Stirling; later

[1] Berwick, *op. cit.*, Vol. 2, p. 249

he was reinforced by several regiments from England and Ireland. George also asked Parliament to grant him 6,000 men which they were obliged to provide under a previous treaty made with Queen Anne to secure the Protestant succession if ever it were in danger.

On 20 September by the French calendar, Stair was informed by his spies that James had two vessels awaiting him, fully equipped, at Le Havre, and he demanded of the Regent that they should not be allowed to sail. The Regent could do nothing but comply with the ambassador's request, and he was also obliged to seize the arms in the ships. If James had had the money to buy more weapons he would not have been allowed to purchase them in France or, for that matter, in any other European country, without the ruler's permission. This happened only a few days after Mar had raised the standard at Braemar but, of course, with the time lapse in communications, the King was still unaware of this.

After Mar had taken Perth he was master of all Scotland north of the Tay. Argyll was content to concentrate his forces, small as they were in the beginning, at Stirling whose castle commanded the crossing of the Forth and the best entry from England into Scotland. The two other key fortresses were the castles of Edinburgh and Dumbarton which also overlooked the central rift valley of Scotland, and England to the south. Mar decided to try for Edinburgh Castle first because of the stores and cannon it contained as well as its gold, which was part of the money granted to Scotland under the terms of the Union Treaty.

Lord Drummond was put in charge of the party of some hundred men, many of whom were Highlanders, and a sergeant and two soldiers inside the castle had been suborned into aiding the Jacobites. If the eventual outcome had not been so tragic, the story of the attempt to take the castle would have made a comedy. Too many people talked, some to their wives; too many people drank, stopping to 'powder their hair' at an inn on the way up to the castle; and too little attention was paid to the detail of the operation; otherwise how could the scaling ropes have proved to be too short when they were thrown up against the walls? The attempt failed. Mar, although he was virtually master of the area squared off approximately by Inverness, Perth, Aberdeen and Montrose, sat in Perth doing nothing until the end of September. By then the rising in the north of England was beginning, and Lords Derwentwater and Widdrington and Thomas Forster took up arms.

Early in October, while the King was still unaware that the rising in the West had failed completely, he was told by Bolingbroke that Spain would be sending money and that another ship was ready to carry him across the Channel from Saint-Malo. Still James could not pin Berwick down, and his bitter disappointment was beginning to curdle into suspicion. At any rate he wrote to Bolingbroke on 10 October that Berwick 'is now a cypher and can do no more harm, and if he withdraws his duty from me, I may as well my confidence from him. . . . I cannot but suspect that he hath been sooner or later the cause of the strange diffidence they have of me at the French Court.'[1]

Utterly unwilling to believe that his dearly loved and respected brother could really be deserting him, James sent him a commission, addressing him as 'Captain General and Commander-in-Chief of all our forces by land and sea in our ancient Kingdom of Scotland'. This was in spite of the fact that Mar had assumed, without contradiction, that he was in command of the Scottish forces. The letter continued as from a king to his subject: 'Our will and pleasure is that immediately upon receipt of this order, you will repair in the most private and speedy manner you can to our ancient Kingdom of Scotland, and there take upon you the command given you by virtue of our commission of this date. So not doubting of your ready compliance herein – etc.' He followed this with a more informal letter from Bar the next day:

At the time you receive this will be the conjunction in which I shall see the sincerity of your frequent and sacred promises to the King, my father, and to the queen. I shall not indeed doubt of them till I see to the contrary, but as a proof of your good intentions, I hereby require you [word undecipherable] either to come and join me in person with as many officers as you can get to follow you, or to give me some other public and signal mark of your loyalty, such as declaring openly for me with such as 'tis well known you have influence over, and that out of hand, to the end that if you cannot save me in person, you may at least cause a considerable diversion to the usurper's forces. It is now not words but deeds that I expect from you; that is all and the only answer I will receive to this letter, to which I have nothing to add, but that your future happiness, your honour and your all, are now in your own hands.[2]

On 7 October Berwick had written to the King: 'Your Majesty knows where the difficulty lies and that I am not my own master . . .'[3]

The Queen obviously felt great distress over this sad business; on 21 October she wrote to Mr Dicconson at Saint-Germain from her retreat at Chaillot: 'The Duke of Berwick is just gon from me. I suppose he will tell you the small progress he has made in his affair, but Lord Bullinbroke has delivered him the King's order and commission. He says he must consult

[1] HMC CSP, Vol. I, p. 592
[2] *ibid.*, p. 434 (Mahon Vol. I, Appendix, p. xxxii)
[3] *ibid.*, p. 415

mor yett, before he resolves.'[1] On the following day the King wrote to Berwick:

> It would be doing a great wrong to Belley [Berwick himself] to doubt of his willingness to accompany Robinson [the King himself]. Robinson knows that nobody can hinder Belley if he be resolved to go, so he does count he will, the minute he shows such a desire of it. I have said all that can be on that subject already, so I shall add no more of it here, but desire you'l read over my former letters on that subject. I have no time to say more, the post is parting.[2]

Berwick wrote to James on 3 November:

> I have ever since consulted men of sens, able lawyers and casuistes, with a full resolution to goe as farr for your Majesty's service as I can in honour and conscience but I find the reasons alledged against my leaving France without the Regents' leave so strong that it is with the deepest concern I am forced to ask your Majesty's pardon for not complying with your commands. . . . Whatever happens, in all times and places your Majesty shall find me as ready as ever to give real proofs of my true zeale for your person, welfare and restauration.[3]

In desperation James confirmed Mar's appointment as Commander-in-Chief, giving him full powers, and he also created him a Duke. Later, the Duke of Berwick commented:

> King James, at the same time as he commanded the Duke of Ormonde to leave Paris for England, also sent me a commission and instructed me to go to Scotland and take up the command of the army there. As, with the consent of this Prince, I had been naturalized French and had thereby become a subject of his Most Christian Majesty, and as I was moreover an Officer of the French Crown, pledged by several undertakings not to leave the Kingdom without written permission, and that far from granting it on this occasion, the late King and the Regent had expressly forbidden me to do so, I did not think that in honour and in conscience I could obey the order I had received.[4]

It was a terrible choice for Berwick to make, that much is clear: whether he ever succeeded in reconciling the promptings of heart and blood with the dictates of a clear, sensible mind is an open question.

[1] HMC CSP, Vol. I, p. 441
[2] *ibid.*, p. 429
[3] *ibid.*, p. 451
[4] Berwick, *op. cit.*, Vol. 2, pp. 259–60

Chapter Fourteen

The response of the Earl of Derwentwater, James's cousin and childhood friend, to the call to arms was entirely different from that of Berwick. He was allowed to return, as we have seen, with James's permission, to England in December 1709. He arrived with his brother, Francis, via Holland, after having spent the whole of his minority on the Continent. His uncle, Dr Radcliffe, a celebrated man, had been physician to Queen Anne and had founded the Radcliffe Library at Oxford; on 6 December 1709 he wrote to Sir William Swinburne, Derwentwater's cousin: 'Lord Derwentwater intends to be with you very speedily in the country. I do not doubt but that you will extremely like his conversation; for he has a great many extraordinary good qualities, and I do not doubt that he will be as well beloved as his uncle.'[1] Everyone who came into contact with the twenty-one-year-old Earl seems to have liked him, and his kindness and generosity to his dependents and to the needy became legendary in the Northumbrian countryside. A short time later his uncle reported that the Earl's guns had arrived from France, and Derwentwater appears to have settled down to a pleasant life as a wealthy country gentleman with extensive estates.

In 1712 he married the eldest daughter of Sir John Webb, of Canford in Dorset, a strong Jacobite supporter, who had sent her to the Ursuline Convent in Paris, and it was in Paris that she had first met her future husband. They lived at Dilston Hall, overlooking the Lake of Derwentwater in the shadow of Skiddaw, and were prominent members of a pleasant social community chiefly concerned with the raising of young families and the maintaining of their estates, and horses. The Earl visited a Jacobite society which had been organized by his father, and among the guests was the Catholic Duke of Norfolk. It was evident that his sympathies, his religion and his affections were for the Stuarts, and therefore it was not surprising, that when the government became alive to the possibilities of Jacobite insurgence, a warrant was issued for his arrest and that of his brother, Charles. His other brother, Francis, had died earlier in that year of 1715.

He was warned by friends that Government agents had arrived at Durham on their way to arrest him and he went immediately to a neighbouring Justice of the Peace demanding to know on what charge he was to

[1] W. S. Gibson, *Dilston Hall*

be taken, but received no satisfaction. That day, on 27 July 1715, he wrote from Dilston Hall to a Mr Hunter:

> As I know nobody is more ready to serve a friend than yourself, I desire the favour you will keep my gray [sic] horse for me, till we see what will be done relating to horses. I believe they [the Government] will be troublesome, for it is said the D. of Ormond is gone from his house. God send us peace and good neighbourhood – unknown blessings since I was born. Pray ride my horse about the fields, or any where you think he will not be known, and you will oblige,
>
> *Sir, your humble servant,*
> *Derwentwater.*

He is at grass.[1]

In view of the growing disturbances in the West and in other parts of the country, penal restrictions had been laid upon Catholics owning horses of military suitability and they were confiscated.

Derwentwater was completely unprepared for any kind of insurgence: all he asked was to be allowed to live in peace as a Catholic whilst retaining his own personal allegiance to his king and cousin. If he had wanted to take up arms against the Government, he had the means and the opportunity to have gathered together a small army, but he was not of a militant disposition.

He went up alone into the hills and remained there during the end of August, the whole of September and the first few days of October. Then he made up his mind to take a positive line and returned to Dilston. Once decided, he devoted himself wholeheartedly to the cause. He sent messages to a few friends, arranging a time and place of meeting, then he ordered every able-bodied retainer of Dilston to follow him. On the evening of 5 October he drew all his family and dependents together and invoked God's blessing on his enterprise. At dawn the next morning, his men massed in the courtyard, and arms were given out to them; then the Earl of Derwentwater set out with his brother Charles at his side. As he did so his favourite dog howled, and his horse suddenly became restive; only with difficulty could it be urged forward. They crossed the Devilswater, a tributary of the Tyne, at Nunsburgh and went forward to meet a small band of friends which had gathered to join them there. Another score or so of gentlemen were waiting at Greenriggs which is a little to the south-west of Hexham; they decided to ride to the top of a nearby hill called the Waterfalls from whence it was easy to see anyone approaching. After a short while the Earl appeared riding with his friends and servants; some of these were mounted

[1] Quoted from private collection by Gibson, *Dilston Hall*

upon his coach horses, and they all bore arms. They crossed the Tyne near Hexham, gathering in supporters on the way until there was a party of nearly sixty horse. On the morning of the following day, 7 October, they marched to Warkworth where Lord Widdrington and his two brothers and about thirty others joined them.

They had chosen Thomas Forster, eldest son of Thomas Forster of Etherstone, to be their general because he was a Protestant and both Derwentwater and Widdrington were Catholics. Hearing that there was a warrant out for his arrest, Forster had fled the day before from his family home at Bamborough Castle and set out to meet Derwentwater. On the morning of 6 October, Forster proclaimed James King at Warkworth and, after Derwentwater's company arrived, marched with them to Alnwick and thence to Morpeth, proclaiming James in both places. They were now three hundred strong, having welcomed a large number of volunteers who were mounted but not armed; they then proceeded towards Newcastle.

Here they found that the inhabitants, who were for the most part Protestant, had already prepared their defence. There was an old and very solid wall surrounding the city, and all except two of its strong gates had been bricked up. Newcastle also possessed two pieces of cannon which were posted at these gates, and they sent word to the Government's General Carpenter, asking for aid. He turned at once in their direction, whereupon the insurgents turned aside to Hexham. From here they sent urgently to Mar asking for help, emphasizing their lack of infantry.

In the south-west of Scotland the Protestant Lord Kenmure had organized another body of Stuart adherents. Kenmure was a good man, beloved by the people of Galloway and Nithsdale; he was also strong and reliable. With about two hundred horsemen he crossed the border and rode in the direction of Rothbury. As with Derwentwater's company, none of the riders merited the name of cavalry: they were mostly gentlemen riding their hunters and servants and cavalry mounted on carriage horses, farm-horses or barely-tamed wild ponies. Their arms varied from fencing swords and dress swords carried by the gentlemen to bill-hooks wielded by the peasantry. From the very beginning the King's army was ill equipped.

Derwentwater's army had remained three days at Hexham, then they rode to Rothbury where they met Kenmure on the 19 October. Mar had now sent reply that he would despatch to their combined forces William MacIntosh of Bolum with a body of the troops spared from those he had with him doing nothing in Perth. After Berwick, Brigadier MacIntosh was perhaps the most accomplished soldier in the Jacobite army. He had held a captain's commission in the army of James II before the Revolution in 1688, and had followed the Stuarts abroad thereafter. He was a gentleman of a friendly and amiable disposition, who nevertheless, could discipline his troops with an iron hand when necessary, and necessary it was going to be in the case of the rough, tough Highlanders and green recruits of the Northumbrian army. By now the army was about 1,600 strong.

On 23 October, a Sunday, they were in Kelso and their chaplain, the Reverend Patten, preached on the text 'The right of the first-born is his'. Soon the news reached them that General Carpenter, with nine hundred men, had left Newcastle and was advancing in their direction. Hurriedly, the leaders of the insurgents consulted together: should they march south and engage Carpenter – they knew that his troops also were very raw recruits – or should they march north, attack Argyll from the rear and join with Mar at his front? No counsel prevailed: the English officers mostly declined to go further into Scotland, and the Scots, almost to a man, refused to advance into England. As a sorry compromise, they marched along the Cheviot range. Carpenter advanced further and the Jacobites marched from Kelso to Jedburgh, remained there for two days and then marched to Hawick. They were in Hawick on 30 October and Derwentwater, who, with several others of the leaders, was staying with the Duchess of Buccleuch, declared that some decisive action must be taken; he and his brother favoured endeavouring to take the whole of Scotland, thereby giving them a solid base from which to march on England and a place for retreat if necessary. And at least the King would have had one kingdom to call his own.

But the rest of the English leaders disapproved, so they marched on and, as they did so, Carpenter's men fell in with their track and followed them along, almost accidentally, and this gave to the Jacobite troop an appearance of retreat which was psychologically disturbing. Riding through the Border country, they decided to descend into Lancashire, much against the will of Derwentwater, who prophesied it would be their undoing, but no one would listen to him except his brother Charles. Even MacIntosh was for this plan but, in spite of his discipline, five hundred of his Highlanders turned back and marched homewards to the north. However loyal they were, the average Highlanders, recruited by the chiefs of their clans in causes which were often not of their own making, had their own ideas of what constituted warfare. They fought to the death, and whichever side won took its booty and returned home as quickly as possible to enjoy it with their families. Therefore the idea of penetrating deeper and deeper into an unknown and foreign country without definite promise of booty held little attraction for them.

On 1 November the main Jacobite body took up quarters at Brampton in Northumberland, and Forster showed the others the commission which he had received from Mar during their march which authorized him to be general commanding the troops of the King in England. They moved towards Penrith where the local militia, assisted by a motley assortment of ploughmen, cowherds and shepherds, had taken up a line of defence on Penrith Fell under the command of the Earl of Carlisle and Lord Lonsdale. They waited for a number of hours and as each hour passed so the rumours about the strength of the insurgents grew. They themselves numbered about ten thousand. Added to the rumours which were destroying their confidence came the pangs of hunger; the rustics were used to regular meal-times so that, by the time the red and white cockades of the English rebels and the blue and white of the Scots came into view, only a small number of the would-be defendants of Penrith Fell remained and these were soon put to flight. On 2 November, at three in the afternoon, James's army, about 1,700 strong, entered Penrith, where Forster proclaimed him King. They levied dues to about the sum of £500 on the town and then ate well, the leaders enjoying a supper which had been provided for the Bishop of Carlisle and his entourage, before retiring to beds for the night.

The next morning they intercepted Government letters on their way to Appleby, and gained useful information thereby. Now they learned that the Government had arrested many of the Catholic gentry in Cumberland and Westmorland, and some of them began to feel the first twinges of misgiving; one, a Mr Ainslie who had joined them at Jedburgh, left them at Appleby with sixteen other gentlemen from his part of the country. They were marching on Lancashire now, through country familiar to Derwentwater and his brother. Through the bare branches the wintery sunlight glinted occasionally on swords and harness, and the subdued murmurs of the men and the clop of horses' hooves were the only sounds to break the silence of the fells; mists rose from the lakes, hiding the head of the column from those at the rear, and their footsteps echoed morosely through the dark and narrow ravines. It was raining when they entered Kendal, quietly, on 5 November. James was proclaimed, but without any show of pomp or circumstance; owing to the rain there were few people to witness it or to stand listening to the bagpipes skirling. It was different at Lancaster on the 7 November when they entered the city in clear weather with their swords drawn, banners waving, drums beating and bagpipes playing. The English nobles and gentry, some two hundred of them, rode in first with their mounted men, then the Highland foot soldiers, then two hundred Lowland Scots followed by the Scots horse. The Stuart standard was borne without opposition to Lancaster Castle, and the Lancastrians joined in the cries of 'God save the King!' A number of the local gentry and townsfolk joined them, and arms were taken from many houses in the town. What was more important still was the fact that they had been able to seize six pieces of cannon from a ship, the *Robert* from Sunderland, which was moored in the estuary of the Lune River. They were made welcome in the town: they had behaved well and created no damage, and the officers had paid their way, much to the satisfaction of the shopkeepers. So well received were they that the gentlemen of the army were invited to drink tea with the ladies of Lancaster, everyone clad in the best he or she possessed.

On the morning of Wednesday, 9 November, they left for Preston, the horse arriving there at 11 p.m., the foot the next morning. No opposition was offered by this affluent town either, for its militiamen had pulled out two nights before when they had heard of the approach of the insurgents to Lancaster. Here again they were encouraged by the local populace; a number of Catholic gentlemen joined them with their followers, but these too were unarmed and unused to army discipline. Meanwhile the Jacobite leaders hoped that they would soon be joined by the Duke of Ormonde with three thousand trained men. They had also heard rumours of the strong Stuart inclination of Manchester, and councils were held debating whether or not they should march southwards towards Liverpool and Manchester. And again the local ladies entertained the gentlemen to tea.

While they were thus engaged, General Carpenter was busy catching up with them again, descending towards Newcastle and Durham. What was worse, he was liaising with General Wills, an able soldier now commanding the Government troops in north-west England. When Wills marched to Wigan on 11 November he learned that Carpenter was proceeding towards Preston, so he set out the next morning, preparing to join him.

The Jacobites had finally decided to march to Liverpool but, as soon as the Liverpudlians heard of their approach, they threw up barricades and put seventy pieces of cannon about the town. Derwentwater now felt sure that they had made a mistake, and he was realizing more and more just how inept Forster was as a general: he had no power of command and no faculty for taking decisions. The counsels of war were divided and this, he knew, would eventually spell their ruin. On the evening of 11 November he received a letter from a friend warning him of the advance of the Government troops towards Preston.

This news completely overwhelmed Forster, and he was incapable of devising any form of action: it was left to Kenmure to point out to him the gravity of the situation and to call a council of war. Half a mile from the town was a bridge over the River Ribble which Forster should have guarded well, but did not. The road to and from it ran through a valley between two steep slopes: this would have been a very advantageous place in which to take one's enemy, but Forster did nothing whatever about it. On the morning of 12 November, when he was told that the Government troops were in full advance on Preston, Forster decided to withdraw to the town and to confine his defence there. If he had contested the passage of the bridge and made the two nearby fords impassable, he might have overcome the Government troops, or at least hampered their advance farther.

In the town Brigadier MacIntosh took no notice of Forster and made the best of a bad situation by erecting four barricades across principal thoroughfares, putting his men and ammunition in all the houses adjacent to the barricades. Derwentwater threw off his coat and got down to it with the men, working against time. The first barricade was held by Mac-Intosh himself, supported by gentlemen volunteers in the churchyard commanded by Derwentwater, Nithsdale, Wintoun and Kenmure. The second was defended by a party of Highlanders under Lord Charles Murray and this was at the end of a lane leading to fields. The third barricade was at a windmill on the road to Lancaster, and it was defended by the Chief of MacIntosh and his clan. The fourth barricade was on a road leading to Liverpool and was held by gentlemen and their men from Berwickshire and Teviotdale, with some of the regiment belonging to the Earl of Strathmore, and commanded by Major Miller and a Mr Douglas. Each barricade had two pieces of cannon.

When General Wills arrived at the bridge about an hour after noon, he could not imagine that it had been left undefended, and so he surmised that the Jacobites had retreated already. But when he tried to enter the town he realized his mistake. He promptly gave orders for two barricades to be charged simultaneously. Both the attack and the defence were full of spirit, and in the first ten minutes 120 of Wills's men fell, and another 140 when they attempted to enter the town from the lane and fields behind it. Both sides fought with the determination until midnight, and Derwentwater and his brother encouraged their men by their own example. He even had enough men to spare to send to Lord Charles Murray holding the second barricade who were hard pressed. Finally the Government troops withdrew, setting fire to houses as they went, but the fire did not spread owing to lack of wind. Nevertheless, the distant fires did provide a signal for General Carpenter, who hurried his men on to join Wills. He arrived in Preston in the forenoon of the next day. The fires encircled the Jacobites and, although they were still superior in number to the combined forces of Wills and Carpenter, they were enclosed by the enemy who had encircled them beyond the ring of burning outposts.

Their only escape lay in cutting their way through the enemy troops. Such a course inflamed the ready courage of the Highlanders, but the English gentlemen, with the exception of Derwentwater and his brother, were dubious. Forster was completely demoralized and, without consulting anyone, sent Colonel Oxburgh with an offer of capitulation. When this was discovered, had Forster been rash enough to appear in person before the rebel army, the officers would have had a difficult task in preventing their men from cutting him into pieces. Now nothing could be done but to surrender in the hope of preventing more bloodshed in what was likely to be a protracted but losing battle for the Jacobites. Derwentwater offered himself as a hostage for the English insurgents and a Colonel MacIntosh for the Scots. At 7 a.m. on 14 November the Government troops entered Preston and took their prisoners: 75 noblemen and gentlemen from England, mostly Northumbrians, 400 English of the ranks, 143 Scots noblemen and gentlemen and over 1,000 Scots fighters.

All this time Mar had been sitting in Perth, with Argyll waiting at Stirling for him to move. Finally, he decided to try to cross the Tay above Stirling and work down to join Forster in Lancashire: obviously as yet he was unaware of the fortunes of the English contingent. Argyll learned of Mar's design and set out for Dunblane which lay in the Jacobites' path. At Sheriffmuir, to the north-east of Dunblane, an indecisive battle was fought and, although Mar, at nearly 9,000 strong, was at three times the strength of his adversary, he never pressed his advantage: he was incapable of doing so. There was little to choose between Mar and Forster in terms of military ability, and Berwick rightly accused the latter of having lost his head, 'as did most of the other leaders, so they capitulated'.[1]

At Sheriffmuir the right wing of each side broke and gave chase to the other's left and each claimed victory, but Mar chose to withdraw to Perth leaving Argyll's men still in good order and ready to fight another day if necessary. In this encounter the twenty-year-old Earl of Strathmore died fighting for James killed by the sword of a Government dragoon whose life he had spared.[2] Shortly afterwards Inverness surrendered to Government troops. Their only hope had lain in beating Argyll at that point, as Berwick pointed out but, as they did not press the Government for an outright victory, it had time to summon troops from the Continent. Sheriffmuir spelled disaster: this was the end of James's hopes in Scotland and England but, as yet, he knew nothing of it.

[1] Berwick, *op. cit.*, Vol. 2, p. 252
[2] Petrie, The Jacobite Movement, The First Phase, Vol. 1, p. 189

Chapter Fifteen

All that October the King waited in Bar for news from Scotland to be filtered through to him, but nothing except rumours came. It had been decided that Ormonde should go ahead of him by about four days, and his own departure was fixed for 14 October 1715. Bolingbroke in Paris blew first hot, then cold about the King's leaving Bar, but, on receipt of a more despondent report about England's unreadiness, he advised him to wait another fortnight; reluctantly James did so. He wanted Bolingbroke to leave with him, but he said that his presence was necessary in Paris, to conduct the administration of the campaign. He still kept as far away as was possible from the Queen, who would be Regent in James's absence, and she, naturally enough, resented it. By now the King was in a fairly tense state. He was poised for instant action, with conflicting counsels of 'stop' and 'go' in his ears from Bolingbroke and from Berwick who, although he was not committing himself, still continued to give the King advice. Added to all this were the pleas of the Queen that he should not risk his person unduly, and complaints all round that nobody was informing anyone else what they were doing. Even if it had not been his own campaign he was about to fight this time, it would not likely have seemed a relief to James to leave Bar and its interminable exchange of notes from Paris, Chaillot and Versailles to go to fight a campaign anywhere to regain his peace of mind.

Bolingbroke had come to some private arrangement with Orléans to provide arms and men against the marrying of James to his second daughter, Mademoiselle de Valois,[1] but this condition did not suit James himself and in any case the whole arrangement came to naught when one of the two ships promised by Orléans was seized by the English, to the French Regent's apparent surprise.

Ormonde also began to make his own private arrangements with Orléans, who made a great display of friendship for James,[2] promising 20,000 stand of arms and ammuniton. The next morning he sent a representative to Ormonde to confirm the arrangements and to stress that they should be kept secret from Bolingbroke. Orléans was proving as adept as Louis XIV had been at confusing the issue for the Stuarts, while at the same time preserving a sincere and lively concern for James's own personal welfare.

[1] HMC, Vol. II, p. 165. Townshend Papers
[2] HMC CSP, Vol. I, p. 442

When Ormonde did reach the coast it was to find that all their plans had been betrayed to the British by his secretary, Sir John MacLean.

Every movement James made was watched by Lord Stair's spies, and it was impossible for him to leave for any destination without the French Regent being aware of it. But he still had a good friend in the Prince de Vaudémont who conveniently invited him to a *fête* in his château at Commercy. There was nothing unusual about his accepting the invitation, as he had done on so many previous occasions. On 18 October Bolingbroke wrote from Paris to James at Commercy, informing him that two of the King's men had left from different points on the coast to sail for England to prepare everyone concerned for the King's imminent arrival. Three days later he reported to him on the beginning of the failure of the risings in the West: but then James was determined that nothing should prevent his setting out.

He began by sending memorials and letters to the Emperor and to all the European princes, to the universities in England and to the officers in the army and navy. These were dated 18 October and announced his intention. He also re-drafted a memorial submitted to him by Bolingbroke: he was prepared to accept advice if the advice were good, but he did not agree to his letters to the outer world being written for him. This was not capriciousness, but a minute attention to detail. In this particular case Bolingbroke had referred to Queen Anne as 'our sister of glorious and blessed memory': James omitted the 'blessed'; a reference to Charles I as 'our Royal grandfather, that blessed martyr, who died for his people' was altered to 'who died a sacrifice to rebellion'. It was natural that James, as a Catholic, should object to the use of the word 'blessed' in connection with anyone other than a candidate for sainthood and, as much as he cared for his ancestry, he did not feel that the use of such a term to be justified.

He packed up the royal seals and, together with a little golden heart and a sealed packet of letters as well as a devotional book, sent them in a shagreen case to the Queen. Lord Nairne made a list of small personal legacies which included his old inkhorn and portfolio. His books were to be left to his former tutor, Dr Ingleton, who also was to take care, jointly with Sir William Ellis, of the four volumes of memoirs written by James II. His letters and copy-letters he made up into orderly bundles and he sent two keys, one of a strong-box containing his clothes and the other – 'the King could not well remember what it was' – to the Scots College in Paris so that they could be forwarded to the Queen at Chaillot. He also sent a note to the Queen asking her to see that Lords Nairne and Middleton were sent to him before any others when the time came for him to request their presence in England.[1]

[1] Carte CCXI, 211, p. 328

They hunted well at Commercy, and James gave every appearance of enjoying the sport, but on the night of 26 October it seemed as if he were about to suffer another attack of ague: he left the supper-table in some distress and retired to his apartments. He was emphatic that no notice was to be taken of his indisposition and that the party should continue without him. The Prince de Vaudémont was most considerate and, although he sent to make enquiries about the King's health, did not disturb him or allow others to do so. A day and a half later he announced to the company that the King had departed for Scotland, and suggested that they should celebrate this fact by continuing with their merry-making. He also raised the draw-bridge.

So, thanks to the Prince, there were no pursuers on the King's trail, and he made his way entirely alone to the forest outside Commercy where he changed into the violet cassock of an abbé and rode on to Paris. He arrived there on 30 October, and stayed with the Comte de Breteuil, the husband of the former Mademoiselle de Clare, Berwick's niece by marriage. She may have been the 'Mademoiselle de C.' to whom James paid a tender farewell before setting out on his 1708 expedition. Their house was a focal point for the Jacobites in Paris and many came to pay their respects and to kiss the King's hand. It says a great deal for James that, unused as he was by virtue of his position, to making even the smallest journey alone, he should have been able to make a journey of 170 miles or so in disguise, sleeping in an ordinary inn with a strongbox of 27,000 golden *louis* under his pillow. The gold was a parting gift from the Duke of Lorraine. Money for the cause was now beginning to arrive: the Pope had sent 300,000 *louis* and the Spanish ambassador to France another 300,000. This was divided up and sent to various people who would be looking after strategic points.

He made a very good impression on those who came to greet him at the Breteuils' house, but lost no more time than courtesy demanded before proceeding to a general council which lasted well into the early hours. After a few hours sleep in the little house belonging to the Duc de Lauzun at Chaillot, he paid a visit just after dawn to his mother, who was staying at the neighbouring convent, then drove off in the carriage belonging to the Comte de Breteuil. He carried with him his doctor, Mr St Paul, who also acted as a valet, his surgeon, William Erskine, and both the coachman and the attendant were his own men as well. This party had preceded him to Paris and were now all disguised in the Comte's livery.

It took Lord Stair several days to catch up with the fact that James had left Lorraine; then he demanded that the King be prevented from crossing France. According to Berwick, the Regent replied that as soon as anyone told him where he could be, he would see that he was taken back from whence he came, but that he, the Regent, was not obliged to be either the spy or the provost of King George.[1]

A few days later Stair informed the Regent that James would arrive at Châlons in Champagne on a certain day, so the Regent agreed to send someone to find him and bring him back, not to Paris, but to Bar. He sent a certain Major Contades, whose sympathies seemed certainly to have been on the King's side, because he delayed in setting out and took a very out-of-the-way route. Berwick wrote afterwards: 'On his return Contades made a great story out of all he had done when reporting to Stair and the latter pretended to be satisfied although at heart he was pretty certain that the Regent was not very keen on impeding the Pretender's journey and that Contades had no desire whatever of succeeding in his mission.'[2] Stair sent emissaries everywhere to find James, but he had been so well disguised and had travelled to Paris quite alone that 'he was never informed before it was too late to make use of the information'. There were rumours that Stair had tried to have James assassinated, but Berwick discounted them: 'I believe him to be too much a man of honour to ever to have had such a thought. The Duke of Mar, whose interests were quite the opposite of those of Stairs [*sic*] always spoke of him in the same way; and when he speaks well of his enemy one should believe him.'[3]

And yet there was the affair at Nonancourt. When Stair eventually caught up with the news that James had left Chaillot, he rightly guessed that he would be making for the coast via Alençon. It may have been pure coincidence that Colonel Douglas, the same spy as it had been assumed had visited Bar the previous August,[4] was also on the road to the coast via Alençon with two companions[5] who may have been a Mr Macdonald and a Mr Elliott of Stair's embassy. One of the two embassy men met Douglas at Nonancourt, a village nineteen leagues from Paris, three from Dreux and three from Evreux. Colonel Douglas, who arrived first with his servent, was accepted in the best Parisian society, was well-mannered with a reputation for personal bravery, but was of poor means, and Stair paid well.

They ate their midday meal at the post-house in Nonancourt, and were joined by the third man after they had eaten. The postmaster was absent, but his wife, who seems to have been an exceptionally intelligent woman, and may well have been a Jacobite agent herself, was in charge of the post-house. When Douglas arrived with one of his confederates he asked so many questions about the expected arrival of a post-chaise which he feared

[1] Berwick, *op. cit.*, Vol. 2, pp. 255–6
[2] *ibid.*, pp. 256–7
[3] *ibid.*
[4] See p. 167
[5] A. Shield and A. Lang, *The King over the Water*, Ch. 17, p. 234

might have already gone through, and seemed so precise in his description of its occupants that Madame Lospital, the postmistress, became suspicious, particularly when they began alternately to threaten and promise her rewards for any information she might have. She was sure that they were English, and guessed that it concerned King James. She was not only an intelligent woman, but also a very brave one, for, having come to this conclusion, she decided that it was up to her to prevent them achieving their aim. So she allayed their fears by telling them that the chaise had still to arrive, and that she would warn them of its coming. Douglas, to pass the time and doubtless wanting to be out of earshot, took a walk with the first man, leaving the other and the servant to the dismay of Madame Lospital, at the house. As the late arrival had not been offered anything to eat by Douglas, she set before him the best of her meat and wine, and, while he was thus occupied, sent one of her servants to keep watch and warn her when James's post-chaise was approaching. It was now overdue, and the men in the post-house were becoming impatient, so she persuaded the third man to take a rest in her room, while she slipped out unnoticed to a friend whom she trusted, and who agreed to taking James and his company into her house. Then Madame Lospital went on to a relative who was a priest and borrowed an abbé's cassock and periwig. When she returned, she found the English servant waiting at her gate much to her concern. She pretended to sympathize with him and got her postilion to make him drunk, which he did in the shortest possible time: then she locked him up with the other man who was also sleeping under the influence of wine, and went on waiting. A short time later her servant reported the arrival of a post-chaise which did turn out to contain James, while his three friends and servant rode alongside.

Madame Lospital presented herself to James, told him her story and begged him to trust her. If she had been a Jacobite agent, James probably would have done so; if she were not, then it says much for her honest face that he decided to do so in any case. He and his companions followed her to her friend's house and they remained hidden there for three days, the King once more disguised as an abbé.

The brave and resourceful postmistress then sent her postilion to inform Torcy, so she might have already been in his pay, if she was not a Jacobite. James expressed his indebtedness to her and gave her a letter for the Queen which she duly presented some time later at Saint-Germain. The Queen thanked her warmly, made much of her and gave her her portrait. When he had time some months later, James wrote to her repeating his thanks. The three spies were, of course, furious that they had missed their prey and one of them, either Elliott or Macdonald, threatened to strangle her, but, fortunately for her, it did not come to personal violence. Nothing is known of Douglas after this failure, except that he was ostracized in Paris and that he later disappeared altogether, leaving his family dependent on charity.

This episode occurred on 2 November, and so it was not until 8 November 1715 that James arrived in Saint-Malo and his safe arrival there convinced Stair that the Regent was not being so helpful to the British government as he might have been. For his part, the Regent told Bolingbroke and Berwick that he could only delay his searchers so long if he wanted to escape the bad humour of King George. Berwick, who seemed to be entirely unaware of James's feeling about him at this time kept writing to James urging him to sail at once for Scotland. This was entirely James's own wish too, but he resented Berwick making the point, and considered that now Berwick had made it clear that he could not become his commander in the field, there was little point in his handing out advice in such a way. More often than not, he was in any case thinking along the identical lines held by the Duke.

When James reached the coast it was to find the Duke of Ormonde, who had left Paris at the same time as he had left Commercy, waiting for him. In the meantime the Duke had sailed for Cornwall and discovered that all was indeed over for them in the West. He learned then that MacLean had betrayed their plans, that King George had changed the officers of the Plymouth garrison who had been won over to the Jacobite cause, that he had sent an infantry regiment to Bristol, and that Lord Lansdowne and Sir John Wyndham had been taken. On 11 November James wrote to the Queen's almoner, the abbé Innes, from Saint-Malo:

On my arrival here on Friday the 8th it was thought convenient that the Duke of Ormonde and I should wait for fresh accounts from England and without which it was then thought absolutely impossible for the Duke to return thither after the reception he last met with, but considering the danger of delays, the instances that Staire [sic] has made to the Regent, and the little probability we had of having soon accounts from England, the wind being contrary, and the impatience with which the Scots expected me, joyn'd to the good news of last night received from them; it was resolved that wind and weather serving, I shou'd forthwith imbark and set sail, and go to the place appointed in the west of Scotland, and the Duke of Ormonde shou'd go upon the coast of [blank in original] with some arms we have got here, and those few men of Nugent's Regiment which we expect in a few days.[1]

[1] HMC CSP, Vol. I, p. 456

Berwick reported later in his memoirs[1] that Ormonde had sailed to Cornwall with twenty officers and twenty-five dragoons of Nugent's regiment; whether these men, who presumably returned with Ormonde, were extra to those mentioned by James is not clear.

While James and Ormonde were waiting for fair winds on the coast, Bolingbroke was trying to provide arms and ammunition which should have already preceded the King. The Regent made it apparent that, despite his good personal intentions, he could not afford to be mixed up in the affair himself, and so he delegated negotiations. The Arms were promised, but only fair words materialized, 'and to tell the truth', said Berwick, 'I believe that the Regent, beginning to have a bad opinion of this enterprise, was not too concerned to carry out what he had led us to hope for; moreover, there were *cabales* among our people which contributed not a little to the failure of everything. Bolingbroke was hated by the Irish who did not cease to complain about him.'[2] How hard Bolingbroke tried is a matter for speculation: certainly he did not achieve much in the matter of supplies. There is no doubt but that he had a difficult job to do, but he was using the Jacobite cause as a means to his own reinstatement in power, and his heart was not really in the cause itself: when that ran into trouble his interest slackened, to judge by the results. When the Regent, acting on Stair's demand, had seized the arms and ships at Le Havre, about three thousand rifles hidden in another ship higher up the Seine were overlooked. Berwick wanted to send these to Scotland, but Ormonde, 'who only had his English expedition in mind',[2] kept them back and they served no purpose.

Day after day James paced through the rushes and dried heather covering the tops of the cliffs at Cap Fréhel, looking out over the mountainous seas of winter hurling themselves at the red cliffs two hundred feet below. Anxiously he looked for a sign of a ship or for a change in the wind. On 15 November he wrote to Bolingbroke: 'I never wanted you so much in my life, for we have been in a strange confused chaos here these eight days. . . . I have been harassed to death since I am here, and have been a little sick to boot, but I hope 'twill be nothing, for I am well today, but if I have life in me, shall not let slip the first fair wind.'[4] On the same day Bolingbroke wrote to him that his faithful Alan Cameron had been arrested in Mons but had made his escape and was on his way to join him there, and James Murray and Lord Clermont, Middleton's son, had also been arrested in Flanders.

[1] Berwick, *op. cit.*, Vol. 2, p. 257
[2] *ibid.*, pp. 261–3
[3] *ibid.*, p. 264
[4] HMC CSP, Vol. I, p. 485

Captain John Hay joined him with despatches, but after that there was silence from Paris and this was becoming unbearable to the King: on 20 November he wrote to Innes:

> The Post has arrived and there are still no letters for me. Since the arrival of Mr Haye I have no idea of what is happening. I am surprised by your silence because I cannot believe that there is the least negligence on your part. Nevertheless, this is a terrible situation. The winds continue to be contrary and have every appearance of remaining so. Whilst waiting, the world could have changed entirely in the last ten days and we know nothing of it, and things may have altered so much since our plan appeared to be a good one that it could now be bad, depending on whether our affairs have changed for better or worse. I am worried in case there has been an accident of some kind to our subjects but, in any case, if we have no news we shall have to act in the dark and we may spoil everything. I am writing to nobody but you. So as to lose no more time, please deliver this letter to Mr Belleville [Bolingbroke] and to Mr Raby [the Queen]. It is destined more for them than for you.[1]

The weather continued to be stormy and he felt tired, depressed and pulled first this way then that by the rumours flying around his small company who were themselves feeling the strain of waiting. On 24 November he sent a long letter[2] to Bolingbroke, reminding him how they had agreed in Bar that he should follow Ormonde to England, conditions in Scotland not having reached the point of intensity at which they now were: 'my departure was indeed a little precipitate but my patience was no longer proof, I freely own, against all the attacks made on my reputation'. Had the Duke of Ormonde succeeded in his expedition, his timing for his own arrival would have been correct. Then he gave a description of the appalling lack of security he had found on his arrival in Saint-Malo: 'The secret of my passage being in my own breast was, I think, well kept and the length of my journey unavoidable all things considered.' All those lonely miles ridden in disguise to Paris, all the hazards of the Nonancourt affair and the tedium of waiting there until the danger had passed and then he had come to find such a state of indiscretion as this:

> At my arrival at St Malo I found the D[uke of] O[rmonde] with a crowd of followers, which joined to Sir Nicholas' [Giraldin] indiscreet zeal soon made my being here suspected, and afterwards publickly known as it now is, nay the crew of my ship knew before I came who they were to

[1] HMC CSP, Vol. I, p. 460
[2] *ibid.*, p. 461 *et seq.*

carry, and the secret so gott out was necessarily more and more divulged by the length of time the contrary winds obliged me to stay on shoar. At the first appearance of a favourable wind I went in a boat on board the ship with the resolution of going round Ireland, upon the advices Mr Haye brought me strengthened by your opinion which was incontestably most reasonable, for, if the first time the D[uke of] O[rmonde] parted and it was not thought advisable I should go with him, *à plus forte raison* was it unfitt the second, considering the circumstances of his disappointment, and tho' by your advice by Mr Rothe you seemed not much inclined then for my going to Scotland, the great and good change there did by consequence produce a change in your and all men of sence's opinion.

When Scotland had been decided upon, James called his naval men together to hear their opinions:

. . . and their opinion was that by these delayes the season would be so far advanced and that, considering also their experience of the winds and the different ones riquisite to go round Ireland, that that journey was absolutely impracticable, nay Cammocke said in his blunt way that he would give his head if any of us were more heard of, did we take that course.

The next point was as to St George's Channel, as to which the seamen were divided and Cammocke was for it as to the navigating part, but then there was insurmountable difficulties in that, the secret was divulged, the contrary winds gave time for advices to be sent into England, the seas there are very narrow and rough, the season tempestuous, no harbour to retire to on either side, and even I may say needles to thread before I could get to Dunstafnage, besides the article of troops coming from Ireland. After this to run with our ship in a publick manner as I say the gauntlett could not, I think, be called anything but madness. But still my presence in Scotland was necessary and I resolved to go, but the way was the question.

He then consulted Alan Cameron and John Hay, who were convinced of the impracticability of going either via Ireland or by St George's Channel. Captain Hay said

. . . that the delayes had been so great that it was to be hoped Duke Marr would be marched into England, which would make the security of my landing in the west verry uncertain whatever precautions he might have taken for that before, besides that from Dunstafnage to the army was a long journey thro' roads that Hayes plainly said were next to impracticable in the depth of winter; *enfin*, after reasoning the point and turning the matter every way they agreed that my landing on the east coast [erased but legible] was not only the shortest but the securest all things consider'd, tho' surrounded also with difficulties so that the party was taken that I should go to Dunkerque and embark privately from there.

He admitted that the journey would be long and tiring, but his health was good

. . . and I can bear hardships, and for the passage, as my being gone with the D[uke of] O[rmonde] will be published, and that I shall get a ship there privately and will be able to go perfectly disguised, it will be infinitely less subject to accidents then [*sic*] to go in the strange publick manner I must have done from hence at the mercy I may say of fifty men that knew me on board and of all ships I could not chuse but meet on this coast, especially since by a strange fatality the wind is now fair and yet the ships cannot gett out, at the same time the wind is fair from the Downs here.

They had to act in one fashion or another, he continued. Either he set out on this enterprise quite publicly, or else the last secret must be kept. In any case, it was hazardous in the extreme to leave in one small ship which would have all the naval force of England against it, but there was nothing left for him to do but to take this last desperate course. He was sending Cameron back to Bolingbroke so that he could explain to him more fully why he had to take the course he did: after that, Cameron was to meet him at the place he would make known to Bolingbroke. John Hay he was sending into Scotland with a letter for Mar, and his actual landing-place in Scotland was to be told only to Mar and to nobody else. He left it to Bolingbroke and the Queen to decide how much should be divulged to the Regent and Torcy: something had to be said, but only those on the spot would know how far it would be safe to go with the Regent at that moment. Whatever he and the Queen decided should be told to Cameron who would report it to the King when he met him again.

On no account, he emphasized, must Berwick be told:

. . . and it is my positive orders that none but the Queen, and you should, the secret is all, and the want of it sure will, you plainly see, ruin both my reputation and interest with Mary [England]. . . . *Enfin*, all must yield to the secret, nobody know of my design, nor anybody suffer'd to follow, the point is to gett there, and rather than fail that I must sacrifice every thing. Advice is necessary, but when a party like this is taken there remains nothing but the execution, and that alone must be regarded. After that I can own to you that it has gone hard with me to be oblidged to take a party like this on myself, but there was a necessity for it, and I saw no other so little bad.

The Duke of Ormonde, he said, was going to make for Lancashire, in accordance with Bolingbroke's advice, unless contrary winds made him put in on the coast of Cornwall, in which case he would attempt to see what could be done in the West once more: 'he is very full of going to that side of the country but I am intirely of your opinion and so is Campion, tho' he hath still a little hankering after the old project'. The Duke was obviously a difficult man to manage. In the ship carrying Ormonde there would be nearly a hundred men and three hundred sets of arms.

One way and another, James was not sorry to see the back of Ormonde:

The D[uke of] O[rmonde] had a crowd of people with him who were inconvenient in all respects, they were continually whispering notions and jealousies into his ears, and he, I fear, trusted them too much, every body knew every thing and would play the minister. Every resolution was known and blamed, while there was nobody capable of giving good advice, nor nobody would give or do any thing but find fault with what was a doing, every thing was desperate where I was not to be in person and every thing easy in that suposition, in fine all these whispers made so much impression on the D[uke of] O[rmonde] that with all the zeal and courage immaginable he goes about the business now with an uneasiness and a diffidence he cannot dissemble, so great, that had I not been there to spurr him, I know not when he would have been parted, and very much apprehend that if he finds not all ready to his hand that he will not succeed; but one must still hope the best. I can't say he approves quite my present resolution, tho' he never seemed to hint my going over with him. I fancy he had rather I waited somewhere on this road for newes, but delayes you see are dangerous, and not to be harkened to; 'tis plain there is a little emulation between the English and Scotch who shall have me, but after that I must without partiality take the party I think best. On the whole I wish the Duke had spoke a little freer his thoughts to me, but he is a little reserved and afraid of contradicting me which is not right altho' I acted with him with so much kindness and confidence that I am sure he cannot reasonably complain; and after all he is a worthy gentleman who, if he has not all the great qualities necessary on this occasion, 'tis his misfortune and not his fault, and I must needs do him the justice to say that he is entirely attached to me, and would do much better were he not obsessed with such as are incapable of helping him.

It is clear that now James had formed his own judgement of Ormonde: had weighed him in the balance and found him wanting. The Duke was given to rash actions, had no capacity for leadership, was indiscreet but faithful: with no one else to help him James had to make the best of what he had.

Another gentleman who was not as helpful as he might have been was the Earl of Rothes, or 'Mr Rothe' as James named him in this long letter. He had asked Rothes to accompany Ormonde, 'seeing the need he had of a man of spirit and sence about him', but Rothes declined, saying that he would rather remain with the King. This James was determined he should not do, because he was well known by sight now, and would be in great danger if he continued to stay with him. Rothes then said that he would prefer to stay a month in the neighbourhood after the King had gone rather than go with Ormonde: he, too, had obviously had enough of the Duke.

> After this [wrote James] I cannot say I am over satisfied else wise with Rothe. He putt himself more on the foot of a director than adviser, he could not answer the reasons for the present resolution, he was without rime or reason for my passing to seas where he could not well tell himself, nor reply to the objections made to him by the D[uke of] O[rmonde] and myself, and because his advice was not followed nor he now to go along with me, he fairly has given up the cudgles [*sic*] and declared to me he would think no more of anything but to pass the rest of his dayes in quiet; all the calm reasoning I could make with all the kindness immaginable to himself was all in vain, and he so peeked that, were he not too honest a man to say what he thinks, my reputation would very much suffer.

Unfortunately for James, he had already told Ormonde that Rothes would go with him and, what with the Duke feeling slighted and Rothes sulking, his position was not an enviable one: the greatest tact was needed, for it would not take much to upset Ormonde entirely, yet it was really due to his initial panic that they found themselves in the position they were now in.

He was, and rightly so, obsessed with the idea of absolute secrecy and refers once more to the question of whether to tell the Regent and, if so, whether Torcy should also know: 'for you may depend that what the Regent knows of me t'other will hear, and be disgusted, if not trusted by us, besides that I must needs say the man is truly affectionate to me and can advise better than any body what way is to be taken in this case, if you think the Regent should know the truth'.

Then he came back to the subject of the Duke of Berwick, and this appears to be the only time in which James lost control of his temper as well as his pen, and wrote with malice. It was indicative that the person in question should be his half-brother whom he had loved and trusted so completely:

> I am not a little concerned that Mary [Berwick] begins to monopolize all. I plainly see that she will serve you just as she did Ld. Mid.[dleton],[1] not to say the Queen herself, and as she will any body that is my man and employed in France by me. You may depend on't that she only makes use of the pretext of my business to introduce herself; her affaires will prosper by that mine will go at sixes and seavens as they have done these seaven years in her hands. She will act, you'l see, on her own head, she will tell the Queen and you but what she pleases and rule the roast her own way, and I doubt if she be so well as she pretends to be with the Regent; after this I cannot pretend to decide in this matter; the Queen and you must act in it as you find most for my service. I am supposed gone and shall write to him [here James, in his bitterness, forgets to write in the sex of Berwick's codename] no more, and must suffer the humiliation of courting a disobedient subject and a bastard too, rather than risk everything in the main point.

Once the control had snapped not only acrimony but spite issued forth: James cannot in his heart have believed that Berwick had been working against him for his own good during the past seven years, which would have been since the abortive attempt of 1708, and the last thing with which he would have taxed Berwick in normal conditions would have been the circumstances of his birth. There was no doubt but that the King was tired, overwrought and living on his nerves, trying to deal with men much his senior who were behaving like fretful children at a time when he needed the strength of Berwick behind him, but it hardly excuses such terms written in a letter to a man who was ten times more devious than Berwick knew how to be.

He next mentioned Clermont and Murray, who had been taken in prisoners on their respective ways to him: 'Clermont being in the service cannot, I think, suffer, but for Murray I am realy in pain for him. I hope he had time to destroy his papers, tho' as it has happened, there was no secrets of consequence in them.' He was also concerned about the man who had done most after Ormonde to ruin their chances of stealing away unnoticed: 'Sir Nicholas Giraldin apprehends being brought into trouble on account of all the *mouvements* he has given himself on my account. If that should so happen, pray do him all the service you can with the French Court.'

He continued the letter the next morning with some relief:

[1] James apparently blamed Berwick for keeping Middleton from his court at Bar, although he did join him later, but this could equally well have been Bolingbroke's doing, opposed as he was to Middleton

Maria Clementina Sobieska from a contemporary portrait attributed to
Trevisani. (*Scottish National Portrait Gallery*)

De Rome ce 7 Fevrier 1719.

Que l'adieu que j'ay a vous donner ma tres
chere Clementine est triste et accablant pour moy
et comment puis je m'y prendre pour vous l'annoncer.
Que dans le temps que votre Pere m'a donne les
dernieres preuves d'une constance heroique, par une
conduite [...] je croy votre [...] que dans
un temps que vous allez mettre le comble a touts
vos [...] pour moy, par une suitte accompagnée de
tout de risque et de fatigue, que dans un temps ou
votre [...] va paroitre avec tout l'eclat, et d'un
merite [...] touchant et engageant pour moy, que
dans ce meme temps, je vous quitte je vous [...]
pour aller vous avoir loin dans un autre monde
et voici la nouvelle que j'ay a vous apprendre.
Reveillez le vous supplie tout ce que vous avez de

Cara Clementina

Je benis Dieu Caro mio [...] par votre
[...] que vous et vos enfants se porte bien
et je puis en dir de meme, les medecine
ayant tres bien fait, ainsi s'il plais
a Dieu je vous verrois jeudi en [...]
je vous prie de ne pas oublier celle
qui est tend a vous et le sera a jamai
C R

8. *Above.* The b
ning of a let
James to Cle
warning her
imminent de
for Spain in
February 17

Below. A let
Clementina w
written durin
period of con
cence away f
Rome.

(*Both from t
Stuart Paper
Windsor by t
gracious perm
her Majesty
Queen*)

At last I hope, the Duke of Ormonde is now on ship board, and expect tomorrow, before noon, an account of his having sett sail. Rothe hath at last taken the party of a man of honor and goes with him, which was indeed but nessessary [*sic*] and it is most agreeable to the Duke, who, as soon as he and I parted two dayes ago, was cruelly plagued with disponding discourses, especially Cammock who retracted all he had said to me of St George's Channel, and would no more undertake to carry the Duke into it. There was an odd innuendo's [*sic*] also as if I had slipt my neck out of the colar, and sent them to be sacrificed, so to calm and quiet all, I took an occasion to writ the enclosed letter which, join'd to Rothe's last resolution, to Cammock's coming into better humour and to Campion's reason as well as a former letter I writ of which I have no coppy, hath calmed and quieted all and they part now with a verry good will and heart, tho' I find by Flannigan that they are cruelly *entesté* with Cornwall, pray God it turn for the best.

Ormonde did, in fact, sail the next morning with a moderate wind in his favour, bound for Cornwall, which the King regretted. He told Bolingbroke that he could do no more: he had told Ormonde his reasons against it and also those of Bolingbroke, but the whole business was so dangerous that it was right that in the end Ormonde should decide for himself. Before leaving, Ormonde tried once more inadvertently to confuse the issue, but the King refused to listen to him:

I should have said before that one of our fine projects was that I should sail with the Duke and lye on the coast towards Land's End 24 hours to hear what the Duke had done or at least till by winds or ships coming towards us I was forced away. This the Duke himself gave enough into and Rothe too, but I did not, nor I believe you would not have done so either,[1] but enough of our confused proceedings and indeed too much of such details, were it not to demonstrate by experience that all depends on secrecy and that a good party once taken is to be pursued without more ado or running into a labyrinth of unnessessary and confused reasoning when there's no change in affaires that require it, but a crowd of people will allwayes run into that inconvenience; and I do not forgett what you told me of the danger of any body's following me.

He also pointed out that it was impossible for him to say, in the circumstances, where he would be on any given day; he was travelling once more under the name of Du Puis on the road. He was still worried about Ormonde: 'I am in pain for him, for it is not naturall that after all the noise we have

[1] Writing under stress, James, for once, loses command of his English syntax

made here that the English ships should neglect a fair wind to come on this coast, and yet there appearing none makes me apprehend that as the surest game they may be waiting for him on the western coast.' His fears were, in fact, well founded, for Ormonde was forced to return eventually to the coast of Brittany and never reached the English shore at all. He remembered the man in whose house he was sheltering:

> The man of this house, as Cam[eron] will tell you, has been the heartiest man alive and indeed far beyond what could be expected, for to cover the secret he goes along with me himself and Flannegan has directions to banter everybody in these parts and on his road to you. I part on Monday and will carry on this gentleman at least to the place I meet Cam[eron]. I wish I had some handsome present to make to him *en partant*. If the Queen could send me by Cam[eron] a ring for him it would do mighty well.

Then, after asking Bolingbroke to let the Queen see any letters he sent him, he concludes this long letter with: 'Nothing but the secret's getting out can I think make it fail, but indeed I think secrecy is banished the world and we may well call it *rara avis* etc. for I never saw so much indiscretion in any as since I came to these parts.'

Disguised as an ordinary sailor, he set off on the road to Morlaix and Dunkirk, on 2 December 1715, accompanied by Berwick's son, his dearly-loved nephew Lord Tynmouth, similarly attired. Even if his faith in the young man's father had swerved, his esteem for and trust in Tynmouth had not diminished. On the contrary, he was the one person he chose to be his companion in this most hazardous of adventures. There is no further mention of their former host travelling with them. The seas all along the coasts of Brittany and the Côte du Nord were filled with British ships on the lookout for this man who was, according to their information, about to set off at any time across the Channel to try to regain a crown. The price of £100,000 on his head was more than sufficient to tempt any pro-British spy astute enough to fall in with his trail.

As usual, James's weather for such an important operation as this was foul: blizzards struck the northern coast of France, and they suffered from the intense cold as they battled along roads deep in snow. They had to take shelter in ordinary inns, sleeping on rough and dirty beds, eating abominable food, and talking as little as possible so as not to betray themselves by their mode of speech. Somewhere around Morlaix, on 12 December, they heard that Ormonde had returned to France and also managed to see a printed news-sheet account of the Battle of Sheriffmuir which had taken place a month before. They realized that it was not a defeat, but could not, at that distance in time and place, evaluate it for the Pyrrhic victory it really was. If it were any kind of a victory, James knew that it had to be backed up by the arrival of fresh supplies or it would be worth nothing.

Towards that end the Queen had arranged for a gift of 200,000 crowns from King Philip of Spain to be sent with Sir John Erskine and Francis Bulkeley (one a friend, the other a relation by marriage of Berwick) to Calais for shipment to Scotland. Tynmouth was sent by James to join the other two men at Calais while he trudged on alone to Dunkirk, battling against the strong winds which raged all along the coast.

At Dunkirk he found that Bolingbroke had, for once, been successful, and waiting for him was a small ship of two hundred tons which carried eight guns, as well as all the arms and men its small capacity would allow. It also carried a cargo of brandy, in an attempt to allay suspicion should they be stopped by a British man-o'-war. On 27 December the wind changed and blew fair and the King embarked, accompanied only by Alan Cameron and two servants. For five long days the little ship struggled through the North Sea, forcing James into another period of physical inactivity. In spite of the unknown situation into which he was advancing, it is not difficult to imagine the state of exhilaration he must have experienced, being so close to his aim at last. But exhilarated or not, he was sea-sick, which, in the prevailing weather, was not surprising.

On New Year's Day (22 December Old Style and English Calendar), they were within sight of the coast of Scotland, off Montrose where they had hoped to make landfall. But James's patience was to be tried a little longer because there was a suspicious-looking vessel lying just outside the harbour. They put out again and sailed northwards to the harbour of Peterhead, where they landed the next day, Captain Park carrying James, still in a weakened state, on his back through the last few yards of water to the shore. No one was expecting them in the small herring-port where the scattered, granite cottages vied in their greyness with the leaden sky, but they were in friendly country, since Peterhead had been founded some generations before by the Keiths, the family of the Earl Marischal. James was on British soil for the first time in twenty-seven years.

Chapter Sixteen

His joy at being on Scottish ground, even in the deep snow of mid-winter, at first overshadowed all other considerations; it was only gradually, as James moved on with his small company of friends towards Aberdeen, that the true colours of the picture that the Earl of Mar had presented to him became visible. In reality, affairs were in a deplorable state: in his letters Mar had said that the army stood at 16,000 men, but there were barely 5,000, all badly armed and ill organized with little or no provisions. The ship carrying the gold ingots from Spain, with Tynmouth, Erskine and Bulkeley aboard, had still not arrived, yet it had left Calais before James had set out from Dunkirk. There were still no supplies from Bolingbroke, and no news of any to come. But the warmth of the welcome given to him in this Keith country did partly allay his misgivings. He spent the night of the 23 December (Old Style) at the house of the Earl Marischal at New-burgh. The Earl and his brother, James Keith, were two of the most faithful and most valiant adherents of the Stuarts, and it was their very great honour that they were the first to shelter their King on his arrival in his own country. From Marischal's house at Newburgh, the royal party, with James still in disguise, passed *incognito* through Aberdeen to the Earl's main seat at Fetteresso. Here Mar and General Hamilton and a number of the nobility came to acclaim him and kiss his hands; for the first time he was able to behave as a king in a country which was rightly his.

It was here that he came to realize exactly what the Pyrrhic victory of Sheriffmuir meant, and he determined to proceed to Perth, asking Lords Huntly and Seaforth to meet him there. Support from these two lords was necessary if he wanted to hold the greater part of Scotland, but the north was the territory of the Earl of Sutherland, who was pro-Hanover, and his estates bordered on theirs. Sutherland was rich and powerful, and both Seaforth and Huntly knew that they were liable to be invaded by Sutherland should their support of the Jacobites become too overt. The Marquis of Huntly had, in fact, already made his peace with the Government and ex-cused himself to his King because the bad weather made travelling so difficult and it would take some time to re-assemble his chiefs, since they had all returned home. Seaforth said pretty well the same, and further stated that if he left his country he would be leaving it wide open to invasion by Sutherland. Short of definitely antagonizing them, the King had perforce to be content with this poor show of loyalty, and buried his pride to the extent of sending them some officers and money in order to hold their allegiance.

The command of the left wing at Sheriffmuir, which had broken, had been in the hands of General Hamilton, who was regarded with something less than esteem by the rest of those who were there. When he arrived to present himself to the King he was a considerable embarrassment: James could no longer rely on him, yet his innate kindness prevented him from castigating Hamilton either privately or publicly. It was necessary for reports to be sent back to France and Spain, and Alan Cameron was to carry them as one of the King's most trusted servants. One way, then, of getting rid of Hamilton, whose personal loyalty was not in question, was to send him with Cameron, and this is what James did. So unaware did the General seem to be of his transgression, that he went on a private shopping expedition in Paris and sent James some blue ribbon, and Mar some lace, in addition to a large number of bottles of champagne in which, no doubt, to celebrate the King's eventual coronation; it was really very kind of him, but it hardly made up for his conduct at Sheriffmuir.

Monotonously and remorselessly, the snow blotted out the countryside which, at its best, was far bleaker than any James had yet known. News was filtering in, despite the weather, and nothing was for his encouragement. Seaforth and Huntly now made no pretence of joining him. Inverness, which at the beginning of the campaign had been taken for the Jacobites by Colonel John Hay, was now held for the Government by the infamous Lovat aided by Duncan Forbes of Culloden. And the Seaforths and the Huntlys decided that their charity began at home: they had no men to spare for the King, since all were needed to defend their own lands.

He knew now that hundreds of his followers languished in prisons in Carlisle, York and London for his cause, and that Derwentwater and his brother, Wintoun and brave Kenmure were in the Tower. Bolingbroke appeared to be a broken reed, and Mar and Ormonde were of little use: he had absolutely no one to whom to turn for discussion or advice. The Keiths were loyal to the last breath, but they were soldiers and, of necessity, had little comprehension of the wider implications of the campaign. All they could do at this moment was to look after the King, and this they did to the best of their ability. His depression and general malaise progressed towards its inevitable culmination – an attack of the quartan ague, augmented by the physical strain and the exposure to the elements he had known since leaving Commercy. As always, he alternately shivered with the ague and was consumed by a raging fever. Unable to leave Fetteresso with Mar, who was making his way back to Perth, James had to remain indoors until 30

December, hearing meanwhile loyal addresses from the magistrates of Aberdeen and the Episcopal clergy. On the 30 December, he moved on to Brechin and Kinnaird, and on 4 January he reached Glamis as a guest of the Earl of Strathmore. Because the Earl was a minor his estates had not been forfeited when his elder brother had been killed at Sheriffmuir. Later the young Earl was to describe James as a very fine gentleman, very punctual, very religious, but a lover of dancing, modest, chaste and of a great and unusual understanding. He was also reported to have touched for the King's Evil in Glamis and the patients, it is claimed, recovered.[1]

Everywhere James was moved by the display of affection and loyalty shown him by those of high degree and low and, now that his fever was past, he began to regain his spirits, although he was still weak. From Glamis he rode into Dundee and a royal welcome, with Mar on his right hand and Earl Marischal on his left. All the way through the city, under its triumphal banners, the people cheered and acclaimed him and by the time he had reached the market-place he had collected a retinue of nearly three hundred horsemen who had rallied to his standard. He delighted in this show of affection by his people and, because he was relaxed and happy, they sensed this delight and returned it with love. They would not let him dismount, but kept him there on his horse until the early afternoon, and his hand was kissed by all who approached him. The next morning, 6 January, he rode on to another seat of the Strathmores, Castle Lyon, then on to Fingask, belonging to Sir David Thriepland, where he slept that night. The next few days he knew must be the most important of his time in Scotland, for they were approaching Scone, where he hoped to be crowned, and Perth which was the Jacobite stronghold. It was essential that he should be at the peak of his mental and physical condition and, being so lately recovered from illness, he would not have been human if he had not worried to some degree lest this should not be so.

The Scottish regalia had been kept at Scone, but disappeared mysteriously at the time of the Union with England in 1707. No king of Scotland had been crowned there since Charles II had signed the Covenant with Scotland, so those of the ladies of Scone and Perth and the wives of the nobility affected to James's cause began to gather their jewels together to make a crown for him. He had no objection to being crowned by a Protestant bishop as his father had been, or a Moderator of the Church of Scotland or even, if necessary, by the Earl of Mar; and the sacrament was to be a relatively simple one. Nevertheless, the Catholics in his party began to make difficulties over the terms of the new Royal Declaration which he would presumably have uttered at the time of the coronation.

[1] A. Shield and A. Lang, *op. cit.*, Ch. 18

He stayed the night of the 7 January at the Royal Palace at Scone, because the house he intended to inhabit in Perth was not yet ready for him. The next morning, in the bitter cold, he arrived in Perth. Because all the coal-mines in Fife were in the hands of the enemy, there was no fuel to be had in Perth, and consequently, the townspeople were not in their most cheerful mood to begin with. A form of military inspection had been planned in Perth, and James was as eager to see the Highlanders mustered there as they were to see him, but, unfortunately, their numbers were few. Although the Seaforths and the Huntlys had had little intention of arriving, other well-intentioned clans had had genuine difficulty in reaching Perth through the inclemency of the weather. He was dejected by their fewness of number, and his disappointment must have shown on his face, for they, on their side, were disappointed in him. It is not difficult to imagine the confrontation of the wild, tough, roaring warriors of the hills with the tall, slender, black-eyed, olive-complexioned young man, virile, and brave without doubt, for how many would have undertaken such a journey against so many odds and with a price on his head to come to them in the depths of a winter which had dismayed even themselves by its unusual ferocity? But he was quiet, gently spoken and seemingly withdrawn from them. When James realized the effect he was making on the Highlanders, he became nervous and inhibited to such a degree that he seemed to be stern and cold. He still did not feel well, and could not find the energy to put a false and bright face on the matter. The Highlanders needed someone outgoing towards them, someone likely to grab a claymore and rush roaring into battle at their head, someone with the zest and *panache* which a later generation was to find in his son – but not the quiet, introverted young man before them whose fires smouldered too deeply for them to see the flames.

There was no doubt but that Perth was a personal disaster for James. Apart from all other considerations, the troops gathered there had expected him to come with reinforcements and with money. The talk about the plans for the coronation, which had originally been planned for 23 January, grew less and less until it was heard no more.

Even Mar realized that they were in desperate straits, and he commendably put aside his own pride and wrote to Berwick, asking him once again to come to Scotland as their general; but even then Berwick delayed his reply, and went through the, by then, all too well-known ritual of explanations as to why he could not come. Apart from the fact that the Regent would not let him leave France, Berwick was never a soldier to spill blood in an already doomed cause. Bolingbroke had still not sent supplies and, on 12 January, James had news of the ship carrying the Spanish ingots. It had been delayed by winds and enemy shipping in Calais until 20 December and then it had had to battle through the same kind of stormy weather that James's own ship had faced. Then, stranded off Dundee it had been shattered to pieces. Lord Tynmouth, Sir John Erskine and Francis Bulkeley all managed to escape, and it was in fact Tynmouth who brought the news to the King. Mar wrote from Scone the same day to General Gordon near Dundee:

> The ship was broke to pieces but the bulk where the gold was still lies on the sandbank where she stranded. They think that at the springtide, which is Saturday, Sunday and Monday it may be dry and so recovered. Lord Rothes was advertised of her being stranded by the disaffected thereabouts and desired to send a party, so I am apt to believe the party we heard of today at Falkland have been going there. The King thinks it best for us to appear to give the ship and all that was in her for gone, and to neglect her by recalling the party sent to Cupar today and letting it be as much known as can be though it is not fit to mention any considerable sum having been in her, in case of that making the enemy look the more narrowly after it. This, 'tis likely, may make them recall their party tomorrow and if they do, on Saturday or Sunday our people may look after the recovery of the gold, though I am afraid it is gone.[1]

In this case, as during the whole expedition and during the attempt seven years before the weather was James's second enemy. He hoped that it might have deterred the Duke of Argyll from marching against them, since, so far, he had been strangely quiet but even this bonus was not to be allowed him. Argyll, in fact, only reported hearing 'a rumour' that James landed on 11 January. The Duke had been accused of not being vindictive enough in his hounding of the Scots rebels after Preston: his own nationality seemed to render him suspect. And, to prevent any lack of zeal on his part, Lord Cadogan was sent by King George to assist him. The Government now had some ten thousand men and thirty guns in the field, and, when Cadogan prepared to march, Argyll objected because the roads were completely under snow. Cadogan insisted, and orders were given to the local people to clear the roads before the English and Dutch troops as they marched towards Stirling. Argyll assembled all the carts he could find in his neighbourhood to carry not only munitions, but also wood and coal to warm the troops. He had a large artillery train and everything necessary for subsistence in a long siege.[2]

In Perth, James knew that it would not be very long before their position there would become untenable. Now the Spanish gold had gone he had very

[1] HMC, Vol. I, pp. 486–7
[2] Berwick, *op. cit.*, Vol. 2, p. 266

little money left; most of what he had taken with him from Lorraine had been paid to the loyal troops for subsistence and to buy gunpowder, to say nothing of the money he had sent north to Huntly and Seaforth. Recently he had also sent them General Echlin, one of his more trusted commanders, to see if they could retake Inverness, but he must have known that it was a lost cause. Still nothing came from France, no money, no men, no arms, no gunpowder. On 31 January, Bolingbroke wrote to Mar (whom James had now created a duke), that in England 'Every creature who might stand up in the defence of his country is imprison'd, dispers'd or dispirited; the people are still the same, or rather their resentments run higher than ever, but there is not a Duke of Mar amongst the nobility or gentry . . .'.[1] Bolingbroke was not lacking in soft words, even if more active things were missing.

James could see that the weather might help them after all, for, if the ground were frozen solid, Argyll's men would not be able to dig themselves in for a siege, whilst the Jacobites would be able to come out of Perth, cross the frozen River Tay and fight on open ground on the opposite bank. All the Highlanders were aching to come to grips with the enemy, but Mar was depressed and did not favour the idea. If James had not listened to him something might have been achieved, but he followed Mar's advice and remained where he was.

Argyll set out from Stirling to march to Perth on 29 January 1716. He reached Perth on 1 February around 2 a.m., although the distance between the two cities was less than thirty-five miles: the weather was worse than it had ever been. This, combined with the fact that the Jacobites had lost all the towns they had held north of the Tay, finally convinced James that there was no point in trying to hold out in Perth. He determined, at a council of war held on the same day as Argyll left Stirling, to retreat north via Dundee. He also reluctantly agreed to Mar's 'scorched earth' policy, and put his name to the order to burn all the hamlets which lay in Argyll's path (due warning having been given to the inhabitants), so that he would receive no assistance from them. Mar wrote to General Gordon: 'The burning goes mightily against the King's mind.'[2]

On 3 February, James wrote to the Regent asking him for aid to carry on the rebellion from the north. He wrote from Montrose that night, and on the next morning received the news that the enemy was only four miles away. It was clear that he was to be their quarry, and that he was a source of potential danger to all the friends and supporters who were with him. From Montrose he sent Sir John Erskine to tell Berwick that he intended to

[1] HMC, Vol. I, p. 493
[2] *ibid.*, p. 496

retreat to the north as the enemy advanced, and to raise his standard again a little beyond Aberdeen, where there was an excellent position which five hundred men could defend against ten thousand. The right of the position was covered by the mountains, and the left by the sea; in front was a bog which could only be crossed by one particular track.[1] He had obviously worked out exactly what he was going to do, but he was not allowed to do it. The Duke of Mar and others around him made him realize that he could not afford, while he had no heir, to risk the royal person; furthermore, conditions now were such that they would probably have to seek terms with the enemy, and that was impossible while the King remained with them having a price on his head. Berwick wrote:

> One may be curious to know why King James returned so soon from Scotland and why, in accordance with what Chevalier Erskine told us, he had not retreated to a place beyond Aberdeen: all that I have been able to discover is that Mar persuaded him that it was no longer possible to carry on the attempt, that those of his party would be completely ruined and thus it was necessary, by his withdrawing, to give them the chance of coming to terms, and this his presence rendered impracticable. It is true that this reflection could have been made before the departure of Erskine: but I am convinced that if a fault was committed, it was only because of the too great deference paid by this young Prince to the advice of others.[2]

Berwick seems to have been totally unaware of the irony in this last sentence.

The pity of it was that Mar stage-managed things in such an undignified fashion: the soldiers were told that a retreat had been decided upon, and James's baggage horses were brought round to the front of the building in which they were sheltering, while Mar hurriedly led him to the back door, where horses were waiting to take them and the wounded Marquis of Drummond to the nearby shore. James was most reluctant to leave in such a way, and wanted to take Lords Tullibardine, Linlithgow, Tynmouth and Edward Drummond with him, but they were all scattered within a radius of a few miles on various errands, so messages were sent to them and to the Duke of Melfort telling them what was happening and warning them to make their escape without further delay. Tynmouth and his friend Bulkeley, who were never far apart during this campaign, decided to chance making their way to Aberdeen, which they did successfully. There they waited eight days until they could hire a small boat to take them to Holland, whence they travelled to France. The Regent was most annoyed with them and took

[1] Berwick, *op. cit.*, Vol. 2, p. 268
[2] *ibid.*, p. 269

away Tynmouth's regiment from him: 'In taking the regiment from my son, they gave it back to me,' was the laconic comment of Berwick.[1]

The King left on 4 February and the night before his departure he wrote some letters which he left with General Gordon. One was addressed to the Duke of Argyll, but it appears never to have been sent to him. In it James repeated how much he had disliked giving the order to burn, and said that he had asked Gordon to give all that remained of the royal purse to him so that the Duke could make some kind of compensation to those who had suffered. He also wrote to the Highlanders, thanking them for their services and their devotion, but they, when they heard that the King had gone, simply gave up in disgust and turned their heads towards home.

Mar's last effort at least was crowned with success: more adept perhaps at organizing failure than initiating success, he had arranged for a small boat to be standing by – the *Marie Thérèse* of Saint-Malo – which carried them to Waldam near Gravelines in French Flanders. Melfort, Drummond, General Dominic Sheldon and ten other gentlemen followed in two other small boats. James was never to see Scotland again.

[1] Berwick, *op. cit.*, Vol. 2, p. 269

Chapter Seventeen

King James and the Duke of Mar landed at Gravelines on 26 February 1716 after 'an enterprise marked by two kinds of failure: prevailing ill-fortune and the greater difficulty of re-mounting such an enterprise with the hope of success in the future'.[1] The King's first action was to send two ships back to Scotland to bring off as many of his men as possible. Then he set off in the direction of Paris, accompanied by Lord Drummond; perhaps he had had enough of Mar's company on the ship coming over, for in any case the Duke had to make his own way to Paris.

In no way could the failure of what was to be known henceforth as the 'Fifteen' be attributed to James himself: he had been single-minded, almost to the point of fanaticism in his planning, but the information on which he had had to base his plans was false. No one could have faulted his courage, but one man alone, no matter how brave, could not have held all the strands of the operation in his hands; when he received any counsel at all it was rendered useless by a conflicting opinion from another source. But the chief reason for the failure was the fact that he had had no general. It was all very well for the Duke of Berwick to say afterwards that if he had been consulted he would not have agreed to the expedition because it had lacked prudence almost from the beginning:[2] his absence from the operation in the field had made all the difference between success and failure.

There was no doubt but that Berwick had been on the horns of a dilemma: he sought to reassure Mar that he and Bolingbroke had left no stone un-turned in doing what they were able to do for the cause in a letter written in February 1716:

> I know not what those who have been heare backward and forwards may have imagin'd or say'd, but this I can averr, that I never promised to follow the King anywhaere without the proviso of the French Court's giving me leave. The King may very well remmember, that three yeares agoe of my own accord I made him the offer of my services under the above said proviso. His Majesty thought it then so reasonable that he thanked me for it and writt to the French Court to obtain the leave. It was then granted; but after Queen Ann's death the late King of France

[1] Montesquieu's *Eloge* in Berwick, *op. cit.*, p. xlvii
[2] *ibid.*, p. xlviii

thought it necessary to avoid any occasion of quarrel with the new Gouvernement of England, and therefore not only recall'd his leave, but even forbid me positively from stirring; I did all that lay in my power to obtain the recall of that prohibition, but in vain, as I can prove by an original letter under M. de Torcy's hand dated of the 19th June last. Since the King of France's death I have used all my endeavours with the Regent but to as little purpose.

This being my present case, all I can say is, that I am still ready to part, whenever the Regent will allow me, but 'tis neither consisting with my honour, my duty, my oaths, nor even with the King's interest or reputation, that I should desert like a trooper; it was with his Majesty's leave that I became a Frenchman, and I cannot depart from the vast obligations that I now have incumbent upon me, without breach of publick faith and gratitude. Your Grace is to much a man of honour not to approve of this my conduct and resolution. If ever proper occasions offer you shall find me as zealous as any man to render the King service, and of giving your Grace real proofs of the great value and esteem I have for your person.[1]

There was a great deal of sense in Mar's insisting that the King should leave Scotland when he did: it was the manner of his departure which the Duke arranged so strangely. If James had remained, there would have been a house-to-house search for him throughout Scotland, and many Jacobites who had managed to elude the long arm of the Government until then would have been discovered, and consequently transported or imprisoned. His presence could have brought them nothing but danger and grief and this was the bitterest part of his regret.

Little by little news was coming in. On 28 February (Old Style) 1716 a Captain Stratton wrote to the Duke of Mar the following letter which seemed to imply that perhaps there was some truth in the Government's fear that Argyll, left to his own devices, might not be pursuing the rank and file so vindictively as George I would have liked:

The Scots rebels, after the Pretender left them, march in a body northward, first to Aberdeen, then further north towards Strathspey and to Badenoch. Argyle did not pursue them much further than Aberdeen, but sent detachments to Peterhead and Fraserburgh, and, which is odd, in all that pursuit there was few or no stragglers catched, and not one of note that I hear of taken, but I hear of about a dozen of gentlemen that have rendered themselves prisoners. What treatment they will meet with God knows, but nothing of clemency is yet expected. The clans and all

[1] HMC, Vol. I, p. 506

other Highland men are got safe into their own country, some say there is yet a body of them together, but little certainty whether it be so or not, but it is certain that most of the Lords are with the clans, particularly the Earls Marischall, Southesk, Linlithgow and Viscount Killsyth. Most of the gentry are dispersed to various places, many have crossed Murray firth to Kaitness, and no doubt some of them are gone to the Western Island, particularly to the Isle of Skye, and some with the clans on the main land, and some few skulking in the Low Country. The generality have either lost their horses or so sold them for little or nothing.

The troops are cantoned at Dumbarton, Glasgow and Stirling, but the bulk of them at Dundee, Arbroath, Montrose, Brechin, Aberdeen, Peterhead, Elgin, Inverness, and some little garrisons in houses of Braemar and Cromar. Some say that the Marquises of Huntly and Seaforth's houses are likewise garrisoned, and these two worthy Lords are gone to the Highlands. If this be true they are not like to get much by their fine doings.[1]

There were many things such as these for the King to think about as he travelled via Boulogne, Abbeville and Beaumont-sur-Oise to Malmaison, where he stayed in order to be near his mother at Saint-Germain without infringing the interdiction on his presence at the château too overtly. While at Malmaison, he tried to see Orléans, but in vain: the Regent was no longer interested, now that the Stuart expedition had failed. From Malmaison, James went on to Mademoiselle de Chausseraye's busy little Jacobite house in the Bois de Boulogne where he received Bolingbroke and the Duke of Ormonde. There seemed at that time nothing unusual in his treatment of Bolingbroke. The Duke of Mar joined them there as well: this was at the end of February 1715. Stair had by now realized that James was once more on French territory and demanded that the Regent should order him to leave France at once, and Orléans, who could now see the advantages of a possible alliance with Britain against the growing threat from Spain, readily complied.

Elisabeth Farnese, Queen of Spain, had made it clear that she would not have James in her country; King Philip was kinder and sent a present of money to his royal cousin. And this was accepted with gratitude, for James was now nearly destitute. Bills were coming in for supplies and for the ships he had used in his journey to and from Scotland, as well as for those he had sent to bring back the men he had left behind. He realized that he was now a source of embarrassment to most of the European courts to whom he might turn for shelter. There was an increasing struggle for the balance of

[1] HMC, Vol. 2, p. 9

power in Europe, now that France was no longer supreme. France, Spain, the Netherlands, the Empire and Portugal were all, in their various ways, seeking an alliance of one kind or another with England. To remain on friendly terms with her, they had to refuse King James. Even the Duke of Lorraine and the Prince de Vaudémont withdrew their whole-hearted support although it was tacitly understood that if he could find no other home then, in the last resort, they would give him their hospitality again. The Pope was ready to welcome him, but James knew that once his cause was linked with Rome in the eyes of his Protestant supporters in England his motives would be suspect. The situation was becoming desperate: he had to get out of France or suffer the ignominy of arrest by the Regent. Finally, it was to Avignon, a Papal possession, that he decided to go. On or about 3 March, just before leaving Malmaison, and without consulting anyone, James sent Ormonde to Bolingbroke with an order for his dismissal as Secretary of State. No one seemed to know what inspired this action: it may be that he had learned from some of Mademoiselle de Chausseraye's visitors more than he had ever imagined about Bolingbroke's relations with Claudine de Tencin, and realized how information about his plans could have leaked out to his enemies. Or he may have thought that Bolingbroke's burning personal ambition would spur him on to continue a struggle which, at that particular moment, was useless. Nevertheless, it was neglect in discharge of his duties with which he charged him and this, in any case, could have been attributed to the Secretary's signal failure in supplying the King's army in Scotland.

Berwick was shocked by the King's treatment of Bolingbroke, and was still immovable in his admiration of the latter. This was remarkable in a man of such clear perceptions, but when Berwick placed his faith in anyone his trust was not shaken by gossip, and he was convinced that all the short-comings attributed to Bolingbroke were simply the fabrications of the *clique* of women in the house in the Bois de Boulogne. Never given to talking much himself, idle chatter antagonized him completely and, as he did not listen to it, he did not realize that there might be a grain of truth deeply hidden in the piles of chaff. Later he wrote in his memoirs:

The Prince gave, as his reason for what he had just done, the fact that Lord Bolingbroke had totally neglected to send to Scotland any supplies of arms, money etc., and that that was the cause of the failure of his affairs. The gossips of Saint-Germain added that it only depended on him to obtain from the Regent all kinds of help, but that he did not wish it in order to ruin the Pretender whom he was secretly betraying, but the real reason for his disgrace arose out of other motives: one might even believe that King James, who wanted to exonerate himself from all that the malice of his enemies might invent against him, was not sorry that everything was thrown upon Bolingbroke. Also, the Duke of Ormonde had always been jealous of Bolingbroke whom he considered to be a superior genius and, consequently, one to be respected more than himself. A thousand little politicians, who were unable to make any headway with so enlightened a Minister, and who thought that they would be assured of doing and knowing everything if Ormonde were in power, did not cease their efforts to arouse the latter against him, and to make the least of his actions seem odious. Mar also had his own interests in view: he wanted to make the public believe that, if he had been succoured by Bolingbroke, his expedition would have succeeded: he also wanted to be the sole Minister and to govern everything and for that he had necessarily to get rid of Bolingbroke for, knowing the small genius of the Duke of Ormonde, he did not fear to find him in his way. Mademoiselle de Chausseraye and several other ladies, whom I have mentioned above as being annoyed with Bolingbroke because he did not consult them any longer, joined the rest of his detractors; and it would appear that the Ministers of Saint-Germain, if they did not exactly put their shoulders to this wheel, at least did nothing to hinder his dismissal. One must be deprived of all good sense not to see the enormity of the fault King James was making in getting rid of the only Englishman capable of managing his affairs, for whatever some people of more passion than good sense may say, by the acknowledgment of all England, Bolingbroke was one of the ablest Ministers who have existed.[1]

He could not understand, he added, why the King should have dismissed Bolingbroke in such a preremptory manner; surely he could have found ways to explain why he was taking such a step, perhaps blaming it upon the coldness which existed between the Secretary and the other ministers? In this, Berwick was thinking out of character, for no one was given more to the blunt statement, even if it were politely presented, than himself and, also, seemingly in wilful dismissal of James's own approach to the truth. They were both alike in this and, although neither was clumsy, both resembled their father in pressing on regardless of the opinions of others. Berwick repeated that he believed that Bolingbroke would have moved heaven and earth to obtain help, but that he had been the plaything of the French government, and although he knew this there was no other European power to whom he could turn for help.

Had James acted unwisely in dismissing Bolingbroke? Certainly Lord

[1] Berwick, *op. cit.*, Vol. 2, pp. 270–6

Charles Edward Stuart, Prince of Wales, from a contemporary portrait attributed to A. David. (*National Portrait Gallery, London*)

10. Henry Benedict, Duke of York, from a contemporary portrait attributed to A. David. (*National Portrait Gallery, London*)

Charles Edward Stuart, Prince of Wales, from a contemporary portrait attributed to A. David. (*National Portrait Gallery, London*)

10. Henry Benedict, Duke of York, from a contemporary portrait attributed to A. David. (*National Portrait Gallery, London*)

Stair had reported to London that Bolingbroke had published the secret plans of his master and, thanks to the Claudine de Tencin liaison, most of the Jacobite plans had been known in advance by the English government. It was also to be remarked that the only time when they were not known was when James was in Scotland and far from Bolingbroke. Every secret betrayed meant the loss of Jacobite lives, and James could not afford to lose any time in removing the source of the betrayal which had probably been brought to his notice by the pro-Jacobite Bishop of Rochester, Francis Atterbury. Later that year he was to make the bishop his Resident in England. Bolingbroke left the court and retired to a private life in Paris and the provinces until he eventually received a pardon from the British government in 1722. It was an ironic coincidence that he should cross Atterbury's path when he took ship for England; the bishop, who had refused to sign a declaration of fealty to the Hanoverian King after the Fifteen, had grown steadily in Government disfavour until the time arrived when it was only logical, and much safer even with its inherent risks, to join the 'King over the Water'. The latter was the title given to James by the faithful in the United Kingdom: those who drank his health surreptitiously over a bowl or glass of water.

The Duke of Mar wrote to Colonel John Hay on 13 April 1716:

> You will have heard of Lord B[olingbrok]e's being out which indeed could not be otherwise, not only from the odd and negligent part he had acted, but things were so 'twixt D. O[rmond]e and him that they could no longer have confidence in one another, so they could not be both employed, and there was no choice hard to be made betwixt them. For want of a better I am now in the post he was, but all this only to yourself, and if you come by Paris, as I suppose you will, keep your mind to yourself, see who you will.[1]

Hay had been sorely puzzled by the sudden departure of the King and did not mince matters in the letter written on 3 April which had occasioned the reply from Mar above. As he wrote from Dunkirk,

> After that the King went aboard at Montrose, the army had orders to march towards Aberdeen, General Gordon, my Lord Marischal, Tynmouth, and in short all of us moved about twelve at night. Some got to Aberdeen the next day, the others the day after, when all the general officers and gentlemen of note were called, to advise what was to be done. It was very melancholy to think that nobody proposed anything, nor thought but of preserving themselves, and making the best terms they

[1] HMC, Vol. II, p. 55

could. They all agreed that the best way to get anything that could look like honourable terms was by sticking together and asking in a body. . . .

The King's leaving Scotland, your Grace may imagine, was a great surprise upon me. Since that was the way his Majesty was determined to take, I own it was a secret not to be entrusted to any except those who were immediately concerned in it, though I must own it gives me a great deal of uneasiness to think that your Grace should leave one in the situation that I was in to the mercy of a merciless enemy, from whom I could expect but the honour of dying for my King and country's service which I should never shun if in a honourable way.[1]

John Hay had been responsible for the taking of Inverness, the one decisive action of Mar's campaign in Scotland, and if he had been captured, his life would have been worth very little.

It was this kind of reflection which weighed upon the King's spirits during the cold and wet April when he arrived in Avignon. It was still Lent and the pontifical city did not present a very cheering aspect, but the time of the year and the weather matched his mood. Besides the Duke of Mar, he was also attended by the captain of the cavalry attached to the Archbishop of Avignon and the Marchese Salviati, the Papal Vice-Legate. The Duke of Ormonde arrived two days later, on 4 April, followed by Lords Tullibardine, Nithsdale (who had made an extraordinary escape from the Tower of London after Preston), Drummond and Panmure. Soon the Earl Marischal and his brother, and Lord George Murray, Lord Southesk, Sir John Erskine and other gentlemen arrived on the French coast and made their separate ways to Paris, Saint-Germain and, eventually, Avignon. Some, such as Erskine, made the best of a melancholy journey 'home':

Our master, I know, loves Burgundy for his ordinary drink; here is the place to have it both very good and as cheap as anywhere, for the Pomar, and what is particularly called Vin de Beaune, grow both within half a league of this, and the gentleman who came with us can and will assist us in procuring it.

We never fail once a day at least to drink our Master's and your health in Vin de Pomar or Beaune, but never exceed half a bottle at a meal, save last night, being Saturday we took each a whole to drink to our wives and mistresses etc.[2]

Others did not accept their fate so philosophically; on 4 April Mr Moray, or Murray, of Abercanny wrote:

[1] HMC, Vol. 11, p. 55
[2] *ibid.*, p. 63

His poor wife and children being brought to great hardships and his family being like to be extinguished, presuming his Grace will not reckon it immodest, if he lays the case before him and earnestly begs him to acquaint the King with it. If his losing an estate of 1,500 l. sterling a year, his raising a troop of the best horse in the army for His Majesty's service, standing by his cause to the last, his family never being out of their duty to his Majesty and his ancestors can merit a share of His Majesty's favour, it could never come more opportunely. . . . [1]

Many, many letters such as these reached Avignon and, more often than not, they were followed by their writers who, singly or in groups, made their way to the King, now becoming desperate in his attempts to help them. His financial situation was worse than ever, taking into account all the debts he had incurred over the expedition. Then there was the rent of the house in Avignon which had been vacated for him by the commandant of the Pontifical Guard, and the neighbouring house, both with contents, as well as nearby houses for members of his suite. He lived in a frugal simplicity, but exterior appearances had to be maintained if he were to be taken seriously by the governments of Europe. Mar wrote to Innes on 10 May 1716: '. . . there is a great addition to the cruelty of Patrick's [James's] situation, that it will not be in his power to do for so many worthy people what their merits justly deserve; nay, I am afraid will not be able to give them bread. . . .'[2]

Sir William Ellis, his treasurer, arrived from Saint-Germain, bringing with him 80,000 crowns raised by the Queen, which was just enough to pay the first year's rent. Indefatigable as ever, although she was suffering from the cancer which was to kill her in two years' time, the Queen was the nucleus of all that occurred at Saint-Germain, and she it was who suggested that the *Mary Magdalene* should be sold, one of the five ships loaded with provisions, arms and ammunition which James had sent to bring off as many of those left in Scotland as he could. The sale, as her secretary Dicconson advised Mar on 14 May,[3] would bring in 11,000 *livres* and the Queen had advised him to accept it.

Dressed in sombre colours, chiefly black, James walked the ramparts of the palace of the Popes, outpacing with his long strides the rest of his gentlemen, never talking and smiling little. Before Easter he had heard pretty well every Lenten sermon in the city, and they were many: he had walked in religious processions and attended Mass daily. He seemed to be immersed in solitary thought, and he gave the appearance of a man in

[1] HMC, Vol. 11, p. 89
[2] *ibid*, p. 165
[3] *ibid.*, p. 150

torment. His old governor, the Duke of Perth, died on 5 May 1716, and this added to his depression: the ranks of those who had known him in his childhood were beginning to thin.

All through April and May and for many months to come, the Jacobite refugees kept pouring in and, on 19 May, Mar wrote to Lieutenant-General Dillon, who was in Paris, that James was seeking help from Charles XII of Sweden in the hope that he might take some of them into his own army:

> They had no choice but to stay and be hanged or come over, and, now that they are come, have no other earthly resource to give them bread but the King who, as long as he has or can get it, cannot in honour see them starve, when they have so gallantly ventured and lost their all upon his account. They are unwilling to be a burden to him if they could help it, and as few will be so as possible; a great many of these are willing and desirous to serve anywhere in the wars till the King have occasion again for their services himself; some of them are men of estates and, though they be forfeited, have saved a little which may be some help to them; but this class is small, others are men of quality who had lived at their ease and too old to begin to be soldiers abroad so must fall on to the King for bread.[1]

With all this on his mind, with the knowledge that his mother was the only one whom he could trust implicitly, now that Berwick had deserted him, it was remarkable that his health should have withstood the strain, but, so far, it did. However, at twenty-eight, his inner fire and the natural gaiety which he had begun to find again over the years following the death of Louise Marie were rapidly being extinguished. It is not difficult to understand why. Born into a royal failure, he had spent all his life dreaming of the time when he would retrieve a crown; twice the occasion had arisen, and each time he had been betrayed by the ineptness of those around him. In his unhappy attempts to regain his own he had spilt the blood of hundreds of men from his Three Kingdoms, men of all ranks, high and low, and it was with these ghosts he was to live for the rest of his life. Small wonder then, that the English lampoonists, who had a field-day after the failure of the Fifteen, caricatured him as 'Old Mr Melancholy'. If he had been short, fat and fair he would not have earned such an epithet, but he was tall, slim and dark, dressed with a sombre elegance, and he was beginning to take on the strange Stuart charisma of solitude.

The Duke of Lorraine's regretful refusal to give him shelter again within his dominion had not prevented him from writing to him from Châlons on the way to Avignon:

[1] HMC, Vol. 11, p. 167

I should be the lowest of mankind if I cherished any other sentiments. . . . You know my heart and I know yours: I do justice to your feelings, as I trust that you do to mine. Excuse this little expression of my emotion, which I cannot resist. It will convince you that my gratitude and affection will never change with changes of time and place. Believe me, I hope sincerely that absence cannot undo our close friendship, which I trust may exist between us till the last moment of my life. . . . French regards for French interests does not allow me to remain long in France; my own regard for your interest prevents me from staying in Lorraine, and it has been decided that I shall go to Avignon to await replies from Sweden. . . . Our poor Scots have fled to the hills; it is a death by slow fire for them; God knows how they will exist or what conditions they will obtain in the end, being without all help or resources. I have sent two ships immediately to try to save some of them and to take them some powder which might be useful to them while they wait to come to terms, but I doubt very much that this small succour will reach them where they are at present.[1]

He was to send five ships in all.

There was one outcome of the defeat at Preston which had an especially sad significance for the King – the death of his childhood friend, the Earl of Derwentwater. Reports brought to James told how the tall young man, who was so near to him in age, family, religion and integrity, had been brought in a coach from the Tower of London to the Transport Office on Tower Hill. He was left to wait there a short time and then conducted through an avenue of soldiers to a black-draped scaffold which had been erected opposite the Office. He turned pale when he saw it, but soon regained his natural composure. Then he spent about a quarter of an hour in prayer and advanced to the edge of the scaffold where he read aloud, in a firm voice, a speech he had written with the permission of the Sheriff of London. First of all, he asked forgiveness of 'those I might have scandalized by pleading guilty at my trial', because, in doing so, he had tacitly admitted the authority of men who were judging him in the name of King George. He continued:

But I am sensible that in this I have made bold with my loyalty, having never any other but King James III for my rightful and lawful sovereign: him I had an inclination to serve from my infancy, and was moved thereto by a natural love I had to his person, knowing him to be capable of making his people happy. And though he had been of a different religion from mine, I should have done for him all that lay in my power, as my

[1] HMC, Vol. 11, p. 35

ancestors have done for his predecessors, being thereto bound by the laws of God and man.[1]

His friend and confessor, Father Pippard, gave him absolution, then he took off his black velvet hat with its long black feather, his fair periwig, his gold chain and crucifix and his black velvet coat and waistcoat and laid his head upon the block. He gave his executioner two golden guineas and begged his forgiveness, repeated a prayer calling upon the name of Jesus three times, and then his head was severed from his body at one stroke. Father Pippard said afterwards that the voice of the crowd was like the sigh of the sea.[2]

James concluded his letter to the Duke of Lorraine:

You will no doubt have been moved by the death of poor Lord Derwentwater, but his death has also been one of a true Christian hero. I have sent Mr O'Rourke his speech which it is worth having explained to you. This is very sad news but, alas, I have no other at present, and it is crushing to me who would have thought myself to some degree content if I were alone in my misfortune, but the death and misfortunes of others of which I am the innocent cause pierces my heart.[1]

[1] Jacobite Tract, Brit. Mus. C.115 a.3 (25)
[2] Gibson, *Dilston Hall,* p. 108
[3] HMC, Vol. 11, p. 35

Part Three

THE PALAZZO MUTI

Chapter Eighteen

The atmosphere at Avignon was one of perpetual turmoil, and the Jacobite court was the vortex. Soldiers in threadbare uniforms filled the streets of the town, as once they had in Saint-Germain, and rich and strange were the variations of the French tongue to be heard on all sides. Some stayed; others, after resting their weary bodies and tired minds in the ever-increasing warmth of the early Provencal summer, travelled on to foreign courts where they could earn their living by using their swords or their wits. The episcopal authorities of Avignon were concerned about the number of Protestants in the Jacobite ranks, and by the fact that James had provided two Protestant chaplains for his subjects: Doctor Charles Leslie and Ezekiel Hamilton. There was no Catholic chaplain for the very good reason that the papal city was full of clerics anyway. His Protestant subjects were constantly in James's mind, and this was apparent in his letter to Cardinal Imperiali of 12 May 1716:

> With regard to my residence, since His Holiness leave it to me to choose, I may say to you in confidence that Avignon is the only one of his states which is conducive to the well-being of my affairs, Rome and Italy being too far, and in no way suitable for the relations which I have to maintain with my Protestant subjects. Also is it not true that my enemies are seeking to force me to go there only because they regard that place as a certain means of ruining all hopes of my re-establishment?[1]

If he preferred Avignon for the conduct of his affairs, he did not feel settled there personally. In July he wrote: 'These southern climates agree less with my inclination than with my health which, I thank God, is very good.'[2] Gradually, he began to ease out of his melancholy, at least to outward appearances, and to take part in the social life of Avignon, which was dominated by the Salviatis, the family of the Vice-Legate. In the early mornings he would ride as he used to do in France, and perhaps later, when the great heat had subsided a little, he would drive about the countryside, on one occasion visiting Vaucluse, home of Petrarch and his Laura. For his delight a dispensation was given to an operatic company to visit the papal city of Avignon, and he attended assemblies, even dancing now and then.

But if his body was thus occupied, his mind was still revolving around

[1] HMC, Vol. 2, p. 147   [2] *ibid.*, p. 268. Letter to Lady Elizabeth Hatcher

more serious things. The greatest problem he still had to face was how to provide for the hundreds who had flocked to join him. Then there was the possibility of another attempt – when and how it should be made and how financed – and, lastly, an ever-present source of disquiet: the factions at court. The *immigrés* brought rumours with them: some ill-founded, others not so. And they also brought reports of how London was reacting to the aftermath of the Fifteen. There was an opinion that George had been too severe on the Scots, and that the Duke of Argyll's comparative leniency had resulted from his encounter with the funeral cortège of the Earl of Derwentwater. On 11 June 1716 (Old Style), one Hugh Thomas wrote from London to 'Thomas Bayard', the code-name for Lewis Innes, the Queen's almoner at Saint-Germain: 'The town is now become like a garrison; 3,000 foot guard it day and night, besides the horse dragoons. Three people were killed yesterday, being the Pretender's birthday, in the streets for wearing white roses, and a multitude sent to prison . . . and the whole nation through all the towns yesterday distinguished themselves with white roses, especially where they wore not dragooned.'[1] Young Lord Clerment, newly arrived from captivity, went so far as to say that nine out of ten Englishmen wanted James on the throne, and to make war with France. He maintained that, although the officers were Whigs, the men were Tories and would rush to join the King if he landed with eight thousand soldiers. James had heard this all before, and this time he was determined that he would not make any landing unless he was sufficiently backed by men and supplies. So he began to explore possibilities again with France, Spain and Sweden. Yet nothing was possible unless he could obtain some measure of unison among those nearest to him.

There were the old disagreements between the Irish and the Scots, and the Scots disagreed among themselves as to the real culprits of the failure of the Fifteen. The Duke of Mar was jealous of the Duke of Ormonde and the Earl Marischal. He said that the Earl was angling for the vacant Garter appointment caused by the death of the Duke of Perth, but in fact this was filled by the new Duke of Perth who, in turn, was dissatisfied with the green colour of the Order of the Thistle which was also his. The Earl Marischal was inclined to believe someone called Smith of Methven, who claimed that Mar had negotiated with Argyll to get better terms for himself before leaving Scotland. Strangely enough, Mar did not entirely deny being in contact with the Duke, but said that he had only tried to find out the extent of Argyll's authority. 'Bobbing John' Mar had odd ideas about the extent of loyalty to a cause. He was more concerned with trimming his sails to the prevailing wind than with formulating any plan of treachery: when he had

[1] HMC, Vol. 2, p. 227

failed with George of Hanover he had turned to the exiled King. At least he was open in his waverings with those principally involved, even if he seems to have been incredibly insensitive where his own reputation was concerned. When Colonel John Hay arrived in Avignon, he was another to swell the ranks of the anti-Mar faction.

Lord Galmoy was reported to be a traitor in a letter sent to James from a Mr Thomas Wescombe, although the King does not seem to have taken this very seriously. More to the point were the accusations against Lords Huntly and Seaforth, whose withdrawal from the campaign at a crucial time in order to safeguard their own interests had contributed not a little to its failure.

As the heat of summer progressed and the situation grew more tense, James became more restless. He knew that George was trying to put pressure on the Pope to get him out of Avignon by threatening to bombard the Papal territory of Civitavecchia. Because relations were strained between the Vatican and France, the Pope was less inclined to carry out hastily a request from an ally of France, as England now was, and he did not rush James's departure untowardly.

James knew that it could not last so for ever, and that sooner or later he would have to move on, but where was he to go? The very last place he wanted to be in was Rome, which would mean the end of his hopes where the Protestants were concerned. It was therefore all the more important that he should move as swiftly as possible in organizing another invasion. So he wrote to Charles XII of Sweden on 16 July 1716: '. . . the more I appear to be abandoned by the rest of Europe, the more confidence I have in the justice of my cause and in the heroic qualities which have led your Majesty to take the side that is unjustly oppressed . . .'[1]

Determined to leave no stone unturned, he reopened correspondence with the Earl of Oxford in England, and sent to find out how Marlborough's inclinations lay, but neither of these were of any use: it was about this time that Marlborough had suffered a stroke, and no definite reports as to his condition of health could be obtained.

He sent Colonel O'Rourke to Vienna to entreat the Emperor for the hand of his niece, the daughter of the Elector Palatine. On 10 June 1716 a name crept into the royal correspondence which was ultimately to have a sinister effect upon the latter Stuart fortunes, that of Major James Walkinshaw of Barrowfield. He was then at Sens and wanted to know what he should do. When he had been at Saint-Germain, 'I had not one groat in my pocket', but the Queen had given him 150 *livres* with which to buy clothes and food.[2] A month or two later he was also on his way to Vienna,

[1] HMC, Vol. 2, p. 283   [2] *ibid.*, p. 215

to find out for James what the internal political situation was there, and if it could be used to the advantage of the Jacobites.

Spain had been tried as a possible place of residence for James, but although Philip and his *éminence grise*, Cardinal Alberoni, were with him in spirit, they were not prepared to harbour him when such an action would of a certainty have plunged them into war with France while their economic situation was at its worst. For that reason, too, they could not do anything to ease James's financial state.

The Regent of France, the Duc d'Orléans, was also determined in no way to become involved again with the Stuarts. James knew only too well now that the days of the personal commitment of Louis XIV had long passed. Then, too, there had been a large consideration for France's interests, but Louis had at least done his best to reconcile the two. With the Regent, the Jacobites had no value whatsoever unless they were victorious or, at the least, could be used as an irritant. But while England and France were in the early stages of courting each other, James was an embarrassment for Orléans. In a letter to the Earl of Oxford in London, dated 21 September 1716, the Duke of Mar expressed himself very clearly about the Regent's methods:

> Mr Pink [the Regent] is a fellow that can keep nothing, so not to be trusted with this affair of Lambert's [Sweden's] . . . but, without letting him into it, I cannot but think that you may fall on ways to make him see what may certainly be his own personal interest as well as that of Monsr. Furbin's [France] if such an affair could be brought about. His joining in it, though it were only in his beloved sneaking, underhand way, would be of vast advantage, and make the game, I think, sure, which other ways he makes very hard and difficult more ways than one.[1]

To do them justice, it was not surprising that neither the Regent nor Philip of Spain should have much confidence in James's chances of success when it was so patent that he had no commander-in-chief to put into the field. Everyone had seen the extent of Ormonde's and Mar's abilities in this direction, and there was still no change in Berwick's position. By this time the Duke of Berwick was in his forty-fourth year and had made twenty-six campaigns, eleven of which he had commanded. Together with his uncle Marlborough and Prince Eugène, he could be said to rank among the greatest military geniuses of the century. He was on excellent terms with the Regent, who had got to know him well during the Spanish campaign of 1707, and when he sent him to take command in the province of Guienne in July 1716, the Regent wrote to him on his arrival in Bordeaux: 'Nothing

[1] HMC, Vol. 2, p. 464

is difficult in your hands, and I beg you always to count upon my friend-ship.'[1] Orléans said that he did not have much confidence in honest men but, if there were one completely honest man in the world, it was the Maréchal Berwick.[2]

Before leaving for Guienne, Berwick gave his son, Lord Tynmouth, all his possessions in Valencia, including the duchy of Liria, and sent him to Madrid to become a Spaniard. He was one of the few remaining personal and family ties James still had, and it was with a great degree of sadness that he heard of his departure about which, naturally, Berwick had not con-sulted him. But the young Duke of Liria loved his royal uncle and was anxious to remove any bad impression others might give of his leaving for Spain, so he wrote to ask for his consent when his marriage to the daughter of the Duke of Veragua was being arranged, and the King replied: 'A small ailment hinders me from telling you in my own hand how pleased I was to find by yours of 7 September that your marriage was at last concluded. . . . The cheerfulness with which you followed me to Scotland is what I shall never forget.'[3] The marriage negotiations had taken some time to conclude because, however justifiably proud Berwick might have been of his royal lineage, his position as Maréchal de France and his military background, the Duke of Veragua was even prouder of *his* family name, and had been wor-ried by the fact that Berwick himself was illegitimate.

The 'small ailment' to which James referred was, in fact, much more important than he made out, and, once again, it was to coincide with a period of decision, for negotiations were on foot for an agreement with Charles XII of Sweden who would provide sufficient troops – and these would be Protestant troops, moreover – to mount an invasion upon Britain. On 20 October, James was successfully operated for a *fistula in ano*. The operation, which he endured with immense fortitude, these being the days before anaesthetics, lasted five minutes and necessitated ten cuts of the knife and scissors made by the famous Parisian specialist Guérin who was sent by the Queen. Afterwards he remained calm and tranquil without any appearance of fever, although he was naturally very weak for a long time. The church bells of Avignon were muffled and he was allowed no visitors until well into the month of November. One good result of his illness was that it was impossible for the Pope to insist on his going elsewhere so, for the time being, the court rested at Avignon.

Although he was out of imminent danger with regard to his physical condition, his friends were always concerned with the possibility of

[1] Berwick, *op. cit.*, Vol. 2, pp. 280–2
[2] *ibid.*
[3] HMC, Vol. 2, p. 473

assassination. The King himself treated this possibility lightly and took no extra precautions in his walks and rides around Avignon before his operation. In the September of 1716 a certain Henry Douglas wrote to a lady at Saint-Germain:

> . . . I have learned today from a gentleman just landed from England as follows, which please acquaint her Majesty with. There are four villains, one Burell, a person of an ill aspect, about 5 ft 10 inches high of a sallow, muddy complexion; his comrade, one Harrison of a low stature, thin bodied, of a pale, melancholy complexion; and two others he cannot describe. The assassination is designed to be prosecuted with a bow and not fire-arms, the first person being an expert archer, if ever they have an opportunity for their treacherous designs. It will be attempted at night. The arrow is to be poisoned. . . .[1]

On 10 September, Archangel Graeme, a Scottish Capuchin, wrote to Mar from Calais (where he was keeping out a watchful eye during his religious peregrinations) that there were a number of new arrivals from across the Channel including the faithful Lord Wintoun, a Mr Wauchope, and also an English parson said to be a spy sent by Townshend, and who had formerly been at Saint-Germain. He continued:

> I am informed that John Mackintosh, the Brigadier's brother, keeps correspondence with Mistress Muchette, a whore in London, and acquaints her with every thing that passes at Avignon, though she has neither honour nor discretion sufficient to be entrusted with news of the least consequence. . . . If I be not very much mistaken, Douglas, who undertook to murder the King,[2] arrived here yesterday by the packet-boat, and went straight towards Paris. . . .[3]

Many of the *immigrés* were unused to the sophistication of large European cities and sometimes, in all innocence, let their tongues run away with them. Stair's men were everywhere waiting for any crumb of information which they could pick up with regard to the activities of the Pretender, as James was now known to all in Britain, except the Jacobites. This was the name which Anne had given to him in her dismissal of Parliament of 1708, the time of his first attempt at invasion.

Guérin, the surgeon, stayed with James until early January 1717 and, soon afterwards, the pressure on the King to leave Avignon was renewed. By this time he had learnt that the Elector Palatine preferred the Electoral Prince of Bavaria as a husband for his daughter, but the news does not seem

[1] HMC, p. 506   [2] See above, p. 266   [3] HMC, p. 448

to have surprised him overmuch. It took a great deal to surprise him now, in any case. He was thirty – just past his youth – and the whole of his life had been directed towards one objective, to take his rightful place on the British throne. He had made two attempts to do this, and had driven himself to the utmost to make both of them succeed: ill health, inclement weather and inept generals had all combined to make them fail. Berwick's defection, Bolingbroke's betrayal, conscious or unconscious as either, or both, might have been, had left him few illusions about human nature. More and more, he sought refuge in the Quietism which he had learnt from Fénélon, but, although this quality was an admirable one for a ruling monarch to possess, philosophical acceptance of the blows of fate was not a doctrine easily appreciated by Highlanders spoiling for a fight to place their king upon his throne.

It was about this time that Charles XII of Sweden had begun to show interest in the Jacobites again. The bishoprics of Verden and Bremen had been secularized and made over to Sweden in 1648 by the Treaty of Westphalia; in 1712 they had been conquered by Denmark and then sold by Denmark to Hanover for a large sum of money and a promise of support against Sweden. It was natural, therefore, that Charles should harbour a grudge against Hanover and be likely to throw in his lot with James. The matter was concerted between Baron Görtz, Swedish minister to the Hague, Baron Spaar, another minister, Count Gyllenborg, the Swedish ambassador in London, and General Dillon, James's representative at that time in Paris. For the supply of 12,000 foot and 2,000 horse, Gyllenborg and Spaar wanted one million *livres*, one half of the original sum asked. Charles himself was away in the north, fighting, as usual, for Sweden's existence, and it is doubtful whether he ever knew of the hard bargain struck by his ministers, who may well have been intent on feathering their own nests. Where James was to obtain the money was, of course, a major problem. General Dillon rose to a superb height of Celtic bluff. He obtained credit for the whole sum in Paris, and gave bills which were payable in twelve months. Dillon commanded his own regiment in the Regent's army, and was as much subjected to his authority as Berwick was. It was Orléans' wish that Arthur Dillon should go to James and personally escort him out of Avignon. The task was repugnant to the bluff Irish Jacobite, and he employed all his powers of persuasion to make Orléans see that his arrears of pay were made up as a recompense. Altogether he was paid 180,000 *livres* and this was sent immediately to Stockholm, and also used to buy six ships in France to be sent to Sweden. When the money was received in Stockholm, the bills were paid up in Paris and Dillon had momentarily saved the day. Shortly after this, Spain annexed Sardinia; the Triple Alliance of England, Austria and the United Provinces objected, as did France, and the result was that Spain declared itself with King James, Cardinal Alberoni sending him a million *livres* which could not have arrived at a more opportune moment.

In days of rain and snow James left Avignon. Never once did he have the benefice of good weather for any of his departures. It was 6 February when he set out to cross the Alps with his baggage carried in small handcarts covered with waxed cloths. Most of the court, which numbered about seventy now, went by sea, but James himself had no desire for this method of transport, preferring the hazards of snowstorms in the mountains. His mother wrote him many letters along the way and before he left Avignon he received from her a lock of his sister's hair and the last ring which remained to her, the diamond of her marriage.

Accompanied by the Dukes of Mar and Ormonde, he set out from Avignon *incognito*, as the Marquis de Cavallone. The horses, handcarts and carriages slipping and sliding on the snow, they crossed Mont Cenis and dropped down to Turin. Before they reached Turin, Mar left them to return to Saint-Germain to see the Queen and to rejoin his wife who had recently arrived from England.

Turin was the chief city of the Duchy of Piedmont and Savoy, and its Duchess was the daughter of his aunt, Henrietta, the ill-starred *Madame* of France. The Duchess's husband, Victor Amadeus, was also King of Sicily, which he was shortly to exchange for Sardinia, and if James had died without issue she would have been the nearest *de jure* claimant to the British throne. They welcomed him with a certain amount of ceremony, but not too much, and privately, for they, in common with most of Europe, did not want to antagonize England; even so, the British envoy was somewhat disgruntled by the reception they did give him. James realized, quickly enough, that his being there in their city was only a source of embarrassment to them, so he stayed only a few hours. It was the first time he had suffered this form of humiliation in person; in Lorraine he had had time to get used to the idea that the Duke and his son had needed to sacrifice their personal feelings to the good of their dominions, and the letters[1] passed between them revealed the understanding which existed; but the sheer expediency of the attitude of these, his near relations, seemed unusually callous.

He travelled on, as the spring began gradually to make its presence felt, through Piacenza and Parma where the duke afforded him a most royal welcome, to the court of his mother's uncle, Rinaldo, Duke of Modena. Ever since his infancy, he had heard about the beauties of Modena and the delights of the court where Queen Mary Beatrice had spent her first sixteen years. He arrived on Friday, 12 March, and went straight to the ducal palace

[1] See p. 213

where the Duke and his two sons received him in the courtyard with every mark of warm friendliness. James took to the Duke on sight and, unusually for him, talked so openly and easily that in half an hour they were as good friends as if they had known one another a lifetime. It must have been a relief for him to feel that he was on real family ground at last: his likeness to this family, as well as to Charles II of England, was remarked upon, and in the three motherless daughters of the Duke (who were looked after by their grandmother, the Duchess of Brunswick) he saw much to remind him of his mother. The two elder girls, particularly, were beautiful, and all three were dark, tall and with good figures, and well educated.

He loved Modena; with its beautiful buildings, its art treasures and its library, it was one of the most civilized cities in Europe and, probably for the first time, James felt that he was just as much Italian as English. And, also for the first time, he really fell in love. Against the background of a north Italian spring, in May when, with the slightest effort in the world, every sky, every hillside, every cypress looked as if it had been painted by Botticelli, James fell in love with his cousin Benedicta, the eldest of the three Princesses. Apart from the youthful yearning after 'Mademoiselle de C.'[1] of ten years before, he had never lost his heart. In a period when attachments, romantic or otherwise, were lightly regarded in the artificial society of a court, it is remarkable that even James's enemies never tried to attack him on these grounds. His father's warning, his happy family life with his mother and sister, his particular station in life which he regarded as God-given, together with the fact that most of his adult working life had been spent in the company of diplomatists and soldiers, all combined to make him a 'man's man'. The court at Saint-Germain was not the same as that of Versailles, and that of Avignon was even less so. These were not places for silken dalliance, but down-to-earth quarters for people who had suffered much, often losing kith and kin as well as their material well-being in their attempt to put the Stuarts back on the throne. Their wives and daughters were busier repairing well-worn clothes than losing their virtue. James respected all these people as individuals, and knew only too well the debt which he could never repay to them unless he came into his own. He liked women, except for the gossiping clique which congregated at Mademoiselle de Chausseraye's, and he was always courteous to them, but he had never wanted to become involved. Marriage was another thing: it was necessary because he had to have an heir, but he would have to be very fortunate in-deed to fall wildly in love with the person he was to marry.

But he did fall wildly in love with Benedicta, and lost no time in proposing marriage to her; how much her resemblance to his mother

[1] See p. 89

counted in his devotion to her is a matter for conjecture. Apart from his feelings for the Princess, it would also have been a most suitable marriage; the family was respected, well-to-do and Catholic.

Duke Rinaldo was puzzled by the whole thing and gratified, but he refused to be rushed, and said that he needed a little time to think it over. James lost no time in informing his mother and the Pope, both of whom were delighted. Clement XI offered to perform the marriage ceremony himself when a date was decided upon. Duke Rinaldo did not invite him to stay permanently in Modena, which would have been a solution to the question of his place of residence; so James, full of love and hope, travelled on to the Papal States via Bologna, where he stayed for two days, at the Palazze Belloni, the residence of a rich banker.

The town was illuminated in his honour, and he received visits from the Archbishop of Bologna and a number of its nobility. All the time he was in Modena and while he was travelling, he had the Swedish affair in his mind, and, on reaching Pesaro, a pleasant, small seaport backed by gently rising hills, he settled down to work again. He liked the town, which had been built principally during the Renaissance by the Sforzas and the dukes of Urbino. Walking by the seashore he relaxed in the early spring sun and spent the evenings quietly 'sitting by the chimney side'.[1] He had arrived at Pesaro on 20 May 1717, and on 26 May he heard of the collapse of the negotiations with Sweden. Correspondence between Spaar in the Netherlands and Gyllenborg in London had been intercepted by George's men, in spite of the immunity of the diplomatic bag: all the plans for invasion were now revealed. Görtz was arrested in the Netherlands, and a number of the 'well-intentioned' were taken up in London, including Lord Lansdowne. Strangely enough, none of the sentences were too severe, and most were set free before long. One, a brother of Colonel John Hay, was sentenced to death, but managed to escape without undue difficulty. After the reactions following Preston, George may well have considered it the better part of discretion not to antagonize the people any more by cruel sentences.

This time something in James seemed to break. There had been one disappointment after another, and it seemed that everything he attempted to achieve crumbled into dust before he could reach it. Nothing poor Ormonde was able to say could touch him, and his health, which had been on the mend, began to falter again. Ormonde suggested that perhaps the time had come for him to go on to Rome, and James was in such a state of despondency that he did not care where he went. The Duke himself did not go, perhaps because he was a Protestant, but returned to be with the Duke of Mar in Paris. Some of James's other Protestant followers preferred to return

[1] Carte CCXVII, 180, p. 341

to Paris or Saint-Germain rather than to travel on to the Papal city. But if some returned, others such as Lords Southesk and Panmure rejoined him in Rome and Lords Nithsdale and Kilsyth were waiting for him there when he arrived on 26 May. He stayed with Cardinal Gualterio, the Protector of England, in his palace near the Lateran, and the Cardinal came to meet him in two coaches, with six horses to each coach and all the pomp and panoply of a prince of the Church. Shortly afterwards Gualterio became Secretary for a newly formed office dealing with missionary countries, but he always remained closely attached to the King's cause.

The thought of Benedicta, the company of old friends and companions, and the warm hospitality of the Romans conspired to raise his spirits, and he showed his gratitude for all that was being done for him in the Holy City. He visited the English and the Scots Colleges in Rome and received their clergy: he attended receptions and other social functions and appreciated the illuminations at night. On 20 June he spent his twenty-ninth birthday in Rome with pomp and great circumstance, and he visited Tivoli with its fountains.

Neither Clement XI nor Cardinal Gualterio felt that James should remain too long in Rome at the cost of reduced Protestant support, so the Pope suggested that, for the time being at least, he should reside in the fifteenth-century palace of Urbino, once the home of the *condottiere* prince, Federigo da Montefeltro, now a papal possession. On 3 July 1717 King James set out once again on his travels.

Chapter Nineteen

In one of the two three-horsed carriages winding their way up the precipitous path leading to the palace of Urbino there sat King James with Colonel John Hay; in the other Charles Booth swayed and bumped along with the royal doctor, Mr St Paul, and the King's valets. The hill they were so laboriously climbing was nearly 1,500 feet above sea-level, and on its summit the cliff-like walls of the palace sheered into the air until its twin pinnacles seemed to pierce the sky.

As soon as they entered the gates of the town and drove through the narrow, crooked streets, they were able to see that the palace dominated all else: it was grotesquely, yet superbly out of proportion to the little town at its feet, and far more in harmony with the Appenine peaks which formed its background. The atmosphere of timelessness, of being isolated in centuries past, which prevailed over the whole town was most concentrated in the tiny *piazza*; this seemed to be but a threshold to the palace gateway and to the Gothic church of San Domenico which faced it. They alighted and passed through to the inner courtyard where all was quiet and all was calm. Even at a first glance, there was a mathematical perfection to be discovered in the Corinthian columns lining the sides of the square; above them, and of equal height, rose slender pilasters and arched windows.

The Renaissance beauty of the interior matched the outside: the rooms were large but perfectly proportioned, light and airy. One of the most outstanding features of the whole building was the exquisite detail of its doorways: they were of sculptured marble and the doors themselves masterpieces of *intarsia*, the different-coloured woods forming *trompe-l'oeil* pictures of still-life, war-trophies, and subjects related to science and literature. There were two chapels, one to the glory of God, and the other to the glory of the Muses; the former was built entirely in sculptured marble. The library, which had been so dear to the heart of Duke Federigo, was one of the finest in Europe for size and content. This was a palace for people with peaceful minds, who loved beauty and quiet days spent in cool, airy rooms away from the glare of the summer sun. To anyone ill or depressed, or dependent upon regular outdoor exercise, it was a beautiful prison.

The Pope, thoughtful as ever for the King's personal well-being, had sent ahead Salviati, the Vice-Legate of Avignon, and a friend of James, to be the Governor of Urbino. Another more positive mark of his generosity was

228

a pension of 12,000 *scudi* a year which, although for James personally was, divided among the needy of the court. They were now about fifty or so, which was by no means too great a number to occupy the empty spaces of the great palace.

Now that the Swedish plan had failed, the matter foremost in his mind was whether or not Duke Rinaldo was going to accept him as a son-in-law. His closest intimates knew how much his heart was involved, and Mar wrote to Dillon on 26 July 1717:

> Since ever I heard the account he gave of that lady, I have always thought that she had made an impression on him, and now I find it was true and I wish him with all my heart good success in it. I am so pleased with his having resolved to marry anybody that I am almost blind to any bad consequence it can possibly have, and the character this lady has is so good, besides her being so well born, that I hope it will have none, but on the contrary be what all concerned in him will be pleased with and reap all the advantages that could be expected from any.[1]

He wrote to the King himself on 13 August and advised him not to be 'too hasty in taking a refusal', and added, 'I imagine that Patrick [the King] is a good deal possessed of an inclination for Mrs Masters [Princess Benedicta] which, joined to the good character I hear of her, makes me wish the success of this affair so earnestly, and heaven prosper it.'[2]

Worn out by waiting, James became despairing, restless and depressed. He could not follow his usual distractions of long hours of riding and hunting, since he was not yet fully recovered from the effects of his illness and also, what was much more significant, it was impossible to ride around Urbino unless one used a mountain goat to leap from crag to crag.

At last, on 30 August, the Duke of Modena addressed his reply to the King's request for his daughter's hand, and it was an unequivocal 'No'. He sent a canon of the Church with his letter, and to him James made a verbal reply to be transmitted to the Duke. He made a copy of what was said, and entered it in his records for 12 September: 'Finding myself now free of any commitment by the brief, significant and positive reply of my uncle, I have nothing more to add, unless it is to hope that he never has reason to repent of such conduct which is far removed from the frank and sincere manner which I have employed towards him since the very beginning of the affair in question.'[3]

The Duke of Modena had joined the ever-increasing company of European rulers who decided to play for safety rather than risk offending the Emperor and England by sponsoring James in any way. The King had

[1] HMC, Vol. 4, p. 468   [2] *ibid.*, p. 516   [3] *ibid.*, pp. 457–8

grown accustomed to refusals of military aid for a reason, but this was different. It affected him most personally, and very deeply, yet pride and his own private philosophy prevented him from taking Mar's advice: pride because, since he was a king, he could not plead; philosophy in so far that this was another blow from fate which he had to learn to accept and to bear.

More and more he continued to chafe at the natural restrictions of Urbino and he felt deserted and cut off from the rest of the world. There was a similarity between the situation of the palace and the château at Saint-Germain: both had a panoramic view, but no mountains lay behind the château, and at Urbino there were no woods where he could ride all day when he wished to. He did his best to live with this too, and began to find a solace in music, for which he had always had an inclination. In that November, Mar, who had rejoined the court, wrote to his friend Dillon in Paris:

> Amongst other things that I am glad to find in our master, he begins to be a convert as to this country music, and I am sure it will grow upon him. I brought some music with me from Venice and Bologna, and there [are] some pretty good voices and instruments here so I hope we shall make a shift to amuse ourselves with it, till better days come. The house is an excellent one, but for the part of the country it stands in there are few places of the Highlands of Scotland that are not champaign level countries in respect of it. The K[ing] goes a promenading for about half a mile or so, but it is on the tops and ridges of hills from one to another, in which I see very little pleasure, and that walking about the large rooms and galleries of the house is a much more agreeable exercise. The air, I believe is good, but we shall certainly grow very dull and insipid for want of a little good wines to enliven us, and give a fillip to our spirits now and then.[1]

It seems that the King was not the only man in Urbino to feel depressed from time to time. Mar enlarged upon his own attitude to the place and the consolations of making music among themselves in a letter addressed to Sir John Erskine:

> Our distress here is cruel, and the place of the country we are in is a damned one. We have more snow than is, I am sure, in Lochaber or Badenoch, and nothing but hills, not so much as the least valley near us, so that our promenade before the snow was on roads cut out on the sides of one hill to the top of another where there is nothing to be seen but hills on three sides and hills on the fourth quite to the sea. We have a fine

[1] HMC, Vol. 5, p. 239

house indeed, where you would be surprised to see so much music, and so little drink that can make one merry, the old stock of that is out and the new not come. . . . I have music in my rooms thrice a week, a voice thoroughly good, an excellent violin, one that plays well on the harpsichord and sometimes Painter [Lord Panmure?] plays on the bass fiddle and Mitchell's [Earl Marischal] Jack on the flute. The King looks in often when they are at it, and is really come to like it, which is a pleasure to me. I know it will be no small one to you. Perhaps you will think it dear of the postage, but here I send you an air which is a mighty favourite of his. . . . We have much less company here than at Avignon, but full as good agreement which is some amends. . . . In the meantime, for want of wine etc., I should die of the spleen, were it not for building castles in the air of several kinds, for which I have more time than formerly, the post being but once a week.[1]

John Mar's ebullience and eternal optimism kept him going in a situation which was taking its toll of more introverted characters.

Autumn turned into winter, and the snow came down; the novelty which it first brought with it soon changed into a deadly monotony, isolating their minds as well as their bodies from the outside world. Now they were confined entirely to the palace, and this was a debilitating experience to those, especially the Scottish gentlemen, who had been used in other days to spending the greater part of their time in open-air pursuits. If Mar was not good as a general in warfare, nevertheless he was proving his worth as a social organizer and, in all fairness, it has to be admitted that he probably did much to keep a number of the unfortunate exiles from giving way entirely to their depression. He also did his best to keep them warm, which was no mean achievement in a building of that style and proportion:

'We have been busy these two or three days about shuttlecocks or cleckings to give us some exercise but, now they are made, we have nothing but tennis rackets and battledoors to play with. Could you not send us some shuttlecocks and light rackets, which would be a great present. Clephan wrote to you or the Earl for some drawing materials which I hope you'll send.'[2]

Lack of warmth was one of the things which contributed most to the misery of the Jacobites, living like caged birds in that huge palace suspended, as it seemed, in the cold air. James was probably grateful that his study, which had been the study of Federigo himself, was one of the smallest rooms in the palace, for he spent most of his time there. It was also one

[1] HMC, Vol. 5, pp. 367–9
[2] *ibid.*, p. 382. To Col. Stuart of Inverrity, possibly at Rome.

of the most famed studies in Europe, decorated in marquetry of coloured woods with *trompe-l'oeil* allegories, architectural perspectives, and still-life of books, hour-glasses and other subjects of literature, art and science. If he let his gaze wander to the upper part of the walls, he could see twenty-eight portraits of philosophers, poets and theologians such as Dante, Ptolemy Thomas Aquinus and Pope Sixtus IV, all serving for inspiration.

As the year wore on he had returned to positive thinking. Putting all thought of Benedicta behind him, he decided to concentrate on marriage purely from a dynastic viewpoint. There were two other matters which occupied his mind: the trouble over Spain's arbitrary annexation of Sardinia, which had aligned France with England, Austria and the United Provinces against her; and the uneasiness between the Catholics and the Protestants at Saint-Germain. He felt that his mother, her almoner, Lewis Innes, and General Dillon, his agent in Paris, were not as tolerant towards the Protestant Jacobites as they should have been. He wrote to Père Honoré Gaillard, a friend of the Queen Mother, on 28 February 1718:

Alas! all Catholics are not saints, and there are only too many among them who have still more ambition than true zeal. With such people the solid foundations of religion is little regarded; and when they think of this situation in which it has pleased Providence to put me, of the necessity under which I lie of living among Protestants, of the necessity under which I shall lie of giving them preference in posts, honours, etc., and of the little part they themselves will have in business, this great resemblance to the primitive church is unbearable to those who lack its true spirit. . . . Who does not know the prudence and even charity with which the Protestants here behave towards the Catholics? Who does not know that there is no longer any question of my personal religion? . . . I am a Catholic, but I am a king, but as the Pope himself has said to me, I am not an apostle, I am not obliged to convert my subjects except by my example, nor to show an obvious partiality for the Catholics which would only injure them effectually in the long run.[1]

This statement, which was not meant for publication even, encapsulated all James's intense desire for toleration for the Protestants. It was not merely a matter of expediency, but was sincerely felt by a man whose temperament led him more to moderation than to violence in all things.

To everyone's surprise, his health held good, and he was determined to keep it so, for his one desire was to try to mount another expedition at the earliest possible moment. Mar wrote to a certain Monsieur Stiernhock in

[1] HMC, Vol. 5, p. 513

February 1718: 'We are in a country that I cannot say is a good one, and the winter is severe enough to try the hardest constitution, and his Majesty walks abroad every day in the cold and snow, while others of us are glad to keep indoors.'[1]

But he was restless; the religious trouble at Saint-Germain had produced a coolness between the Queen and himself at a time when he knew that she was a very sick woman and the distance between them was as great as if it had been half-way around the world. Only a personal *rapprochement* could have helped now, but that was not to be. He wrote to the Prince de Vaudémont in February of that year:

> With regard to politics what can I tell you from this remoteness? You are in the land of the living, and I am here in a desert, among mountains covered in snow, where we only know what is happening in your country a long time afterwards, when things have often changed before we know the situation they were in when the letters were despatched. As to the rest, my hopes are well-founded, my effort is constant, and the darkness permanent, with the certainty of incertitude about everything concerning me, and with a boredom which is only too reasonable in a remoteness I shall do my best to end at the earliest possible moment and yet, in spite of everything, my health, thank God, has never been better and helps me to banish any despondency. We have almost no company here, nor amusement, apart from a little Italian music that I begin to acquire a taste for, and the snows hold us virtually prisoners in the palace, which is one of the most comfortable and most magnificent that you could see, being perched on a high mountain, the summit of which is scarcely large enough to hold the building, shored up as it is in one place by vaults to stop the earth from crumbling.[2]

In addition to the coolness between the King and his mother, there had also been slightly strained relations between the Pope and himself. There had been rumours in the autumn of 1717 that the Earl of Peterborough had set out from London with the intention of killing James. The ubiquitous Douglas was also reported to have been seen again on the road to Italy. No one saw any more of him, but Peterborough's movements were closely watched by the agents reporting to the Pope and Cardinal Gualterio, both of whom begged James to be on his guard. James said that he did not think Peterborough capable of being such a villain, and refused to take the matter seriously, to the dismay of Gualterio and annoyance of Clement. Seeing that if he did not do something, Peterborough would be in grave trouble as soon

[1] HMC, Vol. 5, p. 489   [2] *ibid.*, p. 484

as he reached the Papal States, James asked Cardinal Origo, Archbishop of Bologna to have the Earl arrested and his papers examined, but he was to be subjected to no ill-treatment or lack of respect. He then forestalled the Pope's intention of examining Peterborough by telling Origo to send the gentleman to him. This again annoyed Clement. When James, after talking freely and in private with Peterborough, declared that he could find no intention of malice in him, he demanded that he should be released, Clement thought that matters had gone far enough, and warned James that his sojourn in papal territory depended upon his good conduct there. But, as it happened, George of England played right into James's hands for once, by threatening to send a naval expedition to the Mediterranean in retaliation for the humiliation done to a peer of his realm. With the fear once more in his mind of Civitavecchia being bombarded, Clement's wrath subsided, and the Queen Mother appealed to the Regent who, in turn, used his good offices with George, and no more was heard of the affair.

While all this was going on, James had been more interested in the visit to the palace of the Italian antiquary and astronomer, Bianchini. He had read his books and wanted to meet the man himself. They had watched the eclipse of 20 September 1717 together, and Bianchini paid another visit to the King a little later; this time he brought greetings from the Pope, together with a considerate enquiry as to whether James's wants were entirely fulfilled at the palace. All that James wanted was a clock with bells, which would tell the time in English fashion and not in the twenty-four-hour European way. His court apparently did not understand the latter method, and was continually unpunctual. He watched another eclipse in the autumn of the following year: his was the interest of an educated layman of his time, no more, no less.

Ormonde had returned with Mar to the King in October 1717 and, although Stair reported that Mar had called and talked of general matters at the English embassy on the way, there was no indication that Ormonde had ever thought of assuring his possible future in the same way. Whether James had any suspicions of Mar's activities is unknown, but he had absolute confidence in Ormonde. So much so that he entrusted him with a very special mission.

Consolidating their allies, the British had bought off the Emperor Charles VI with a secret subsidy in 1718, and this now meant that there was a Quadruple Alliance in Europe, made up of England, France, Austria and the United Provinces. This could stand against Spain or any other power likely to support King James. It also meant that he could not hope to raise men or arms in the Austrian Netherlands. Although the negotiations with Charles XII of Sweden had collapsed, a wild hope was suddenly born of what seemed to be a well-founded rumour that the two erstwhile enemies, Sweden and Russia, would be likely to unite in order to overthrow the Quadruple Alliance, and that they also would be willing to promote James's cause as an irritant against England. Ormonde was sent to sound out Tsar Peter as to the possibilities of this scheme, and at the same time to see what his master's chances would be of marrying either the Tsar's daughter or his niece. Ormonde was accompanied by Colonel O'Brien, Lord Buchan, Mr Jerningham and Mr Charles Wogan, one of the young veterans of Preston. The negotiations, or preparations for negotiation, between Sweden and Russia dragged on with little effect – and in effect came to nothing when Charles XII was killed at the siege of Friederichshall in December 1718. The marriage project dwindled when the Tsar decided that he would need a surer *parti* for his daughter than a king as yet without a country; his niece, the Princess of Courland, was illegitimate, and therefore could not be considered as a candidate for the furtherance of the British royal line.

In the meantime, James had managed to rid himself very diplomatically of General Dillon's services as his agent in Paris. Dillon boasted that the Regent had offered to send him at the head of a military contingent to Italy. James said that he thought it was a very good thing for Dillon, although he would regret the loss of his services; however, Dillon was not to worry because he had already sent a Mr James Murray of Stormont to take his place in Paris. Murray was to travel a good deal between Paris and Urbino during the next twelve months, but he was only holding the post in Paris until Colonel O'Brien should take it over permanently. This was the beginning of a trust which the King placed in Murray to the detriment of a peaceful atmosphere in his court.

Murray was two years younger than the King, and the second of the fourteen children of Lord Stormont. He had become a barrister at the age of twenty but never practised, had had the beginnings of a political career under Queen Anne, was disappointed when he failed in re-election as an M.P., and went to France where he became secretary to Bolingbroke and first came within the King's orbit. He was an ambitious young man, vain and pretentious, and with a rare gift for upsetting people: he seemed to have a monumental lack of tact. James had a strange failing, inherited from his forebears – he was incapable of choosing wise or helpful advisers and more than once he placed his trust where it was lightly valued. Against this, one can only say that once he discovered anyone who betrayed that trust, or failed him in any other way, he lost no time in getting rid of them from key posts, as he had in the cases of Bolingbroke and Dillon. Murray was strongly anti-Mar, and when he found himself within the King's inner circle he began to do his best to oust Mar; and this was made all the easier by the

Chapter Twenty

If the location of Urbino had not been so isolated, the Duke of Mar would probably have been happier there than in Paris or Saint-Germain: he had just enough responsibility but not too much, the King was there to take the major decisions, and it was a pleasant enough society to be in. So far, he had no inkling of Murray's attitude towards himself, and it was with a certain air of a trusted servant doing his duty well, and knowing that he was doing it well, that he wrote to Thomas Forster's former *aide-de-camp*, Charles Wogan. Captain Wogan was barely twenty-one, but he had seen action at Preston and was one of those who had escaped from Newgate in 1716. He had made his way by stages to Avignon, where he had met the King, and a mutual liking had been engendered. After that, he had joined Dillon's Regiment (attached to the Regent's army) in which his uncle, Colonel Richard Gaydon, also served. They were then stationed at Sélestat.

Mar's letter told the young Irishman that the King had a very high opinion of him, and that he wanted to employ him in an affair which needed the utmost discretion, secrecy and good conduct, as well as zeal and diligence. He continued:

> You will be very glad he thinks now very seriously of setting about what all who wish him well so much desire, marriage. There are amongst others two princesses proposed to him; one, the Princess of Baden Baden, the late King Lewis's daughter, the other a Princess of Saxe, cousin to the King of Poland. It is reasonable he should be well informed of their persons, etc. by one he can trust, before he make any advances towards any of them, and you are the person he has pitched upon for going to see them and giving that information.
>
> If any other Courts fall in your way through Germany, where there are princesses, it will not be amiss that you endeavour to see them and inform yourself about them, for there are many in that country, and in some of them there may be princesses as fine women as any of the two we have been informed of.[1]

On James's instructions, Mar added a postscript: 'Prince James Sobieski, son to the late King of Poland, has several daughters, who, I believe, are

[1] HMC, Vol. 5, pp. 234–5

somewhere in Germany. You may inquire about them and endeavour to see them all, if they fall in your way or be not much out of it.'

None of the ladies mentioned in the body of the letter came up to Wogan's idea of what the King's wife ought to be. He travelled on through West-phalia, Swabia and Bavaria, with no result. Then he came to Ohlau in Silesia, saw, met and approved of Prince James Sobieski's youngest daughter, and returned triumphantly to Urbino. James wrote to Ormonde, who was still engaged on the Russian mission, that he had seen Wogan who had 'performed his part very well'.[1] But it was not Wogan who was chosen to carry the King's request for his daughter's hand to Prince James Sobieski. Several of the King's advisers, including Mar, were of the opinion that to send an Irish Catholic on so important a matter might damage James's standing with the Protestants in Britain. So James Murray of Stormont was sent instead, to Wogan's fury. Murray received his instruc-tions on 24 June, and set out for Ohlau shortly afterwards with a letter written in French for Prince James. It read as follows: 'Monsieur Murray, gentleman of quality from Scotland, who will give you this, is empowered in my name, Monsieur, to ask in marriage the Princess Clementina, your daughter, being furnished in this respect with my full authority in order to bring to a happy and prompt conclusion that which I so ardently desire.'[2]

More than ever, James needed someone close to him, for the Queen Mother had died from cancer in May 1718. Mary Beatrice of Modena had been one of the greatest and certainly the most consistent influence in James's life: some said that her influence had been too great. There is no denying that while she was regent during her son's minority she was the person to have the most influence on the young king; this was natural in the case of a widowed mother with an only son. But her influence was balanced by the very strong presence of Louis XIV. During the King's adult life, no one ever made him do anything against his own inclination, and it was this factor which accounted for the difference between the Queen Mother and himself in 1717, made all the more tragic by its occurring so near to the end of the Queen's life. Almost to the very last days she acted as his repre-sentative to the court of France and, although she had been in pain for a number of years past, she had never complained about the many demands made upon her. Hers was the last disinterested love which James was to know, and there was never anyone who was to possess such a large part of his affections again. Proscribed from travelling outside the Papal dominions, he had to rely entirely on the post for news of the Queen's health and, as he had already pointed out to the Prince de Vaudémont, news reached him

[1] HMC, Vol. 6, p. 233
[2] Lubomirski, *Lettres et Mémoire*, No. 1, p. 1

long after the event was past. It was nearly one month after Mary Beatrice had died that he received the news and her papers, which he opened in the presence of Lord Middleton, her grand chamberlain, Dominic Sheldon, her vice-chamberlain, Mr Dicconson, her treasurer, and General Sir Arthur Dillon. It was well known that Lord Stair's spies had been briefed to get those papers, as her correspondence with James would have proved invaluable for the British government. As it was, they had managed to obtain access to her rooms at Saint-Germain while she was dying, but there does not seem to be any proof that the papers had been tampered with. Pope Clement, who seems to have been another kind of father-figure for James (though not wielding the same influence as Louis XIV had done) prevailed upon the French Regent to continue the Queen Mother's pension to the King, and James was assured that, although France was bound by the Treaty of Utrecht to forgo the Stuarts publicly, he would always have the sympathy of France. That sympathy was shortly to be stretched to the utmost.

The whole of Europe seemed to be in a ferment of suspicion that summer, and with cause. The basis of most of the trouble was Spain's greed and the necessity felt by her Queen, Elizabeth Farnese, to provide her sons with possessions abroad. It was by her inspiration that Spain first laid covetous hands upon Sardinia. The Spanish landed in Sicily in 1718, and it was known that Naples and Sardinia also looked attractive to Queen Elizabeth. Any accumulation of power by Spain was regarded with the highest disapproval by England, as it always had been in the past, and this time England was allied to France, the Holy Roman Empire and the United Provinces of the Netherlands.

The British fleet, commanded by Admiral Byng, had been sailing the Mediterranean since June that summer, and immediately after Spain's successful landing in Sicily, war was declared between Britain and Spain. Alberoni, who was the power behind the Spanish throne and who partly owed his cardinal's hat to James's mediation with Clement XI, recognized (as others had done before him,) the irritant value of the Jacobite cause, and decided that Spain would help to promote an invasion on James's behalf. Allied to this reason was also the thought that if England had a Catholic monarch it would, sooner or later, return to the Mother Church; Alberoni seems to have taken little account of James's own intention of a tolerant monarchy.

So Ormonde was recalled from his mission to Russia and sent to consult with Alberoni in Madrid, together with the Earl Marischal and his brother, James Keith. The Cardinal had already sent Sir Patrick Lawless, an Irishman in the Spanish service, to Charles XII of Sweden to try to ensure his co-operation but, as usual, Charles at that point was too involved with his own affairs to be in any way operational with regard to those of James.

Two simultaneous landings were to be made: one in England, under Ormonde's command; the other in Scotland, under the Keiths. Ormonde was to have between 4,000 and 5,000 men (which was just over half of what he thought necessary), 1,000 foot soldiers and 1,000 horse soldiers with 300 mounts, the rest of the mounts to be furnished locally, ten cannon and arms for 15,000 foot. Marischal was to have six companies of Spanish soldiers and 2,000 pieces of arms. There were to be ten men-o'-war and nineteen frigates to convey Ormonde's expedition to England from Corunna and three frigates to carry the Earl Marischal to Scotland from San Sebastian. The King was to travel with Ormonde.

Shortly after learning of his mother's death, James had fallen ill again with the quartan ague, and this time it was a very severe attack which left him considerably weakened. Summer had made little difference to his dislike for Urbino, but it would probably have been the same in any place where he was force to live by the will of others. He had never known a home of his own choosing; he had grown up from an infant to a young man in Saint-Germain but, once past childhood, he realized that this shelter depended upon the friendliness and generosity of Louis XIV; and the home that was rightly his he was unlikely to see again without his creating a major upheaval among the states of Europe.

He asked the Pope to allow him to reside elsewhere than Urbino before the coming winter and suggested Castelgandolfo, which was the Pope's summer residence, or Viterbo. This considerably ruffled Clement: he had no intention of giving up Castelgandolfo, and it was really overoptimistic on James's part to imagine that he should, or would. Viterbo, said the Pope, was too dangerous – there were too many spies in that area – and he assured James that cool heights of Urbino would be much more comfortable than anywhere on the plain, where the heat was apt to become intolerable; why did he not try Pesaro? Cardinal Gualterio, who was acting for James in this argument, said that James had tried Pesaro, and it did not suit him. The Pope said that Castelgandolfo was damp, and made some more suggestions: what about Albano, Perugia or Foligno? But only Castelgandolfo would do for the King. By now Clement was so angry that Gualterio thought it only wise to warn James that he might alieniate the Pope altogether. This does not seem to have disturbed the King at all, and he continued to ask for Castelgandolfo for his future residence. Perhaps only Booth would have known how to deal with James in this mood, for the King was exhibiting all the 'bloody-mindedness' of his father and was being quite unreasonable. In the end the Pope, like a fond parent brought to the point of exasperation, agreed, but stipulated that James must never expect to occupy Castel-gandolfo before mid-November, thereby ensuring that he would be certain of his usual papal vacation.[1]

In the meantime, confined to Urbino, James decided to write to Clementina, now that Murray would have delivered his letter to her father. His first letter to her read:

After having asked for your hand in marriage from the Prince, your father, and the Princess, your mother, I thought it suitable that I should address myself to you, Madam; that I may have the pleasure of owing to yourself, as I do to them, the happiness that I hope for from your individual consents, since your merit as well as your person have long been the object of my admiration and of my proper desires, as I am now of the persuasion that everything I have heard of you is well below the truth. Flattering actions and vain speeches can only shock a heart and mind fashioned as yours are, but I hope that you'll not find unworthy of them the offer of the heart which I give to you by inclination before I give it in duty as a token of assurance that my care and my consideration for the present and for the future are equally engaged in making you as happy and contented as you deserve to be. Your merit, Madam, can only draw from above new blessings for the righteousness of my cause and give a new ardour to the zeal and devotion of my faithful subjects. May Heaven grant that the summit of my own personal happiness may be the beginning of that which I shall henceforth share with you, unable as I am to envisage any that is not involved with you.

James R.[2]

Clementina was sixteen years old, very small, brown-haired, black-eyed and vivacious. She had a great deal of spirit, and a courage which she had inherited from her grandfather, the great Polish patriot and warrior Jan Sobieski. It was a strange coincidence that, from her early childhood, she had dreamed that one day she would be Queen of England, so there was certainly no opposition on her part when the *de jure* King of England asked for her hand. Charles Wogan was delighted with his discovery, and his only criticism, if such it can be called, was that she was 'healthy but somewhat thin, and has the hopes and wishes of the family for growing more tall, though I fear they won't succeed in any considerable degree'.[3] She was also very religious and observed the rites of the Catholic Church to the very last letter; as she was not very robust, her frequent fastings sometimes led her

---

[1] See A. Shield and A. Lang, *The King over the Water*, Ch. 22
[2] Lubomirski, *op. cit.*, No. 1, p. 1. Tr. Author
[3] HMC, Vol. 6, p. 95

to faint. Although of a pious nature, she was nevertheless light-hearted and all that a pretty princess of sixteen, who was the darling of her father's court, should be.

What amounted to a streak of hysteria in her character seems to have passed unnoticed while she was still young, but it should have surprised no one later had it been remembered that her paternal grandmother, who was French, was an outstanding woman, intelligent, but extremely volatile, and her own mother, a daughter of the Prince Palatine, was a very silly woman. Her father, Prince James, was somewhat of a depressive nature and had suffered throughout his life by comparison with the fearless extrovert who had been his father; her natural family inheritance was therefore not an entirely stable one.

Her material inheritance was another matter, for the Prince had inherited vast estates, money and jewels from his father. On marriage her dowry would consist of 600,000 *livres* in French *rentes*, 800,000 *livres* in Polish estates, 250,000 *livres* owed by the Elector of Saxony to Prince James Sobieski, and many jewels. In immediately realizable effects she was worth about 900,000 French *livres*. Her heirs would inherit a large part of the family estates in Poland, since Sobieski had no sons. She was also very well connected, being not only the granddaughter of the great Polish 'Saviour of Christendom' and a beloved god-daughter of Pope Clement XI, but also the cousin germain of the Emperor Charles VI and of the King of Portugal, niece of the Electors of Trèves and Bavaria and niece of the Prince Palatine. From all points of view, she could not have been a better choice for James, nor a worse one in so far as England and her papal connection were concerned.

When James received the consent of the Princess Maria Clementina's parents to the marriage, he wrote to thank them and to express his happiness. Then he turned to practicalities:

> It seems to me of the greatest importance that our Princess should begin her journey to Italy and that it should be carried out in the most careful manner and in secret. A simple white dress will suffice for the ceremony as convention and the mourning which I wear make everything else superfluous; as to the persons who should accompany her, I leave this to you, but as it seems the most convenient thing for her journey to be absolutely secret and *incognito*, I do not see anything in this respect which could or should delay it. She will find here gentlemen-in-waiting of quality and two ladies who, until others are allocated, will serve her personally and will suffice for her train and to accompany her. For the rest, that which makes me hasten the whole of her journey is not simply

an unreasonable haste on my part, but the fear of events which are bound to be disagreeable and embarrassing for you and for me, above all when, after the contract is signed and ratified by both sides, envious people take sides. It is impossible to foresee everything which could happen but it is certain that, as soon as England learns of the marriage in question, he will move heaven and earth to hinder it if he can and that he will write strongly to the Emperor on the subject. For that matter, you are aware of the close union that exists between these two Princes. . . .[1]

Murray having performed his part, the plan was for John Hay to conduct the Princess and her mother from Ohlau to Bologna, where the King would be awaiting them. Murray was to return home. Whether he was indiscreet, or whether John Hay was recognized, the fact remained that England did come to learn about the proposed marriage and did do its best to prevent it. Clementina's mother departed *incognita* with her daughter, two ladies, each with her maid, two counts, her chamberlain Monsieur Châteaudoux, four chambermaids, a chef, a *maître d'hôtel*, ten footmen and four carriages. It was given out that they were going on a pilgrimage to the shrine of the Holy House at Loreto, a very fashionable thing to do at that time. The Princess Sobieska dallied in Augsburg whilst staying with her brother, the Bishop, and took the opportunity of having her jewels reset, since Augsburg jewellers were renowned for their skill. This gave King George of England time to put heavy pressure on the Emperor; but he, it seems, was rather reluctant to imprison his young cousin, so he allowed enough time for the ladies to have moved out of danger before sending anyone to arrest them. But he had not reckoned with the Princess Sobieska's indolence and frivolity: still she lingered. In the end, they left Augsburg so late that the Emperor's troops were able to arrest them at Innsbruck, where they were imprisoned in the Schloss Ambras.

James, meanwhile, had left for Bologna. He travelled with only a small suite and stayed at the house of the banker Belloni, as he had done on his previous visit to that city. He received only the Legate Archbishop, and his friend, the Marchese Francesco Monti. While waiting for his princess's arrival, he passed the time agreeably enough by going out each day and visiting places of interest in the neighbourhood. One day he sent to Clementina a hundred branches of silk flowers which he had bought at the Monastery of St Agnes, but by that time she was under lock and key.

He learned of her detention on 15 October 1718, and wrote to her the next morning, full of consternation both for her and for their marriage. Although he had never met her, Wogan's account of her had given him a

[1] Lubomirski, *op. cit.*, No. 5, pp. 2–3

great deal of cause to hope that she would be the one person to make his life, in Urbino or elsewhere, more bearable. Wogan had said that she was spirited and gay, but not too ebullient; she was quick and intelligent, and she shared his religion. She was also attractive and pretty. Surely it would not have been too much to ask of fate that at least his marriage might have been achieved without complications? But apparently it was. He could not know, could only guess at the extent of her courage, but in his letter he exhorted her to stand firm and not to return to Ohlau. At the same time he tried to implant in her mind the necessity to make her escape if she possibly could:

> The assurance which I have of your good sentiments for me leads me to write to you so freely and, as I am sure that I am not mistaken, so I am that you will be ingenious in your determination to discover every possible means for coming to Italy to be at my side. Madam, I am always at your command and, if you think a journey on my part would serve a purpose, you have only to ask, I shall take wing as you speak, and I shall despise fatigue and danger when it is a question of serving you, preferring to be a prisoner with you rather than to reign without you and, being unable to take care of you myself until that time, I beg you to count on Mr Hay and to pardon the liberty which I take in writing thus to you, as it is my heart rather than my hand which writes, and I have decided this time not to restrain it, but to give it its freedom. I hope this letter will come into your own hands; I beg you to console me with an answer, being more to you, as you deserve I should be, Madam, than to myself.
>
> *James R.*[1]

Murray had failed, Hay had failed, and there was no one who could advise the King what to do. No one, that was, apart from the fiery young Irish Catholic who had found Clementina, but was not allowed to go back and bring her to the King in triumph. Now Charles Wogan had a plan for rescuing the Princess, and James was desperate enough to agree to it.

On 21 October 1718 Maria Clementina wrote to her *fiancé*:

> The letter which your Majesty did me the honour to write in such touching terms is a great solace in the affliction which they cause us by holding us here without reason; I hope that God will not permit us to suffer for long, and that is why, Sire, I pray you to be patient and to preserve your health. Do not hazard anything, above all in coming here – the risk would be too great for your person, and nothing stands to be gained by it. The

[1] Lubomirski, *op. cit.*, No. 7, pp. 3–4

Princess, my mother, holds firm and will not give way on the subject of our journey; as for me, I feel too much that it is a question of my happiness and my honour to fail to imitate her in this obduracy. Besides my heart speaks to me and, whatever happens, I shall endure in my resolution never to give my hand to another than your Majesty and to live all my life to your command.

Clementina, Princess of Poland[1]

The last sentence must have given James some twinge of conscience because he had left for Rome early in November in order to ask the Pope to put pressure on the Emperor – after all, Clementina was his godchild. At the same time, he and Clement discussed the question of his freedom to contract another marriage if the one proposed did not take place. Among those suggested by Clement was the Princess Maria Vittoria di Caprara, who would have made him a suitable consort both from the point of view of her person and her dowry. There was no disguising the fact that the King could not afford to be overly sentimental regarding the question of marriage: if the marriage with Clementina did not come to pass, then another one had to be arranged for the sake of the dynasty, whatever his personal feelings might be. Cardinal Gualterio was, however, on the side of Clementina, and refused to discuss any other marriage.

James passed that winter in Rome, writing letters to Clementina and the Princess Sobieska in Innsbruck, urging them to keep up their spirits and await a deliverer, and to Prince Sobieski who was sorrowing in Ohlau and wishing every now and then he had never agreed to the marriage. Wogan was meanwhile dashing around Europe on his own, disguised as a Flemish merchant, which gave him a good excuse to post from Rome to Bologna and thence to Innsbruck, where he managed to arrange a meeting with the Princesses and tell them that they must rely on him. Then he travelled through Austria and Bohemia to Silesia, journeying in the depth of winter on roads which were little more than cart-tracks and, what is more, through enemy territory for the most part. When he reached Ohlau, Prince Sobieski was in one of his depressed moods and, although he received Wogan with the greatest courtesy, said that he wanted to call the whole thing off, and told the young man that, although he trusted him implicitly, this was not the time for 'quixotry'.

All this was taking time, and James had begun to lose patience with the Prince and Princess Sobieski. Finally, he wrote to Clementina:

You are at present the acknowledged mistress of yourself and, although I am too reasonable to ask you the impossible, I think I should be lacking

[1] Lubomirski, *op. cit.*, No. 8, p. 4. Tr. Author

in my duty to you and to myself if I did not propose that you should avail yourself of this letter from the Pope to make your Mother let you depart secretly with a lady. I flatter myself that she will not oppose me nor my design, and that she will be sufficiently authorized by the Pope's letter without waiting for a sealed order from your father, the Prince. . . .[1]

One month after that letter was written, the King was writing to Clementina again, from Rome on 7 February 1719:

Take, I pray you, all your courage in your hands and listen to me with patience. It serves no purpose to talk to you of political reasons and you will, I am sure, believe me when I tell you on my honour I find myself in such a great and pressing necessity that not to submit to it would be to renounce all reason. My love for you, dear Clementina, is without limits, it is true, and when it is joined to prudence and honour it only becomes stronger and more stable as I do not doubt but that your feeling for me is of this kind – far from thinking I shall shock you in doing my duty, I do not know how to give you a surer indication of my unswerving constancy and love for you.[2]

Although all hope of Swedish assistance had faded with the death of Charles XII in December 1718, another development arose which was to further Jacobite plans. A plot to make Philip V of Spain regent of France instead of his uncle, the Duc d'Orléans, had been discovered, and it was said that it had been instigated by Cardinal Alberoni through Cellamare, the Spanish ambassador to France. England had been at war with Spain for some months past; now it was the turn of France to declare war on Spain, with unexpected complications in some quarters. The Duke of Berwick, who had been partly responsible for establishing Philip on his throne, was now to fight against him. His own son, whom he had encouraged to take Spanish nationality and to whom he had given the dukedom of Liria, was put in command of a Spanish regiment stationed at Gerona in Catalonia, and Berwick found himself fighting against his son, his uncle and his half-brother, James. Once more an opportunity had presented itself for James to try to reclaim his own, and once more he seized it. Again it was winter, a time of high winds and snow.

Wogan had battled his way back to Sélestat and had gathered round him two companions, Captains Misset and O'Toole, and his uncle, Colonel Gaydon. Misset's wife insisted on accompanying them; she was several months pregnant and also brought her maid. When all had been prepared,

[1] Lubomirski, *op. cit.*, No. 18, p. 22
[2] *Ibid.*, No. 30, pp. 13–15

the six, with Michael Vezzosi, a devoted valet to James, set out *en route* for Innsbruck and Clementina.

The King told Clementina that he was leaving a procuration for their marriage in the hands of James Murray which was only to be used if she obtained her liberty and was mistress of herself, otherwise it would be dangerous for her to be considered as his wife if she were recaptured. Whatever their relation to one another, he had made his will in such terms that she knew that he held her dear to him:

> As I not at present in a position to arrange a settlement, my Will is in such terms that your Dowry will revert to you. If I die before I am in a position to give you the settlement you should have, whether the procuration is used or not, in the case of my death you will have convincing proof that you were uniquely dear to me. . . . The few jewels I have I leave for you in the hands of Mr Murray. I also leave with him for our marriage my little diamond which has no other value than that it was put to a similar use by the King my father. . . .[1]

Should she arrive while he was away, she could stay either at the Palazzo Muti, in the Piazza dei Sant' Apostoli, which the Pope had given to him for his residence while in Rome, or, and it might be preferable, she could stay at the Ursuline Convent in Rome. The Duchess of Mar (who had come from Paris to Rome), Lady Nithsdale and Mrs Hay, the wife of Colonel John Hay and sister to James Murray, would wait upon her on her arrival. He concluded his letter: 'When you are mine, I shall be happy but, without you, greatness and the Crown itself will be a burden to me. Duty makes me seek them, but they have no attraction for me unless you share them.'[2]

On 8 November, James left for Spain, and Alberoni's plan for a two-pronged descent on Britain was put into action. The two Keith brothers had recently been in France collecting Jacobites to fight for the cause, and they made their way to Madrid, calling upon the Duke of Liria at Gerona on the way. It was as well that they did, since he had not been informed at that stage of the Jacobite aspect of the war with France. He offered every assistance to his uncle, no doubt regretting the while that they were on the opposite side to his father, Berwick. Everything was left in the hands of Murray, which added greatly to that young man's conceit. He was still busy working for the exposure of the Duke of Mar, whose wife was suspected by a number of Jacobites to be an English spy because she had remained so long in England and also because her sister, Lady Mary Wortley-Montagu,

[1] Lubomirski, *op. cit.*, No. 30, pp. 13–15
[2] *ibid.*

was certainly no Jacobite. Just before the King left for Spain, Mar told him that he would willingly give up the seals of office, but James refused to take up his offer to remain just a Gentleman of the Bedchamber, and said that he would be of great use to him in laying a false scent at the time of his departure. Mar, to whom the idea of the Duke of Ormonde being in command in Scotland was not a happy one, recommended Lord Tullibardine for the post, but nothing was done to remove Ormonde from the command.

While the King was slipping secretly out of Nettuno harbour, accompanied by John Hay and Colonel O'Brien, on the evening of 9 February, bound for Cadiz, the Dukes of Mar and Perth, John Paterson, a Father Brown and two other gentlemen left Rome, bound for the north in the direction the King would have taken had he been setting out on an expedition to rescue Clementina. Travelling via Florence, Bologna and Modena, the party was arrested at Voghera; their passports were taken away and they were held for four days, the time which it took to send a messenger to Lord Stair reporting that King James had been taken. After the four days were up they were sent to Milan. In the meantime the Emperor had heard of what had happened and was furious with Lord Stair: he had become involved in the arrest of the Princess Clementina much against his will, and this last occurrence was too much – he ordered the release of everyone in the party, whether it contained James Stuart or not.

All this confusion and delay served James admirably, giving him several days' start before anyone guessed that he had left or for where. Of course, Stair's spies did eventually learn of his departure and made up for lost time by correctly forecasting when and where he intended to land in Britain. Extra troops were rushed to the west of England to await the arrival of Ormonde's expedition.

The King had set out in a small French vessel flying Genoese colours and commanded by the same Timon Cannock who had carried him on the ill-fated 1715 expedition. No sooner had he stepped aboard when, as if at a given signal, the skies became overcast with clouds, and a great wind whipped up the ocean to a storm of ferocious intensity. He became very sea-sick, and the ship had to put in at Cagliari until the weather showed signs of abating. There was little improvement and they were forced to go on, but were blown northwards off their course, and then had to lay up three days in Marseilles before they could put to sea again. His sea-sickness subsided but was replaced by an attack of the ague: he had a raging fever and there was no doctor with him, so they put into Villefranche and used what local aid they could, and he was bled. After a twenty-four hours' stay there, they set out again but were blown ashore at Hyères where they had to lodge in a dirty tavern crowded with peasants, and, because it was carnival time, the King, disguised as a sailor, was forced to dance with his landlady although he could hardly stand on his feet. After this nightmare they re-embarked and finally reached Las Rosas in Catalonia on 8 March, one month after they had left Italy.

The Duke of Ormonde had been waiting for the main Spanish fleet since 24 February, but it too had been delayed by storms and did not leave Cadiz until the day before James had landed at Las Rosas. On 11 March the Earl Marischal sailed from near San Sebastian with a small Spanish force and landed successfully on the Island of Lewis. The Earl's younger brother, James Keith, had raised Brigadier Campbell and General Gordon at Bordeaux, Lord Tullibardine at Orléans and Lords Seaforth, Glendaruel and Lord George Murray in Paris. All brought their followers and also their clan jealousies. But most were united in their disapproval of the Duke of Ormonde as Commander-in-Chief because he was an Englishman, apart from the fact that his military capabilities were dubious. To make matters worse, Tullibardine still held an old commission of James which gave him the command of any troops raised in Scotland; this had been issued in 1717.

This common dislike served to unite them for once and, somehow or other, they made a concerted embarkation in two frigates from Le Havre on 19 March, landing in Lewis on 4 April, where they found the Earl Marischal had just landed with his two frigates at Stornoway. Then Tullibardine found that the Earl Marischal was apparently in charge of this force, and there were more quarrels. They went by sea to Kintail in the territory of the Earl of Seaforth, but bad weather delayed them and it was over a week later when they landed in Loch Alsh and set up their headquarters in the castle of Eilean Donan. Some three hundred Spanish troops with arms and ammunition were landed, besides the Jacobite officers, and the troopships returned to Spain. They were joined on their landing by about a thousand Highlanders of the Seaforth and the Cameron clans. Split into two camps, one for Tullibardine and one for Marischal, they settled down to pass their time bickering until the arrival of Ormonde. And, of course, Ormonde never came.

Totally exhausted, James made his way from Las Rosas to Gerona, where he was met by his nephew, the Duke of Liria. Together, and rejoicing in each other's company, they travelled to Barcelona and thence to Madrid where they arrived on 27 March. All the weight of Spanish ceremonial splendour was poured into the welcome which King Philip and Queen Elizabeth gave him at the palace of Buen Retiro, but he stayed the shortest possible time due to courtesy and then, still accompanied by Liria, pressed northwards over very bad roads in foul weather towards Corunna, where he proposed to join Ormonde before sailing to England.

He did not know, could not know, that once more he was travelling towards disaster. Two days after his arrival in Madrid, the Spanish fleet which had left Cadiz bound for Corunna had encountered, off Cape Finisterre, storms of an extraordinary ferocity which had lasted over ten days. The ships were scattered: some sank; others were damaged beyond repair; a few limped back into port. When James arrived at Corunna on 17 April he was greeted by Ormonde bearing this news. So many men and animals had been lost, in addition to the ships themselves, that Ormonde and Alberoni agreed that it would not be possible to remount the expedition until August at the earliest.

The fatal pattern of the Stuart fortunes was reasserting itself: as in 1708 and in 1715, the season was wrong, lack of leaders resulted in senseless bickering and recrimination, the King's health cracked at the crucial time, and the elements were spiteful. If his own money had been involved in the failure of the expedition it would have been bad enough, but there was further humiliation in the fact that it had been financed with Philip's money.

At the same time in April, as three British men-o'-war appeared off Corunna, presumably looking for James, Charles Wogan and his friends, against all odds, had managed to carry off the Princess Maria Clementina from the Schloss Ambras. They bore her over the Brenner in the worst of weather, through the Emperor's territory, encountering enemy spies, bad food and broken axles with more or less equanimity, until they reached the Papal States on Sunday, 30 April. About eight o'clock on the morning of 9 May 1719, Clementina woke up in a small house in Bologna and put on a simple white dress, a white *batiste coiffe* with a broad white ribbon and the famous Sobieski pearls. After confession and Communion, she was married by the proxy of James Murray to James Francis Edward Stuart, *de jure* King of England, Scotland, Wales and Ireland.

Chapter Twenty One

Far away in Scotland, on 9 May, the same day as the proxy wedding in Bologna, a British squadron sailed into Loch Alsh, blew up Castle Eilean Donan and its store of ammunition, and took most of the Spanish garrison prisoners. On the whole they were treated reasonably well, and were sent first to Edinburgh then back to Spain. Lord Marischal was able to retire in safety with most of the Scots to Glenshiel. On the way they had heard the news of the dispersal of the Spanish fleet, and knew that, whatever happened now, they could not be reinforced and were therefore doomed. Nevertheless the small force stood up to an onslaught of Government troops from Inverness commanded by General Wightman, but was heavily outnumbered in the battle fought at Glenshiel on 10 June (Old Style), which was White Rose Day, the King's birthday. Marischal, Lord George Murray and Brigadier Mackintosh were all wounded, but they and a great number of the Scots managed to escape to the Western Isles and thence to the Continent.

Although Alberoni had said that he would not be able to do anything for James before August, it was gradually becoming apparent that it was unlikely that he would be able to do anything at any time at all, because the war was going very badly for Spain. Philip had sent his Irish diplomatist, Sir Patrick Lawless, to Russia to investigate the possibility of an alliance with Peter the Great. But Peter's terms were a large subsidy from Spain for Russia and, as an extra insurance, an alliance to include Prussia. That country, however, could see little use in tying itself to an ailing power and joined England instead. This now meant that Spain had a most formidable opposition lined up against her: England, Hanover, the United Provinces, France, the Empire and, also Prussia.

James meanwhile was staying in Lugo in north-west Spain, awaiting news of those who were able to escape from Glenshiel. The old problem of providing for his faithful followers was ever more acute, and very much at the front of his mind. He was depressed and anxious and yet, in a fatalistic way, he was eager for yet another attempt: he watched the course of the Franco-Spanish war with a keen interest. With ties of family and friendship on both sides he was personally a neutral spectator, but the Stuart interests depended upon a Spanish success.

It was not until 10 June that he received news of the escape of Clementina from Innsbruck, but still he remained in Lugo. It was as if he were unable to leave Spain while there remained the slightest hope of further aid for an invasion of England. On 18 June the Duke of Berwick, at the head of the French forces, took Fuentarrabia, and Spain's chances of being able to spare either men or money for the Jacobites became correspondingly remote. On 3 July he heard that Maria Clementina had arrived in Rome, where she had been royally welcomed by the Pope, who had sent his nephew and niece, together with Cardinals Aquaviva and Gualterio, to greet her when she entered the city. Clement also arranged for his god-daughter to receive the same pension that he had granted to the King. Everyone was kind to Clementina, for, as Wogan said, 'the majesty of her countenance, agreeableness of her air, beauty of her features, sweetness of her temper and vivacity of her wit were a match for the greatest prince or monarch in the world'.[1]

All the loyal Jacobites who had remained in Rome when the King had gone to Spain were anxious to meet their young Queen, but complications arose. The Duke of Mar, after his arrest and subsequent release at Voghera, had gone to Paris and again there were rumours of meetings with Lord Stair. John Hay was with the King, but his wife had attended the Queen during the proxy wedding. Clementina, then, was in Murray's hands and he chose to try to keep everyone away from her. Lord Pittsligo, a devoted follower of the King and much respected in Jacobite circles for his integrity, was one of the number who had sought audience of the Queen but had been kept from her by James Murray. He had already had his suspicions about Murray's 'climbing' and his patent desire to oust Mar, and had asked Mar how Murray 'came to be kept about the K. He told me he had no hand in it, and he was surprised when he saw him appear publicly at Urbino. For he had been sent by some of the King's friends in England who, I am informed, are growing weary of him, though they expected his return but he thought it fitt opportunity to change the situation and it seemed the K. was persuaded to keep him.'[2] Later he added to this:

> The substance of what I learnt from Sir Charles Wogan and Sir John Misset was that the Q. was very much disgusted with M––y and his sister, and also with Mr Hay though she was acquainted with his management later. That her maid she brought from Germany was mortified and an old gentleman of Prince James' Mr Chatteau-doux and Mr Misset's lady. The particulars are too many and too frivolous to insert. He said the Q. was not only angry with Mr M––y but despised him and was content to see old Chatteau-doux and Misset mimic his grimaces.

[1] *Historical Register,* Vol. IV, p. 189
[2] H. Tayler, *The Jacobite Court at Rome in 1719,* Lord Pittsligo's narrative, pp. 50–1

Hereupon Mr Misset fell to work before us and acted him to the life. I protest I was sorry things were so low, the Q. might have had more proper diversions but it is natural to a young body to like such comical representations.[1]

Lord Pittsligo, it should be noted, was about ten years older than his master, the King, who was then thirty-one.

Murray was undoubtedly a careerist and, more than once, in the correspondence of various people at this time he is described as 'giving himself airs'. When Lord Pittsligo and others asked when they might pay their respects to the Queen, having gathered outside her lodging, he merely answered them with a shrug, and there was an incident in a coffee-house in Rome in which he announced very publicly that he had told Mar not to set out in the direction he had taken, and if he had got himself arrested he had only himself to blame. This so outraged the Jacobites present that Pittsligo unwisely determined to warn the King in a letter that Murray was taking too much upon himself. James, tired beyond belief of all the petty quarrels which had sprung up in Saint-Germain and Urbino, was not at all pleased now that they seemed to be recurring in Rome. At any rate, he reprimanded Pittsligo instead of Murray, and it was a long time before he could go so far as to admit that there might have been something in what Pittsligo had written, or before he could apologize to him.

Thus the foundations were unfortunately laid for a distrust, on Clementina's part, of at least one of the King's intimates. At that time she did not seem to take too much exception to Mrs Hay, in spite of Pittsligo's report, but the Colonel's lady was sister to James Murray and very attached to him.

It was becoming apparent that nothing was likely to be done for the Stuarts in Spain: Alberoni was losing his influence, to the gratification of the Spanish Queen, and there was very little money in the exchequer. Spain had to make peace with England soon or perish, for Berwick was making his way down from Bayonne with his eyes on San Sebastian. This was at the end of July. While James was on Spanish soil it was obvious that no peace negotiations could begin, and he was not slow in realizing that his absence would be preferable to his presence. So, having done all that he could to settle some of the brave men who had been at Glenshiel with the Spanish forces, he prepared to move on. There was only one place for him to go, and that was Rome, the city which he had resisted so long. It was an ironical fact that the cradle of the religion to which he belonged, and which meant so much to him personally, was the last place in Europe to further his

[1] Tayler, *op. cit.*, p. 95

cause. But there was no help for it. Now nothing seemed to matter to James any longer: there was absolutely no opportunity of advancing his cause no matter where he might turn: Rome was as good as any other place. In a very depressed frame of mind he left Lugo for Valladolid; he was also suffering a great deal from the intense heat of the Spanish summer. Ormonde joined him at Valladolid, and they waited there a few days to learn what had happened to San Sebastian, then under siege by Berwick. It surrendered on 2 August, and James recognized the end of his hopes of help from Spain. He left Ormonde and took ship from Vinaroz to Livorno accompanied by Colonel John Hay and the rest of his suite who had been with him in Spain. For what must have been the first time in his life he sailed in good weather and a favourable wind blew him to Italy and his wedding.

Though the wind was hurrying him along, it was obviously with no undue haste that James approached the marriage ceremony to be held in Montefiascone about seventy miles north-west of Rome. He was accompanied by Hay and Murray, the latter having left Rome to meet him on his arrival in Italy. James had been too much preoccupied by events in Spain to be swept off his feet by thoughts of marriage to a princess who had just passed her seventeenth birthday. He himself was now thirty-one and, although from his letters it is easy to see that he had a great deal of affection for the young girl who had undergone so much for his sake, he never gives the impression of a man at the mercy of his passion. For one thing, he was much too level-headed to pretend to himself to feel undying love for someone he had never even seen: even if the reports about her were enthusiastic, he had to see and decide for himself as he always did in other matters. And, as has been pointed out before, this was not a romantic love, but a dynastic arrangement such as kings and those born to be king had had to accept for generations. Probably Maria Clementina did not approach the marriage in the same manner: her childhood dreams, her youth, the pictures and descriptions she had had of James, the very adventure of her journey to him, to say nothing of the wild gallantry of her rescuers, may have made her imagine a man who would be a great deal less preoccupied with affairs of State and more predisposed to give her the major part of his attention than he actually was. But there was no flaw in their first meeting.

James had arrived at the papal fee of Montefiascone on 28 August and took up residence in the Bishop's palace. The Bishop of Montefiascone was to perform the ceremony in the cathedral on the summit of the hill, which was the type of eminence forming the background of so many Umbrian landscapes. The small town was built up the sides of the hill and was surrounded by a defensive wall at its foot. In this wall were two massive bronze gates left perpetually open as a symbol that the Bishop was always ready to welcome his lord and master, the Pope.

The surrounding country around Montefiascone and Viterbo was scoured by the Bishop's agents, for provisions for entertaining the King and Queen of England on the occasion of their wedding. The local gentry gave willingly of their game and their dairy produce, to such an extent that James was embarrassed by their generosity and promised to reimburse them when he should come into his kingdom. 'Never was such faith shown in Israel,'[1] wrote a local chronicler, as the mountains of food piled up in the Bishop's palace.

On 2 September, Clementina arrived with five of her six 'faithful marmosets' as she called her rescuers. All the men had travelled with her, but Mrs Misset had stayed behind in Rome to be delivered of a healthy baby boy. Mrs Hay was her female attendant. She and James first met alone in a room in the palace.

They made a handsome pair: the King, tall, dark, slimly but strongly built, still with that mysterious air of being set apart by destiny, and Clementina, seventeen, tiny (so tiny that they had had to buy children's shoes to fit her when they reached Bologna on her epic journey), dark-eyed as he was, with long, brown hair and a round and pretty face given to mercurial changes of mood. From appearance alone, it would have been hard not to love Clementina, and she was as good as she was pretty. She had intelligence too, but it was of the instinctive variety and not always informed with reason. To a certain degree she would always remain a child, and James had been an adult in mind since his accession at thirteen. He was also of the kind who, once they have given their heart as he had done to Benedicta, never love again with all the fire of their being. But he was prepared to love Clementina with the love of which he was capable, and to love her alone.

They were married in the cathedral and, after the wedding banquet, they returned to the cathedral for an oratorio sung in their honour. This was followed by a play in honour of Hymen performed by the students of Montefiascone. More histrionic manifestations were offered but politely declined by the King and Queen of England who, by this time, must certainly have been feeling tired. He gave to the cathedral, as a mark of his gratitude, episcopal vestments, insignia and an altar frontal embroidered in gold; and Clementina gave a chasuble adorned with priceless oriental pearls which had formed part of her Sobieski dowry. Also in that dowry was an enormous bed (sent ahead to the Palazzo Muti in Rome) which had been taken by Clementina's grandfather from the Sultan's personal baggage after

[1] Quoted in P. Miller, *A Wife for the Pretender*, p. 145

relieving the siege of Vienna. It had a framework of wrought silver gilt, enamelled and encrusted with precious stones. The curtains of the bed were made of Smyrnan brocade worked with seed-pearls and gold; once they had sheltered the standard of Mahomet and a most precious copy of the Koran as well as the representative of the Prophet himself.

As a proof of his gratitude to Charles Wogan, the King made him a knight baronet and conferred knighthoods on John Misset, Lucas O'Toole and Richard Gaydon; and, although he could not do the same for Mrs Misset, he made her father, who was then a captain, a colonel. To Wogan he said: 'You have behaved as I expected from your zeal, from your spirit and from your courage, and you may count upon it that, if I wish to be seated on the throne which belongs to me, it is partly because I wish, if it is possible, to make you as happy and contented as I may, for you have well merited it.'[1]

He was as happy as he could know how to be, as happy as a man of his temperament could be whose solitude was peopled with the ghosts of men who had laid down their lives for him. Autumn came creeping up the hill to Montefiascone, so they returned to Rome, and it rained.

[1] Sir John Gilbert, *Narratives of the Detention, Liberation and Marriage of Maria Clementina Sobieska . . . by Sir Charles Wogan and others*, pp. 104–5

St Ouen ye 10th July 1747
104
RP.

Sir

I have received yrs of ye 13th & 20th Iune
and I got a Dager throw my heart it
could not have been more sensible
to me than at yr Contents of yr first
my Love for my Brother and Concern
for yr Case, being the occasion of
it. I hope your Majesty will forgive
my not enterjng any further on so Disagreable
subject the shock of which I am sure
will be other wise so shall referr to next post
anything in yours, to be answered I
lay myself full of Respect, at yr
Majestys feet moste humbly asking
Blessing.

your Moste
Dutifull Son
Charles. P.

A letter from Prince Charles Edward to his father after receiving the news that the Duke of York had become a cardinal. (*From the Stuart Papers at Windsor by the gracious permission of Her Majesty the Queen*)

Rome Oct 31st 1758.

By what the Nuntio at Paris writes here, I remark with satisfaction the concern you are in about my health, which I cannot but take very kindly of you, and I thank God I can give you now a better account of it. I am at last able to take the air in the coach, and tho' I am still very weak, yet by degrees I hope my strength will return in some measure to me, so you need be in no present pain for me. As for our affairs, I can say little upon them, after all I charged Lumisden with for you; but I should hope that the misfortunes the French have had in America would animate them to take our cause in hand, & the advantages they & their allies have lately had in Europe should I think naturally both encourage & enable them to do so; tho' if what I hear be well founded, I am affrayed we have little to expect during this winter, but I can at least please myself with the thoughts of your profiting of this dead time to come & make me a visit, which can never be too soon for me, & which is the temporal comfort I most desire. I have seen all your letters to Edgar, and have nothing further to add here, but to besceech God to bless you, & send you soon to me. I tenderly embrace y and am all yours.

James R.

12. A dictated letter from King James to Charles Edward with the final sentence and signature in his own handwriting. (*From the Stuart Papers at Windsor by the gracious permission of Her Majesty the Queen*)

Chapter Twenty Two

A papal guard was mounted daily outside the Palazzo Muti, and it was the only residence besides the Vatican and the Quirinale to be so honoured. It was not a building of great architectural distinction, but of reasonable size, built, as most of the Roman *palazzi* were, around a square courtyard with ochred walls overlooking a small fountain in the centre. The staircase facing the entrance door was dark and steep, and it was not until the *piano nobile* was reached that any sense of atmosphere or of regal dignity was achieved. They settled in easily and comfortably enough, and were readily accepted by Roman society, only too eager to welcome the King and Queen of England. On one side of their *piazza* was the fashionable church of the Santi Apostoli and, as James and Clementina went to daily mass there, it was not long before she became known as 'Regina Apostolorum'. The Pope also gave them the Savelli Palace at Albano for a summer residence.

Their return in that sad, wet autumn was bedevilled by the beginning defection of the Duke of Mar. After his secret contact with Lord Stair in Paris in 1717, Mar had tendered his resignation to James on grounds of getting too old for the job of Secretary, but the King had refused to accept this, even when the Duke had made it dependent upon the King's coming into his own again. Mar seemed to have a talent for getting himself arrested: on the way to join James in Spain in 1719 he had been imprisoned in Geneva at the request of the British agent there. He wrote to Lord Stair asking for permission to cross France because his health was failing and he needed to take the curative waters at Bourbon. Stair agreed, and went so far as to suggest that, if Mar made his peace with the Hanoverians, he might receive a pension from the British Government. He went to Bourbon, where he was joined by his Duchess, and, on being cured, he returned to his house in Paris which he had been sorely missing for some time past. Once there, he asked Dillon what he thought he should do about submitting to the British government. Loyal Dillon thought this a very odd thing to ask, and said so, adding that he knew what *he* would do, but Mar must certainly lay his problem before the King who was the only one qualified to give him an answer.[1] Mar's imprisonment in Geneva had been a fairly social one – to the extent that he had been able to incur debts amounting to a thousand pounds sterling which were paid by Stair. This was the first stage of the

[1] Carte CCXXXI, p. 51

Duke's 'rehabilitation' with the British government. James had also been sending him as much as he could afford all the time he was in prison, in spite of the fact that his absence was causing considerable inconvenience – since the Queen Mother's death the conduct of business had been in the hands of Mar, Dillon and Lansdowne in Paris, and there was no doubt but that Mar was the most efficient organizer of the three. John Hay and James Murray worked under the King in Rome but, because of their youth and Murray's conceit, they were not trusted by the rest of the court and, whether he agreed or not, James knew that he dare not delegate to either of them. As he was fully occupied with the Roman end, it was vital that there should be someone reliable with Lansdowne and Dillon. In London Bishop Atterbury was in charge, and this was a key appointment because the Prime Minister, Robert Walpole, was a much more determined opponent of the Jacobites than they had yet known. The general situation in London and the greater part of England was gradually becoming easier: peace and prosperity were acceptable after so many years of war. The economy still left a great deal to be desired, but optimism was rising – to such a degree that it resulted eventually in the South Sea Bubble.

All the time Mar was in Geneva, Murray lost no opportunity in denigrating him. Although the Duke was by no means universally liked, this attitude on the part of one regarded as a young upstart was not appreciated by a great many at the court, including, of course, Lord Pittsligo whose criticism resulted in temporary exile. On 26 November 1720, Murray wrote from Rome to his brother-in-law, John Hay, who was then in Paris, that he would soon be setting out on his travels but, as he had no money of his own, he feared that he might be an expense to the King in his retreat. If he could no longer be of service to the King he would not be sorry to be going, but Murray was under no doubt whatsoever but that James owed him at least a living.

By now Clementina was expecting a child, and Murray was not slow to try to turn even this to his advantage. He wanted a title which he considered (probably correctly) would help him wherever he decided to go after he had left the King. In November or December 1720 he wrote to James asking him for a public mark of favour, pointing out that unless something like this was done for him the world at large might think he had been ignominiously dismissed. The best time for making the announcement of such a favour would be after the Queen's delivery for, after all, he had been vitally concerned in the marriage.

Charles Wogan's part in the rescue of Maria Clementina obviously counted for little where Murray was concerned. The King was eventually to create him the Earl of Dunbar, but in his own time and not yet. So

Murray left the court in Rome and, among the ranks of those closest to him, only Colonel John Hay remained about the King. There was no one of the calibre of the Earl of Middleton, who had died in 1719, nor of either of the Dukes of Perth, the second Duke having died in the spring of 1720. Wisdom and experience were necessary in the delicate manoeuvres involved in trying to win both the Earl of Oxford and the Duke of Argyll to the Stuart side. Oxford, true to his old form when, as plain Mr Harley, he had delayed and procrastinated with the Duke of Berwick, would not commit himself, although he corresponded occasionally with James. Argyll was to be lost to them for ever when George I realized that he would be more useful working with him than against him, and appointed him Lord Great Chamberlain. Division among their leaders depressed the English Jacobites, and this was deepened when the Scottish adherents began to press for separate treatment for religious affairs north of the Border. Eventually James had to agree to a commission being set up to manage Scottish religious affairs. In London, in addition to Bishop Atterbury, there were – working in a loose kind of committee and endlessly quarrelling among themselves – Lords Orrery, Grey, North, Gower and Arran, but not one of them possessed the consistency and clear-sightedness which Berwick had shown in the years before the Fifteen.

There was still a desultory kind of correspondence passing between the King and the Duke of Berwick; they were on friendly terms but, henceforth, the Duke was to play little part in James's life and plans. He wrote to the King on 9 November 1720 from Bordeaux, expressing a hope that the times might soon be favourable for the restoration, and added a comment on the Queen's confinement: 'I do not wonder at the Queen's being mistaken in her reckoning, it happens often at first being with child, but I hope she will repair the delay, by giving us a prince at the end of this month.'[1] Clementina was wildly out in her calculations as was shown by James's letter to the Duke of Ormonde in Spain written two days after Berwick's letter: 'The Queen returns to you her kind compliments and continues very well. It is indeed a little singular to have mistaken so much as 3 or 4 months in her reckoning.'[2]

On the last day of the old year of 1720 a son was born and was baptized by the Bishop of Montefiascone (who had performed the marriage ceremony) with the names Charles Edward Louis Philip Casimir Sylvester, and he was immediately created Prince of Wales. The baby was bonny and strong and, although she had had a long, exhausting labour, Clementina was soon physically restored. Berwick wrote again from Bordeaux on 25 January 1721:

[1] Windsor: The Stuart Papers (WSP) 30.3   [2] *ibid.*, 50.30

Give me leave to make my most hearty compliments to your Majesty on the birth of the Prince, it is the most agreeable news we have had this long while, and fills all honest men with joy: none can wish your Majesty more happyness and prosperity that I do. I beg you will be pleased to lett me advise the Queen of my most dutyfull respects and to congratulate with her on her happy delivery.

Berwick[1]

Jacobites celebrated the arrival of the Stuart heir all over the Catholic countries of Europe: bonfires were lit at Saint-Germain, and Versailles was euphoric with *feux de joie* and Te Deums. A royal salute was fired from the Castel Sant' Angelo in Rome, and the Pope made the royal family a gift of 10,000 *scudi*, besides celebrating a mass in the English church. As for Charles Wogan who, by this time, was attached to the Spanish army in Carthagena, he wrote to the King as soon as he had received the news in his customary ebullient vein:

This old town has been all in a flame for three nights with fire-works, illuminations and Artillery. The Dames have ventured abroad for the first time to Balls and Assemblyes, and their husbands have for the first time gott drunk. Sober Don Pedro de Montemayor hopes, he says, in a few days to come to his right Senses; and our whiggish Consul here has been provoked by his Spleen and our mirth into a feaver; the like train of rejoycing has been at Muraia and all the towns about us.[2]

In the early spring of 1721 Wogan and the Missets returned to Rome for a while, and Mrs Misset was appointed a lady-in-waiting to the baby prince.

Domestically, this was the happiest period in James's life: he loved Clementina with a deep affection and she was still in love with him. She saw him still as a figure of romance, which in one way he was; yet loving in a mature fashion, loving the man for what he really was apparently was beyond her. But this was the best time for them: they were a happy, young married couple with a delightful baby son. And it was as a happy family that they were seen by a young English traveller who arrived in Rome on 20 March 1720 and wrote to his father on 6 May, describing first how they had entered the Holy City at the time of the ceremonials subsequent upon the Pope's death. On his arrival he had found a letter from his father advising him not to mix in the circle of the 'Pretender' as King James was now widely known in Britain. But he admitted that he had a great curiosity 'to

---

[1] WSP 51.90
[2] Quoted in H. Tayler, *Jacobite Epilogue*

see this man who daily makes so great a noise in England'.[1] As it happened, he struck up acquaintance with a Doctor Cooper, an Anglican clergyman, whom he did not suspect of being a Jacobite, and whom he liked very much. On Easter Saturday the genial divine invited them to a Church of England service: 'Such language at Rome appear'd to me a jest; I stared at the Doctor, who added that the PRETENDER (whom he called King) had prevailed with the late Pope to grant Licence for having Divine Service according to the rules of the Church of England perform'd in his Palace, for the benefit of the Protestant Gentlemen of his Suite, his Domesticks and Travellers'.[2] Both Doctor Cooper and his friend, Doctor Berkeley, who was a Church of England chaplain at the Stuart court, assured the young traveller that James was an

> upright, Moral Man, very far from any sort of Bigotry, and most averse to disputes and distinctions of Religion, whereof not a word is admitted in his Family. They described him in his Person very much to the resemblance of King Charles II to which they say he approaches more and more every day, with a great application to business, and a head well turned that way, having only some Clerks, to whom he dicttates such Letters as he does not write with his own Hand.[3]

But, alas for his parent's admonition, the young man and his friend went to take the evening air in the park of the Villa Ludovisi and came face to face with King James and Queen Maria Clementina before they realized what had happened, or so the young man said, making his excuse that 'common civility obliged us to stand sidewise in the Alley, as others did to let them pass by'.

> The PRETENDER was easily distinguish'd by his Star and Garter, as well as by an air of greatness, which discovered a Majesty superior to the rest. I felt in that instant of his approach a strange convulsion in body and mind, such as I never was sensible of before; whether Aversion, Awe or Respect occasion'd it, I can't tell. I remark'd his Eyes fixt upon me, which I confess I could not bear. I was perfectly stunn'd, and not aware of myself, when pursuant to what the standers by did, I made him a Salute; He returned it with a smile, which changed the sedateness of his first aspect into a very graceful countenance. As he passed by, I observ'd him to be a well-siz'd-clean-limb'd Man.[4]

This description of the particular aura which surrounded James, marking him out from other men, is all the more interesting coming, as it does, from

[1] *An English Traveller at Rome*, Brit. Mus. C115.3.55, pp. 1–3
[2] *ibid.*   [3] *ibid.*   [4] *ibid.*

one who was not a Jacobite. Clementina he described as being well-shaped with 'lovely Features: Wit, Vivacity and Mildness of Temper are painted in her looks'.[1]

The King asked Doctor Cooper if they were English, and then asked them how long they would be in Rome, assuring them at the same time that they would be welcome in his house: 'The Princess [Maris Clementina], who stood by, addressing to the Doctor in the prettiest English I think I ever heard, said, pray Doctor, if these Gentlemen be lovers of Musick invite them to my Concert tonight. I charge you with it, which she accompany'd with a Salute and a Smile in the most gracious manner.'[2] How could he have refused, he asks? He discussed with the learned Doctors the points of the case, and they all decided that he should go. So he went to the Palazzo Muti that night where he found gathered the flower of Roman high society and the best musicians in the capitol, as well as a 'plentiful and orderly collation'. James came to him and gave him and his companion a general invitation to visit him there in his house, and he spoke of the young man's grandfather and of his being a constant follower of Kings Charles I and II and 'added that if you, Sir, had been of age before my Grandfather's death, to learn his Principles, there had been little danger of your taking party against the rights of a Stuart . . . 'The traveller was surprised to learn that James knew so much about the families of English society: 'His answer was, that from his infancy he had made it his business to acquire the knowledge of the Laws, Customs and Families of his Country, so that he might not be reputed a stranger, when the Almighty pleased to call him thither.'[3]

They were invited, and stayed to dinner:

There is every day a regular table of Ten, or Twelve Covers well serv'd, unto which some of the qualify'd Persons of his Court or Travellers are invited: It is supplied with English and French Cookery, French and Italian Wines, but I took notice that the PRETENDER Eat only of the English Dishes, and made his Dinner of Roast Beef and what we call Devonshire Pye: He also prefers our March Beer, which he has from Leghorn, to the best Wines. At the Desert he drinks his glass of Champagne very heartily, and to do him justice, he is as free and chearful at his Table, as any Man I know. He spoke much in favour of our English Ladies, and said he was persuaded he had not many Enemies amongst them: then he carried a Health to them. The Princess with a smiling countenance took up the matter, and said, I think then, Sir, it would be but just, that I drink to the Cavaliers.

[1] *An English Traveller at Rome, op. cit.*
[2] *ibid.*   [3] *ibid.*

They all then drank toasts to their respective friends: 'I assure you, Sir, said he, that the friends you mean can have no great share of prosperity till they become mine, therefore here's prosperity to yours and mine.'[1]

After the meal Clementina took them, as any proud young mother would have done, to see her son:

> He is really a fine, promising child, and is attended by English Women, mostly Protestants, which the Princess observ'd to us, saying that, she thought fit to have him bred up by their hands; and that in the Country where he was born, there was no other distinction but that of honest and dishonest. These Women and particularly two Londoners, kept such a racket about us to make us kiss the young Pretender's Hand, that to get clear of them as soon as we could, we were forced to comply. The Princess laughed very heartily, and told us she did not question but the day would come, that we should not be sorry to have made so early an acquaintance with her Son: I thought myself under a necessity of making her the compliment, that being hers he could not miss being good and happy.[2]

With regard to the Protestant nurses, either the Queen was to make a complete *volte-face* within a short time, or else perhaps her quick intelligence warned her that here was a chance not to be lost of proving to a non-Jacobite stranger eventually to return to London society that the young Prince of Wales was being brought up outside the influence of Rome which, whether she approved of it herself or not, happened to be true.

The next day was the day on which the post-bag from England was scheduled to arrive at the Palazzo Muti, so the two young men went again to see James. There were letters indeed, but nothing very encouraging in them either for the Stuarts or for the good of the English nation. The King remarked that there was 'no great prospect of amendment in the affairs of England'. He bemoaned the misfortune of England 'groaning under a load of Debts, and the severest hardships, contracted and imposed to support Foreign Interests' and the bad treatment of the old nobility by a 'new Set of People, who must at any rate enrich themselves by the spoil of their Country. . . . Thereupon he rose briskly from his Chair, and expressed his concern with Fire in his Eyes.'[3]

He turned to an old English gentleman in his company and said then, 'I have been told by several of the most eminent Prelates of the Church of Rome, particularly my friend the late Arch-bishop of Combray [Fénélon] that it should never be my business to study how to be an Apostle, but how

[1] *An English Traveller at Rome, op. cit.*
[2] *ibid.* [3] *ibid.,* pp. 6–7

263

to become a good King to all my people without distinction, which shall be found true, if ever it please God to restore me.'[1]

The young man concludes his letter to his father:

> I am not sorry to have contented so far my curiosity and that were he not the PRETENDER, I should like the Man very well. We should truly pass much of our time in dullness, had we not the diversion of his House but I give you my word I will enter no more upon Arguments of this kind with him; for he has too much wit and learning for me: besides that he speaks with such an Air of sincerity, that I am apprehensive I should become half a Jacobite if I continued following these Discourses any longer.[2]

The discourses revolved around James's expressed conviction that all clergymen, with the exception of those requested to serve the State, should be confined to the bare duties of their vocations and, if they did not comply, they should be removed from the opportunities of creating mischief. Ever present in his mind was mistrust of the Jesuits, first inculcated by Fénélon.

The over-all picture of James drawn by the well-bred young man on the fashionable Grand Tour of Europe is very different from that so often presented by the lampoonists of the London broadsheets who had only the barest superficial appearances to work upon. If he were tall and dark, and had once been seen enduring grief, as after the failure of the Fifteen, to the anti-Jacobite cartoonists of the day he was 'Old Mr Melancholy'. But it was noticeable that the worst which they could do was to try to make fun of him, as they did with any of their opponents, or to attempt to revive echoes of the 'Warming-Pan Mystery' in which it was claimed that James was not the true Prince of Wales, but that another infant, probably one of the Oglethorpe boys, had been substituted by means of a warming-pan into the Queen's bed shortly after the birth of a still-born Prince. And even the Whig satirists refrained from concocting falsehoods about his moral outlook: it seems to have been tacitly agreed that he was an 'upright' man.

There were pro-Jacobite ballads which redressed the balance in no uncertain way, however, as witness this song written for his birthday in the month following the young traveller's visit:

The Bonny Black Laddie

My Laddie can Fight, my Laddie can sing,
He's fierce like the North-Wind, yet soft as the Spring,
His Soul was designed for no less than a King:
Such Greatness shines in my Black Laddie.

[1] *An English Traveller at Rome*, op. cit., pp. 6–7   [2] *ibid.*

Then comes a symbolic verse, personifying James supported by his three kingdoms:

> With soft Downs of Thistles I'll make him a Bed,
> With Lilies and Roses I'll pillow his Head,
> And with my tun'd Harp I will gently lead
> To Ease and safe Slumbers my Laddie.[1]

Perhaps the Lilies signified the support of France but, at that moment, it could only have been wishful thinking, for that country had no intention of going to war again yet, after the peace with Spain in 1719. The Duke of Berwick was able to forget the necessity of having to fight his own son, and stayed at the French court until June 1720 when he went first to Bordeaux and then, in the following year, to Marseilles where plague had been raging for a long time and had to be contained. The Regent asked Berwick to take over Provence and, in addition, he was given the command of Auvergne, the Bourbonnais and the Limousin. The plague was to last for another year or more, but Berwick applied stringent measures of quarantine, and eventually he got the better of it. But all this meant that, even if either he or James had wished for a *rapprochement*, Berwick's situation was not any better and still prevented a physical meeting. Their relations were cool and polite from casual references in letters, but nothing more; though James was still on the friendliest terms with Berwick's son, the Duke of Liria.

There had been another visitor to the Palazzo Muti a week or two before the arrival of the 'English Traveller', and he had been brought stealthily up the back stairs by Mrs Hughes, chief nurse to the Prince of Wales. This visitor was Christopher Layer, a young London barrister who had come with talk of great disaffection in the whole country and in the army, which was borne out by the letters James had been receiving from Bishop Atterbury of Rochester, Sir William Wyndham and Lord Bathurst, among others. It was known that George would soon be returning to Hanover for a visit, and Layer had thought out a plan by which the Tower was to be taken and the family of King George abducted. This time, all would be centred on London; Mar and Dillon would leave for Scotland, Lansdowne for the West Country, Lord Strafford for the North, and Lord Arran would be General of all the forces of England and Ireland. The King planned to leave Rome and travel to Rotterdam via Frankfurt; he would wait there until he received information as to the best place for him to land in England. Much hope was placed in the economic confusion and general unrest prevailing in England after the spectacular failure of the South Sea Bubble in July 1720, but the great weakness of the plan was that James had to delegate

[1] Jacobite Tracts, Brit. Mus. C115.a3

the organization to the Jacobite lords in London, and to Mar, Lansdowne and Dillon in Paris. With his grasp of detail and clearness of mind he was far better equipped than any of them to get such a project moving, but he was forced to stand back and watch from a distance and trust his men.

Once again, the problem was how to obtain sufficient finance to back the venture. The sister of Charles XII of Sweden, reigning after his death, was asked in vain for the return of the money James had sent him five years before. The new Pope, Innocent XIII, was not so friendlily disposed towards the Stuarts as his predecessors had been, and he refused to lend the King money without security. All the old familiar pattern was repeating itself, and James became increasingly worried and depressed. This was the first major project which he had undertaken since his marriage and it meant that he must, to some degree, neglect Clementina. Neither could he confide in her: she was so far unversed in the desperate need for secrecy in the smallest detail of such negotiations, and James was fanatically anxious about leakages – with justification. Clementina had, until now, been in the centre of the stage: her romantic escape, her marriage and then the birth of the much-desired Prince of Wales had all followed one upon the other, so that she had become accustomed to the role of heroine and did not understand that state affairs sometimes must take precedence over private ones.

In spite of all the precautions taken from Rome, the Jacobite plot was betrayed to the British government: some said that Mar had had a hand in it, but there was no definite proof. One of the chief couriers between Paris and London, a non-juring clergymen called George Kelly, was one of the earliest to be arrested. He was thrown into the Tower, but not before he had had time to burn his papers: he gave no information to his captors. Fourteen years later, he escaped from the Tower and made his way to Rome where his career was to join itself eventually with that of the Prince of Wales.

England was now altered: the Lord Mayor of London was warned of a 'wicked conspiracy', and assistance was sought from the United Provinces in the form of troops. The historian Thomas Carte was arrested, and Lords Orrery, North and Grey, and then Christopher Layer himself. At first Atterbury was untouched, then a strange thing happened: Mar wrote to Atterbury under codenames, but in clear characters, saying that he was sending him a present of a little dog called 'Harlequin'. He sent this letter through the ordinary post, knowing full well that all their mail in either direction was carefully watched, and the dog served to identify Atterbury. He was asked by Robert Walpole either to cease his opposition to the Government, or to leave the country, which he did, to enter James's service. On arrival at Calais he heard that Bolingbroke, having made his peace with the British government at last, was in the vicinity on his way back to England – which seemed to the Bishop to be a fair exchange.

On the whole, and possibly because it was thought there was not enough evidence to hold them, the Lords in the Tower were treated fairly lightly, but Christopher Layer was condemned to death on 31 November 1722. His sentence was delayed in its execution until the following May.

During that summer, Charles Wogan's younger brother, Nicholas, had been cruising around the Mediterranean with three ships waiting to convey the King to England. James had taken a country house at Bagnani to cover his retreat when it should become necessary, and Cardinal Aquaviva waited for him there. Two officers, relatives of Ormonde, were also to join him there, while Ormonde himself left Madrid for Ventosilla, ready to sail as soon as he had received news that George I had left for Hanover. But all was hopeless. As usual, it took a long time for the news of the discovery of the plot to reach them. On 30 June, John Hay wrote to his brother-in-law Mar that it was 'mightily important that the post comes in to know whether this plot be a sham or not'.[1]

It was about this time that there began to grow an atmosphere of tension between the King and his wife. Perhaps she was disappointed at the outcome of the latest attempt, perhaps she was bored with nothing constructive to do while James was giving all his time and mind to salvaging what could be rescued from the failure – whatever it was, Clementina decided that it would be good for her health to leave Rome for the curative baths at Lucca. Even if she did not command the same amount of affection from the new Pope as she had from his predecessor, who had been her godfather, she still had the whole of Roman society at her feet: they were enchanted by her charm, her gaiety, her pretty little accent in Italian and French, and the mixture of sweetness and gravity in her expression. But when the Pope veered away from James, Roman society began to do likewise, and the sympathy was all for the Queen, who welcomed it; whereas the King would not stoop to seek it for his person even if he were prepared to do so for his cause if it were necessary. She had a temper, and so had he, and, although he had had longer practice in controlling his, there were times when he lost his equanimity. Colonel John Hay watched this growing incompatibility with dismay and wrote to his brother-in-law Mar: 'Their tempers are so very different that, that tho' in the greatest trifles they are never of the same opinion, the one won't yield one Inch to the other; the dread of being governed and the desire of governing, passion, youth ingrafted by a little mean education, will even afford matter for supporting their differences, which must end in something very dismall, their healths are equally ruined

[1] WSP 60.98

by it, and it is impossible they can hold out so. . . .'[1] This was written as early as 21 April 1722, and it could be that the Duke of Mar was the worst person possible for Hay to have written to in such confidence.

She went to take the baths at Lucca under the transparent *incognito* of the Contessa di Cornevaglia (Countess of Cornwall), and she was accompanied by Mrs Hay. Once there, she obviously began to miss James and wrote him a long letter, on 31 July 1722, in her sprawling, untidy, childish handwriting which ran upwards across the page. Her spelling in French was appalling; she had obviously learnt the language by ear and spoke it idiomatically. She told him that his letter had been 'a great consolation' because it showed that distance had not diminished his love for her and, although their separation cost her much, she was convinced that it could only serve to consolidate their mutual love. Then comes a pathetic little statement: 'I am trying now to overcome my bad temper so as to appear to you in the future as the best girl in the world. I am delighted to learn that one no longer thinks about the nasty plan 'D' which has deprived me of the satisfaction of being with my Carissimo. . . . I shall not know rest or quietude until I am in the arms of my Carissimo.'[2]

His tenderness for her was clear when he rushed to Lucca at the end of September 1722 to cushion her against the shock of her mother's imminent death. He was with her when the news finally reached them, and he stayed with her in Bologna, doing his best to distract her by driving her around the countryside so that she could visit the religious communities at Certosa, San Dominico, Sant'Agnese (where he had sent the silk flowers during his early courtship of her), and Corpus Domini.

They stayed in the Palazzo Belloni where James had stayed in the year previous to his marriage, surrounded by a magnificence of crimson velvet and hangings of gold. He was well liked by the society of Bologna, who did everything to make his consort feel welcome too. The attitude of the Bolognese towards him personally was always very different from that of the Romans. In the first place, they accepted him as one of their own: he was partly of north-Italian extraction and a member of the house of Modena. In the second place, they had no reason to complain, as some Romans did, that his presence was a drain upon their State's finances. And, lastly, their social climate was less influenced by the personal likes and dislikes of the Pontiff.

As on the King's earlier visit, the Cardinal Legate of Bologna sent precious gifts, this time to the Queen as well. From the balcony of the Palazzo Almandini they watched the racing horses and silken banners of the medieval *palio* of San Petronio, and James himself revived the ancient

[1] WSP 61.29 Tr. Author   [2] WSP 61.64

English ceremony of touching for the King's Evil. This supposed God-given power of a king of the legitimate line, through the laying on of hands, was thought to cure scrofula, and a line of children suffering from the disease were brought to the King as he knelt on a velvet cushion with Clementina's Dominican confessor at his side. After a reading from the Gospel containing the line 'You shall lay hands on the sick and they shall recover', the King laid his hands upon them and in several cases, apparently, they were healed.

In October they returned to Rome, as he hoped that he would still be able to get away to Spain and thence to England in one of the three ships which Charles Wogan, with his usual pertinacity and persuasive charm, had managed to extract once again from the King of Spain. But all Wogan's efforts were to be set at nought when three British ships set out from Gibraltar, on information received, to give chase to the Spanish vessels.

Rome was rife with spies at that time and, as Baron Philip von Stosch, alias 'John Walton', wrote to London for Walpole's benefit, even the tapestries on King James's wall spoke,[1] and he was constantly asking for more money to pay all his informants. Besides this network which enmeshed not only the Palazzo Muti, but also the Stuart summer palace at Albano, much could be gleaned from the gossip of the King's friends and acquaintance in Rome and Paris. Walton was friendly with the Princesse des Ursins who had now made Rome her home, and with the Cardinals Gualterio and Alberoni; while Lady Lansdowne, wife of James's representative in Paris, was on friendly terms with Marlborough's brother, Colonel Churchill, who was frequently visiting the Continent from London. John Walton quickly estimated that the man who was of most use to the King was John Hay, and it became part of the British government's plan to remove Hay from James by any means possible. It was precisely here that Mar was to have such value for them: if they had given him a pension and paid his debts it was not merely because they felt philanthropic: he had to render service in return.

Whatever suspicions James may have had earlier on, they were confirmed when Mar, entirely on his own initiative, gave the French Regent a memorial (supposedly backed by the King but of which he was completely ignorant), asking for Orléans's support of the Stuarts, since France had remained neutral in the last venture. But the condition which Mar suggested to the Regent for this support was that autonomy should be given to Scotland and Ireland. This was bound to offend the English and Mar could not have been ignorant of the fact that it was more than likely, in view of the French and British alignment, that it would eventually reach English ears.

After the betrayal of Atterbury and now this latest piece of outrage, the

[1] Lesley Lewis, *Connoisseurs and Secret Agents in Eighteenth-Century Rome*, p. 71

Chapter Twenty Three

Death began to remove a number of the characters in the Stuart drama: Cardinal Dubois who, since he had received his hat through James's intervention, had been much more favourably disposed towards the Jacobites of late, died in August 1723; the Duc d'Orléans, Regent of France, died in the last month of the year and the Duc de Bourbon succeeded to his position; while Pope Innocent XIII, who had not cared nor done very much for the Stuarts, died in March 1724. Cardinal Orsini was elected Pope Benedict XIII, and this was in the King's favour.

On 16 January 1724, Wogan wrote from Madrid to inform the King that Philip V of Spain had abdicated in favour of his seventeen-year-old son, Luis: 'A King of 40 years and in good health, abdicating freely his Kingdom to become an hermit in a wilderness, with a wife of 31, reserving for his society the Marquises of Grimaldo, Valouse and his confessor. . . .'[1] But the young Spanish prince died soon after and Philip was forced to resume his crown, leaving a spiritual kingdom for a temporal one.

All these changes, plus the fact that he was once more trying to engage the interest of Tsar Peter the Great, kept James very busy during 1723 and 1724, and this did not help the already strained relations between himself and Clementina. Mar had strongly recommended a Mrs Sheldon, sister-in-law to General Dillon, for the position of governess to Prince Charles Edward, and the Queen who, as she was against John Hay, necessarily often fell in with the ideas of the Duke, agreed to employ her. Now Mrs Sheldon became Mar's chief instrument in stirring up trouble between the King and the Queen, and between the Queen and John Hay. She was a Catholic, and resented the presence of the Protestant under-nurses about the little Prince. She was adept at fanning the flames of Clementina's wrath when directed against her husband or Hay, and also at playing upon her little vanities. Clementina appeared to stand in need of a confidante, or a woman friend; she never seemed to make particular friends about the court and this would have been as well, for nothing was needed to give rise to petty jealousies. She had not long lost her mother, and her sisters were far away, therefore she was forced to rely upon the friendship of a subordinate: it was unfortunate for everyone concerned that she should have chosen Mrs Sheldon.

Clementina's bursts of gaiety became rarer, and she developed a state of

[1] Quoted by H. Tayler in *A Jacobite Epilogue*

depression which may have had some origin in the after-effects of the birth of her child, but certainly was to some degree congenital. Perhaps, if the resources of modern medicine had been available then, something as comparatively simple as an excess or a deficiency of the thyroid gland would have been diagnosed, but such speculations are fruitless. She refused to go out socially, and then complained that she was bored and practically a prisoner in her own house. James encouraged her to go out, but to no avail. Religious duties took up more and more of her time, but they had not yet assumed the proportions of the obsession they were to become a few years later.

Though requested to by the writer, the Duke of Mar did not burn the letter which John Hay sent to him on 21 April 1722 referring to the state of tension between the King and Queen, and it is more than likely that Mar showed the letter to her. Whatever happened, her dislike of John Hay grew and everyone was aware of it.

James's distrust of Mar was now so great that he sent Hay to Paris to try to find out what plan the Duke was concocting. Hay was away in August 1723 on this mission, and both Gualterio and Atterbury wrote to warn him not to stay away too long, because his enemies never rested from their work in his absence.

One thing immediately apparent, and that was that Mar knew far too much about the negotiations with Peter the Great. As early as February 1722, John Walton had reported to London details of a Jacobite agent's work in Russia.[1] Matters were not helped in 1724 when John Hay's elder brother, the Earl of Kintoull, who was inclined to listen to Mar, decided to take the oath of allegiance to George I: Hay was still not accepted by a number at the court, and it was felt quite likely that he might go the way his brother had done. But in this they were wrong: whatever Hay's shortcomings were (and he was credited with being cunning, avaricious, overbearing, etc., although not disliked as much as Murray had been) his fidelity to the King was without question, and his letters show a sincerity which is lacking in many others sent to James.

The news of the difference between Clementina and James over the education of their child, and her resentment at the Protestant element contained therein, seemed as nothing in comparison when it became rumoured that the Queen had some reason to be jealous of Mrs Hay. There is no indication that Clementina ever accused the King of infidelity nor, for that matter, that he was ever unfaithful to her. Even if he had ever had the inclination to be so, his reputation would have been at too high a risk, and he certainly would not have been able to ask the Pope or any of the Catholic powers of Europe for help, to regard it only in a material light. This

[1] Lewis, *op. cit.*, p. 65

Henry Benedict Stuart, Cardinal York, from a contemporary portrait by
Batoni. (*National Portrait Gallery, London*)

14. Charles Edward Stuart in middle age, from a contemporary portrait by
Batoni. (*National Portrait Gallery, London*)

'infidelity' seems to have existed in the mind of Mar alone, and it was he who insinuated it into his dealings with the British government's representatives in Paris, and also with John Walton in Rome, who began to spread the rumour about in the shortest time possible and in a way calculated to do the most damage to the King's reputation. John Hay wrote to the Queen, referring to a letter written by a person of high degree which mentioned the rumour, and he suggested that the Queen's mind should be put at rest with regard to Mrs Hay. He stated that there was no need for him to proclaim his wife's innocence, but that he was prepared to send her far away if the Queen should desire it. He continued:

I was not ignorant, Madam, even before your Majesty had been six weeks married, of endeavours then used to raise jealousy in yr. Maj. as to ye King's conduct in relation to Mrs Hay. I was so much persuaded then of the King's virtue as well of Mrs Hay, who I did believe would not throw away her reputation upon any King or Prince in the World, and seeing yr Majesty's goodness towards Mrs Hay continue, I then believed that these were only assertions and contrivances of some people by which they might be enabled to gett att their own ends and that they had no manner of impression upon yr Majesty. But since the same story is renewed again, I beg yr Majesty would lett me know what would be agreeable to you yt I should do to remove uneasiness – that yr Majesty may be persuaded that I am ready to sacrifice everything that is dearest to me for your satisfaction, since there is nothing that I'll stick at one moment to make yr untion with the King flourish. I most humble beg of your Majesty that this letter may be seen by nobody, for a Lady's character is a nice thing to expose and as I have said nothing in Mrs Hay's vindication which the design of it does not lead me to do, yr Majesty may easily perceive that I have calculated my letter for yourself alone. To which I beg yr Majesty will be graciously pleased to send me two lines of ane answer. This is a subject the King is intirely a stranger to and I hope yr Majesty wont mention it to him. You'll do me a particular favour if you are so gracious as to return me the letter yt I may putt it in the fire. Had I been able to putt on a coat, I would not have dared to trouble yr Majesty with so long a letter, to which I shall only add, that the King has not these 6 weeks past mentioned the least thing to me of any family uneasiness.

Allow me to subscribe myself with all profound sumission, Madam, Your Majesty's most dutifull, most faithfull and most devoted servant,
John Hay.[1]

1 WSP, 64.93

That the letter itself is still extant, and that there is no record of the Queen's having replied to Hay's decent appeal gives some indication of her disturbed state of mind at this time. The letter is undated, but seems to belong to some time during the period 1723 to 1724.

Clementina appears to have held nothing against Mrs Hay at this time. When Lord Kintoull made his peace with the Hanoverians there were various family matters to be settled between him and his brother and, although John Hay himself could not return to England under pain of death, his wife was able to do so with a certain safety, particularly since she was not under the same penalty. So Mrs Hay set out for England, completed her business, but was arrested as she attempted to return, and was put in Newgate. The Queen was pregnant with her second child at that time, and so anxious was she to have Mrs Hay with her that both she and the King asked the French authorities to intercede for them and to obtain the release of Mrs Hay. This was achieved but not before the Queen had given birth to a son on 6 March 1725. He was baptized Henry Benedict Maria Clement Thomas Francis Xavier by the Pope, and was created Duke of York.

In that same month in which James was able to rejoice in another son to help perpetuate the name of Stuart, he learned of the death of Peter the Great. This meant in fact the end of their hopes of outside assistance and, virtually, the end of the Stuart hopes of mounting any invasion of Britain for the time being, unless they were to depend on Scotland alone, since all of Europe that mattered was tied up very cleverly on England's part in some form of alignment or alliance which precluded help for the Jacobites. Neither the Scots nor James felt that the time was right for him to depend upon an entirely Scottish operation, so there was nothing he could do but wait, enduring meanwhile an unforeseeable term of practical inactivity. It was all the more important now that he should keep in touch with his adherents in Britain lest their interest should flag, and his correspondence continued to increase: probably no previous British king had ever written or received so many letters.

The birth of two sons to the King did much to inspire the Jacobites 'over the water', and particularly when they learned that both children were strong and healthy and good to look upon. Prince Charles Edward was reputed to possess a devastating charm even at that early age and – as was only to be expected, considering his parents – a great determination and will of his own. When Pope Benedict XIII was elected, the Prince of Wales was presented to him shortly afterwards in the Vatican gardens, but refused to kneel to His Holiness, a fact which greatly pleased the Protestant Jacobites.

By August 1724, James had decided that it was time that Charles should be removed from the care of women as it was becoming clear that he was needing a firmer hand to guide him; also it was time for his formal education to begin. He had already shown a precocious feeling for music and, at the age of four was performing quite creditably upon the violin. James had always had a love of music, perhaps inherited from his Italian ancestors, and this seems to have passed on to his son. Both boys, particularly the Duke of York, had attractive singing voices as well. That August, James recalled James Murray, who had been travelling around Europe in some style and had passed a most agreeable stay with James's friends in Lorraine. He created Murray Earl of Dunbar and appointed him governor to the Prince of Wales. This was a deliberate step to show that where his training for becoming a king was concerned, Charles was not entirely in Catholic hands. But, in order to ensure his religion was properly looked after, he also appointed Sir Thomas Sheridan as under-governor. Nothing was more calculated to infuriate Mrs Sheldon, who saw the new appointments not only as a slur upon her own work, but also, in the case of Murray, as a deliberate attempt to convert the little Prince for political ends. She lost no time in working up Clementina into an equal demonstration of anger. In March 1725, James had definitely appointed John Hay as Secretary of State instead of Mar, who was, however, still attached in a nebulous fashion, to the Paris headquarters, although James tried to ensure that nothing of any importance went through his hands. With the office of Secretary, James gave John Hay the titular earldom of Inverness, and this, too, did not please the Queen. When the Protestant Lady Nithsdale was put in charge of the infant Duke of York, it was more than Clementina could stand. She demanded that James should dismiss the Hays, and he refused. Murray, or Dunbar as he was now to be known, was an old and trusted servant to James, but he was now aware of the man's personal limitations, and during the previous four years he had come to rely upon John Hay, or Lord Inverness, more than anybody else.

Clementina became more and more disturbed and hysterical, threatening to leave James unless he dismissed the three people she detested. He was equally determined not only to be master in his own house but to be free to appoint whoever he chose to any position he might choose. If once he allowed Clementina the right to interfere in those appointments of the royal household, which were necessarily of political origin, he would be subjected to the same persecution in affairs of state.

Their domestic situation was now the gossip of the courts and coffee-houses of all Europe. It created untold damage to the reputation of the Stuart cause and, if George I had ordered such a situation, he could not have managed it better. Cardinal Alberoni, still an exile from the court of

Chapter Twenty Four

There could have been no greater irony in James's life than that the wife he loved so dearly should accuse him of deviating from the religion which was costing him his crown. Apart from the facts that she just could not see that the Protestant appointments were simply a matter of political expediency, and that his seeming neglect of her for attention to minute details of state was necessary to regain the crown and safeguard the lives of those dedicated to helping him to do so, the disparity in their ages (thirty-seven and twenty-two) and their temperaments was too great. The marriage, which had begun so well, foundered on the rocks of incompatability. But nothing could alter his deep affection for her. Her lack of maturity and of inner resources, apart from a hysterical yet sincere religious observance, made her incapable of responding to his overtures of reconciliation with anything but petulance.

Benedict XIII, more politically naïve than his predecessor, was on the Queen's side, as was a great part of Roman society. The day after her flight, the Pope sent a bishop to tell the King that he would not tolerate the education of the Princes as Protestants, nor his adultery with Lady Inverness. James lost no time in telling the Pope to mind his own business: he was not asking for advice on how to run his own family.[1] He could not believe that the Pope meant to charge him with adultery, or that the bearer of the message, a bishop, had not made some mistake, otherwise the messenger would have 'run the risk of having to leave the house by the window instead of the staircase'. Benedict then sent two cardinals to see the Queen; she had already refused to see Cardinal Gualterio, Protector of England. The Cardinals asked about her feelings, particularly with regard to Lady Inverness, but all she would reply, over and over again, was: 'Je n'aime pas ces gens-là' – 'I do not like those people.'

James refused to believe that she alone was responsible for her attitude, and wrote to her uncle, the Duke of Parma, to the Spanish Queen and to the Duke of Ormonde: 'This is the work of our enemies who have misled the Queen to her ruin. . . .'[2] He wrote to her father, explaining what had happened and imputing it to her high ideals of conscience and honour in which she had been misled by 'persons of high rank and virtue'. He asked him to take her back into his palace at Ohlau because 'it is noways decent for her to remain in Rome.'[3]

[1] WSP, 87.L54   [2] WSP, 87.82   [3] WSP, 87.81

To Clementina herself he wrote:

Your conduct towards me, the manner in which I have been threatened, and the public damage done to me by your retreat into a convent, although I feel them as I ought, touch me less than the misfortune and shame to which you will expose yourself by so strange an action. I feel no resentment against you, for I am convinced that the malice and cunning of our enemies have imposed upon your youth and the weakness of your sex. . . . Return to reason, to duty, to yourself and to me, who await your submission with open arms, to restore you to peace and happiness as far as depends upon me.[1]

But to submit was just what Clementina was not going to do and it was not tactful of James to remind her of her youth and the 'weakness' of her sex when, in escaping from Austria, she had undergone an experience which a much older member of the opposite sex might well have shirked. He continued, two days later on 11 November 1725: 'It is certain, Madam, that I have loved only you and that I have never wished for anything more than to please you in everything except where reason, my honour and the good of my affairs are concerned.' He refers to the patience over the past two years with which he suffered her petulance and, 'when at times you scarcely wished to speak with me or look at me, I have had recourse only to silence'.

With regard to the rumours flying about the Invernesses, he pointed out that there was not a single fact to support them. He had taken away the direction of the household from Lord Inverness some time ago in order to please her, and since then

his wife has never appear'd before you, but when you have asked for her. . . . In our present circumstances, I could not turn him out, without ruining my Interest and putting my affairs in the utmost confusion: and yet, tired and afflicted to see himself the perpetual mark of your unjust anger, as he has so long been that of my enemies, he has often desired his discharge, and nothing but my positive command could keep him near me. See, Madam, the difficulties in which you put me, and where is the honest man who, after such scenes as you have shown the world, will dare to serve me?

In so far as the Prince of Wales was concerned, it was true that he had given orders that Charles Edward's governor and sub-governor should accompany him everywhere: they had been with him continually in his own chamber, although that had not applied always when they had taken him to visit his mother. The reason for this order was to prevent him run-

[1] WSP, 87.94

278

ning off 'to the servants where children learn nothing good' (perhaps a reference to some a lack of surveillance on the part of Mrs Sheldon?) 'But all the world could see that your excess of anxiety only began and reached their peak since I have taken my son from her [Mrs Sheldon's] hands and from the women's.' He ends '. . . do not resist any longer these last efforts of my love which only awaits your return to re-awaken, never more to falter or to end.'[1]

Recapitulating this in less personal terms, the King sent a memorial to his representatives in London and abroad. Some explanation was necessary, for there were those among his own entourage who believed Clementina's story, including Bishop Atterbury. This, in itself, was sufficient to bring joy to the heart of Walpole.

Alberoni visited the Queen every day and was indefatigable in his efforts to 'help' her. Whether or not he was a spy for England, the Cardinal certainly had an axe to grind regarding his personal position *vis-à-vis* the Pope. After his rejection by Philip V, he had come to Rome and had risen to eminence in the counsels of Innocent XIII, but everything had changed when Benedict XIII was elected in 1724, and he had lost much of his influence. If he could have engineered the dismissal of James' Protestant servants, he would have risen in the new Pontiff's estimation. He still had some influence with Elizabeth Farnese, the Queen of Spain, and at first she naturally took her cousin Clementina's side. Spain's attitude was reflected in its treatment of poor Wogan who had gone there in the hopes of preferment in the army. But all hopes of promotion ceased, and he was regarded 'like a Dog in a nine-pin Alley' and told that he should 'think himself happy in keeping what he had got'.[2]

When Clementina was not spending long hours on her knees in chapel, she wrote, at Alberoni's dictation, to the Queen of Spain, the King of France, to Ormonde and to Atterbury, and also to her sister, the Duchesse de Bouillon:

> Mr Hay and his lady are the cause that I am retired into a Convent. . . .
> al the civilities I have shown them have only served to render them the
> more insolent. . . . I would rather suffer death than live in the King's
> palace with persons that have no religion, honour nor conscience, and
> who, not content with having been the authors of so fatal a separation
> between the King and me, are continually teasing him to part with his
> best friends and most faithful subjects.[3]

On his side, James wrote to Atterbury, then in Brussels: 'The Queen neither hath nor indeed can have any reason for leaving of me, and her

[1] WSP, 87.94   [2] WSP, 233.170   [3] Lockhart, *Memoirs*, Vol. 2, p. 265

pretended motives all centre in matters quite out of a wife's sphere, and entirely subservient to D[uke]. of Mar's projects.'[1] In the following month, December 1725, he wrote to Ormonde in Spain: 'It would seem that the project has been long layd and by letters of D. of Mar's I can see that his voice has been for several years to remove Lord Inverness by the Queen's means.[2]

The most immediate material effect of Clementina's action was the suspension of the papal pension to James, which was disastrous not only to himself but to all the Jacobites dependent upon him for sustenance. In February 1726 the King offered to replace Lord Dunbar (who, like Inverness, was growing weary of so grave a dispute of which he was an innocent cause) with the Duke of Ormonde, then in Spain. Ormonde he would replace with the Earl Marischal. But Ormonde, too, was a Protestant, so nothing was accomplished.

Economy necessitated a withdrawal from Rome to Bologna, where living was much cheaper, and also it is likely that James would have felt himself to be in a more friendly atmosphere in the north and in a city he knew well and liked. The Pope tried to prevent this by offering to act as a go-between with Clementina, providing James got rid of his Protestant chaplains. All that the King would concede was that he would send them to Florence. Then the Pope demanded that he dismiss Dunbar, and the King lost his patience: everybody, including the chaplains, was to go to Bologna. He was given back three-fifths of the pension, the rest being made over to the Queen for her private maintenance.

He wrote to her in September, asking if she would join him and the children in Bologna, but she refused, saying that she was at last enjoying peace of mind. On the October night before he left he went to see her accompanied by a small suite. As he entered the convent reception room the Queen bowed low, but he raised her in his arms and led her into an inner room where they remained for about half an hour in private conversation. Nothing was known of what passed between them, but James came out of the room alone. He returned to the Palazzo Muti.

The English and Scottish Jacobites were appalled at this turn of events: since Clementina was second cousin to the Queen of Spain, first cousin to the Emperor and closely related to Maria Leszczynska, the Queen of France, it seemed as if she had wilfully disposed of all possible sources of assistance. But, of his own accord, the Emperor had decided to curb England's power if possible, and he began to show an interest in the Jacobites during the winter of 1726, but said that he could only help them with the assistance of

[1] WSP, 87.97
[2] WSP, 87.138

Spain. As no help from Spain was forthcoming, at least while James was separated from Clementina, this scheme fell to the ground.

For the most part his mind was now occupied with how Sir John Graeme, his representative in Vienna, was progressing with the Emperor, also whether there would ever be any sign of Spain changing its mind, and whether anything was to be achieved with Peter the Great's widow, the Tsarina Catherine I; but James also had to play a social role in Bologna out of courtesy to his hosts. He was invited to all the large houses of the district; in the evenings he attended receptions and assemblies, where he played 'ombre', a card-game he liked, with the aristocratic ladies of Bologna; he walked in the gardens of the beautiful Villa Mirabella; and from a special box he watched more than one performance given by the Duke of Parma's theatrical troop.

The children were sincerely admired wherever they went, and James was proud of them. Six-year-old Prince Charles must have had a constitution of iron, since he was invited to many functions along with the King his father. He danced with the newly married Contessa Popoli and with the little daughter of Senator Bargellini, 'admired by all the nobility for his gallantry and wit'.[1] A magnificent ball was given in the Casa Marescotti in honour of his birthday on 31 December, and the light of thousands of candles, indoors and out, danced over the satins and diamonds of the guests in their gala costumes, while the King himself led a suite of English dances. There were more diversions for the carnival season in February, with a grand ball at the Casa Fibbia in honour of the King of England, at which twelve ladies, including Lady Inverness, danced – magnificently dressed and bejewelled in the Spanish style, a gesture which, no doubt, it was hoped the Spanish court would come to hear of. The Cardinal Legate of Bologna gave a sumptuous repast at his palace on 22 February and, the King and the Prince of Wales, and even little Henry, attended a further ball at the Casa Fibbia on 1 March. To this day, Italian children keep late nights, but the social round of the small Prince of Wales in 1726 and 1727 in Bologna was, to say the least, extraordinary.

They were housed comfortably enough; Lord Inverness wrote to the Duke of Ormonde in Spain just after their arrival in October 1726:

> Nothing has occurred since my last – the King has got into his own palace which is one hired from Senator Fantucci and has a noble staircase which most of the strangers that pass this way, come to see. There is but little conveniency in the house, but by a Communication that is made to another place, the royal family will be well lodged. I have got a little

---

[1] L. Frati, *Maria Clementina Sobieska in Italia*

house, pretty near, built by a whimsical physician who has laid out so much money on it that he is obliged to quit for the payment of his debts, to my no small ease. It is very like an English house, and if it were on the road betwixt Bristol and London, I would make you an offer of it, but where it stands I should be very sorry to see you in it.

By the sharp weather that is already come in we don't doubt of feeling here a pretty severe winter, which will do well to season us that are used to a Roman climate and prepare us for colder weather which I hope we shall soon feel at home.[1]

All the social gatherings, the necessity of the outward show of charm and affability must have made tremendous demands on James as well as on various members of his suite. An added complication at this time was the resignation of the Duke of Mar, because, welcome to James though it was, it meant that he had to leave the Paris agency to Lansdowne and Dillon alone. A little later, Mar wrote a fulsome letter to the King, underlining his devotion to the royal family:

How to be of service to your Majesty and the Royal ffamily, [*sic*], on which the interest of my country depends, having been from my infancie the chief object of all my views and wishes, to be under your displeasure, as I have had the misfortoun (the innocently I think) to be for these two long years, could not but be the greatest and most sensible affliction to me. All my consolation was that time would show and make plain to you the uprightness and sincerity of all my actions and intentions towards you, and how groundless were all the assertions and culumnies maliciously thrown upon me. . . .[2]

At the end of March, James returned to Rome, determined to do something, anything, to end the deadlock with Clementina. There was, in reality, only one thing he could do. Lord Inverness had offered to resign rather than to become the innocent cause of the end of all the Jacobite hopes. Reluctantly the King accepted the resignation and, on 9 April 1727, the Invernesses left for Pisa and Lucca in case the Queen should decide to go to Bologna. Told by Cardinal Bentivoglio that Lord Inverness was going, Clementina replied that it 'was a great point, but not all'.[3]

While he was in Rome that April, James took his elder son to call upon the Pope and recite his catechism. This he did perfectly, and thereby convinced His Holiness that his young soul was in no danger of conversion by the Protestant Lord Dunbar. Having at least made this point, and waiting to see what Clementina would do next, James and the little boys left for the

[1] WSP, 98.19   [2] WSP, 106.88   [3] WSP, 106.40

north again, this time to Croce de Biacco, outside Bologna, where he had bought a holiday house, the Palazzo Alamandini. The children travelled after the King, arriving a few days later on 4 June. The two children were now the only respite in his solitary, dedicated life and he was devoted to them. Now and again the files of the letters written in his own neat, clear and precise hand, to the Pope, to princes of the Church and to heads of state, are interrupted by one written in slightly larger characters than usual to 'Dear Carluccio', his pet name for Charles, telling him and his brother that he is looking forward to seeing them, or is thinking of them. Such are the few lines written while he was waiting for Charles to come to him at the seaside resort of Pesaro on 7 October 1726: 'Dear Carluccio – I long to know you are over past the hills and to see you again, be very good and give my blessing to Henry. God bless you both, adieu, *J.R.*'[1]

On 11 June 1727, George I died suddenly at Osnabrück, but the news did not reach James until a month later. It was at this time that the Duke of Liria visited the King, on his way to take up his post as Spanish ambassador at St Petersburg, and, as nothing had been heard from Clementina in spite of the fact that Lord and Lady Inverness had gone, he wrote to her, in the name of the King and Queen of Spain, stating that it was time that such a disagreable affair should come to an end because it was ruining Jacobite hopes all over Europe.[2] To this, Clementina replied in a curt few lines of thanks, adding that she was incapable of doing the least wrong to her honour and conscience.[3] However, it did seem to have some effect on her, or perhaps it was due to a hint discreetly dropped that she might be refused the sacraments if she continued to fail in her duty, but whatever the reason was, she left the convent as suddenly as she had arrived, and set out for Bologna and the Palazzo Alamandini.

As soon as James knew that George was dead, he summoned Inverness from Pisa and, together with Sir John Graeme, they set out from Bologna under cover of going to meet the Queen. Liria was instructed to keep Russian interest alive in the Jacobite cause, and he left for the east. The King did not yet know Spain's reactions, what the English attitude to him now was, or whether he could hope for French help again. He rushed across northern Italy, through northern France and arrived in Lorraine in less than a fortnight. Here he realized that, very far from receiving any help from France, the chief minister, Cardinal Fleury, was only too anxious to prevent him entering the country. If he had allowed James to do so, there was every possibility that the new-found goodwill between France and England might be shattered. Nevertheless he did restore the pension James had received from France, suspended since 1724.

[1] WSP, 97.148   [2] WSP, 106.82   [3] WSP, 106.112

He could not look for help from Sweden either, because George II managed to buy off Queen Ulrica for a sum of £50,000 a year. The Scottish Jacobites reported back to the King, while he was staying with the Duke of Lorraine outside Nancy, that he would not be able to rely upon any solid support in numbers from them and, on the receipt of this news, he knew that there was no point in persisting further. The French were also putting pressure on the Duke of Lorraine to cease harbouring him and, rather than cause his old friend any more embarrassment, James left for Avignon. The Duke of Liria and Mr O'Rourke, who had replaced Graeme in Vienna, did their best to try to rouse the Emperor to some positive interest, but to no avail; neither could Colonel O'Brien (who was then in Paris while Graeme was with the King) move the inflexible Cardinal Fleury.

While James was away, Clementina arrived at the royal residence, embraced her sons and wept. The Pope had given orders to the Bolognese authorities that she must be entertained royally, but she said she did not want to see anyone, and gracefully declined the many invitations sent to her by the ladies of Bolognese society. She had no inclination to do anything but visit the shrines and religious monuments and houses of the neighbourhood. She was especially taken with the convent of St Peter the Martyr. There she struck up a very close friendship with one of the nuns, Sister Maria Laura Chiarini who was, apparently, of an 'artistic' turn of mind. Clementina paid her more than 108 visits during a year and a half, and Sister Maria Laura painted more than one hundred votive saints for her edification! As a further mark of her devotion, the Queen donated a beautiful gown of crimson velvet to make a rich baldacchino for the convent chapel. There was no doubt that she was happiest and found her greatest fulfilment in the religious life. She could leave her husband and her children without an apparent qualm and find the utmost satisfaction in driving from church to convent and from convent to church. Her piety was patently sincere and, if it had not been for her strict religious upbringing and conviction, she might well have resolved her disappointment with James and all that he represented in the much more usual Italian fashion of taking a lover; but this was not Clementina's way.

While James was at Avignon he asked Clementina to join him, but she refused, perhaps because Lord Inverness was again with the King, but, as soon as he had seen James settled in, Inverness returned to his wife at Pisa. Sir John Graeme was not doing too well in his new position as Secretary of State: he had not been long in the position before there was a mishap in his correspondence, resulting in the betrayal and arrest of one of the most reliable of James's couriers, George Lockhart of Carnwath. Lockhart managed to escape to Holland, but denounced Graeme as a traitor. Later he was to discover the real traitor, a man called Strahan, and to admit his mistake; but by then James had decided that Graeme might be too great a risk, even though he himself knew he was innocent. So he arranged for Graeme to go to Spain for a few months, and then just before he returned to Italy, he recalled him to Avignon where he could do little damage. He retained the title of Secretary, but James looked after his own affairs and correspondence from then onwards.

Lord Dunbar was fully occupied in Bologna in keeping Clementina in a quiet frame of mind, and delegated more and more of his governorship of the Prince to the under-governor, Sir Thomas Sheridan. Sir Thomas was devoted to the little boy, but his teaching capacity was not of the greatest, and it is from this period, when his father was absent, his mother preoccupied with religion, and with discipline generally lacking, that the seeds of Charles's future shortcomings were probably sown.

Clementina, against the express wishes of James, had brought Mrs Sheldon with her to Bologna, and this did not help the situation with the King's intimates at court. Dunbar was more acceptable to the Queen than Inverness had been, but she treated him with scant civility and did her best to make his position untenable, although he was wise enough not to take offence. This would have been disastrous in the absence of the King, for then the Queen would have been left in command, and the Princes would almost certainly have fallen again under the bigoted influence of Mrs Sheldon.

All the time she was in Bologna and separated from James, Clementina was sending him short and affectionate letters, assuring him of her love and submission: it seemed as if, while they were apart, she could play the part of a loving wife: a typical letter written on 5 August 1727 ends, 'Your very humble, very obedient and ever-faithful wife, *C.*' with a post-scriptum: 'our children continue in good health'.[1]

James returned to Bologna when the English government once again threatened the Pope with the bombardment of Civitavecchia, an ever-effective menace. Added to this, there was a certain hint that the papal pension to James might be stopped if he did not leave Avignon and, because so many beside himself were dependent upon that pension, he had recourse to nothing other than to go.

Clementina had wisely despatched Mrs Sheldon to a convent a few days before the King's return on 9 January 1728. On the following day he wrote to Inverness in Pisa: 'I returned here on Wednesday and found the family in very good health. I was much pleased to find the Duke [of York] remember me and so well pleased to see me.' He had not seen either child for

---

[1] WSP, 109.31

just over six months, and it would have been no surprise if little Henry had forgotten what his father looked like. He continued:

> I have some hopes that matters may be made up in the right way at last betwixt the Queen and me; I have behaved myself with more *disinvoltura* on this occasion than I really thought I was capable of, and I have already settled in a friendly manner with the Queen by giving her and taking to myself an entire liberty. She leads a most retired, melancholy life, and though I have encouraged her to alter it, I don't believe she will, but that's her own business, and I shall not constrain her.[1]

The following March he wrote again to Inverness about the Queen's way of life which was beginning to show some signs of religious mania:

> She leads a most singular life, she takes no manner of amusement, not even taking the air, and when she is not at Church or at Table, is locked up in her room, and sees no mortal but her maids or so; she eats meat this Lent, but fasts to that degree that I believe no married woman that pretends to have children ever did; I am very little with her. I let her do what she will. . . . She has quite left off dressing parure. . . .[2]

It was about this time that Clementina had two false pregnancies: she was suffering from self-delusion but, in any case, as James had said, her state of health at that time was not conducive to child-bearing. He did all he could to surround her with love and affection and she, on her side, allowed him to do so whilst doing her best to love him as far as she was able in return. But it seemed as if her preoccupation with religious devotions created a wall of glass between them: there was no hostility, not even an armed neutrality, but rather an atmosphere of mutual toleration. This led to a sense of strain on James's part, and it cannot have been a very relaxed atmosphere for two young children, much as he tried to make it possible for them. Clementina loved her children too, but it was a rarified kind of love she gave them.

Not very long after James's return to Bologna, he took the Prince of Wales, now eight years old, on a tour of northern Italy, with the expressed intention of taking him to see his great-aunt, the Dowager Duchess of Parma. This visit was a great success and James called Lord Inverness to Parma while they were there, and asked him to return as Secretary of State; but Inverness asked permission to decline, knowing that such an appointment was bound to meet with the disapproval of the Queen.

James badly needed a Secretary of State: at this time in Rome he was carrying the burden of all correspondence himself: since Atterbury had come

[1] WSP, 113.37   [2] WSP, 114.16

to France there was no one he could completely rely upon in England. Lords North and Grey had also crossed over to France, leaving Lord Cornbury in charge, and he was not very effective. There was also the Duchess of Buckingham, half-sister of the Duke of Berwick, a devoted Jacobite, whose heart was in the right place but her head not always. It was the 'emotional' Jacobites who proved to be a greater danger to the cause than any spy of the Georges. Atterbury was beginning to feel the effects of age and he was becoming renowned for his displays of bad temper. He quarrelled with Colonel O'Brien in Paris, and retired in a fit of pique to the country. In March 1728, Cardinal Gualterio died: he had been a good friend to James and had often provided a buffer between the Pope and the King in moments of mutual exasperation. Another hope was extinguished when it was learned that the Tsarina Catherine of Russia had died at the age of thirty-nine, and before the Duke of Liria had time to reach St Petersburg. She was succeeded by the young Tsar Peter II, a sickly boy of fourteen.

A peace congress was held at Soissons in June 1728, attended by representatives of Spain and the Alliance, and James sent a priest, Father O'Callaghan, as an observer and to confer with the Spanish and the Austrians about Jacobite interests. Spain tried to insist on the return of Gibraltar and Port Mahon, but Lord Stanhope, the English representative, threatened to leave the congress if this were granted.

At the same time another vain attempt was made to obtain his mother's dowry for James. The peace negotiations dragged on, and were only concluded at the end of the following year when Spain buried its differences with France and England in the Treaty of Seville and an end was made to the hostilities begun in 1725. In the House of Commons the division between the Whigs and King George II on one hand and the Tories on the other became more marked and, at the same time, some of the Tories showed themselves to be more overtly Jacobite. So, at a time when James had reason to hope for better things in London, Ormonde and O'Rourke, his men in Madrid and Vienna, were rendered virtually ineffectual. Towards the end of 1730, Walpole, following some devious plan of his own, let it be seen that he too was interested in the Jacobites, but James was not deceived: '. . . I have not the least reason to think that Walpole or any other of the present Ministers are anyways favourably disposed towards me.'[1] He had learnt a hard lesson with Bolingbroke.

In February 1730, Pope Benedict XIII died and was succeeded by Cardinal Corsini as Pope Clement XII. The King was a personal friend of the Pope's nephew, and the Corsini family was generally well disposed towards James. One of the first things the new Pontiff did was to try and make the

[1] WSP, 140.195

Queen see sense over the recall of Lord Inverness. She had gone out with James socially on one or two occasions, and there were times when it seemed as if she might be about to alter her way of life, but sooner or later she would return to her drastic fasting and the hours upon her knees: James's only joy and relaxation at this time were his two children; Charles and Henry were now becoming companions for him and he wrote with affection to Lord Inverness: 'My children give me a great dale [*sic*] of comfort, I am really in love with the little Duke, for he is the finest child can be seen.'[1] He knew that he was wanting in some of the parental virtues and that he sometimes lacked patience and calm, but he directed his spiritual reading towards conformity with the will of God. The quietism of Fénélon's teaching was now so deeply implanted in the character of the King that the formidable spiritual strength it gave him was also in danger of becoming merely resignation where his material affairs were concerned. While his sons were so young, he knew that he could not afford to cease from fighting for the cause which had been his since birth, but he also knew that if the Divine Will did not choose to place the sceptre in his own hand, he now had heirs to whom it would pass as their inalienable right.

His methods of fighting were straightforward: where deeds were not possible he would rely upon his declarations and memorials sent to England and elsewhere in Europe, as well as upon the good word of the faithful. He never stooped to print the kind of pamphlets which the Whig gutter-press scattered over London and other cities. Never once did he consider selling out his religious conscience for the crown, and he remained as adamant about this as he had ever been: '. . . I and my children are Catholics, and it is in vain to expect a change . . . . What have my Protestant Subjects to fear after all the assurances I have, and shall be willing to give for the security of the Church of England; Or would they have the Royal family to be the only persons in England constrained in points of Religion ?'[2]

Towards the end of 1730, Clement XII informed Cardinals Imperiali and Alberoni, both still of the Queen's party, that the existing situation between her and the King must end. She refused to explain her attitude to the Cardinals, so the Pope himself consented to give her an audience. He advised her to see the King's point of view, and to recognize his need of a servant and secretary such as Lord Inverness. Clementina said that she could not reconcile her own conscience and honour by accepting the Invernesses, but if the Pope would take it upon his conscience she would submit. Clement said that he had no intention of taking anything in the affair upon his conscience: it was a clear-cut case, and either the Queen acquiesced in her husband's choice, both as King and head of the family, or she had to

[1] WSP, 131.7   [2] WSP, 145.58

recognize herself at fault. At last Clementina knew that she was beaten: two months later, in December, she told James that she would welcome Lord and Lady Inverness with all courtesy. Writing to invite Lord Inverness back to Rome, James added: 'So, thank God, the affair is ended.'[1] Clementina was seen in company with her husband on several occasions, but still maintained her austere regime inside the Muti Palace.

At some time during 1730, Baron de Pollnitz, a visitor to Rome, met the royal couple. He had less to say about the King, describing him as tall, spare, beginning to stoop, dark and with an air of sadness about him and greatly resembling Charles II and James II. Clementina had obviously still retained her old magic, for he describes her eulogistically. But even allowing for eighteenth-century extravagance of expression, there is no doubt but that the Queen was still a very attractive woman at twenty-eight:

> The Queen is a Princess, who deserves in reality to be a queen, and though not a sparkling beauty, it may be said that her person is infinitely charming. She has, indeed, the character of a most accomplished lady, and never was there a better-natured person with more humility. She is friendly, compassionate, charitable, her piety is exemplary and, in truth, she leads the life of a saint, without affecting the show of ceremonial devotion; for she has nothing more at heart than to do good, and her love of one sublime virtue is incredible; for though she is heartily attached to her own religion, she has no rancour against those who differ from her in opinion, but would fain reclaim them by her good example and good nature. Were she mistress of a kingdom, she would certainly make it her rule to discharge the duties of her rank as became it; and indeed, nature has given her great advantages to acquit herself worthily in such a sphere, for she has a wonderful quick comprehension, an admirable memory, and she speaks Polish, High-Dutch, French, Italian and English so well, that it is not easy to distinguish which of those languages is most familiar to her. I own to you that of all the Princesses whom I ever had the honour to approach, I do not know one more deserving of the veneration of the public. I should be glad to see her happy: and if that respect and duty, from which I shall never depart, did not bind me so strongly to the King and Queen of Great Britain, I could wish to see her wear the crown of the three Kingdoms.[2]

One is always confronted by the strange dichotomy in Clementina's attitude: her publicly expressed religious toleration and her domestic bigotry with regard to her sons' education and to the King's intimates.

All through the year 1731 the Duchess of Buckingham was busy with her

[1] WSP, 141.37   [2] C. L. de Pollnitz, *Memoirs*, II, p. 196

schemes to effect the restoration. She had the moral support of Bishop Atterbury, but James himself did not become involved; indeed he seemed to stand apart from all the planning. He knew that without foreign aid nothing could be accomplished, and Berwick, who for the first time in his life was living as a country gentleman on his estate of FitzJames while still in close contact with the French court, advised him to give up all hope of aid from France for the time being[1] and to concentrate on winning the support of the Protestants in England. This was almost the last piece of advice – and certainly it was of sound sense – that the Duke of Berwick was to give his half-brother.

The plot was based upon dangling the promise of preferment before various people highly placed in the English government, the army and the navy in return for their support. Much reliance was placed upon the Jacobite-leaning Tories in the House of Commons. The plot failed in the most unlikely way. The Duchess went to London, bearing letters and lists of names, and there met Robert Walpole. She was completely taken in by him, thought that she had won him over to the Jacobites and revealed all their plans. James had already cautioned Cardinal Fleury, who was acting as Louis XV's representative with regard to Jacobite affairs, to take every safeguard against Walpole being involved: 'To penetrate our designs and make our projects miscarry, I cannot but have very bad opinion of Mr Walpole. . . . In two words, I beg of you, if you have undertaken my Restoration, to confide in as few persons as possible. . . . The Duke of Ormonde may be trusted as soon as things are ripe. . . .'[2] Lord Orrery was to have been the go-between with Fleury, but after the Duchess's indiscretion, France lost all interest in the Stuart plans for the time being.

There was, in fact, a general lack of interest in Europe, and James could do nothing but wait for a more propitious moment. Walpole had won over the Emperor by giving British assent to the Pragmatic Sanction which guaranteed the succession of his daughter, Maria Theresa, as ruler of the Austrian Habsburg lands, and the young Tsar Peter II had died of smallpox. He was succeeded by Peter the Great's niece, the Duchess of Courland, whom James had declined as a bride, so there was small hope of sympathy from Russia. Since the Treaty of Seville, Spain was lost to them, and all the members of the Grand Alliance stood firmly by England as they had done since the beginning.

James had every reason to feel isolated in his personal relationships, as well as in affairs of state. During 1731 both the Duke of Wharton and Lord Inverness were converted to Catholicism. In the case of the former, there was not much effect on the general course of Jacobite affairs, since the

[1] WSP, 145.57   [2] WSP, 145.7A

dissolute, drunken Duke was to die shortly afterwards in a monastery near Barcelona, leaving a young wife dependent upon the King for support. But Inverness's conversion made him even more unpopular in certain Jacobite quarters, and certainly suspect to the King's Protestant supporters in England. Inverness was a wholly devoted and good friend of James, but he had many enemies about the court. Although Clementina had agreed to his return, with Lady Inverness, the atmosphere between them was hardly a relaxed one and, all things considered, it was not a surprising turn of events that Inverness should ask the King's permission to retire from his position as Secretary of State. With great reluctance and personal sorrow James let him go, and Inverness went to Avignon where he remained until his death in 1740. The implacable enemy of Inverness had always been his brother-in-law, the Duke of Mar, and he was to die in the following year, 1732. After living for some time in Paris, he finished his life in Aix-la-Chapelle, where he had devoted his time to the study of architecture. By this time, Mar was no loss to the Jacobite cause, but at the beginning of his service with James he had been a good administrator, if a disastrous soldier. He was an eccentric, and one who could not bear to be on the losing side: he had spent most of his time running with the hare and hunting with the hounds.

The conversion of Inverness thoroughly upset the irascible Bishop Atterbury, champion of the Protestant Jacobites, but he did not have much time in which to express his anger for he too died, in March 1732, not long after Lord Orrery who had died in the previous autumn. In Atterbury of Rochester, James lost one of his most faithful adherents ever – a man of the strictest Protestant principles who had given up everything he possessed to follow a Catholic king because that king alone had the right to rule. Robert Carte, the historian, who had been Atterbury's secretary, returned to England shortly afterwards.

Totally alone now, James was dealing single-handed with his usual piles of correspondence. He tried to get the Duke of Ormonde, then attached to the King of Spain, to join him, but there was a great delay as Philip did not want to let Ormonde go. In any case, Ormonde was now nearly sixty-eight and had never been the administrator that Mar had been. Ormonde did eventually leave Madrid, but settled in Avignon near to Lord Inverness and Sir John Graeme.

Meanwhile James had summoned the honest Earl Marischal from Madrid, and he came at once to his master's side. He was more the fearless soldier than the statesman: nevertheless, the very fact that there was someone there whom the King could implicitly trust was worth a very great deal. Marischal was too much admired in most of the European courts – where he was respected, together with his brother, as representing all that was best in the Jacobites – to be allowed to stay with James without some interference being instigated by the English government. They had deprived the King of Mar and, through Mar, of Lord Inverness, and of Clementina, and now they began to work upon Marischal, principally through a Mr Hamilton, a Protestant chaplain attached to the Stuart court in Rome. The number of spies in and around the Palazzo Muti at this period was formidable, and Baron von Stosch, alias John Walton, did not have to exert himself overmuch to obtain information about the King's actions, since he had so many friends, highly placed and otherwise, in the social and artistic circles of Rome. One of his closest friends was Cardinal Alessandro Albani, youngest nephew of the Pope who had supported James's father after his flight from England. But the Cardinal was no friend to the present Pope and, as he was sympathetic towards the King, it was natural for Albani to take the opposite course. By his very position he was often in James's circle, and any odd scraps of conversation were grist to Walton's mill, although not always of much use to London.

Gradually the English people were becoming used to the Hanoverian rule, even if many of the Scots were still against it. For the English, George II did not carry the same mark of the usurper that his father had done, and economically and politically the country was at a better advantage than for many years past. But some voices in Parliament were heard complaining that France had not yet dismantled the port of Dunkirk as promised in the Treaty of Hanover. This, naturally enough, set up repercussions in France and Fleury began once more to look towards the Jacobites. Colonel O'Brien was still the King's man in Paris, and James issued his usual warnings about the need for secrecy and Walpole's power to destroy anything they might concert together. But he need not have worried: in the by now accepted ritual, France refused to move without the guarantee of English troops and the English Jacobites would not declare for the King without the promise of practical French aid. So nothing was done. In a spirit of near-despair the King wrote to Ormonde on 9 June 1732 stating that their supporters were so jealous of one another and so afraid of committing themselves before troops were landed, that he could see no way of inducing them to speak their minds freely. He felt that he understood their attitude, especially that of the English Jacobites but, although they had his cause at heart, there seemed to be few who acted from disinterested motives and did not think first of their own preservation and fortunes.[1]

The Earl Marischal did not stay very long: he could not stomach all the intrigues and devious actions of many of those in the Stuart court which, he declared, was no place for an honest man. Having always been of the

[1] WSP, 154.29

anti-Inverness party, he warned James once more about the Earl. Sickened at heart, James did not look for another Secretary of State, but employed as his amanuensis a man devoted to himself and his cause, James Edgar, who was unlikely to create any contention anywhere because he was not of sufficient importance.

Chapter Twenty Five

By the summer of 1729, the royal family had settled down to a fairly equable routine. James travelled a good deal between Albano, where the air was so much fresher than in Rome, and the Palazzo Muti; but Clementina preferred to stay in Rome, even in the heat of summer: she was near to her beloved Santi Apostoli, and could visit the convent in Trastevere where she had previously stayed. James did everything in his power to make life with her and his sons agreeable to all concerned. Short of allowing her to interfere in State affairs, and he considered the Princes' education as such, there was nothing that he would not have done for Clementina. Writing from Albano that June he reminded her: 'If you have a mind to have any company to see the Fire-works my close apartment below is at your service and you have but to give your orders to Sir Wm. for anything of Refreshments you may have mind to.'[1] In vain he encouraged her to go out or to entertain: she rarely left the Palace.

Prince Charles Edward never learned to spell, although he could always turn a graceful compliment, especially with the help of Lord Dunbar. He wrote to his father on 10 June 1729:

Dear Papa,

I am glad you find the weather at Albano so favourable to your health tho it hinders me so much longer from the happinesse of seeing you. Whether absent or present I hope you will always continue your love to me. My brother is very well and so i is Dear Papa,

Yours most Dutifull Son,
Charles P.[2]

Two days later James wrote to Clementina:

I am very impatient to see Harry in his Breeches, wch. will not be till Wednesday morning. Tho' I shall God willing be with you to morrow before 9 a' cloke at night. Dont come out to meet me, no more than Carluccio, to whom my blessing, as well as to his Brother. I continue well enough and I hope to see you tomorrow. I need say no more to yours of yesterday.

James R.[3]

[1] WSP, 129.62   [2] WSP, 129.16   [3] WSP, 129.29

294

His father's pet name for Charles was the Italian form of 'Carluccio', while Clementina used the Polish diminutive of 'Carlusu' when she wrote him affectionate notes in her sprawling, manic hand which, even she admitted, must have given him some trouble to decipher.

On 25 June 1729 the King wrote to Ormonde in fatherly pride: 'The Duke is now dressing in men's clothes and begins to be a great comfort to me. He is mighty strong and lively and seems to have already a good dale of reflexion.'[1] In 1732 he wrote to Bishop Atterbury: 'I am glad my Children's medal was agreeable to you. The Duke is now entered into his 8th year. I thank God thay are both a great comfort to me as I hope they will be one day to others.'[2]

Early in 1733, Prince James Sobieski (who signed himself in a loving letter to Charles Edward as 'Your Royal Highness, Your very humble and obedient servant and loving Grandfather, James Prince Royal of Poland') suggested that James might like to be considered as a candidate for the elective crown of Poland, now that Augustus of Saxony, its last possessor, had died. But James had only one crown in mind as he wrote to his father-in-law on 28 March: 'My own country takes up my entire heart and inclination, and its laws and interests have been my principal study . . . I admit that I heartily regret that my son, the Duke of York, is not of the age to be a candidate. The blood of the Sobieskis runs in his veins and, by what may be judged of so young a child, he will not be unworthy of it.'[3] It was impossible for Charles to be considered because he was the heir to the British throne *de jure*.

Tribute was paid by both Jacobites and their enemies to the unusual attractiveness of the two little boys: John Walton was annoyed by all the attention paid to them by English visitors to Rome. They were well made and moved gracefully, and their fair complexions were emphasized by dark eyes inherited from both sides of their family. From both their parents they inherited quick tempers, but they were never to learn to govern them as James had done as a young man. Charles, particularly, was as volatile as Clementina, soaring from flights of elation to abysses of despair. Henry was more studious and introspective than Charles, who was inclined to value physical prowess more than study as a way of fitting himself to win back the crown. From a very young age the Prince of Wales had been an unusually good shot, as well as a rider, and these things were naturally noted and made much of by the Jacobites who could see that in the young Prince they had the makings of a romantic and inspiring leader. James did all that he could to make them good Englishmen: English was spoken at court, and English food preferred. He was proud of his sons' proficiency in music, and

[1] WSP, 129.63 [2] WSP, 152.46 [3] HMC, X, app. I.164

allowed them to perform at private *soirées musicales* – Charles playing his violin and Henry singing with a pure, sweet note. Although Lord Dunbar loved the Princes with a faithful devotion, he was not entirely blinded by Charles's great charm to the fact that it was impossible to get him to study as he should and, although he spoke French and Italian easily, his Latin left a lot to be desired. All the adulation he received, combined with his natural zest for living, made Charles extremely hard to handle at times, and the King was very much aware of this. He wrote to Inverness on 12 August 1733: 'There is no question of crushing the Prince's spirit, and no danger of its being crushed, for he is mightily thoughtless and takes nothing much to heart; but I hope he will soon begin to think a little, and that with the natural parts God Almighty has given him, and the pains that are taken about him I hope that he will be good for something at last. . . .'[1]

From their earliest days the two boys had been accustomed to appearing in public. They would be seated, one on either side of the King, at the dinner table laid for a dozen or more guests. Their mother, because she observed stringent fasts on certain days, had her own little table nearby. Like his father, Henry had a delicate digestive system and they were both excused from rigorous fasts by order of the Pope. After dinner, Clementina would usually retire to her rooms, leaving her husband to amuse himself with his sons and his gentlemen for a little while until he retired to his study and the eternal correspondence.

With the beginning of the War of the Polish Succession in August 1733 the correspondence increased. This was to have two effects upon the King and upon the Jacobite cause in general: one direct and one long-term.

Louis XV had decided to back by force the claim to the throne of Poland made by his deposed father-in-law, Stanislas Leszczynski, against that made by the Austrian candidate, Augustus of Saxony. The war was fought not in Poland but first in Italy and then on the Rhine, because France, Savoy and Spain were united in a greedy desire to get their hands upon the Austrian possessions there. At this stage Lord Cornbury came from London to Paris to urge the French ministry (Fleury in particular) to send an expedition to England. For the moment it seemed as if the French would be prepared to do so, then the Tsarina of Russia decided to assist Austria, not from any altruistic motive, but because Russia never missed an opportunity of carving up Poland. She threw 30,000 troops into Poland, a step for which France, for one, had been totally unprepared. No more thought was paid to the Jacobites now, but all money and troops were concentrated on the Rhine where the Duke of Berwick was rushed to take command against Prince Eugène leading the Austrians.

[1] WSP, 164.16

Partly owing to the good offices of Bishop Atterbury and the young Duke of Liria, and partly to the healing effects of time, James and his brother had been slowly growing together again, although circumstances and distance still held them physically apart. When Berwick began the campaign in a masterly fashion by taking the town of Kehl, James wrote to wish him as[1] brilliant a finish to the campaign as was its beginning, but Berwick was never to read the letter. He arrived in Strasbourg on 30 March 1734 to find nothing prepared for the heavy warfare which was obviously imminent. Fourteen years of command had not yet given him the trust of the French ministry, and he still had to beg for men or money.

The weather was very warm, and the snows of the Jura had melted to flood the waters of the Rhine, but Versailles took no heed of Berwick's warnings of the danger and difficulties involved. Louis XV insisted that Philippsburg on the Rhine should be besieged immediately and, as nothing was prepared there either, Berwick began on 12 June to supervise personally the digging of the earthworks, striding about the muddy trenches from early morning on. Part of the time he was engaged in work near a slight eminence on which the French guns were trained in case of a surprise attack from the Austrians at its rear. He climbed up on a bench, in his usual fashion, to view the field, in spite of the fact that a sentinel was posted at the spot to see that no one stopped there (as they had already lost one or two of their men in cross-fire). Whether the sentinel was too awed to stop his commander, or whether Berwick was too heedless of the danger to halt his observations at that place, no one knows, but Berwick was killed, his head carried off by a cannon-ball in a cross-fire between the French and the Austrians.

Peer of England and France, grandee of Spain, a commander of the armies of three of the first monarchs of Europe, the Duke of Berwick was not only a military genius but also a great and well-loved man. He was honest and direct to a fault; his rather severe air and classically handsome face hid great humanity and sweetness of temper. He always knew exactly what he was going to do, and did it, and was as careful as his contemporary, Marlborough, in looking after the welfare of his troops – so far as the French ministers would allow him. In the most difficult of operations, said his friend Montesquieu, he preserved a tranquility of soul and a *sang-froid* which produced a natural intrepidity. Of the twenty-nine campaigns he had made throughout his life, he had commanded fifteen. 'One could say with truth', wrote Montesquieu, 'that he had in him more grandeur than he had occasion to let appear, acting, as he did, always in the simplest way and never seeking estimation.'[2]

James had lost not only his half-brother, but the man who had been the

[1] WSP, 169.1   [2] Berwick, *op. cit.*, p. 375

greatest influence upon him during his youth and early manhood. The *impasse* of 1715 and Berwick's apparent desertion of him had hurt him more deeply than either of them knew, but, even then, he could not cut him out of his life entirely. They corresponded, Berwick informing the King of what was going on outside Italy, and whether or not there was anything to be hoped for the Jacobites therein. He was sixty-two when he was killed, eighteen years older than James.

France and its army mourned. A grief-stricken Versailles directed that all public amusements should be stopped until after the funeral, and every public place was hung with black. Crowds wept along the route as his body was borne back from Philippsburg to the chapel of the English Benedictines in Paris, where he was laid to rest beside his father. In Rome, James and his family attended a requiem mass at the church of St Louis of France.

It was fitting that Berwick and his son, the Duke of Liria, should have been fighting on the same side at the last, for while Berwick was in command of the French troops on the Rhine, Liria commanded the Spanish contingent in southern Italy. He had passed through Rome on his way to the south, and had stayed at the Palazzo Muti, once again renewing his happy relationship with his uncle and aunt, and making friends with the young Princes, particularly Charles, to whom he stood in the same position as Berwick had to the young James. Charles admired him greatly, and desired nothing more than to follow him in his exploits in the south. After Liria, to the Palazzo Muti came Don Carlos, son of the King of Spain, on his way to claim the throne of Naples. So, for a little while, the Stuarts led a gay and sociable life. It was not until their distinguished guests had left, that the news of Berwick's death reached them. Liria himself received the news on 27 July and, overwhelmed with grief, retired to Naples for a month of mourning. James wrote to him, immediately telling him that he was sending Charles to Gaeta, on the coast halfway between Rome and Naples, to learn the art of war with his cousin, Don Carlos, and under the command of himself, the new Duke of Berwick. Perhaps he intended that Liria should interpret the gesture of sending his elder son to him at that time as a measure of comfort, so that he should feel that there was someone, no matter how young, of his own family with him. As he had made his own first campaign under the first Duke of Berwick, so Charles was to make his under the second Duke, but his son was much younger, at thirteen, than he had been.

Charles' sojourn at Gaeta was to have an indirect influence upon James and all the Stuart fortunes thenceforward, because it was while he was away from home and parental discipline at a critical period in adolescence that the character of the man he was to become began to form. James had the normal doubts of any father about how his son should behave away from home on his own for the first time, as he wrote to Berwick – Liria:

. . . for as well as I love him I had rather lose him than he should not behave as his birth and his honour require of him. *Enfin*, I put him absolutely under your care and direction and if he observes my orders you will find him very docile.

I earnestly beg of you to let me know, freely and without flattery, how he behaves in every respect for after all he is very young, and one cannot expect from him what one might do were he some years older.[1]

The Prince travelled *incognito*, using his father's old *nom-de-plume* of the Chevalier de Saint George, and he was attended by Dunbar, Sheridan, two gentlemen, and two friars as chaplains. The latter provision was a mistake, as the physician to Don Carlos pointed out to Lord Dunbar, adding that it was by such small details that kingdoms were lost, since their presence would be recorded in all the English and Dutch dispatches.

From the moment he arrived, the Prince made a great impression: 'When the King [Don Carlos] arrived the Prince went to the *sale des gards* to meet him and there made a compliment very prettily and without the lest embarras after which he followed H.M. into his room and spoke to him with the same ease as he used to do to any of the Cardinals at Rome.' Dunbar went into great detail about the Prince's arrival in a letter to the King dated 5 August 1734. Everybody who met Charles fell under his spell: the King of Naples called him 'lively and charming' and the French ambassador praised him 'in all companyes and told me he would not only give *ane* account of what he remarked in him to the court of france, but that he would write on this subject to all the french ministers in all the different courts of Europe. This surely deserves that Y.M. should take notice of it in some shape or other for it marks a particular affection to yet interest and may do H.R.H. considerable service.' He assured the King that he was not flattering when he declared himself to be extremely satisfied with the Prince, and that already people there were saying 'que c'est un homme formé [he's already a man]'.[2]

The King of Naples was kept out of harm's way, without his knowing it, by being taken to a certain part of the trenches every day where was no action, but where officers were specially posted so it might look as if there was every likelihood of being some. This would not do for Charles, who wanted to be where the action really was, and then the problem arose of how to keep the King of Naples' illusions intact when he could see the thirteen-year-old Prince running a graver risk. On the first day the Duke of

[1] WSP, 171.90   [2] WSP, 172.51

Berwick 'intends to carry him today at eleven a clock to view one of the batterys where he says he will run little or no risque; he choses that hour because he says the Ennemy dont fire at that time of the day, which is all I can write to Y.M. at present on that subject but shall give Y.M. an account of what passes'.[1] Later he wrote that the Prince 'is teasing both the D. of Berwick and me every day to shew him these trenches of which he hears so much discourse',[2] and that it would be a good way of letting the Prince earn a reputation without incurring too much risk.

James wrote loving fatherly letters to the boy, telling him how pleased he was to have such good accounts of him and warning him to look after his diet. Charles replied with constrained little notes of a minimum length, obviously penned from a sense of duty:

> *Sir,*
> I am very glad that you are contented with me. I have been very good and hope with the Grace of God to continue so and umbly ask your Blessing.
> *Charles P.*[3]

> *Sir,*
> My Lord Dunbar has excused me for not having writ to you hetherto. I have been very good and humbly ask your Blessing.
> *Charles P.*[4]

This sets the tone for all the correspondence between Charles and the King henceforth: affection, patience and clear-sightedness on the part of James; impatience at parental authority and a non-involvement on Charles's part.

Gaeta fell to the second Duke of Berwick on 9 August, and Don Carlos, King of Naples, attended a Te Deum in the cathedral, accompanied by Prince Charles. A triple salute was fired in the Piazza, and then Charles rode down the narrow streets descending to the harbour where he was staying in a house overlooking the sea. The crowd huzza'd all the way. The next day Carlos left for Naples by sea, attended by a squadron of Spanish ships, and Charles followed him in a special galley. He stayed in Naples for a month, until after Carlos's coronation, and then he returned to Albano, perhaps not before time where the Spanish prince was concerned, for Charles was attracting a great deal of attention and was fast becoming the leading figure on the stage.

Charles did not return *incognito*, as he had departed, but in full state as Prince of Wales, with a guard of fifty soldiers, and two beautiful Spanish horses with superb harness, the gift of the King of Spain. From then onwards he was established as a romantic, dashing young leader in the hearts

---

[1] WSP, 172.51   [2] *ibid.*   [3] WSP, 172.90   [4] WSP, 172.134

of the Jacobites, and a potential menace in the minds of the Whigs. It was almost symbolic that James should ride out to meet his son on the road to Albano, for it was about this time that the emphasis began gradually to shift from the King himself to the Prince, in terms of the hoped-for restoration.

The new Duke of Berwick stayed behind in command of the Spanish troops at Naples, and proceeded to besiege Capua. But he had inherited tuberculosis from his mother, Honora Bourke, the first Duchess, and all the time he was fighting he was spitting blood. James was worried about him: he had seen his namesake grow up from a child to a young man when, as Lord Tynmouth, he had accompanied him on the lonely, hazardous journey to the coast in 1715, and then to become a responsible young military commander who seemed to show every sign of following in his illustrious father's footsteps.

He was approximately of the same age as Clementina. However, she began to fail slowly during the year 1734, to die in the following January in her thirty-fourth year. James and she had lived in an affectionate peace for the past nine years, and, although he had done everything short of constraining her, to see that she did not destroy herself with her injudicious fastings and penances, her small, weakened body had eventually to succumb. On 12 January 1735 she received the last sacraments and retained full consciousness throughout. She died in tranquillity. The Princes were wild with grief and could not control their weeping: the self-possessed young man that Charles had been only a few months before at Gaeta was transformed once more into a boy of thirteen crying for the mother he had lost.

Pope Clement XII decreed that she should be buried in full regal state. Followed by her sorrowing ladies, her servants and all the courtiers of the Palazzo Muti and the Jacobites of Rome, her body, clothed in normal dress, was carried into the near-by church of Santi Apostoli where it was embalmed and clothed in a Dominican nun's habit. She lay in state for three days, and an incredible number of people from all walks of Roman life came to see her lying there, for her charities had extended far and wide. Then her ladies re-clothed her in royal apparel, in gold and ermine, and a red velvet cloak with matching shoes, and with her hair loose about her little neck. She was placed on black velvet fringed with gold, and laid upon a bed of state under a baldaquin of purple velvet. Her crown of gold was placed upon her head, and her ivory sceptre in her hand. Around the bed of state thirty-two cardinals knelt and prayed while the friars of the basilica of Santi Apostoli intoned the prayers for the dead. Every religious order in Rome sent representatives to walk in procession to St Peter's carrying wax tapers, with the Chapter and clergy of St Peter's, the Queen's household and the King's.

All along the route the black-draped windows were crowded with people. The King and the Princes watched from the windows of the Palazzo Muti: the tall spare man, with a young boy on either side of him, their formal, silvered-white wigs contrasting with the sable velvet of their clothes. After the Requiem Mass her ladies removed the royal robes and put a black cloak over her black and white Dominican habit, with a nun's black veil upon her head. Placed in a threefold coffin, her body was put to rest in the crypt at St Peter's until such time as the King would return to England, when she would be buried in Westminster Abbey. Her heart was given to the church of Santi Apostoli, where she had spent so many hours upon her knees. The King and his sons spent the rest of the day in prayer.

Clementina had done more damage to James's cause than a legion of Walpole's spies could have achieved. Sometimes her actions had betrayed more than a hint of manic-depression and, for all that current rumour maintained, her hysterical jealousy was directed not so much against Lady Inverness as against that lady's husband. It seemed as if she could not bear James to have a close relationship, even that of friendship, and was prepared to go to any lengths to break such a bond. Pity there must be for her: she loved James as he did her, but neither could really understand the other. Pretty, graceful, quick-witted, mercurial, stubborn and charming, devastatingly charming, she had lived her last sixteen years under the cloud of a major disappointment, and the little Princess who had wanted to become 'Queen of England' never knew the weight of the crown on her head during her lifetime, only in her death.

Chapter Twenty Six

James was forty-seven when Clementina died. Except for his sons and his nephew, he had no close relations, and no intimate friend to whom he could talk unreservedly. His health had been intermittently poor since a visit made to Naples in 1731, when he had complained of stomach ills, and he had had to give up his favourite sport of hunting for some time past. His life, so far, had been a case of living from one disappointment to the next, a condition which youth meets with resilience, but lonely middle-age with one degree less than despair. So it was with a genuine affection that he welcomed Lord Inverness back to Rome in April 1736. The Pope and Roman society showed his lordship much esteem, and Inverness was obviously very happy to be back, and delighted to see that the Princes were showing such promise. But, even before his return, intrigues were still fermenting at the court in the Palazzo Muti, and his presence gave fresh impetus to the schemes of those always seeking power about the King. Rightly or wrongly, Lord Dunbar was reputed to be jealous of the attention paid to Inverness and, eventually in July, the latter returned to Avignon rather than once more be a cause of strife.

Thenceforward, his secretary, James Edgar, came closest to knowing the King's mind. Their positions were always clearly marked as being that of master and servant, but a mutual devotion and trust was built up between them which lasted all their lives. Edgar never wanted and never sought power or influence, and he was respected by everyone who came into contact with him. He used to copy a large part of the King's correspondence (although James still wrote a great deal in his own hand) and dealt with all the expenditure of the royal household which, under the King's supervision, was admirably organized. Edgar wrote in a tight, neat, meticulous hand, getting as many lines as possible onto a page, as if he knew only too well that paper cost money. When correspondents knew, for one reason or another, that they could not reach the King, it was to 'Mr Edgar' they wrote so that, next to James, he probably knew more about the state of Jacobite affairs than any other Jacobite alive.

With another shift in the balance of power in Europe those affairs seemed likely to be taking a turn for the better. The French had seized all the Austrian possessions in Italy except for Mantua, and the Emperor Charles VI decided to sue for peace. This meant that if France, Spain and Austria came to terms, there would be a Catholic coalition in Europe ready to use the Jacobites in any attempt that might be made against England. One of the conditions agreed upon was the restitution of Gibraltar and Port Mahon to Spain which meant wresting them from England. Besides the recognition of Don Carlos as King of Naples and the Two Sicilies, Frederick Augustus of Saxony was recognized as King of Poland, and Charles VI's daughter, Maria Theresa, as his heir under the Pragmatic Sanction. She was to be married to Francis, Duke of Lorraine. Lorraine was given to Stanislas Leszczynski for his lifetime, with reversion to France on his death: this was in exchange for the loss of Poland, and the Duke of Lorraine meanwhile was to be compensated with the Grand Duchy of Tuscany. So the map of Europe was rearranged once more and France and Spain professed themselves ready and able to help James. Spain was not in a good enough financial condition or in a mind to help anyone at that time, but Cardinal Fleury, acting for France, was more encouraging: the Porteous Riots in Edinburgh and disturbances in London, where the City Corporation was pro-Stuart, raised Jacobite hopes, although James had remained fairly sanguine throughout.

There was talk of arranging a marriage between Charles Edward and either an Infanta of Spain or an Austrian Archduchess. Spain or France were more likely to help in a practical fashion than the Emperor, and James was inclined to favour the idea of the Infanta more. The Prince of Wales was now nearly sixteen and anxious to prove himself in some military action, so the King asked Charles VI if the Prince could take part in the campaign against the Turks in Hungary. The Emperor delayed in replying to this request so, meanwhile, the King decided to send Charles on a tour of northern Italy with Lord Dunbar; this would not only add to his education but, it was hoped, enlist sympathy for the Jacobite cause through the very attractive personality of the Prince himself. He travelled *incognito* as the Count of Albany, and besides Dunbar, Mr Francis Strickland, a young Englishman, and Sir Henry Goring went with him. Both men were to play their parts, good and bad, in the Prince's life for some years to come. He set out in May 1737 and visited Bologna, Parma and Venice where he was fêted by the Doge and followed the ducal barge when the Doge was ceremonially wedded to the Adriatic. Everywhere he went in Parma and Bologna, balls and assemblies were given in his honour, and all northern Italy rang with his praises. Dunbar wrote to the King from Bologna:

As H.R.H. cannot enjoy the diversion of dancing with moderation, but overheats himself monstrously, I have refused a ball the publick here intended to give him tomorrow night, and have writ . . . that he would accept of a *Conversazione*. . . . The later he comes home and the more he wants to sleep, he will sit the longer at supper, so that it is not possible to get him to bed of an opera night till near three in the morning tho' he be home soon after one.[1]

Already the Prince was acquiring the taste for late-night diversion which was to remain with him throughout his life.

He met the Elector of Bavaria and his wife in Venice and they, too, were enchanted with him, claiming him as a relative on his mother's side. The Doge wrote to a cardinal in Rome that he had been delighted to receive the Prince. When the last of the Medicis, the Grand Duke of Tuscany, died the people of Florence were disappointed at being deprived of an opportunity of seeing the Prince, since, naturally enough, all public processions were cancelled, and they declared that they were sure that he would be chosen as the next Grand Duke. In this they were mistaken, but it did not prevent the English government becoming furious at the success of his tour. They were so angry with the Venetian Doge that they gave twenty-four hours' notice to the Venetian Resident in London; in so doing they drew more notice to the Prince's tour than even James could have hoped for.

But the Emperor's answer to the request for Charles to join the campaign against the Turks was negative, and neither France nor Spain wanted him in their countries, or in their armies. If war were to come with England, they wanted it to come at the right time – one of their own choosing – whereas Charles's mere presence in Versailles or Madrid would be a provocation to war.

In December 1737, Prince James Sobieski died in Ohlau, leaving his estates in Silesia and all sums due to him from the State of Poland to the Prince of Wales and the Duke of York. He also made over to them all the family jewels, including the Polish Crown Jewels. Five years later the land was sold to the Polish noble family of Radziwill, and possession of half the jewels and dues were to be contested over a long period, but in a friendly enough fashion, by the Prince de Turenne and the Duchesse de Montbazon, children of Clementina's sister who had married the Duc de Bouillon.

Also at the end of that year Lord Orrery died, and among the 'Old Guard' only the Earl Marischal was left with any capacity for leadership. But gifted as he was in the military sense, he was not a particularly brilliant administrator. Ormonde was ageing fast, and there was no one of the King's own generation, with the exception of Inverness and Dunbar, whom he could fully trust. The management of Jacobite affairs was passing into the hands of a younger generation and, for the most part, into those of less

[1] WSP, 198.29

significant men without either the rank or style to impress foreign onlookers.

At this time there came to Rome, in his twenty-third year, John Murray of Broughton, the son of a baronet from Peeblesshire. He came from Leiden where he had been studying at the University, and met James Edgar as well as the Prince of Wales and the Duke of York, though he does not seem to have met the King. He was the representative of an association in Scotland for the furtherance of Jacobitism, but like Francis Strickland, he was later to have an unfortunate influence on the Prince of Wales.

At the end of December 1737, or in the following month, a well-known Highlander, John Gordon of Glenbucket, arrived in Rome, sent by General Alexander Gordon of Auchintoul and by Macdonald of Glengarry. He brought optimistic news of the enthusiasm of the Highlanders for the cause, and of a scheme for withdrawing a few officers and men from the west coast of France (with the permission of Cardinal Fleury, with whom he had talked on the way to Rome) and throwing them into Scotland. No more waiting was necessary, according to Glenbucket, and if foreign help was not forthcoming: the Highland Jacobites were willing to proceed on their own. Once more, James was not entirely convinced, and sent Lord Inverness's brother, William Hay, back to Scotland with Glenbucket with instructions 'to see as many considerable people as possible and as few as can be of others',[1] to assure prominent Presbyterians that their religion would be unharmed by the restoration, and to try to estimate the strength and likely support of the Highland adherents.

He knew that the English Jacobites were still wavering, and he wanted Colonel Cecil, whom he regarded as the leader of the Tory, and particularly the Jacobite faction in Parliament to let slip no opportunity of inveighing against Spain, with the help of demonstrations within the City of London, so that an occasion might be found for declaring war on that country, or for giving Spain a reason to attack England – by which means their own ends would be furthered. But Cecil was to die at the end of that year and once again there was no universally accepted leader of the Jacobites in the House of Parliament.

In June 1738 the second Duke of Berwick died, to the great grief of James and his sons. At the time of his death James had been interesting himself in the making of a special state carriage as a gift to the Duke who had been appointed Spanish ambassador to the court of Naples. His son, the third Duke and yet another James Francis Edward, completed his education in Rome and visited the King frequently, thus keeping alive the affection which had originally flourished between James and his grandfather. Besides the personal loss, James now lacked a personal representative at the

[1] WSP, 205.6

court of Spain and an adviser on Spanish affairs. One was sorely needed at this time, since Spain appeared to be completely indifferent to the Jacobite question, while France had signed a treaty with England, Austria and Sardinia, and a separate agreement with Sweden.

On his way back from Rome, William Hay saw Colonel O'Brien in Paris who was of the opinion that they could manage simultaneous landings in England and Scotland with only 9,000 men, and he began to 'work upon' the Spanish ambassador to that end. In like fashion, the Spanish ambassador in London, Thomas Geraldine, formerly Fitzgerald, was worked upon by Colonel Cecil, while Ormonde did what he could in Madrid. Finally, to everyone's astonishment, Spain awoke from her apathy to such an extent that she offered 20,000 men. These would have to be embarked under pretence of making a landing in North Africa, or of reinforcing Spanish garrisons in Italy.

When Hay reported to the King, the situation in Scotland did not seem so promising. There was not much ammunition to be found in the Highlands, the Lowlands seemed to be apathetic, and the Presbyterians might decide either way: too many people were governed entirely by self-interest. One or two representatives of the clans visited Rome, such as Drummond of Balhaldy and 'young' Lord John Drummond, brother of the Duke of Perth. But their visits only served to convince James that there was not enough agreement between the clans themselves: 'I see with sorrow that there is little union amongst our friends in Scotland; however I do not doubt that they are all united to serve me when a good occasion presents itself. But for that to be effective, certain support either from England or with foreign troops is necessary.'[1] This was written to O'Brien on 15 February 1739.

England declared war on Spain in October 1739, principally because of disagreement over the right to search merchant vessels in the West Indies, and there now seemed no reason why she should not assist the Stuart cause both for its sake and her own. This at first she professed to do, asking James to allow either Ormonde or Marischal to take up a command at Corunna where a fleet was supposedly being formed to invade Scotland. The King decided that it was a feint on the part of the Spaniards to keep the British fleet out of the Mediterranean, and when Ormonde and Marischal were ordered to go to Corunna, they refused and left Madrid. Ormonde went to Avignon, but Marischal, for the sake of his livelihood, was obliged to keep his commission in Spain for the time being.

Walpole's position was considerably weakened by the war with Spain and, following Bolingbroke's example of twenty-five years before, he made

[1] WSP, 215.141

approaches to the Jacobites. He went so far as to send Carte, Atterbury's old secretary, back to Rome from London to sound out James, who knew Carte to be sincere but had no such illusions about Walpole.

Pierre de Tencin, Archbishop of Lyons, had retained his old friendship for the King, and when he was made a cardinal with James's help in 1739, he was in a position to be of some use. Fleury had been trying to decide whether or not to help James and, after de Tencin had been made *chargé d'affaires* for France in Rome, the tide began to turn in the Stuarts' favour.

James Erskine, Lord George, came to see James in Rome, as an unofficial representative of the English parliamentary opposition, pledging their support, providing that James sought to control the actions of his adherents. James answered this in a letter dated 24 March:

> We have now been more than 50 years out of our Country, we have been bred and lived in the School of Adversity . . . long experiences teached us how little we can depend on the friendship of foreign Powers. . . . But should it happen that any Foreign Power contributed to place me on the Throne, it must be visible to all thinking men that I can neither hope to keep it, nor enjoy peace and happiness upon it, but by gaining the love and affection of my Subjects, I am far from approving the mistakes of Former Reigns, I see, I feel the effects of them. . . . Therefore I do not entertain ye least thought of assuming government on the same footing my family left it, I am fully resolved to make the law ye rule of my government and absolutely disclaim any pretensions to a dispencing [*sic*] power.[1]

This was probably the most enlightened utterance made by any Stuart monarch, and was typical of James's lifelong attitude towards his restoration.

France blew hot and cold, and Spain made another tentative suggestion for an invasion which it then withdrew. With regard to Fleury, James was very realistic and wrote: '. . . he will not undertake a War merely on my account.'[2]

In September 1740, Lord Inverness died suddenly at Avignon; he had for some time been a sufferer from gout, and complications had developed. This removed the only friend remaining to James apart from Dunbar; outside the family tie his loneliness was almost complete. He had known Inverness for nearly twenty-five years and been a loyal friend in spite of the opposition of the Queen and the schemers at court. Many of his letters end with 'adieu my dear John', and, apart from Clementina, 'Carluccio' and 'Harry', he never addressed anyone else, not even Berwick, by their Christian name in correspondence.

[1] WSP, 232.160   [2] *ibid.*, 235.169

Charles Edward meanwhile, had been waiting in the wings as it were, chafing at the lack of action, as his father had done nearly thirty years before. And, like his father again, he was obliged to carry out his social obligations during this period of inactivity. The Prince Royal, son of Frederick Augustus, King of Poland and Elector of Saxony, visited the Palazzo Muti in the carnival period of 1739, and was welcomed with much grace by the two Princes. There was a masked ball given in his honour, and Charles, who was a good dancer, opened the ball. Both he and fifteen-year-old Henry were dressed as 'shepherds' in white silk and diamonds. Later James entered, in mask and domine, and looked on proudly while his two sons danced English country dances. But dancing was not the limit of the Prince of Wales' physical activity: he continued to ride, run and shoot, and do everything he possibly could to keep himself fit for the opportunity which he knew must eventually present itself.

And it did begin to take shape in 1740 in the form of the War of the Austrian Succession. Both Frederick II of Prussia and Maria Theresa of Austria and Hungary had recently ascended their respective thrones; and already Frederick was filled with dreams of territorial aggrandizement which he lost no time in attempting to fulfil by laying claim to Silesia. Maria Theresa was vastly inexperienced in matters of state and war. This was made apparent in the Battle of Mollwitz, which was a crushing defeat for Austria. At the same time, disregarding the Pragmatic Sanction, the Elector of Bavaria decided that nothing could be lost by his laying claim to, and assuming, the Imperial crown. Augustus, Elector of Saxony and King of Poland, also wanted to strengthen his dominions at the expense of Austria, while France demanded Luxembourg and the Netherlands. Austria was brought to her knees, that is until Maria Theresa was crowned Queen of Hungary: then, with her intrepid and warlike Hungarian soldiery, she pushed the Bavarians out of Munich, and took back Prague from the French who had made great inroads into her Bohemian dominion. England decided to support Austria, along with Sardinia, but as yet there was no war declared between England and France.

Walpole's ministry fell in 1741, and he entered the House of Lords as Lord Orford. Now there was a feverish but mainly unconcerted activity among the Jacobites in Britain: Lord Sempill was James's chief contact in England, and Drummond of Balhaldy and Murray of Broughton the main agents between Scotland and Rome. When the cost of 16,000 troops for use in Hanover was presented to the English Parliament, there was great resentment against the Crown, and James emphasized again and again to Sempill the need for harrying the Whig Opposition. But there were no Jacobite Tories in the new cabinet, so nothing efficacious was achieved.

Cardinal Fleury died in 1743 while France was still engaged in the war with Austria, and he was succeeded as director of France's foreign policy by Monsieur Amelot, a much less effective personality. But Jacobite affairs remained in the hands of Cardinal de Tencin, who became Minister of State. In August 1743, Louis XV sent a spy, one of his equerries, a Mr James Butler, into England on the pretext of buying horses for him; this was unknown to James, but news of the visit reached the ears of Carte who reported back to Rome that Butler now had lists of likely Jacobite supporters, and there about three hundred of them in England and Wales. Butler returned with Drummond of Balhaldy and reported enthusiastically on the general Jacobite situation in Britain. As England, along with Sardinia, had confirmed her support to Austria in the Treaty of Worms of September 1743, France and Spain reaffirmed their family support in the following month, which meant that if France opted to assist James, then Spain was more likely to follow suit than she had been previously.

James was sceptical as to the outcome of all this. He knew that he and his cause were only tools in the hands of the French and Spanish, to be picked up and dropped as occasion demanded. In June 1743 the French army was thoroughly defeated near the River Main at Dettingen by English, Austrian and Hanoverian troops, headed by George II, the last British monarch to take the field in war. The retreat meant that more French troops were released for use elsewhere, and therefore more could be sent into England.

When Louis XV sent Drummond of Balhaldy on to Rome, he instructed him to tell the King it was time for the Prince of Wales to travel to Paris. At this point the King wrote to Colonel O'Brien to say that if France had decided to call for the Prince without a previous declaration of war with England, then they intended to make use of the Jacobites instead of assisting them. He was also worried about letting Charles go: it could have been a trap to get the Prince into France where he had no legal right to be and then to imprison him, for, after all, he only had Balhaldy's word to go upon. Finally, acting against his better judgement, he decided to let the excited and impatient Charles Edward leave for France.

The Duke of York was also anxious to go with his brother, but this could not be allowed: later perhaps, if all went well, he might join him. It was natural enough that Charles should have been in the foreground of the picture at this time, and perhaps James was so preoccupied with State problems at that period that he did not give as much attention to Henry's growing-up as he might otherwise have done. But Lord Dunbar was still keeping a devoted watch over his younger charge and, in 1742 when Henry was seventeen, he sent a report on the Duke's behaviour, which was obviously worrying him, to the King. Henry asked to be called at a quarter to six every morning and rose at six and said his prayers until a quarter past six. At seven he made his toilet and then spent one hour at prayer, half in his closet and the other half in his bedchamber: 'Always says them aloud, so that when he is in his bed-chamber with the doors shut, they hear him in the next room.' His breakfast lasted a quarter of an hour or less. His confessor, Father Ildefonso, was present during his prayers and some part of the rest of his morning:

> . . . sometimes when the dancing master was in the way, he danced his two little minuets with him before he began with Father Ildefonso which lasted but a few minutes, because he has lost the inclination he had to that exercise. When he rid a horseback he went out immediately after his lesson with Father Ildefonso. Then he dressed and went to Mass of which he heard two and sometimes three on holy days, and Saturday last four – to wit two with yr Majesty one with the Prince and one by himself. When he hears Mass with the Prince he stays at prayers in the Chappel about a quarter of ane hour thereafter when the hour of dinner permits it. Since Lent he has heard sermon always twice, sometimes thrice, and perhaps once four times in a week, but of this last they cannot be absolutely positive.

After dinner Henry would wait a certain time with his watch in his hand and then go into the chapel again for three-quarters of an hour or so. When he went out after dinner he would go into a church for half an hour and, on returning to the Palace at four o'clock, he would return to the chapel for another hour or hour and a half. Dunbar was disturbed by the Duke's state of mind: '. . . in reciting or reacting his prayers he puts his mind in agitation, pronounces his words aloud and crowds them with great precipitation one upon another and I often remark him when he goes abroad after dinner with a blackness about his eyes his head quite fatigued and his hands hot and the same thing when he comes from his prayers at night.'[1] Small wonder then that the Duke was always in considerable agitation about never having enough time to do what he should do, and that his studies suffered:

> During the rest of the day he never reads a word on any subject nor could he probably do it, so that were not the course he is in ruinous to his health, as it certainly is, he would arrive at the age of 22 without having cultivated his understanding or acquired a reasonable degree of such knowledge as is the chief duty of station at present both towards God and man.

[1] WSP, 246.139

In this manner, the first capacity in the world with a wonderful memory would be lost, and this I take to be a very great evil and what wants a prudent and ane affectual remedy. I will add to this that when he is not employed as above he is always singing, which I am far from thinking indifferent in regard of his breste.[1]

From this account it would seem that Dunbar had every reason to be worried about Henry whose feet appeared to be set upon the same path trodden by Clementina. It remains a mystery why James, whose own education had been so carefully nurtured, and who was himself if not a scholar at least a cultivated man, should have allowed such a state of affairs arise, let alone exist. One fact is apparent, that good teachers among his small circle in Rome were hard to find, apart from priests, and the King was determined that his sons should not fall under Jesuit or any other priestly influence.

His correspondence with both his sons shows an exemplary patience and he never reproved them for trivial reasons, even if, at times, he seems to have been rather painstaking in indicating the best courses for them to adopt. The older he became, the more impatient Charles Edward appears to have become with his father, and the more he revealed his resentment at any form of control or advice. Gaeta had been his apotheosis so far, and his undoing: he was perfectly convinced that he could stand on his own feet and could deal with any problem that might arise.

When James received Charles's summons from Louis XV and had decided to let him go, he issued a Declaration of Regency:

James R.

Whereas We have a near Prospect of being restored to the Throne of our Ancestors, by the good Inclinations of Our Subjects towards Us, and whereas, on Account of the present Situation of this Country, it will be absolutely impossible for Us to be in Person as the first setting up of Our Royal Standard, and even sometime after, We therefore esteem it for Our Service, and the Good of Our Kingdoms and Dominions to nominate and appoint, Our dearest Son, CHARLES, Prince of Wales, to be sole Regent of Our Kingdoms of England, Scotland and Ireland, and of all other Our Dominions, during Our Absence.

23 December 1743 in the 43rd year of Our Reign,
J.R.[2]

The immediate problem was how to get Charles out of Italy and into France. Conditions of utmost secrecy were necessary, but even so, the King was not happy about sending his elder son away into the unknown. However, as he wrote to Sempill: 'But matters are too far advanced now to go

[1] WSP, 246.139   [2] Brit. Mus. C115.i.362

312

back or suspend, the King of France has called for the Prince and he shall part. . . . The French projects are chiefly grounded upon an immediate expedition upon England, so they would have great ground to complain of us, if at the eve of execution we proposed delays . . . *Enfin*, I take the case to be *now or never* in relation to France, and we must all act accordingly.'[1]

Fortunately, circumstances for once played into their hands. The Duke of Gaetano invited the two Princes to a shooting party on his estate at Cisterna. In the cold dark hours before dawn on 9 January 1744 James said good-bye to his two sons: he was never to see Charles again.

They rode together at first, and then Charles with Francis Strickland galloped ahead, leaving Henry to arrive at Cisterna on his own. A little way further down Charles met Sheridan's nephew, Michael Sheridan, and an Irish soldier in the French army, John William O'Sullivan, who was to be his constant companion thereafter. Strickland rode back to inform Henry that Charles had had a slight accident and had sprained his ankle. Only when it was certain that the Prince was well on his way was Henry told the truth, and when the King wrote asking him to delay his return until the end of the month, so as to keep Charles's secret from the outside world as long as possible, he replied with a certain justifiable peevishness that he was

> . . . very happy but at the same time very impatient to hear news of our 'dear Traveller' which news I do not doubt will be but good for the hand of God seems to be remarquably upon him on this occasion. . . . I shall stay here with a great deal of pleasure as long as your Majesty will think fitt, were it to be of any use. In this oaccasion I would realy be locked up very willingly in an old Tower till Easter.
> Begging your Blessing I am yr most dutiful son,
> *Henry.*[2]

Meanwhile the Prince, in various disguises, reached Genoa. From there he travelled to Antibes, Avignon, Lyons and, finally, Paris, where he stayed with Lord Sempill. Henry wrote to him there, when he returned to Rome on 6 February, assuring him that, without him, he felt like a 'fish out of water'. He was glad that their father had hid the facts of Charles's departure from him 'for certainly the great love I have for you could not but have showed itself, may be imprudently on that occasion'.[3] He continued:

> I have realy been upon thorns untill I heard you safely landed. . . . for the manner in which you have made this journey will guain you a vast deal of honour all over the worled and I don't dought but that you will daily increace it by all your future undertakings. I wish you could see all

[1] WSP, 255.6   [2] *ibid.*, 255.49   [3] *ibid.*, 255.147

the content and satisfaction my heart feels every time I hear any thing that can redound to your honour and Glory, and that I am sure proceeds from the Respectuous love and tenderness I have for you which, I can assure you Dear Brother (were the King but to permit me) wou'd make me fly through fire and water to be with you.[1]

Charles sent him affectionate messages in letters to his father whom he told about his two companions' efforts to keep up with him on the journey: 'And if I had been to go much further I should have been obliged to get them tyd behind the chase with my Portmantle, for they were quite *rendu*: . . . I have mett with all that could be expected from Mr Adams [Louis XV] who expresses great tenderness and will be careful of my concerns. . . .'[2] Louis had indeed received the Prince kindly, but circumstances forbade an official welcome.

Towards the end of February he left Paris and moved on to Gravelines whence he went to Dunkirk to watch the embarkation of over seven thousand men under the command of the Maréchal de Saxe. Other ships and transports from Calais and Brest joined them. Just when things seemed to be moving at last and the Duke of Ormonde had been summoned by Louis XV to Paris, in spite of the fact that Saxe was not entirely happy about the welcome they were likely to receive from sympathizers in England, a fleet of more than a score of British ships under Admiral Norris appeared in the Downs. Fortunately for the French ships, the British were held back first by an ebb tide and then by a calm, but as soon as the wind began to change, a fierce storm arose and all the French transports foundered. No more was needed for the French to call off the proposed invasion, and Charles was left in the depths of frustration in Gravelines. Once more a storm had defeated the House of Stuart and altered the course of its history.

[1] WSP, 255.147   [2] *ibid.*, 255.163

Chapter Twenty Seven

The Maréchal de Saxe went back to his wars in Flanders, and the Earl Marischal, certain that nothing could be accomplished for a very long time, returned to his house near Boulogne-sur-Seine; but Charles remained at Gravelines until summoned to Paris by Louis XV after war had been declared against England at the beginning of March 1744. Sir Thomas Sheridan came out to be with his beloved pupil, and a small house was made ready for the Prince in Montmartre, since his presence was officially ignored by Louis. Soon he was joined by a small group of young men, hot-headed but, for the most part, courageous. But again, there were the usual jealousies and disagreements, particularly between the Scots and the Irish. The King wrote to warn his son against this, but his advice was little heeded. The Prince wrote to complain about Drummond of Balhaldy and Lord Sempill and these were the only Jacobites now in Paris in whom the King had confidence. There were faults on all sides, but it seemed to be sufficient to have the King to advise one course, for the Prince to take the opposite.

News from England was not good: after the failure of the French expedition the defences had been strengthened all along the coasts, the Habeas Corpus Act suspended, and several well-known Jacobites arrested – the usual course of events after a Stuart attempt. There seemed to be little hope of positive action from Ireland, and Scotland alone provided any enthusiasm. But none of this damped Charles's ardour, and he was more than impatient to be on his way to Scotland. All the military preparation he had had was the few weeks spent at Gaeta ten years before, while still a boy, but what he lacked in experience he made up for in enthusiasm and courage.

On 26 March he wrote to his father: 'You may be persuaded that any [no] disappointment whatsoever will ever discourage mee or slacken mee in applying to what is next best to be done for your service. I have lerned from you how to bere with disappointments, and I see it is the only way, which is to submit oneself entierly to the will of God, and never to be discouraged. . . .'[1] At this time Charles was still very serious about his religion and had taken an Irish priest, Father Kelly, to be his confessor in Paris: this again worried James who thought the Irish Catholic influence on Charles's mind might have an adverse effect where the English Protestants and Scots Presbyterians were concerned.

[1] WSP, 256.169

Murray of Broughton visited him in Paris, bringing largely exaggerated reports of the possibilities of money being raised in Britain, and of the time being right to strike while England was cut off from her European allies. Murray went home in October by way of Holland, hoping to enlist the help of officers in the Scots Brigade in the Dutch Service. When he arrived in Scotland and told the Jacobites of the Prince's plan to come to Scotland on his own, without foreign assistance, they were appalled. At least six thousand regular soldiers and enough money to sustain them would be necessary before Scotland could think about putting any idea of invasion of England into motion. The message was to be sent to the Prince with all speed, and it was entrusted to Lord Traquair who, so it seems, neglected or forgot to send it further at the time.

Needless to say, Charles took great care not to inform the King of his plans, and James waited in the Palazzo Muti for him to return, knowing only too well that there was nothing more to be hoped for from France. He was also filled with apprehension that Charles would do something rash if left to his own devices. Henry was becoming a problem too; he naturally enough wanted to join his brother, to whom he was extremely attached, and to share in the honour and glory of regaining their rightful inheritance. But, for the moment, one son abroad was enough for the King.

He was in his fifty-seventh year and beginning to feel the approach of old age. For thirty-nine years he had managed state affairs more or less single-handed, and he was tired out. At a time when he should have been hoping to share some of the burden he was beginning to realize that Charles and Henry were each likely to be a liability in their different ways. During November 1744 he had been ill, and dictated a letter to Edgar on 15 December for the Prince of Wales:

> I thank God I am better and about as usual, the Doctors tell me my ails are not dangerous, yet they increase with age [56] and I cannot apply as I could have done even a year ago, for as for reading or writing myself I can do very little of either, because the least fixing of my eyes gives me some sort of giddyness in my head. So you see my dear Child that you are likely to have but a useless old father in me, but still I thank God my heart is good and if its being all yours could be of any help to you, that will never fail you.[1]

He was pleased to know that Charles was staying from time to time with his Berwick cousins at Fitzjames, and also with his Bouillon cousins at their estate of Navarre, just outside Evreux in Normandy. Here Charles could hunt and shoot, and there were always plenty of amusements to divert him.

[1] WSP, 260.166

At this time in his life he conducted himself with sobriety and, although given to late nights, drank abstemiously: he was still the Prince Charming of the legend. And he still wrote immature letters which carried overtones of the petulance which both he and his brother had inherited from their mother. On 28 February 1745 he wrote to his father excusing himself for not having replied to two letters of the King:

> As I have been so much hurrid between Balls and business, I shall refer to my next. It would be a great comfort to me to have real business on my hands, but I see little of that at present as I shall explen in an other. It is sumthing surpriseing to me not to have herd from Lumley [Lord Sempill] this to weeks and even he ows me an answer to one of mine of that standing, but I esely conceive the reson on't, which is that after making such a noise of his being able to do a great deal, he dos nothing – or he dos not care to lett me in the confidence of his manedgements, which I believe has happened before now to more than he, for I see here everybody thinks himself to be the wisest man in the world.[1]

In answer to this the King counselled him: 'I cannot but recommend you to bear with Balhaldy and Sempil. . . . In truth I was formerly uneasy to see both your person and affairs in their hands alone, but that is no more the case . . . I fear it is what most of our people aim at, and therefore you must be particularly on your guard.'[2] But the Prince had differences of opinion with de Tencin, O'Brien and the Lord Marischal and seemingly everyone who had tried to help with advice or common sense.

Even if Charles had not received the message warning him not to set out for Scotland which Traquair was supposed to have sent him, he must have gathered something of the attitude of the Scots from his various acquaintances in Paris. But in the spring of 1745 he began to organize, and borrowed eighty thousand *livres* from Waters, the banker in Paris who had Jacobite sympathies; and he wrote to his father to ask him to pawn the Sobieski jewels in Rome. James had no idea of what Charles had in mind, since the Prince let him understand that he was still working in co-operation with the French. As he had run up bills, in the region of 30,000 *livres*, during his stay in Paris, there was a considerable drain on James's own resources, so carefully husbanded over the years against the expenses of the restoration when it should come.

Charles bought twenty small field-pieces, 1,500 muskets and 1,800 broad-swords, as well as dirks, ammunition and brandy; and from two French-based Jacobite ship-owners, Walter Rutledge and Anthony Walsh, he chartered a frigate, the *Du Teillay*, which lay at Nantes, and a man-o'-war,

---

[1] WSP, 263.24   [2] *ibid.*, 263.186

the *Elisabeth*, as an escort vessel. With four hundred *louis d'or*, and seven chosen companions – the Duke of Atholl, Francis Strickland, Sir Thomas Sheridan, George Kelly, Aeneas Macdonald, John O'Sullivan and Sir John Macdonnell – he set out for Scotland on 4 July 1745. They left Belle-Île with a handful of attendants, including the intrepid Michael Vezzosi, who had been James's own valet and had accompanied Wogan on the rescue of Clementina. Of the 'Seven Men of Moidart', as they later came to be known, four were Irish, two Scots and one English.

This news contained in a letter dated as from the day of his sailing must have given James a considerable shock when he received it at the Palazzo Muti somewhere around a month later. In the letter Charles explained why he could no longer wait for the French court to make its mind up to help him:

> I cannot but mention a parabole here which is: A Horse that is to be solde iff spurd does not skip or shew some signe of Life, no body wou'd care to have him even for nothing; just so my Friends wou'd care very little to have mee iff after such usage which all the world is sensible of, I should not shew them that I had Life in me. Your Majesty cannot disapprove a son's following the example of his Father; you yourself did the like in the year 15, but the circumstances now are indeed very different, by being much more encouraging. . . . I have presumed to take upon mee the manedgment of all this without even letting you suspect there was any such thing a Brewing . . . had I failed to convince you, I was then afraid you might have thought what I was going to do to be rash, and so to have absolutely forbidden my proceedings. . . .[1]

He said that he had tried all possible means and stratagems to get access to the King of France or his minister, nor could he obtain an audience for Sir Thomas Sheridan, acting as his representative. He felt that Cardinal de Tencin was not much trusted or liked by Louis XV, who was timorous and lacked sufficient courage to replace him. Towards the end of the long letter he told his father he had borrowed about 120,000 *livres* from Waters *fils* and 60,000 *livres* from his father. Nothing in this letter was calculated to give James peace of mind, and he waited anxiously with the Duke of York for any whisper of news of the Prince that might reach Rome.

After the gallant *Elisabeth* had held off the British man-o'-war, the *Lion*, which had tried to waylay the *Du Teillay*, the Prince of Wales landed on Eriskay on 22 July (New Style) 1745. He raised his standard at Glenfinnan on 19 August, and the rest of the Jacobite story belongs thereafter to Charles Edward.

[1] WSP, 265.294

James had lived a little over two-thirds of his life, and all that time he had been waiting for something to happen which never did, but he had never given up his dream. There seemed to be a strange fatality hanging over him, and his line, which could bring up tempests against him, undermine his health at the most inappropriate times, poison his relationship with his wife and finally, provide him with two sons who were ultimately to disappoint him in the furtherance of the Stuart restoration.

After Charles's landing there came his triumphant entry into Edinburgh, his stay at Holyrood where it was apparent that, however briefly, the Stuarts had, for a time, come into their own again. James was proclaimed King James VIII of Scotland and King of England, France (still France!) and Ireland. After Holyrood came the Jacobite victory at Prestonpans on 21 September 1745, following which the greater part of Scotland was for the Prince; the march to Derby; the disagreements between Charles and the leaders of the clans, notably Lord George Murray; the disintegration of the spirit which had infused the rising until then, and finally, the disaster at Culloden on 16 April 1746, which meant the total destruction of all that James had lived for and the end of the movement in Europe.

Moved to action at last, the French government did all it could by sending ships to bring off the unfortunate Jacobites, and a great number were saved in this way; but for six months the Prince lived the life of a solitary fugitive on the run, 'skulking' in the heather of the Western Isles and the Highlands. In one way, this was his finest hour: all the time he had spent in developing his physical powers stood him in good stead, for the life he had to lead was one of extraordinary duress, and his determination to survive was of an almost superhuman intensity. But it was also during this period, when he was sleeping rough, often in wind and rain with a few boughs for a shelter, that he learned to value the warming properties of alcohol.

The ever faithful Sir Charles Wogan was in Spain at this time, endeavouring to drum up Spanish support and money for the Prince: the Spanish Court was enchanted with the Prince as a hero, but the full news had not yet reached either Wogan or the Spanish King and Queen. On 9 October, soon after Prestonpans, Sir Charles wrote to the King about the maddening delay in getting anything done at the Escorial:

All this delay, the uncouth situation I figured to myself the Prince must be in, and some other disagreeable circumstances of letters writ to persons in this Court, blameing ye Prince's enterprise as rash and inconsiderate, not to say worse, fixed my blood to yt degree and fill'd my head with such dismall ideas of the Prince's being abandoned even by this

319

Court, where his addresses had been so kindly receiv'd, yt I was seized with a violent fever and the jaundice, so as not to be yet in a condition to get out of my room.[1]

At last Spanish money and ships were despatched, and Aeneas MacDonald, a Jacobite banker from Inverness, was sent to the Inverness-shire coast to supervise the safe delivery of the money to the Prince. He said that if the Prince had remained only a day longer on the coast he could have had the money, which was buried somewhere near Loch Arkaig and never found, and he could have left in one of the frigates which were sent to bring him off. There were some rumours that the Prince did not want to be taken off, and it could have been that he was working out his own salvation as well as hoping to be ready on the spot when the opportunity for another attempt arose. When the result of Culloden became known to him, Wogan wrote to the King on 15 July:

Sir,
   'Tis with a sorrowfull heart I doe myself the honour to inform your Maty. of my departure this day for Madrid, there being no further encouragement for ye affair I came about, and having received orders from ye Court of Spain to return to my employment there. All this goes to my heart and it would be wrong in me to afflict your Majesty wit the recital of my grief. Yr. Maty. has surer accounts from other hand than I can give of ye way our Prince is in, and may be persuaded yt as long as God lends me life, I shall be allways equally readie to do wt. service I can for ye Cause I have ever much at heart, being with the most inviolable zeal and duty Yr. Majesty's most dutifull and faithfull subject and servant,
   C. Wogan.[2]

This letter was typical of all that was best in the older type of Jacobite, such as the Earl Marischal and his brother, James Keith, the Duke of Ormonde or Earl Dunbar; it was typical of the disinterested devotion which James had been fortunate to receive from a small number of his followers all his life. But the time came when the Earl Marischal sought his permission after the Forty-Five 'to live quietly with a great Plutarch in the way I wish, until there comes an occasion for reall service'[3] and he retired with his brother to Prussia, where James Keith was made a Marshal of the Prussian army, and the Earl was appointed Prussian minister to the court of France in 1751. So, in a sense, he did not retire, but answered the call for 'reall service',

[1] WSP, 269.49   [2] *ibid.,* 275.139   [3] *ibid.,* 224.17

and he was then in a very strategic position for the Jacobites. The Duke of Ormonde died on 15 November 1746; shortly after giving hospitality at his house in Avignon to Henry, then on his way to join Charles who was, so he hoped, in Scotland. The Earl of Dunbar also retired, to live with his widowed sister, Lady Inverness, in Avignon in 1747: it was rumoured that he had had some differences of opinion with the King about the behaviour of the Prince of Wales.

The strength of Jacobitism lay in people such as these, and its weakness, for in Rome, Avignon, Paris and London, the backbone of the movement was formed of the aristocracy and the landed gentry. In England it was eventually to die of attrition for this very reason: it made no attempt to attract the common people who should have composed its main body. As for those at its head, like the Earl Marischal, they were prepared for deeds requiring great valour and skill, but they did not want and did not know how to deal with minor matters of organization and administration. James himself was the exception: King though he was he was prepared to fight, when a young man, and also to spend hours at his desk dealing with matters which touched upon every conceivable aspect of the cause.

The aftermath of the Forty-Five, as of the Fifteen, fell heavily upon the Scots. Of those taken after Culloden, 120 were executed, over 100 were banished, and nearly 1,000 were transported to North America. Some were kept in confinement in prison-hulks on the Thames, and the mortality rate was very high. The Duke of Cumberland's men pillaged the Highlands and whole villages were burned. Many of the lairds and chieftains escaped abroad and, in so doing, made way for the centralization of power in George II and Westminster: never again, were the heads of the clans to have the absolute feudal power they had known until then.

The retribution meted out by Cumberland, the 'Butcher of Culloden', lay heavily upon the mind and conscience of Charles, and of his father who had already experienced the same agony of mind after the Fifteen. Part of Charles's later wild behaviour may well have been rooted in the solitary days and nights in the hills and glens spent in reviewing the terrible balance sheet. Added to this burden on the King's mind was the dire uncertainty of knowing whether or not his son was alive. On 6 June 1746 he wrote to Charles from Albano, the letter being passed out in the usual way through various channels until it was likely to come somewhere in the vicinity of where the Prince was last heard of:

God knows where or when this will find you, my dearest Carluccio, but still I cannot but write to you in the great pain and anxiety I am in for you . . . do not, for God's sake, drive things too far, but think of your

321

own safety, on which so much depends. Though your Enterprise should miscarry, the honour you have gained by it will always stick to you, it will make you be respected and considered abroad . . . and always engage the French to protect and assist you, and to renew in time another project in your favour. . . . *Enfin*, my dear Child, never separate prudence and courage. Providence has wonderfully assisted you hitherto, and will not abandon you for the time to come. . . .[1]

After this, he wrote once a week to Charles, without ever losing hope, casting his letters into a void of unsurmisable profundity.

Henry, too, was suffering during the absence of his brother. The smallness of the family meant that each one of them had only two others on whom to pour their affection, and Henry's lifelong love and compassion for his brother, and later his feeling for his brother's dependents, were one of his most endearing characteristics. He sold his share of the Sobieski jewels to enable him to join Charles in Scotland, and was about to sail at the head of a contingent of French troops from Boulogne when he received the news of Culloden. He waited on the coast, but in vain, and then begged Louis to allow him to fight in the campaign led by the Maréchal de Saxe in Flanders. The permission was granted, after he had already left without waiting for it, using the *incognito* of the 'Count of Albany'. Saxe gave him a warm welcome and, like his father and brother, he gave every evidence of being a valorous soldier. But there was never any fear that Henry would supersede Charles in the favour of the Jacobites. He lacked the 'common touch' which came easily to Charles, as it had to their great-uncle, Charles II, but not to Henry, whose excessive piety and devotion was also daunting to those outside his small circle of intimates. Apart from his religious zeal, his only other interests in life were the arts, particularly music, and he delighted in attending concerts in Rome, in singing and in composing – mainly religious music.

When Charles returned to France six months after Culloden, Henry was there to meet him at Fontainebleau. Sir John Graeme, currently in Paris, was also present, and wrote to the King on 17 October 1746: 'Though the fatigues, the want of all necessarys, and the dangers he has undergone are beyond imagination, yet he looks as well as when I had the honour to see him more than two years ago. Nothing was ever so tender as his first interview with the Duke.'[2] Also accompanying the Prince were the faithful Lochiel and his brother, Dr Archibald Cameron, who was to be the last person beheaded in England, Lochgary and Roy Stewart. Louis XV entertained the Princes in a most regal fashion, and for the first few weeks

[1] WSP, 275.26   [2] *ibid.*, 277.165

Charles was the darling of Paris. Then, as he realized that there was to be no help, or immediate help, from France, his manner changed. He became bitter and distrustful, spurned everyone who was likely to give him good advice, and turned to a few associates, Kelly, Strickland, O'Sullivan principally, who encouraged the weaker sides of his nature. He made fun of Henry and his attachment to religion, and tried to force him to live the kind of life he himself was then leading. His relationship with the French deteriorated into disaster and, in the end, no one in the French ministry took him seriously.

Henry left Paris surreptitiously, unable to bear this state of affairs any longer. Charles kept writing to James about what he considered to be Henry's want of consideration for him, and the King tried his best to keep the peace between them, but it was obvious to all concerned that Henry's absence would be more pleasing to Charles than his presence.

Henry had another reason for coming home and, on 3 June 1747, James informed Charles of the Duke's decision to take holy orders:

I know not whether you will be surprized, My Dearest Carluccio, when I tell you that your Brother will be made a Cardinal the first Days of next month. Naturally speaking you should have been consulted about a resolution of that kind before it had been executed but as the Duke and I were unalterably determined on the matter, and that we foresaw you might probably not approve of it We thought it would be showing you more regard, and that it would be even more agreeable to you, that the thing should be done before your answer could come here, and so have it in your power to say it was done without your knowledge or approbation. . . . After this, I will not conceal from you, My Dearest Carluccio, that motives of conscience and equity have not alone determined me in this particular: and that when I seriously consider all that has passed in relation to the Duke for some years bye-gone, had he not the vocation he has, I should have used my best endeavours and all arguments to have induced him to have embraced that state. If Providence has made you the elder brother, he is as much my son as you, and my parental care and affection are equally to be extended to you and him, so that I should have thought I had greatly failed in both towards him, had I not endeavoured by all means to secure to him as much as in me lay, that tranquillity and happiness which I was sensible it was not possible for him to enjoy in any other state.[1]

Charles's reply was immediate and brief:

Sir,

I have received yrs of ye 13th and 20th June had I got a Dager throw

[1] WSP, 284.103

my heart it would not have been mor sensible to me than at ye Contents of yr first.

My Love for my Brother and concern for yr Case being the occasion of it, I hope your Majesty will forgive me not entering any further on so disagreeable a subject the shock of which I am scarce out of so shall take ye liberty of referring to next Post anything in yours to be answered. I lay myself full of Respect and Duty at your Majesty's feet, most humbly asking Blessing, your most Dutifull son,

Charles P.[1]

Henry wrote to Charles entreating his brother to write to him, but answer came there none. A Father Myles McDonnell, who was near the Prince, wrote to the King, expressing the opinion of many English Jacobites who thought that Henry's decision was one which could only harm the cause and bring suspicion on it from the Protestant adherents:

> . . . I endavour'd to persuade them that when your Majesty's reasons for consenting to the late event were known they wo'd certainly justify the Proceedings. This is all I co'd say, but alas, that will be of little force at home, where all the old bugbears of Popery, bigotry etc. will be renewed with (I am afraid) too much success. . . . His R.H. the Prince (I am told, for I don't go near him) has shut himself up for several hours alone upon his hearing that news, the Duke's health is no more drank nor his name mentioned at his table. He is teazed about his safety and made to believe that his life will be in danger, being now alone and unmarry'd.[2]

There was much truth in all this: not only the English, but the Scots were scandalized by Henry's action and the King's allowing it, and it seems as if James were now finally convinced, although he did not write in such terms, that there was no longer any hope for the cause. Just before Charles had left Paris for Scotland, he had written to him suggesting that he might abdicate, but the Prince's reaction, especially when considered in the light of what the King did not then know, was so violently against it, that James did not refer to it again to Charles, although he did raise the matter in a letter to Louis XV. There was no point in his abdicating while Charles was away, and he could not know that Charles would never return. The rest of his life was to be spent waiting to welcome his son back in Rome.

The personal relations between father and son were good, even though the King did not approve of the way his son was behaving in Paris. In September, Charles sat for a portrait miniature to be sent to the King, and

[1] WSP, 285.104   [2] *ibid.*, 285.126

asked for one in return. Sir John Graeme, now Lord Alford, had taken Lord Dunbar's place at court (officially Secretary of State), and in the latter part of 1747 Charles asked him to meet him in Paris with the idea of arranging a marriage between himself and the daughter of the Protestant Landgrave of Hesse-Darmstadt, but nothing came of it. And nothing was likely to come of it while the Prince's reputation was as low as it was at that time in France. By now he was firmly in the clutches of O'Sullivan and Kelly, having sent old Sir Thomas Sheridan back to Rome to die, shortly before he set out on his Scottish wanderings. He complained that the court of France had not lodged him in royal state at one of the French King's many residences but in a small château or a large villa on the outskirts of Paris; but he remained deaf to every appeal of James for him to return home. He was, in fact, reacting to disappointment – disappointment with the result of the Forty-Five, disappointment with the French, disappointment with Henry – in just the same way as Clementina had done, cutting himself off from those who were closest to him and, as he knew, still loved him. Like Clementina, he chose to go to extremes: where she chose what was to her the highest vocation, he delighted in sinking as low as he could.

In April 1748 representatives of all the countries concerned in the War of the Austrian Succession gathered at Aix-la-Chapelle to draft a treaty, and in so far as Anglo-French relations were concerned, nothing could be achieved without the promise of Charles's removal from France. Charles refused to go. His father pointed out that it was better to go in dignity as he himself had done after the Treaty of Utrecht, and both the Pope and Louis XV offered him recompense by way of a pension from France and a home within the Papal States, but the Prince remained adamant, to the great embarrassment of Louis. Finally, the French King was forced to order his arrest and, as he was about to enter the Opera House in Paris on 10 December, he was apprehended and taken by Louis's emissary to the prison at Vincennes. At 7 a.m. on the 27 December 1749, Lord Dunbar was awakened in his house at Avignon by the arrival of the Prince disguised as an officer of the Royal Irlandais. He then took a house in Avignon, furnished it and left Michael Sheridan and Henry Stafford in charge, with a few servants. He organized a *poste restante* with the banker, Waters, in Paris, under an oath of secrecy not to reveal his whereabouts and, indeed, Waters rarely knew whether the Prince was at the address to which he was forwarding correspondence. He then set off on eighteen years of wandering through Europe before he was to return to the Palazzo Muti. And all the time he was obsessed with the idea of mounting another invasion to regain his own.

James remained in the palazzo in Rome, sharing it at first with Henry who had become a very devout, but nevertheless very social Cardinal. He moved in the highest Roman society and was close to the Pope; he became, to James's dismay, a very great friend of Cardinal Gianfrancesco Albani, nephew of the Cardinal Alessandro Albani who had been so antipathetic towards the Stuarts. There is no doubt but there was a preciosity about Henry which might well have irritated someone like his father. James complained about Albani, and about Henry's chamberlain and personal friend Monsignor Lascari, whom he considered much too 'pushing'. When he asked Henry to get rid of Lascari, he refused and departed, in a Sobieski huff, to Bologna where he remained for some time before returning to Rome. As a cardinal, Henry was 'given' the church of Santa Maria in Campitelli in Rome, and was also made the titular Archbishop of Corinth: these emoluments, plus the livings of two abbeys and the episcopal see of Frascati, made him a very rich cleric indeed, so James was at least relieved of looking after the material welfare of his younger son, who was now known as 'Cardinal York' and granted precedence immediately after the Dean of the Sacred College of Cardinals. In latter years there was always a certain tension between James and Henry. In particular it was Henry's friends who caused misunderstandings: James did not approve of his associating with musicians for one thing. It was a situation which is frequently met with between two different generations.

On the day before Charles's birthday on 30 December 1750, James wrote to him urging him to marry:

> Tomorrow you end your 30th year. May you see many more than double that number, and happyer ones than those you have already past. The hardships you have gone through and do perhaps still undergo are not so small, and it is to be hoped they will contribute at last to what they are chiefly directed. But in the darkness you keep me as to all that relates to you, I can pray and wish, but I can neither judge nor advise, except on one single article, which is so obvious and so important that I should think everybody who really wishes you well should be of the same opinion in that respect, and that is your securing the succession of Our Family by marrying. . . . And therefore I cannot but recommend earnestly to you to think seriously on the matter, and as you cannot now hope to make a marriage suteable to yourself, to endeavour to make one that may be at least as little unequal as possible.[1]

Two years later the Prince was to establish his liaison with Clementina Walkinshaw, and a daughter, Charlotte, was born the year after.

In February 1757, 175,000 *livres* were unexpectedly repaid to the King in respect of the money he had advanced to Charles XII of Sweden in

[1] WSP, 314.124

1715,[1] and he immediately thought of getting some money to Charles. It was not until the autumn of the following year that he heard there was a possibility of the Prince being in Paris and he despatched his young under-secretary, Andrew Lumisden, to Paris with written instructions on what to say to the Prince:

> You will let the Prince know that I could say a great deal here on his politic affairs and present situation, but my health does not allow me to do it, neither is it indeed necessary. . . . In two words, the Prince must be convinced by his own experience, how little he has to expect from the English alone and that he has little to hope for, in any respect, from any foreign power except France, so that if he does not seriously endeavour to gain and cultivate the friendship of that Crown, it is in some manner next to renouncing all human hopes and means of a restoration and put-ting himself in the necessity of leading for the rest of his days the same ignominious, indecent life which he has led for so many years past and which will put the seal to his own and our family's destruction. . . .[2]

Charles wandered over Europe, through Germany, Italy (but not Rome, so far as James knew), France and even England, and there was a rumour that he attended the coronation of George III in London in 1760. On a previous visit to London he had renounced Catholicism and, apparently as a final expedient, had become a member of the Church of England. His many friends in France urged him to return to Paris – the Duc de Bouillon, the Maréchal de Belle-Île and Murray of Broughton. He left his Clementina in 1760, and it was his father who saw that she and her child were given money and decently cared for in a convent outside Paris. Later it was Henry who took care that they were not lacking in the necessities for a decent life.

Throughout his wanderings James's letters followed him, filled with a fear that he would not see him before his death: 'Do not deny me, My Dear Child, the comfort of embracing you before I dy. Could you see my heart, I am sure you would not. May God Almighty shower down all his blessing upon you in the state he has placed you.' This was in his secretary's hand, and then, in large, sprawling characters of an old man, ailing, with bad sight and partly paralysed: 'I tenderly embrace you my dear son, *James R.*'[3] Again, as a pendant to another letter dictated to Edgar: 'I have seen all your letters to Edgar and have nothing further to add here but to beseech God to help, to send you soon to me, [and in his own writing] I tenderly embrace you and am all yours, *James R.*'[4] He was weakened by hernia, attacks of quartan ague (his old complaint), and had suffered from convulsions once

---

[1] See above, p. 266   [2] WSP, 386.55   [3] *ibid.*, 386.30   [4] *ibid.*, 386.112

when walking in the Cardinal's garden, but his lucidity of mind was unimpaired, and he clung to life with an extraordinary tenacity. In April 1760, he had a severe relapse; Henry gave him the last rites of the Church; Pope Clement XIII, a very good friend, came to give him his blessing, and James commended both his sons to his care. The Pope promised to continue the Stuart pension to Cardinal York, but not to the Prince of Wales. But he recovered, although he was never again to take any vital interest in affairs of state, which were now supervised by Lord Lismore[1] and Henry. He was ill again, with convulsions, in 1761, and again in 1762, but each time he rallied, sustained by a determination to live to see his 'dearest Carluccio' again.

Charles had been staying with the Bouillon family in France, and the Duke had been instructed to see that the Prince had as much money as he needed. France and England were in the middle of another war, and there was just the possibility that Charles might be useful again. So he was living in some style, not admitting to his Protestant conversion in Catholic France, but with a priest in his entourage, domestics, a fine carriage, and horses. He was near enough to have visited James without any great difficulty, but still he would not go.

One by one the old friends of the King were leaving him: Lord Lisemore asked permission to resign the seals of State in 1759, owing to ill health, and he died in the following year. He was succeeded by Lord Alford, previously Sir John Graeme, but he retired to Paris in 1763, where he died shortly afterwards. James Edgar was then given the seals, which he surely deserved after so many years of selfless devotion, but he died in 1764 and was followed by Andrew Lumisden.

The old man, partly bed-ridden, warmly wrapped even in the heat of a Roman summer, still continued to dictate his appeals to Charles, in the same way that he had appealed to Clementina thirty-five years before, with the same lack of result. His letters were full of wise advice and fatherly love, and he begged Charles to pull himself together and remember what he once had been – the beautiful Prince who had charmed the courts of Europe and fired the imaginations of the Highlanders:

> Is it possible, my dear sir, you can so entirely forget your past life, the dangers you exposed yourself to, the hardships and fatigues you underwent, and the applause and glory you gained by supporting our just cause and our faithful adherents? Will you let all that be buried in oblivion and yourself with it? . . . If you make no reply to this letter I shall take it for granted that . . . you are not only buried alive . . . but in effect that you are dead and insensible to every thing.

[1] Formerly Colonel O'Brien

The letter is addressed 'For our dearest Son, the Prince', and in James's own hand: 'I am all yours.'[1] With his thoughts no longer centred on his own restoration, he concentrated all his powers on making Charles return to Rome: 'Will you not run straight to your Father. . . . There is no question of the past, but only of saving you from utter destruction for the future. Is it possible you would rather be a vagabond on the face of the earth than return to a Father who is all love and tenderness for you ?'[2] But there was no answer from Charles.

In 1761, Henry, Cardinal York, was obliged to take up residence in Frascati on assuming his bishopric, but James was never able to visit him there. The Cardinal did all he could to induce his brother to return to Rome; with the permission of the Pope, he arranged for the Stuart pension payable to himself to be made over to Charles, and James had already sent the Prince more than enough to enable him to make the journey. Since the French had been soundly defeated in the naval Battle of Quiberon Bay by the British in November 1759, there was little chance of France beginning an aggressive war for some time to come, and Charles himself was by now practically a cipher. But he let it be known that he would only return to Rome if he were given the full state of the Prince of Wales, heir to the throne of England, Scotland, Ireland and Wales. No monarch in Europe would have agreed to such a recognition, nor would the Pope.

It had to be realized by Charles, as it had been by his father, by the Duke of York and by the rest of Europe, that Jacobitism as a practical movement had ceased to exist. In 1763 peace was declared between England and France and neither country was willing to resuscitate war for a hopeless cause. The Pope promised to receive Charles with every mark of distinction, as the Count of Albany or any other title he might wish to assume, to make over to him the palaces which he had granted to James in Rome and in Albano, and to allow him to accept the Stuart pension made over to him by the Cardinal, but he would not allow him regal style. In November 1763 and the December of the following year, Henry wrote begging Charles to come before their father died, and still he refused. At the end of 1765, James had another attack of quartan ague, and Charles was again urgently summoned by Henry, who had made apartments ready for him in the Palazzo Muti. The Prince delayed once more to see how he would be received by the Pope, and considering, rightly or wrongly, that he was now likely to welcome him as Prince of Wales, he set out for Rome.

James had, meanwhile, taken a turn for the better, and was able to hear Mass and take Communion on Christmas Day. He had a slight relapse two days later, but was better after he was bled a little. New Year's Day, 1766,

[1] WSP, 411.24   [2] *ibid.*, 413.115

the day after Charles's forty-sixth birthday, he was able to eat a little, and then took a sudden turn for the worse. He was given Extreme Unction and commended to the mercy of God. Henry was unable to bear the sight of his father dying, and went to rooms near by to await the news of his death. And at a quarter past nine that night James, *de jure* III of England and VIII of Scotland, died in the presence of several officials of the Vatican and of his own household, but without either of his sons beside him.

The King was embalmed, and lay in state in a chamber in the Palazzo Muti, dressed in his usual clothes, with his sword and periwig, wearing his orders and resting upon a bed covered with cloth of gold. Black velvet curtains hung from silver pillars surrounding the bed, and trapped the clouds of incense as they rose upwards. The room and his bedchamber adjoining were filled with the murmur of prayers for the dead, as his servants knelt by his body. Papal guards were placed at the doors of the palazzo and up the staircase. He had asked to be buried in Santi Apostoli, but the Pope ordered that he was to be buried in St Peter's beside Clementina.

On the Eve of Epiphany he was carried into the church of Santi Apostoli dressed in royal robes of crimson velvet, lying upon a bed of purple silk, with his golden crown upon his head and his orb and sceptre in his hands which had never held them officially in life. The next day a Requiem Mass was sung: on this day, seventy-seven years before, as a tiny baby, he had just been joined by his father and Louis XIV on the occasion of James II's arrival at Saint-Germain-en-Laye – on Epiphany Day, the Feast of the Three Kings.

And now, as at the time of his journey out of England all those years ago, and as at the time of every point of decision in his life, the elements vented their fury against the fateful House of Stuart: the sky was dark all day and, in an atmosphere of bitter cold, the cold which James had always so disliked, the wind drove the sleet along the streets of Rome. The streets, nevertheless, were lined with people in such crowds that it was necessary to call out extra guards along the funeral route, although perfect order was kept. All the shops were closed and no traffic was allowed to move in the city; the windows were crowded with mourners and the red, gold and black of the Swiss Guards glowed in the flare of the torches carried by the black-robed students of the English, Scots and Irish Colleges in Rome. Dignitaries of the Church and Vatican followed, while the King's personal guard brought up the rear of the procession. A second Requiem Mass was sung and, after Absolution, Andrew Lumisden performed his last duty to his master by placing on the coffin three seals, gold, silver and bronze, with James's likeness on one side and one of London on the obverse. He was buried in a regal state and a dignity befitting his own, but no outward show of pomp or circumstance could express the fortitude with which he had faced adversity during the sixty-four years he had reigned as *de jure* King, longer than any ruling monarch Britain has known.

Charles returned to Rome that same month, but he was too late.

Bibliography

BOOKS

Ailesbury, Earl of: *Memoirs*. London: Roxburghe Club, 1890.

Baxter, Stephen B.: *William III*. London: Longmans, 1966.

Berwick, Duke of: *Mémoires du Maréchal de Berwick, écrites par lui-même; avec une suite abregée depuis 1716, jusqu'à sa mort en 1734; precédés de son portrait par Milord Bolingbroke, et d'une ébauche d'éloge historique, par le Président de Montesquieu; terminé par des notes et des lettres servant de pièces justificatives pour la compagne de 1708*. Paris: Moutard, 1778; 2nd edn 1780.

Bevan, Bryan: *I was James II's Queen*. London: Heinemann, 1963.

Bosq de Beaumont, G. de: *La Cour des Stuarts à Saint-Germain-en-Laye, 1698–1718*. Paris: Emile Paul, 1912.

Campana de Cavelli, Marchesa: *Les Derniers Stuarts à Saint-Germain-en-Laye*, 2 vols. Paris: Didier, 1871.

Churchill, Sir Winston S.: *Marlborough: His Life and Times*, 2 vols. London: Harrap, 1947.

Cronin, Vincent. *Louis XIV*. London: Collins, 1964.

Dangeau, Marquis de: *Journal de la Cour de Louis XIV*. Paris: Deterville, 1807. (D) and Firmin Didot Frères, 1857 (F).

Deane, J. M.: *A Journal of the Campaign in Flanders*. London, 1708.

De la Colonie, M.: *Chronicles of an Old Campaigner, 1692–1717*. London: John Murray, 1904.

Fénelon, François Salingnac de la Motte, *Lettres*, ed. John McEwen, London, Harvill Press, 1964.

Fisher, H. A. L.: *A History of Europe from the Beginning of the Eighteenth Century*. London: Eyre & Spottiswoode, 1937.

Forbes, Robert: *The Lyon in Mourning*. Edinburgh: Scottish Historical Society, 1857.

Fothergill, Brian: *The Cardinal King*. London: Faber, 1958.

Frati, Ludovico: *Maria Clementina in Italia*. Rome, 1908.

Fuller, William: *A Brief Discovery*. London, 1696.

Gibson, W. S.: *Dilston Hall: or, Memoirs of James Radcliffe, Earl of Derwentwater*. London, 1850.

Gilbert, Sir John T.: *Narratives of the Detention, Liberation and Marriage of Maria Clementina Sobieska styled Queen of Great Britain and Ireland by Sir Charles Wogan and others*. Dublin: Joseph Dollard, 1894.

332

Haile, Martin: *James Francis Edward, the Old Pretender*. London: J. M. Dent, 1907.

Hatton, Ragnild: *Europe in the Age of Louis XIV*. London: Thames and Hudson, 1959.

Hopkirk, Mary: *Queen over the Water*. London: John Murray, 1953.

Jones, G. H.: *The Main Stream of Jacobitism*. Harvard University Press, 1954.

Levron, Jacques: *The Royal Châteaux of the Île-de-France*. London: Allen & Unwin, 1965.

Lewis, Lesley: *Connoisseurs and Secret Agents in Eighteenth-Century Rome*. London: Chatto & Windus, 1961.

Lockhart, George, of Carnwath: *Memoirs concerning the Affairs of Scotland*. Cork: J. Connor, 1799.

Montesquieu, Baron de (*see* Berwick).

Mure Mackenzie, Agnes: *The Passing of the Stewarts*. Edinburgh: Oliver & Boyd, 1937.

Norton, L.: *Historical Memoirs of the Duc de Saint-Simon*.

Oman, Carola: *Mary of Modena*. London: Hodder & Stoughton, 1962.

Petrie, Sir Charles: *Bolingbroke*. London: Collins, 1937.

Petrie, Sir Charles: *The Jacobite Movement, the First Phase, 1688–1716*, London, Eyre & Spottiswoode, 1948; *The Jacobite Movement, the Last Phase, 1716–1807*, London, Eyre & Spottiswoode, 1950.

Petrie, Sir Charles: *The Duke of Berwick and His Son*. London: Eyre & Spottiswoode, 1951.

Petrie, Sir Charles: *The Marshal Duke of Berwick*. London: Eyre & Spottiswoode, 1953.

Pollnitz, Baron de: *Memoirs*. London: Daniel Browne, 1745.

Porcelli, Baron: *The White Cockade*. London: Hutchinson, 1924.

Rankine, Alexander: *Memoirs of the Chevalier de St George*. London, 1702.

Saint-Simon, Duc de: *Mémoires*. Paris: Libraire Hachette, 1873.

Saint-Simon, Duc de (*see also* Norton).

Sévigné, Madame de: *Lettres*. Paris: Editions Lefèvre, 1843.

Sharp Grew, E and M.: *The English Court in Exile*. London: Mills & Boon, 1911.

Shield, A. and A. Land: *The King over the Water*. London: Longmans, Green, 1907.

Tayler, A. and H.: *A Jacobite Exile*. London: A. Maclehose, 1937.

Tayler, A. and H.: *The Chevalier*. London: Cassell, 1934.

Tayler, H.: *The Jacobite Court at Rome in 1719*. Edinburgh: Scottish Historical Society, 1938.

Tayler, H.: *Jacobite Epilogue*. Edinburgh: Nelson, 1941.

MISCELLANEOUS

Anon: *De' Costumi et della Morte di Maria Clementina*. Rome and Bologna, 1737. Brit. Mus. 1203a. 17.

British Museum Pamphlets:

    Earl of Derwentwater: Speech on the scaffold. C115.i.3.25.

    'The Bonny Black Laddie'. C115.i.3.25.

    An English Traveller at Rome, 1721. C115.i.3.55.

    James III R.: Whereas we have a near Prospect. C115.i.3.62.

    Archibald Cameron's Speech intended to have been delivered to the Sheriff of Middlesex, 1753. C115.i.3.

Carte, Thomas: The Thomas Carte Papers, in the Bodleian Library at Oxford.

The Historical Manuscripts Commission (HMC), London: The Stuart Papers.

Lubomirski, Prince Henri: 'Lettres et Mémoire, concernant l'évasion de la Princesse Royale, Clementina Sobieska, promise au Prétendant d'Angleterre en 1719' – manuscript from the Ossolinski Library, Zaklad Narodowy, Wroclaw.

Verdun: Journal Historique pau l'année 1708.

Windsor Castle: The Stuart Papers in The Royal Archives (WSP).

Index

335